# SHAKESPEARE IN MUSIC

# SHAKESPEARE
# IN MUSIC

*Essays by*

JOHN STEVENS
CHARLES CUDWORTH
WINTON DEAN
ROGER FISKE

\*

*With a Catalogue of Musical Works*

\*

EDITED BY

## PHYLLIS HARTNOLL

LONDON
MACMILLAN & CO LTD
NEW YORK · ST MARTIN'S PRESS
1964

MACMILLAN AND COMPANY LIMITED
*St Martin's Street London WC 2*
*also Bombay Calcutta Madras Melbourne*

THE MACMILLAN COMPANY OF CANADA LIMITED
*70 Bond Street Toronto 2*

ST MARTIN'S PRESS INC
*175 Fifth Avenue New York 10 NY*

# CONTENTS

# INTRODUCTION

THERE is probably no writer who has inspired more music, from musicians of widely differing nationalities and dispositions, than Shakespeare, and on the occasion of the 400th anniversary of his birth it seemed fitting to take a closer look at some aspects of this manifestation of his universal appeal than had hitherto been done. The field proved to be extraordinarily fertile, and once the machinery of investigation had been set in motion it became difficult to contain even the initial findings within the covers of a single volume. This is particularly true of operas based on Shakespeare, where enquiry revealed a rich harvest that would in itself provide the raw material for many books. Incidental music, essential for any production, seemed overwhelming, even without taking into account the constant output demanded by radio and television. Most of it has had to be omitted — bearing in mind that it is nearly all unpublished and virtually inaccessible — and attention was concentrated on those works which have survived in the concert hall, or been specifically written for performance there, and on those songs which have taken on an existence independent of the incidental music of which they originally formed part.

It is one of the paradoxes of Shakespearean music that some of its finest examples have no connection with the theatre, and were written by composers who knew no English. We are so accustomed to think of Shakespeare's greatness in terms of his poetry that it is difficult to conceive of a strong and lasting inspiration received only through a translation, which may be unpoetic, unfaithful, or subtly orientated away from the original intention. Yet such is the force of Shakespeare's genius that his characters have taken on a life of their own, and it is possible for a composer to draw a sound-portrait of Hamlet, Romeo, Lear, Falstaff or a score of others, men and women, without reference to the plays in which they appear. There is, as it were, in the world's cultural consciousness, a corpus of Shakespearean figures whose main traits are instantly recognizable to everyone. We all know what Shylock is like; we recognize Othello; we have a constant mental picture of

vii

Hamlet. He may be dark or fair, tall or short, but he is always Hamlet in the essentials. It is this that enables us to use the names of Shakespeare's characters as a form of shorthand — and accounts for Delius's use, for instance, of the title 'A Village Romeo and Juliet', or Shostakovich's original title for 'Katerina Ismailova' — 'Lady Macbeth of Mtensk'. Neither of these works has anything to do with Shakespeare, but we know that the first will be about unhappy young lovers, and the second about an ambitious woman, probably a murderess. It is this universal aspect of the character which the composer will portray. Sometimes the conception of a man nourished in a different tradition may depart from the accepted English conception in detail, but the image will remain recognizably the same. The madness of Lear, the pathos of Juliet, the gaiety of Beatrice cannot be departed from, even in transition from one art to another.

Such universal appeal is not without its attendant dangers, and many musical works have been fathered upon Shakespeare without justification, among them the many operas based on subjects dealt with by him — Julius Caesar, Coriolanus, Antony and Cleopatra, to name only a few. One might be forgiven for thinking that Walton's 'Troilus and Cressida' or Britten's 'Rape of Lucrece' had some basis in Shakespeare, but the first derives from Chaucer, and the second, according to its librettist, from Latin legend and André Obey. Yet who can say how much a prior knowledge of Shakespeare may serve to direct the attention of writers and composers towards his primary sources?

If it is sometimes difficult to disentangle the true from the false in the larger works, matters become even more complicated when we consider the many pseudo-Shakespearean lyrics which were interpolated into productions of the plays from Restoration times onwards, particularly where a musician of genius, like Purcell or Arne, has given them a touch of true metal, so that in many minds they pass for sterling, and achieve the same measure of respectability as Colley Cibber's additions to the text of *Richard III*. It has, however, been necessary, for reasons of space, to exclude them.

In the essays which follow an attempt has been made to survey some of the summits of achievement in music inspired by Shakespeare, who, as Dr. Stevens reminds us in his introductory essay, inherited and enhanced a tradition of theatre

music used not only for embellishment but in the delineation
of character and with accepted symbolic associations. We do
not know how much, if any, of the music originally used was
specially written. We may hazard a guess that much of it was
arranged *in situ*, for performance by the city waits or the
theatre musicians. Hence, perhaps, the prevalence of traditional airs and contemporary forms of military and ceremonial music. But once Shakespeare's creations had escaped
into the public domain, song-writers were quick to annex them,
as Mr. Cudworth shows in his survey of song-settings over the
last three hundred years. Mr. Dean's fruitful researches into
opera have already been mentioned. They open up new fields
of enquiry on the aesthetic, historical and even purely practical
plane, and pose almost as many puzzles as they solve. Why,
for instance, should *The Tempest* have been set to music so
often, and *Richard II*, with all its drama and poetry, not at all?
One small problem Dr. Fiske has solved for us when he
demonstrates so ably that the inspiration for Berlioz's 'Romeo
and Juliet' came not from the play as written, and as we know
it today, but from Garrick's adaptation. Here the musicologist and the theatre historian, who so often seem to run on
parallel lines, are happily met; and one could wish that their
findings might more often be so conjoined, to their mutual
advantage.

This book ends, as, in conception, it began, with a catalogue of musical works based on Shakespeare. It is by no
means complete. But enough has been done to show that in
every composer listed — and there are over one thousand of
them — Shakespeare's poetic genius at some time lit an answer-
ing spark. And whether he was himself a musician or not, at
least he was the cause that music was in other men. And for
that we must all be grateful.

PHYLLIS HARTNOLL

London, 1964

# PART ONE

# Shakespeare and the Music of the Elizabethan Stage: An Introductory Essay[1]

## JOHN STEVENS

IN a familiar passage near the end of *The Merchant of Venice* Lorenzo speaks eloquently to Jessica of the power of music [2]:

> . . . why should we goe in?
> My friend *Stephen*, signifie pray you
> Within the house, your Mistresse is at hand
> And bring your musique foorth into the ayre.
> How sweet the moone-light sleepes upon this banke,
> Heere will we sit, and let the sounds of musicke
> Creepe in our eares: soft stilnes, and the night
> Become the tutches of sweet harmonie:
> Sit *Jessica*, looke how the floore of heaven
> Is thicke inlayed with pattens of bright gold,
> There's not the smallest orbe which thou beholdst
> But in his motion like an Angell sings,
> Still quiring to the young eyed Cherubins;
> Such harmonie is in immortall soules,
> But whilst this muddy vesture of decay
> Doth grosly close it in, we cannot heare it.
> Come hoe, and wake *Diana* with a hymne,
> With sweetest tutches pearce your Mistress eare,
> And draw her home with musicke.

JESSI. I am never merry when I heare sweet musique
>                                        *Play musicke.*

LOR. The reason is, your spirits are attentive:
> For doe but note a wilde and wanton heard
> Or race of youthful and unhandled colts . . .
> If they but heare perchance a trumpet sound,
> Or any ayre of musicke touch their eares

---

[1] I wish to express my gratitude to Dr. Sternfeld, who kindly read a draft of this essay and gave me many useful comments and corrections. It is a matter for regret that his book, *Music in Shakespearean Tragedy* (1963), did not appear in time for me to make full use of it.

[2] The Shakespeare quotations are from *The New Nonesuch Shakespeare* (1953).

3

You shall perceive them make a mutuall stand,
Their savage eyes turn'd to a modest gaze
By the sweet power of musicke . . .

(V. 1)

Lorenzo also describes that grotesque in Nature, 'the man that hath no musicke in himselfe', seditious and not to be trusted, dark and hellish in his emotions; and then he breaks off — 'marke the musicke'. Lorenzo and Jessica listen attentively (perhaps a change of musical mood was timed for the end of his speech); meanwhile, Portia and her maid Nerissa enter and also comment on the music ('Methinkes it sounds much sweeter then by day? — Silence bestowes that vertue on it Madam'). Finally, *Musicke ceases*. The only other music before the end of the play is Bassanio's trumpet — *A Tucket sounds*.

It is a rich passage which raises many of the issues with which we shall be concerned in this essay — the nature of Shakespeare's 'philosophy' of music; the relationship between this and the emotional, even 'atmospheric', music of the plays; the double function of music as affecting characters and audience alike. More mundane questions will also occur to the reader — Where did Stephano go, or to whom did he signal, when asked to bring his music 'foorth into the ayre'? Who came forth, what instruments did they play, and what music upon them?

## I. THE TRADITIONS

*The Merchant of Venice* was perhaps first fashioned by Shakespeare out of an old play in 1594, the year of the trial of the celebrated Jewish physician, Roderigo Lopez. The 'good' Quarto of 1600 refers to the play as printed 'as it hath been diuers times acted by the Lord Chamberlaine his Seruants'; it is known also to have been presented twice (by the King's Men) before the court in February 1605.[1] Two kinds of performance — one in a public playhouse, one at Whitehall — introduce us to a further complication in our study of Shakespeare's use of music, the variety of physical conditions hidden under the misleadingly simple phrase, 'the Elizabethan theatre'. If *The Merchant of Venice* stayed in the repertory of

<hr>

[1] New Cambridge Edition, pp. 116, 178.

Shakespeare's company (Lord Chamberlain's, later the King's Men), then it may well also have been acted in a third type of theatre, the Blackfriars private playhouse taken over by the King's Men in 1608.

Each of these theatres had, or developed, its particular musical tradition; and musical effects, like other aspects of the production (lighting, style of delivery, and so forth) must have been adapted to suit the occasion. But these three do not exhaust the influences to which Shakespeare was open in his dramatic use of music. Principal among these other influences were: the medieval mystery cycles, obstinately slow in dying despite the efforts of Puritan censors; the Senecan tragedies and Plautine comedies, especially beloved by lawyers of the Inns of Court and students at the ancient universities; the court masque, another medieval form, refurbished by the Tudors and soon to have a glamorous heyday under the Stuarts; the English 'chronicle play', with its pomp and pageantry; and the song, dance and fun of the popular stage jig.

From the medieval drama the Elizabethans inherited in palpable and concrete dramatic form that association of music with the divine which is an invariable part of their mental furniture. 'Heaven is music,' wrote Campion, 'And thy beauty's birth is heavenly.' When, in the mystery cycles, 'God appears on a "scaffold", between two angels or more playing musical instruments, we know that God is in his heaven . . . and the sense of a divine order, a cosmic symphony, [is] tangibly conveyed to the ears'.[1] The music in these great cycles of plays is sometimes naturalistic (when Herod feasts at his court, for instance), not consistently symbolic. But it is never 'atmospheric' — that is, specifically directed towards heightening emotional tension in the audience. The distinction between a symbolic and an 'atmospheric' use of music is not an easy one to maintain in every instance. One of the results of the revolution in musical thinking set on foot by the Reformation, and by humanist concerns with music and morals, was to make everyone, including dramatists, more aware of the emotive powers of music. But the deep philosophic basis for the traditional view was not obscured during Shakespeare's lifetime. At the end of his career, in *The Tempest*, the symbolic

---

[1] John Stevens, 'Music in Medieval Drama', *Proceedings of the Royal Musical Association*, lxxxiv (1957), p. 82.

contrast between concord and discord is used to mark the appearance and disappearance of the banquet:

> *Solemne and strange Musicke: and Prosper on the top (invisible). Enter severall strange shapes, bringing in a Banket; and dance about it with gentle actions of salutations . . .*
>
> *Thunder and Lightning. Enter Ariell (like a Harpey) claps his wings upon the Table, and with a quient device the Banquet vanishes.*

(III. 3)

This action is followed immediately by Ariel's solemn speech: 'You are three men of sinne . . .'.

Inherited also from the Middle Ages, and associated with productions of mystery and morality plays, is a symbolism of place. In the well-known miniature by Jean Fouquet (*c.* 1455), showing the martyrdom of St. Apollonia, the trumpeters and shawm-players are on the scaffold next to God and His angels and as far away as possible from the Devil and Hell.[1] Whether this symbolism was always a horizontal one (Heaven = Stage Right) or sometimes a vertical one also, it is hard to say. Leslie Hotson, reconstructing an Elizabethan public playhouse in *Shakespeare's Wooden O*, combines both, and puts the musicians 'aloft on the Walls of Heaven' at Stage Right.[2] To this, and to the associations of instruments, we shall later return.

The tradition of the Senecan tragedy, dating from the early years of Elizabeth's reign, was less fruitful from the musical point of view. 'In *Seneca His Ten Tragedies Translated into English*, published in London in 1581, songs are conspicuously absent. So they are from the first English tragedies fashioned in the image of Seneca, notably *Gorboduc*, acted in 1562.'[3] There is a Chorus in *Gorboduc* of 'four ancient and sage men of Britain', who utter moral verses after each of the first four acts. There is no evidence that they sang. Indeed choral singing of any sort seems to have been rare except in the plays of the boys' companies. The musical interest of *Gorboduc* is that the tradition of instrumental music with dumbshow seems to originate here. 'The order of the dumb show before the first act' reads:

> *First, the musicke of violenze began to play, during which came in upon the stage sixe wilde men, clothed in leaves; of whom the first bare in his*

---

[1] *The Oxford Companion to the Theatre*, 2nd edition, plate 23.      [2] p. 251.
[3] F. W. Sternfeld, 'The Use of Song in Shakespeare's Tragedies', *PRMA*, lxxxvi (1959).

*neck a fagot of small stickes, which they all, both severally and together,*
*assayed with all their strengthes to breake; . . . After they had this done,*
*they departed the stage, and the musicke ceased. Hereby was signified*
*that a state knit in unity. . . .*

What precise instrument was played, whether rebecs (too
coarse and popular?), violins proper (not generally known in
England at this date, and therefore too esoteric?) or members
of the viol family (recently fashionable as an import from Italy;
diminutive, viol*in*?), we cannot be sure. Nor is the function
of the music particularly clear. The likeliest dramatic explanation is that it underlined the prophetic, and so mysterious,
nature of the dumbshow; from the audience's point of view
the music was an added attraction, and theatre-managers
catered generously for their tastes throughout the period. We
shall see that music for the dumbshow was closely linked with
interval-music, 'music for the Act', in many plays. The dumb-
show in *Hamlet* shows the association of music with mime to be
still alive nearly forty years later:

> *Hoboyes play. The dumbe shew enters.*
>
> (III. 2, Folio)

Later dumbshows in *Gorboduc* call for 'the music of cornetts',
'the music of flutes' (probably recorders), 'the music of hautboys', and 'the drums and flutes' (here probably the military
fife).

*Gorboduc* was first acted by the young gentlemen of the
Inner Temple as part of their Christmas festivities in 1561–2.
Many of the actors were, like its part-author Thomas Sackville,
of noble birth. It was a contribution to fashion as well as to
learning. But fashionable circles at Court were served also
with another kind of tragedy, acted by the choirboys of the
Chapel Royal or of St. Paul's.[1] Richard Edwards's *Damon
and Pithias* has little that is classical about it except its name
and some passages of stichomythia.[2] Characters with names
like Will, Snap and Grim lead us to expect that peculiarly
English thing — a tragicomedy. This play, probably first
performed at Court three years after *Gorboduc* (Christmas,
1564/5), gives its all-male cast musical opportunities of a
sophisticated kind. For example, line 691: *Here Pithias singes
and the Regalles play* (the song is 'Awake, ye woful wights'). Or,

---

[1] G. E. P. Arkwright, 'Elizabethan Choirboys' Plays and their Music',
*PRMA*, xl (1914).         [2] Malone Society Reprints (1957).

B

line 1087 : *Here the Regalles play a mourning songe.* Or, line 1894 : *Then the Muses sing* : 'Alas, what happe hast thou poore Pithias now to die'. 'Awake, ye woful wights' survives in a setting for lute and voice, although regals are the instrument specified in the text of the play.[1] But the form in which most of these theatre-songs have come down to us is that of the 'consort song' — *i.e.* a song for solo voice and four accompanying instruments, probably viols.[2] The Muses' song in *Damon and Pithias* has a part for chorus as well as for soloist. The peculiar effect of music in this type of play, if these songs are to be credited, is to intensify the emotional climaxes — moments of parting, of death, of utter misery. This was a new thing ; and it was some years before the lesson could be put into practice by dramatists with a wider public.

One famous tragedy will give an idea of the more slender musical resources of the public theatres in their early years (1576 saw the building of The Theater, the first London playhouse) : Marlowe's *Doctor Faustus.* This was probably first performed between 1588 and 1592. The numerous texts published in quarto between 1604 and 1631 present two widely different versions of the play.[3] The earlier, shorter text concerns us chiefly. The Chorus is, as usual, the one-man prologue of Elizabethan tragedy. The recurrent appearances of 'the good Angell' and 'the evill Angell' seem to call for music, in the contrasting styles we expect from the medieval inheritance. A chorus of singing-men and boys would have been too expensive ; a consort of recorders perhaps signified the divine intervention through their association with the benevolent supernatural.[4] When Mephistopheles enters (line 514) *with divels, giving crownes and rich apparell to Faustus,* they *daunce, and then depart.* In one of the later additions the devils make a military appearance, one *playing on a Drum.* Probably their dances were of the popular pipe-and-tabor variety associated with vagrant minstrels and loose living — disorderly rather than ceremonious ; elsewhere in the play and its additions thunder and lightning and fireworks (an old medieval stage-trick) gave a chaotic air to devilish appearances. For the

---

[1] B.M. Add. MS. 15117. The regal is a small portative reed-organ.
[2] Peter Warlock, *Elizabethan Songs* (1926).
[3] Christopher Marlowe, *Works,* ed. C. F. Tucker Brooke (1910), pp. 139-41.
[4] J. S. Manifold, *Music in English Drama: From Shakespeare to Purcell* (1956), pp. 69-71.

vision of Helen *musicke sounds*, perhaps the recorders again. Other musical effects, more fully specified in the later quartos, are sennets ('solemn noyse of trumpets sound') ; some mock plain-song (*Enter all the Friers to sing the Dirge*) ; and the all-important, imperious bell ('The clocke striketh twelve').

The tradition of Plautine comedy was much richer in song. 'In sixteenth-century editions of that author the songs, or *cantica*, are conspicuous both for their numerous appearances and for the way they are typographically set off from the surrounding dialogue' [1] (this device was a standard practice of the period). Of the earliest English plays derived from Roman comedy, *Gammer Gurtons Nedle* (acted in Christ's College, Cambridge, *c*. 1553-4) is comparatively niggardly with music, though Act II opens with the well-known song, 'Backe and syde go bare, go bare'. But [*Ralph*] *Roister-Doister* by Udall ( ?Eton College, *c*. 1535-40) has songs galore (*Tib, An, and Margerie, doe singe here . . . Then they singe agayne*, etc.) (I. 3) ; a band of musicians on the stage who play for ceremony ('Up with some merry noyse, sirs, to bring home the bride') and for dances ('Pipe up a mery note./Let me heare it playde, I will foote it, for a grote') (both I. 4) ; and *The Peale of Belles rong by the Parish Clerk and Roister Doisters foure men* (III. 3).

The emphasis in these comedies is on popular song and dance. The requirements of *The Commodye of pacient and meeke Grissill* (mid-sixteenth-century) are for songs to be sung to known popular tunes — *e.g.* 'to the tune of Damon and Pithias', a broadside-ballad. The Elizabethan popular audience seems to have been avid for song and dance. Hence the popularity of the stage jig. The jig was a danced ballad in dialogue — 'customarily when a play was finished and the epilogue spoken, the musicians struck up a tune and the comedians came dancing out for the jig'.[2] Although the playwrights do not seem much to have liked jigs (Ben Jonson speaks of 'the concupiscence of jigs and dances'), there is no doubt the audience did. The only printed English jig which survives is *Frauncis new Jigge: between Frauncis a Gentleman and Richard a Farmer*, 1595.

One kind of comedy which certainly had no jig after it was the sophisticated, romantic comedy played by the boys' companies. *Campaspe*, by John Lyly, was 'played before the

---

[1] Sternfeld, *op. cit.* [p. 6 above, n. 3], p. 46.
[2] C. R. Baskervill, *The Elizabethan Jig and related Song Drama* (1929).

Queenes Maiestie On Newyeares Day at Night 1583–4 by Her Maiesties Children, and the Children of Paules'. Lyly had recently been presented with the lease of Blackfriars Hall, and the play was performed there before it was presented at Court.[1] The words for three songs are given in the text: the first, 'O for a bowle of fatt canary', requires three soloists and a 'chorus' (that is, probably, the three together). The light voices of boys, with string accompaniment, would carry well in an indoor theatre, or in Whitehall. The words of the songs were not always specified in the plays. When they are not, it may be a pointer towards their loose dramatic relevance. Nevertheless, a liberal allowance of song was felt to be essential to the plays as *entertainment*; hence, doubtless, the vastly increased number of printed song-texts in the 1632 edition of Lyly.[2] *Endimion*, besides songs, and music for a dumbshow, has a dance for the fairies — *The Fairies dance and with a Song pinch him, and he falleth asleep, they kiss Endimion, and depart* (IV. 3). Thomas Ravenscroft's *Briefe Discourse*, 1614, contains a Fairies' Song which may have been used in some later performances of the play. Marston, a later dramatist, writing for the Children of St. Paul's and Blackfriars, finds it necessary to apologize for the over-musical nature of *Sophonisba*: 'Let me intreat my reader not to taxe me for the fashion of the Entrances and Musique of this tragedy, for know it is printed onely as it was presented by the youths, and after the fashion of the private stage'. The implied contrast with the public theatre should not lead us to underestimate the amount of music, even of song, in the latter. Thomas Heywood's *Rape of Lucrece*, it has been observed, was entirely a public-theatre play; yet when printed in the first Quarto of 1608 it was supplied with twelve complete songs, and in 1638 the fifth Quarto has twenty-one.[3]

In attempting to describe the wealth of dramatic music which Shakespeare as a boy, or a young man, may have heard and later as a playwright adapted to his own purposes, I have spoken almost entirely of music *within* the play. There was, besides, opportunity for music before and after, and between

[1] J. Q. Adams (ed.), *The Chief Pre-Shakespearean Dramas* (1925).

[2] J. R. Moore, 'The Songs in Lyly's Plays', *Proceedings of the Modern Language Association*, xlii (1927), p. 623; he sides with W. W. Greg against W. J. Lawrence and E. B. Reed in questioning their authenticity. The present argument is not affected.

[3] *Idem*, 'The Songs of the Public Theatres in the time of Shakespeare', *Journal of English and Germanic Philology*, xxviii (1929), p. 166.

the acts. We must again distinguish between the practice of the public theatres (the 'common' theatres, as it were, open even to 'penny stinkards') and the private playhouses (catering for more select audiences at far more select prices). The latter present the simpler case.

An oft-quoted passage from the diary of the Duke of Stettin-Pomerania, who visited London in 1602, shows that in a private playhouse such as the Blackfriars there might be quite a concert before the play began:

> For a whole hour preceding the play one listens to a delightful entertainment on organs, lutes, pandorins, mandolins, violins and flutes, as on the present occasion, indeed, when a boy *cum voce tremula* sang . . . . charmingly to the accompaniment of a bass-viol.[1]

This would have preceded the 'three soundings' which heralded the actual start of the play. In *Cynthia's Revels*, Ben Jonson introduces *after the second sounding* three of the children quarrelling as to who shall 'speak the prologue' and wear the black velvet cloak. This 'Induction' is followed by *the third sounding* and then by the Prologue itself. The 'soundings' were trumpet-calls ('Instead of the trumpets sounding thrice, before the play begins, it shall not be amiss . . .'; Dekker, in a preface to his *Satiromastix*); and they were equally used, perhaps originated, in the public theatre. Jonson's *Every Man Out of His Humour*, played at the Globe in 1599, opens, like *Cynthia's Revels*, with an Induction between the second and third 'soundings'.[2]

Musical interludes between the acts of plays in the private theatres are abundantly witnessed by stage-directions such as these for Marston's *Sophonisba*:

> *The Ladies draw the curtains about Sophonisba, the rest accompanye Massinissa forth; the cornet and organs playing loud full music for the Act* [*i.e.* the act-interval, as often];
>
> *Organs mixt with recorders for this Act.*
>
> *Organs, Viols and Voices play for this Act.*
>
> *A base Lute and a Treble violl play for the act.*

---

[1] *Cit.* W. J. Lawrence, 'Music in the Elizabethan Theatre', *Musical Quarterly*, vi (1920), p. 193.

[2] Perhaps cornetts (much softer, wooden instruments) sounded instead of trumpets in some private theatres. Marston, whose stage-directions for music are unusually abundant, never once calls for trumpets. It may be that the trumpet sounded *outside* before the play, while cornetts carried out the trumpet's functions *inside* — to save the spectators' eardrums.

The practice may derive from the custom of presenting a dumb-show between the acts of a play and accompanying it with music (*e.g. Gorboduc, Endimion*). It certainly continued when festival performances at Court were required (Munday's *Fidele and Fortunio*, 1585). We are probably only told about it in the printed editions when the action of the play is dovetailed into the 'music for the Act'. There was an increasing tendency for this to happen: in Marston's *The Malcontent* there is the stage direction:

> *Enter Mendoza with a sconce, to observe Fernezes entrance, who, whilst the Act is playing, Enter, unbraced; 2 Pages before him with lights.*
>
> (II. 1)

In Marston's *The Dutch Courtezan* one of the characters, Mulli-grub, asks 'Is there any Fidlers in the house?' His wife tells him 'Creakes noyse' [*i.e.* band]. He rejoins, 'Bid 'em play, laugh, make merry, cast up my accountes, for Ile go hang myself presently . . .' Thus the music 'for the Act' is worked into the stuff of the play.[1]

Robert Greene's very English medley, *The Scottish Historie of Iames the forth, slaine at Flodden. Entermixed with a pleasant Comedie presented by Oboram King of Fayeries* (1598), makes much use not of dumbshow but of dance between the acts:[2]

> *Enter* Bohan *and* Oberon *after the first act: to them a round of Fairies, or some pretty dance.*
>
> (I. 3)
>
> *Enter* Slipper *with a companion,* boy *or* wench, *dancing a hornpipe, and dance out again.*
>
> (II. 2)
>
> *Enter a round, or some dance at pleasure.*
>
> (IV. 5)

The facts of dancing will be seen to have a bearing on the type of band employed in the theatres.

In the public playhouses, as Greene's Act II hornpipe suggests, the inter-act period and its entertainment was brief; but there is evidence enough that it existed. The style of it

---

[1] Manifold, pp. 15-16; J. Isaacs, *Production and Stage Management at the Black-friars Theatre* (1933), p. 12; W. R. Ingram, 'The Use of Music in the Plays of Marston', *Music and Letters*, xxxvii (1956), p. 154.

[2] Manifold, p. 18, observes that 'there is no very hard and fast line to be drawn between dumbshows, processions and dances'.

is vividly conveyed to us from the conversation between the Citizen and his Wife as they sit on the stage watching *The Knight of the Burning Pestle* by Beaumont and Fletcher, 'an elaborate burlesque of the popular drama'.[1] It is clear that the audience enjoyed calling for their favourite tunes and dances — 'Lachrimae' and 'Baloo', for example. Perhaps it was to avoid this kind of distraction when the stage emptied that Shakespeare in *King Lear* kept the 'storme and tempest' going — if this is, indeed, what the direction *Storme stille* in III. 1 implies.

With a reference to the Court masque we can draw to a close this brief survey of the drama as Shakespeare must have experienced it. The masque was the most costly and elaborate of all the dramatic shows of the age. Its ceremonial nature and its lavish musical effects will be described in connection with Shakespeare's last plays.[2]


## 2. THE HISTORIES

In the introduction to his still standard work, *Shakespeare and Music* (1896, 1931), E. W. Naylor records the following calculation :

> Out of thirty-seven plays of Shakespeare, there are no less than thirty-two which contain interesting references to music and musical matters *in the text itself*. There are also over three hundred stage-directions which are musical in their nature, and these occur in thirty-six out of the thirty-seven plays. The musical references in the text are most commonly found in the comedies . . .; while the musical stage-directions belong chiefly to the tragedies and are mostly of a military nature.

We shall not primarily be concerned here with the hundreds of references to music, though the whole world of Elizabethan music-making can be reconstructed from them; nor, on the other hand, exclusively with the stage-directions as such. The prime object of enquiry is the music which Shakespeare's first audiences heard — its nature and its dramatic function. To this work of reconstruction the spoken text, the stage-directions and the surviving music of the age can all contribute.

There are all kinds of categories which could be employed

---

[1] Moore, *JEGP*, xxviii (1929), p. 168; see also G. H. Cowling, *Music on the Shakespearean Stage* (1913), p. 68.    [2] See below, p. 41.

to sort out the abundant material; but basically, I think, we can regard any song or instrumental piece from two points of view: (i) as part of the Imitation which constitutes a play; and (ii) as part of the Communication which the audience receives. Thus, to take the simplest example, the 'flourish' of trumpets which heralded King Duncan's entry (*Macbeth* I. 4) simply reproduced on the stage, as part of the dramatic imitation, the traditional pomp and ceremony pertaining to a king in real life; those in the audience, on the other hand, receive the 'solemn noyse' of trumpets direct, ringing through their ears, and are emotionally stirred. A more complex example is the famous opening of *Twelfth Night*. The 'sweet sound/That breathes upon a banke of Violets' is, in dramatic fact, a consort of Duke Orsino's household musicians; but in those who hear its 'dying fall' with their own ears it must infuse, as it does in the Duke, the very essence of love-melancholy, both because of its long traditional association with romance, and because of its own languorously expressive beauty.

Shakespeare's use of music as 'imitation' is immensely varied, even considered from a purely naturalistic standpoint. It ranges from the courtly masque in *Timon of Athens* to the balladry of Autolycus in *The Winter's Tale* ('hee singes several Tunes, faster than you'l tell money').

We may begin with the 'pomp and circumstance' of the early Histories: 'flourishes', 'sennets', 'tuckets' and 'alarums' spatter their pages and must have pierced even through the noise of Elizabethan London on many an afternoon. J. S. Manifold distinguishes these puzzling terms as follows:[1] 'The Flourish is a far less precise signal than the military ones: there is little evidence of its having any particular tune, and none of its having any particular meaning . . .; within the theatre it can be played on trumpets, or cornetts, or (to judge by later practice) on any other instrument you please.' Flourishes were probably extemporized and, therefore, brief and simple. 'The Tucket, on the other hand, is a distinctive signal'; it was a sort of heraldic badge in sound, played probably on a single trumpet and consisting of 'a fairly lengthy

---

[1] Manifold, ch. 2, Signals; ch. 4, Brass. This is the best book about Shakespeare's instrumental resources and their theatrical associations; see esp. pp. 26-30. But consult also H. M. Fitzgibbon: 'Instruments and their Music in the Elizabethan Drama', *MQ*, xvii (1931), p. 319.

call — longer at least than the average Flourish'. The Sennet is quite distinct from the Tucket. Its instrumentation is always plural when it is given at all; and it is usually called upon to accompany a fairly lengthy bit of action on the stage. For a later example we have *King Lear*, I. 1 : *Sound a Sennet, Enter one bearing a Coronet, then Lear, then the Dukes of Albany and Cornwall, next Gonorill, Regan, Cordelia, with followers.*

We may suppose that the pomp and ceremony of a royal entrance were considerably foreshortened for dramatic purposes. The naturalism is something less than complete. The representation of battle was inevitably even more circumscribed. Battle in progress is usually indicated by stage-directions such as *Alarum and Excursions* (*e.g.* 1 *Henry VI*, III. 2, where it is closely followed by *Retreat. Excursions*). The 'alarum' and the 'retreat', like the 'parley' and the 'charge', are military signals, sounded on trumpet or drums according to the status of the troops concerned; but in nine cases out of ten when 'alarums' are a mere symptom of battle, so to speak, drums seem to be required.[1] At the end of Henry V's famous speech 'Once more unto the Breach' the crowning line 'Cry, God for Harry, England, and S. *George*' (III. 1) is drowned with *Alarum, and Chambers goe off* — clearly a tumultous explosion of drums and guns. The greatest occasion of all in the Elizabethan theatre for cannonading was a good sea-fight (see 2 *Henry VI*, IV. 1 — *Alarum. Fight at Sea. Ordnance goes off*).

Another feature of the music of the battlefield is signified in stage-directions by the word 'March'; the following sequence from *1 Henry VI*, III. 3 helps establish that it was an identifiable rhythmic pattern which could be played on a drum alone : [2]

PUCELL.  [*i.e.* Joan of Arc]
    Your Honors shall perceive how I will worke,
    To bring this matter to the wished end.
                 *Drumme sounds a farre off.*
    Hearke, by the sound of Drumme you may perceive
    Their Powers are marching unto Paris-ward.
                 *Here sound an English March.*
    There goes the Talbot, with his Colours spred,
    And all the Troupes of English after him.
                 *French March.*

---

[1] E. W. Naylor, *Shakespeare and Music* (1896; rev. 1931), pp. 159-60; Manifold, pp. 24-5.　　[2] Manifold, p. 30.

Now in the Rereward comes the Duke and his;
Fortune in favor makes him lagge behinde.
Summon a Parley, we will talke with him.
                    *Trumpets sound a Parley.*

Outside the theatre a march could take a more musical form
(though the 'nine Trumpets, and a Kettle Drum' that 'did
very sprightly and actively sound the "Danish march"'
(*Hamlet* III. 1) may still be classed as 'field' music).[1]  A Cambridge ms. contains, for instance, 'The Hamburgh March'
in an arrangement for lute.[2]  Besides the national marches,
the dramatist calls sometimes for a 'dead march' : it was used
mainly for funerals, but not exclusively — as witness *1 Henry
VI*, II. 1 :

*Enter Talbot, Bedford, and Burgundy, with scaling ladders;
Their Drummes beating a Dead March.*

'It would seem that any march played on muffled drums was
called a dead march.' [3]

*Richard III* has nothing to add to our knowledge of Elizabethan stage music; but we see Shakespeare's maturing 'art
of music'.  The play as recorded in the Quartos of 1597 onwards occasionally fills out for us a detail which the First Folio
leaves vague.  For instance, in IV. 2 the Folio reads *Sound a
Sennet.  Enter Richard in pompe*; the Quarto *The Trumpets sound.
Enter Richard crowned.* . . .  More strikingly dramatic than the
purely routine militarism of *Henry VI* is the scene where Richard
drowns the piteous exclamations of the Queen and the Duchess
'with the clamorous report of warre' (IV. 4) :

RICH.  A flourish Trumpets, strike Alarum Drummes:
         Let not the Heavens heare these Tell-tale women
         Raile on the Lords Annointed.  Strike I say.
                    *Flourish.   Alarums.*

An interesting hint of the way the later Shakespeare will weave
the musical *effects* and the musical *references* together can be
gathered from Richard's opening speech where he identifies
'merry Meeting', 'delightfull Measures' and 'a Ladies Chamber' with 'the lascivious pleasing of a Lute'.  Richard is not

---

[1] Thomas Dekker, *Works*, i, p. 295: describing the royal entry of James I and
Anne of Denmark into London, 1603 (*cit.* J. H. Long, *Shakespeare's Use of Music*
(1955), p. 46).
[2] Cambridge University Library MS. Dd. ii. 11; Naylor, pp. 200-3, gives
further examples of music.          [3] Manifold, p. 30.

merely a Duke and a future King who is entitled to the pomp
of trumpets — a 'brass-worthy person', to use Manifold's
expressive phrase; he is a man 'rudely stampt', for whom
the blaring stridency of military instruments is both self-
expression and psychological compensation.

The next group of historical plays, belonging to the years
1596 to 1599, contains *Richard II*, the two parts of *Henry IV*,
and *Henry V*. It is less 'stately-written', less Marlovian, than
the early trilogy on *Henry VI*. Shakespeare uses 'the harsh
resounding Trumpets dreadful bray' far more economically.
But this is not all. The whole dramatic texture is richer and
more human, and with it his use of music. The plays form a
chronological, if not a firm dramatic, unit, and we may take
them together.

One could hardly foretell from *Richard II* the enlargement
which the historical canvas will gain when Falstaff takes up
his residence in Eastcheap and entices the young prince to join
him. But one could forecast an increasing subtlety in the use
of music to communicate dramatic intention. Music employed,
apparently, in straightforward naturalistic 'imitation' re-
inforces the weakness, the inner collapse of Richard. At the
beginning he is the king who can require, indeed command,
the judicial combat between John of Gaunt's son, Bolinbroke,
and Thomas Mowbray, Duke of Norfolk. The royal trumpets,
together with a blaze of heraldry, confer the highest dignity
on this quarrel; the chivalric high-spiritedness of the affair is
summed up by Mowbray's 'my dancing soule doth celebrate/
This Feast of Battell'. *A long Flourish* (unusual epithet) marks
Richard's decision to interrupt the fight before it had well
begun, and to pronounce judgement. As if to make the contrast more absolute, even musically, the banished Mowbray
compares himself, as he will be in a foreign land, to

> . . . an unstringed Vyall, or a Harpe,
> Or like a cunning Instrument cas'd up,
> Or being open, put into his hands,
> That knowes no touch to tune the harmony.
>
> (III. 3)

But the basic musical contrast of the play is yet to come.
Richard himself is not merely to be deposed by the man his
trumpets had mastered and to be murdered unceremoniously
in a 'rude assault' by one of this man's minions (there is surely

a bitter irony in the blare of the trumpets for the new king immediately after Exton's guilty speech). He is also to be shown as jangled and harassed by badly-played music of a very different kind; he soliloquizes in prison while music plays in the street outside:

> . . . . Musicke do I heare?
> Ha, ha? keepe time: How sowre sweet Musicke is,
> When Time is broke, and no Proportion kept?
> So is it in the Musicke of mens lives:
> And heere have I the daintinesse of eare
> To heare time broke in a disorder'd string:
> But for the Concord of my State and Time,
> Had not an eare to heare my true Time broke. . .
>
> This Musicke mads me, let it sound no more,
> For though it have helpe madmen to their wits,
> In me it seemes, it will make wise-men mad:
> Yet blessing on his heart that gives it me;
> For 'tis a signe of love.                                    (V. 5)

This dramatic situation reverses the earlier one entirely. The musicians (presumably playing within the tiring-house [1]) are unseen, unidentified, unbidden; their music either is in fact, or at least seems to Richard, unrhythmical and therefore un-satisfying. Whereas as king he had power over his trumpets, and made them express his royal will, now another man's wish imposes this unroyal music on him and puts him into its power. The dissolution of Richard's royal personality is as clearly symbolized by his musical exacerbation as by his breaking of the mirror (IV. 1).

*Henry IV* is far richer than *Richard II* in music and references to music; and not one but several dramatic contrasts are developed. They can only be briefly hinted at here. The first and most important is between the ceremonial trumpets and drums of the Court and the 'vulgar Tavern music' of Falstaff and his companions; then, there is the contrast be-tween Falstaff as he pretends to be (the enthusiastic singer of anthems) and as he is (an addict of the scurvier sort of ballad); another, between the depravity brought on by a surfeit of fiddlers (as well as sack) and the healing potentialities of the

---

[1] The 'disordered string' might seem to suggest a consort of viols; but in the dramatic context this would be inappropriate. A 'broken consort' of standard composition (see below) would contain bowed and plucked strings as well as wind. Or, a single lutenist could serve the purpose.

music which plays for Henry on his deathbed. A more subtle musical paradox lies at the heart of Hotspur's character. On the one hand he is the high-spirited philistine who scorns music and poetry as he does the arts of love and Glendower's Celtic ravings; on the other, he is the epitome of all that is chivalrous and embraces his companions-in-arms to the 'music' made by 'all the lofty Instruments of Warre' (V. 3). In these two plays for the first time four 'worlds' of Shakespeare music meet and blend — the world of the camp, of the Court, of the Church and of the tavern.

### 3. THE EARLY COMEDIES

The Histories show us that however simple the 'imitative' materials Shakespeare uses — a fanfare of trumpets, snatches of bawdy songs sung by a fat rascal, a 'noyse' of musicians in the street — the 'communication' is becoming something far from simple. The Comedies show a similar growth in dramatic complexity; they also show a wide new range of musical possibilities in their variety of song and of instrumental pieces.

*The Two Gentlemen of Verona* is usually dated early in the 1590s. This romantic intrigue of love and friendship provides the occasion for one of the best known of all Shakespeare's songs — 'Who is Silvia? What is she', for which no contemporary setting survives. Proteus, earlier in the play, has encouraged the foolish Thurio to serenade Silvia:

> After your dire-lamenting Elegies,
> Visit by night your Ladies chamber-window
> With some sweet Consort; to their Instruments
> Tune a deploring dumpe : the nights dead silence
> Will well become such sweet complaining grievance :
> This, or else nothing, will inherit her.
>
> (III. 2)

They accordingly go off 'into the City' to hire some musicians — a nicely calculated theatrical touch, since the 'consort' may indeed have come from the City.[1] When they return Proteus sings the 'evening Musique' which he, deceiving Thurio, uses to press his own suit — his false suit, since Silvia is betrothed to his friend Valentine, and he himself to Julia, who in boy's disguise comes in with the Host to hear him. The serenade seems, from the text, to consist of an instrumental introduction,

[1] See below, p. 24.

the song itself, and an instrumental postlude which is played whilst Julia and the Host talk together:

HO.   How doe you, man? the Musicke likes you not.
JU.   You mistake: the Musitian likes me not.
HO.   Why, my pretty youth?
JU.   He plaies false (father).
HO.   How, out of tune on the strings?
JU.   Not so, but yet
   So false that he grieves my very heart-strings.

    .       .       .       .       .

HO.   I perceive you delight not in Musique.
JU.   Not a whit, when it jars so.
HO.   Harke, what fine change is in the Musique.
JU.   I: that change is the spight.

(IV. 2)

If Julia's remarks are to have their full dramatic force, Proteus must not only have sung the solo-part, but also played an instrument in the consort.   The naïve idealizations of the lyric ('Holy, faire and wise is she') lend a certain poignancy to the falseness which Proteus spreads around him.

In *Love's Labour's Lost*, written at about the same time, the use of music is more ambitious.   Whereas in *The Two Gentlemen of Verona* the musicians were adults, now we have boys singing.   'All the evidence . . . goes to show that *Love's Labour's Lost* was a battle in a private war between Court factions.   The large number of parts for which boy-players would be required — the Princess and her ladies, Jacquenetta, Moth — points away from the regular actors' companies to some great household where a troupe of choristers was maintained.'[1]   *Love's Labour's Lost* strikes a note of brilliant artificiality (not a term of abuse for the Elizabethans); the play, Granville-Barker wrote, is 'never very far from the actual formalities of song and dance.   The long last act is half mask and half play; and in song and dance the play ends'.   The courtly 'game of love' is embellished by music on three or four occasions.   The first promise of music, however, is not fulfilled: in I. 2 Armado, the Braggart, says to Moth, his page: 'Sing, Boy, my spirit grows heavy in love', but Moth puts him off 'till this company be past' and eventually does not sing at all. One suspects some kind of revision here: it is unlike Shake-

[1] Richard David, introduction to the Arden edition of the play, p. 1.   One should remember that the professional children's companies were out of action from 1590-9.

speare, or any Elizabethan dramatist, to lead the audience to
the brink of music, as it were, and then withdraw. Act III
begins *Enter Braggart and Boy. Song.*

BRA. Warble childe, make passionate my sense of hearing.
BOY. Concolinel.

Either this is what is termed a 'blank' song (*i.e.* a song for which
no words are given), or Moth's mysterious ejaculation 'Concolinel' gives the clue.[1] There seems, in any case, very little
immediate dramatic point in a song here, except that it gives
Moth an opening for a whimsical fantasy on the singing of
lovers ('to Jigge off a tune at the tongues end, canarie to it with
the feete, humour it with turning up your eie : sigh a note and
sing a note . . .'). The last act is full of theatrical embellish-
ments and music is prominent in them. The 'mask of the
Muscovites' (actually the King and his three lords in disguise),
before the Princess and her ladies, is heralded with trumpets
and brought in by 'Blackmoores with musicke' (in its limited
sense 'music' often seems to exclude loud instruments, trumpets and hautboys). With traditional propriety the lords
invite the ladies to dance, but they refuse. Dance-music
played by a consort of costumed musicians is called for as a
background to the verbal battle of the King and Rosaline
(V. 2). The next show 'in the posterior of this day' is that of
The Nine Worthies, which Dull promised earlier (V. 1) to
accompany on the tabor (a small drum) so that they could
dance the hay, a popular dance. The play ends with a sort
of dramatized debate in song : the Dialogue that the two
Learned Men have compiled in praise of 'the Owle and the
Cuckow'. The first song belongs to *Ver*, 'When Daisies pied,
and Violets blew'; it is answered by *Hiems*, 'When Isicles
hang by the wall' (no contemporary music for either song
survives). The original stage-direction here is *Enter all.*
Whether the non-courtly cast (Holofernes, Armado and the rest)
were divided into two singing groups, or whether each group
had a boy-soloist as 'spokesman', cannot be decided. The
latter seems most likely to be effective.

One cannot without ingenious absurdity argue that the
music is deeply integrated into the dramatic structure of the
play. But it is not mere extraneous entertainment; it does
much to enforce the rarefied atmosphere of this courtly game

---

[1] See Arden edition, p. 45, for a possible Irish derivation.

with its 'trim gallants, full of Courtship and of state'.

*A Midsummer Night's Dream*, written to grace a noble wedding, introduces us to another traditional antithesis in Elizabethan music — between the supernatural and the normal,
everyday.   On the one hand we have Oberon, Titania, Puck
(alias Robin Goodfellow) and a troupe of Fairies; on the
other, a double normality — Duke Theseus and the courtly
lovers contrasting with Bottom the Weaver and his gang.   The
music of fairyland sings Titania asleep, 'You spotted snakes
with double tongue' — a prayer for her safe repose (II. 2).
It plays again perhaps between Acts III and IV, when the
Lovers *sleepe all the Act* (*i.e.* on the stage throughout the act-
interval).   It returns at the end of the play when an air of
supernatural blessing is shed around by the entry of the *King
and Queene of Fairies, with their traine* and their final song, which
embraces the *actual* noble household within the beneficent
sleep-world of the play.   Titania's amorous aberration in loving
Bottom in his ass's head is beautifully pointed by her being
wakened by Bottom's clownish singing of 'The Woosell cocke,
so blacke of hew' (III. 1), a splendid contrast to the fairies'
lullaby; and by Bottom's reply to her offer of music — 'Wilt
thou heare some musicke, my sweet love? — CLOWN.   I have
a reasonable good ear in musicke.   Let us have the tongs and
the bones.' — *Musicke Tongs, Rurall Musicke* (IV. 1).[1]   The
homely rusticity of Bottom and his crew of 'hard-handed men'
is further brought home by the trumpet which, ironically,
introduces their 'palpable gross play'.   There is something
quite topsy-turvy about Bottom's musical, as about his other
artistic, efforts.   So perhaps it is wrong to talk about the
'normality' of his world.   The supernatural is all air and fire;
he is all earth.   The true norm is sounded by Theseus with his
horns and hounds (*Winde Hornes . . . Hornes and they wake*),
bringing back, though not for long, the 'daylight world'.   The
Elizabethan horn was a signalling, not a musical, instrument;
but neither would it have belonged to Bottom's 'skiffle' band.

### 4. THE BAND: THE MUSICIANS: THE MUSIC-ROOM

In our reconstruction of Shakespeare's dramatic 'mirror of
sound' we cannot any longer conveniently postpone certain

[1] This stage-direction is not in the Quarto texts.

practical questions. What, for instance, was the nature of the consort, which played so essential a part in casting the spell of fairyland over *A Midsummer Night's Dream*? One commentator has argued that the stage-direction in IV. 1, *Musick still*, is an inversion of the normal *Still musick* and refers to the music of recorders, associated elsewhere in Elizabethan drama with 'benevolent deities' and the other-world.[1] This fits in very well with its purposes: Titania and Oberon are charming the mortals into sleep again. But grammatically it is unconvincing. If, as is possible, Oberon's own awaking of Titania was accompanied by music, then the direction to musicians to 'go on sounding' is not so nonsensical.

The most likely consort for this play would seem, perhaps, to be a consort of viols, to accompany the lullaby in the manner of the early stage-songs for voice and viols. But was this so? The classic form of consort for theatre music was not a consort of viols or of recorders but a 'broken consort' (that is, a consort of mixed instruments). The constituent members were as follows: lute; pandora and cittern (both flat-backed instruments of the guitar family, wire-strung in pairs); treble and bass viols; and flute (either the transverse flute, or the recorder). The evidence that this was a standard combination lies in the very existence of the *Consort Lessons* of Thomas Morley (1599, 1611) and of Philip Rosseter (1609); these were followed in 1614 by a third collection, Leighton's *Tears and Lamentations* — songs, this time, for the same six instruments with solo voice. Sidney Beck, introducing Morley's *Consort Lessons*, has convincingly assembled much of the evidence that connects this band with the stage. There is its extraordinary versatility — 'Popular tunes, marches, folk and courtly dances, keyboard pieces, a traditional ground, a lute-air, a five-part Italian madrigal, a three-part canzonet — all are scored with equal ease.' And there is its effectiveness: the consort is designed to perform 'music of calculated effect, originally devised, not so much for the pleasure of the participants in private chamber music as for the delight and entertainment of a larger listening audience. Functional in essence, it was music *par excellence* for the festive occasion, yet in its deeper significance . . . an ideal handmaid for the dramatist.'[2] There

---

[1] Manifold, p. 98.

[2] Sydney Beck (ed.), *The First Book of Consort Lessons: Collected by Thomas Morley: 1599 and 1611* (New York, 1959), pp. 2, 6.

C

are, moreover, the circumstances of its production : Morley dedicated his book to the Lord Mayor and Aldermen of London and had the City Waits in mind as ideal performers.  When a band of musicians was required for a theatre, there were two obvious sources, Court (the Royal musicians) and City (the Waits).  It was not unknown for the Waits to meet with official rebuke for being away, augmenting their earnings in a playhouse, when they ought to have been dignifying some civic feast.  The evidence in the plays themselves is not specific enough to clinch the matter ; but such a passage as the following, from Dekker's *Old Fortunatus*, certainly supports the notion that this standard consort was in use for theatre music :

> *Musicke still: Enter Shaddow.* . . .  Musicke ?  O
> delicate warble [flute or recorder] . . . O
> delicious strings [viols and lute] :  these
> heavenly wyre-drawers [cittern and pandora].[1]

That it was a recognized 'unit' of professional musicians admits no doubt — and a recognized English unit, too, as Michael Praetorius, the German musician, shows :

> What the English call a Consort, very aptly taken from the Latin word *consortium*, is when people come together in company with all kinds of different instruments . . .[2]

Such a unit played before Queen Elizabeth on her progresses (1575, 1578, 1591) : 'The Fairy Queene and her maides daunced about the Garden, singing a Song of sixe Parts, with the musicke of an exquisite consort, wherein was the lute, pandora, base violl, citterne, treble viol and flute . . . [The Queen] commanded to heere it sung and to be daunced three times over.'[3]  The consort also played at weddings (Sir Henry Unton's) and for masques (Campion's ; sometimes considerably augmented).

The evidence of the royal progresses is especially interesting because it establishes two points : first, that this band was not too heavy an accompaniment for a solo voice (*e.g.* Arion singing on the dolphin's back) ; and, secondly, that music of six parts could be both sung and danced to while the band was playing. The first means that the serenade in *The Two Gentlemen of Verona* could have been accompanied by a 'broken consort' (the gentlemen came from 'the city', we recall) ; the second

---

[1] *Cit.* Beck, p. 14, see also Manifold, ch. 1, The Band.
[2] Beck, pp. 9-10 ; Manifold, pp. 6-7.          [3] Beck, p. 15.

explains how *A Midsummer Night's Dream* may have been concluded, in its 'private' productions, without the need for Puck's epilogue.

In the Induction to *The Knight of the Burning Pestle* a snatch of dialogue, between the Citizen (imagined as being part of the audience) and the Speaker of the Prologue, shows the casual way in which the professional band may sometimes have been hired for a public theatre:

CIT. What stately music have you? you have shawms? [1]

S. OF P. Shawms! no.

CIT. No! I'm a thief, if my mind did not give me so. Ralph plays a stately part, and he must needs have shawms: I'll be at the charge of them myself, rather than we'll be without them.

S. OF P. So you are like to be.

CIT. Why, and so I will be: there's two shillings; — let's have the waits of Southwark; they are as rare fellows as any are in England; and that will fetch them all o'er the water with a vengeance, as if they were mad.

S. OF P. You shall have them.

The Speaker of the Prologue evidently had the economic aspect of music well in mind. So should we. Musicians cost money, if they could not be found among the cast of actors, and the money came off the profits. Hence, we may be sure, a tendency in public-theatre plays to economize in elaborate musical effects. When the King's Men took over the Blackfriars theatre and acted plays indoors to a select highly-paying audience, music was more lavishly provided, as it had been in the comedies presented at court or in noble households. Popular taste demanded music, song and dance; and it was doubtless in order to meet this demand economically that the Chamberlain's Men (later to be the King's Men) began to employ more musician-actors in the last few years of the Queen's reign — more *singers*, in particular.

Since the earliest professional actors inherited the traditions (acrobatic, mimetic, musical) of the medieval minstrel, it is not surprising to find that two of the Chamberlain's Men, when the company was established in 1594, had been musicians to the Earl of Leicester. Moreover, Will Kempe, famous as a comedian and a dancer (with his nine-days' dance from London to Norwich), could have taken care of all popular and 'rural'

---

[1] The shawm, hautboy or 'wait' was the traditional instrument of the waits as watchmen of the city or township.

music.  At his retirement in 1599 his place was filled by
Robert Armin, who, with Feste's part to play in *Twelfth Night*,
must have been a good singer.  An oft-discussed stage-direction
in *Much Ado About Nothing* records the name of another adult
singer — *Enter Prince, Leonato, Claudio and Jacke Wilson.*  Jack
Wilson took the part of Balthasar and sang 'Sigh no more,
Ladies, sigh no more'.  The company seems also to have
acquired at this time, as apprentices, some boys who could
sing.  There are the two pages who come in in *As You Like It* to
sing 'It was a Lover and his lasse'; and perhaps a Welsh boy,
Robert Goffe, for Lady Glendower in *1 Henry IV*.[1]

There was no orchestra-pit in any Elizabethan theatre.
The musicians either made appearances on-stage as actors or
were somewhere hidden away at the side, back or above the
stage.  On one or two occasions they were certainly *below* the
stage — *e.g.* the scene in *Antony and Cleopatra* (IV. 3) when
Antony's soldiers hear the music of hautboys from beneath
them and draw ominous conclusions.  Music from below had
sinister, indeed hellish, connotations : in *Gorboduc* (IV. 1)
hautboys sound for an entry from 'hell'.

This in itself rather suggests that the normal place for music
was 'above'.  Leslie Hotson's assertion that the musicians
were on top of the mansion of 'Heaven' on stage right has
already been mentioned.  This is only convincing if his general
stage arrangements, in particular the array of 'tents', can
be accepted.  In a theatre with a balcony over the stage (and
the great majority of Elizabethan plays seem to call for one)
the likely place for a music-room is in it — a curtained
space on the first floor level next to the Lords' room.  But it
may have been some time before any fixed music-room became
a necessity for the adult companies working in the public
theatres.

In this as in other matters we must distinguish between the
practice of the private (indoor and select) theatres, and the
public (outdoor and mixed) theatres.  In the private theatres,
such as the Blackfriars, Whitefriars and St. Paul's, there was
indubitably a music-room over the stage — Marston's *Sophonisba* (1606) requires *A short song to soft Musique above*; Middleton's *A Chaste Maid in Cheapside* (performed in 1611) requires

---

[1] See T. W. Baldwin, *Organization and Personnel of the Shakespearean Company*
(1927), pp. 74, 418.

*a sad Song in the Musick-Roome.*[1] The music-room had become
a necessity because of the prevalence of inter-act music. The
room was curtained so that the musicians could be shown
playing during the interval and concealed during the play
itself. The curtains were useful also for discoveries 'above' —
or, for that matter, concealments above. Rowley's *Thracian
Wonder* (performed *c.* 1600) has the stage-directions: *Pythia
speaks in the Musick-room behinde the Curtains . . . Pythia above,
behinde the Curtains.* The increasing popularity of music, and
the need perhaps to be able to adapt new-fangled theatrical
tastes to older plays and playhouses, may have caused this
arrangement to be copied in the Globe and other public
theatres towards the end of Shakespeare's life-time.[2]

J. C. Adams, in his well-known reconstruction of the Globe,
put the music-room higher still, on the second-floor level. But,
as Richard Hosley has observed, this theory, besides being
'architecturally and structurally improbable', is not supported
by dramatic material from the first Globe theatre and, in any
case, strains the common phrases 'come down', 'above',
'music in the air'. Music in the first-floor gallery would fulfil
the natural requirements of meaning.

The bulk of the evidence relating to public-theatre plays
in Elizabeth's reign makes one wish to emphasize the flexibility of the musical arrangements. The band, if there was one,
was mobile. When off duty it probably waited, with the
trumpeter(s) and drummer(s), inside the tiring-house somewhere, trying to keep out of the way. Hence, surely, the
frequency of the simple location (in stage-directions) — *within.*
For example, *Low March within* (*Julius Caesar*, IV. 2); *Musicke
sounds within* (*Troilus and Cressida*, III. 1); Drum *within* (*Macbeth*, I. 3). In Elizabethan stage-directions 'the term *within*
usually refers to the stage level of the tiring-house'.[3]

In the court and aristocratic plays of the same period an
equal flexibility must have been a necessity. Those we have
already examined show the musicians often on the stage as
actors (*e.g. Love's Labour's Lost*, V. 2; *Enter Blackmoores with
musicke*; and, in my opinion, the serenade music in *The Two*

---

[1] This play was performed at the Swan, a public playhouse, but the late date
is significant.

[2] The material and the conclusions of this paragraph are taken from R.
Hosley's interesting and thoroughly documented article 'Was there a Music-Room
in Shakespeare's Globe?' *Shakespeare Survey*, xiii (1960).

[3] Hosley, p. 118.

*Gentlemen of Verona*, IV. 2). The number of cases when *single* musicians perform as actors is, of course, legion throughout the whole period on every kind of stage.

One other purely factual question is timely before we return to the plays themselves : what sources of music were available to Shakespeare? — did he fully use the musical wealth of Elizabethan England? The simple and obvious answer to this is that he only used the musical resources which were guaranteed to be theatrically effective. Hence the notable absence of madrigals and of fantasies for 'whole consorts' especially of viols. These two types of music were aristocratic in their essential refinement and restraint; they were not the music with which to hold the attention of the groundlings at the Globe — nor, to judge from the evidence, the court or private-theatre audience. This latter audience, too, had come to be entertained, not to give that degree of meditative concentration which serious madrigals and fantasies require. The instrumental music best adapted for theatrical, as for ceremonial purposes, was the varied 'broken consort' whose nature and repertoire have already been described. Songs, too, had to make an immediate impression : popular ballads and art-songs for solo voice do this in a way that complex polyphonic songs cannot. A simple dialogue, of course, can be very effective ; so too can simple part-singing — catches and rounds and 'three-man's' songs ; Sir Toby Belch and his boon-companions do a lot of this 'catterwalling'.

Songs and instrumental pieces were sometimes, we may assume, especially written for the plays : Robert Johnson, lutenist at court from 1603 for thirty years, may have composed his settings of 'Wher the bee sucks' and 'Full fathome five' for the original production of *The Tempest*. But precise evidence in this and kindred matters is hard to come by. Generally, I think, we shall be safer in believing that Shakespeare, like other dramatists, adapted music that was already to hand, as he certainly did, for instance, with Desdemona's 'Willow' song. Often, surviving named songs are patently of a later date (*e.g.* 'Take, oh take those lips away', from *Measure for Measure*, in the setting by John Wilson).

The question about sources can be put from another and more practical point of view — where should the scholar and the producer turn today to get the music they need for authentic study and authentic performance of the plays?[1]  For artsongs the repertory of the lutenist song-writers is available in all its immense variety;  for popular songs, there are few direct sources, except the collections of Thomas Ravenscroft, *Pammelia, Deuteromelia, Melismata* (1609–11) — and even here, on Ravenscroft's own admission, there is 'writing up' to be taken into account, 'Art having reformed what pleasing tunes injurious time and ignorance had deformed'.  But in the huge collections of music for solo lute and for the virginals can be found dozens of pieces which embody the popular songs and dances of the age :  'Fortune my foe', 'Heart's Ease', 'Lachrimae', 'Mall Sims', 'Calleno custure me', to mention only a handful.  Courtly dances (pavanes, galliards, almains, etc.) are to be found arranged for virginals and for lute, as well as in settings for four or five viols (a huge repertory, still largely unpublished) and in settings for 'broken consort' (see above). Our knowledge of the music used, and referred to, by Shakespeare is being constantly extended.

## 5. THE MIDDLE COMEDIES

The practical questions raised at the beginning about Lorenzo's speech in *The Merchant of Venice* can now have some sort of an answer.  There is no precise stage-direction in the texts, but it seems as if Stephano, instructed to bring his music forth into the air, will actually bring a group of musicians (a very common use of the term 'music') on to the stage.  They may even have been revealed sitting in the 'discovery space' at the back of the stage, though there is no actual warrant for this.  The circumstantial evidence suggests a consort of strings;  the imagery, especially the word 'touch', applies better to strings than to 'pipes' — 'the tutches of sweet harmonie'.[2]

This scene, quoted earlier at length, raises a new dramatic issue.  Shakespeare is doing two things — changing the dramatic mood of the play by a musical interlude, and talking at the same time about the way in which music does this.

---

[1] The contemporary Elizabethan music edited by Thurston Dart for the complete recorded Shakespeare sponsored by The British Council (Argo Record Company) provides a splendid guide *in sound*.

[2] See *The Oxford English Dictionary*, s.v. 'Touch', sb. II. 8. a.

J. H. Long well describes this scene as a 'nocturne' : the moon-light, the lovers sitting on the bank, the music, the light 'burn-ing in my hall', all combine to make Portia's homecoming romantically serene. Shakespeare seems to have his own 'broken consort' of poetry, action and music for the first time in full play : 'the Venetian incompatibilities of gold and love are finally reconciled, almost as much in the golden music as in the golden ring'.[1]

Other points of interest in the play are : the use of cornetts (slim, curved, woodwind instruments fingered like recorders) instead of trumpets for the various entries of Portia's suitors; and the song, 'Tell me where is fancie bred' (for which no contemporary music survives). The latter is performed in response to Portia's command :

> Let musicke sound while he doth make his choise,
> Then if he loose he makes a Swan-like end,
> Fading in musique.

> (III. 2)

The stage-direction is : *Here Musicke* (Folio) ; *A Song the whilst* Bassanio *comments on the Caskets to himselfe* (all texts). 'Musicke' does not necessarily imply more than lute accompaniment (though the consort may have played here since they were available anyway). Perhaps an arrangement like that re-corded in the autograph working-copy of Massinger's *Believe as you List* was made : line 1968, *Harry Wilson and Boy ready for the song at y^e Arras* ; line 2021, *Metell : the Lute strikes and then the Songe.*[2]

Portia's music is more a 'communication' from the drama-tist to the audience of the importance of the moment than an 'imitation' in dramatic terms — though it has been suggested by more than one commentator that in its rhyming the song conveyed a light hint from Portia to Bassanio as to how he should choose.

*Much Ado About Nothing* and *As You Like It* cannot be dis-cussed at length. The first contains 'revels' with a rudi-mentary masking (*Maskers with a drum; Musicke for the dance*, II. 1) ; the song 'Sigh no more, Ladies' sung, with proper aristocratic reluctance, by Balthasar (II. 3) ; the 'solemn

---

[1] John Hollander, *The Untuning of the Sky* (1961), p. 153.
[2] Malone Society reprint (1927), prepared by C. J. Sisson. There is no evidence, of course, that Shakespeare's 'Tell me where is fancie bred' was sung by a boy rather than a man.

hymne', 'Pardon goddesse of the night' performed at Hero's tomb (V. 1); and a celebratory dance at the end ('Strike up Pipers.' *Dance*). The music's main dramatic function seems to be to 'imitate' the music that such ceremonies as courtly revels, entombment of a princess, and nuptial celebrations, require. Balthasar's song, charming though it is, looks rather stuck on to the play. The fusing power of Shakespeare's imagination does not appear, in this play, to have comprehended music; there are no effects that any other Elizabethan playwright could not have contrived. The popular music that commonly adds depth to Shakespeare's comedies is absent.

Two practical points arise. (i) The identity of the actor who, at some performance or other before the compilation of the First Folio, 1623, played the part of Balthasar, an adult character-actor who could also sing well, has been the subject of controversy for a century; if the name slipped in from a prompt-copy of a late performance, then Jack Wilson may indeed have been the future Dr. John Wilson. But a stage-career does not, and did not then, naturally lead to a doctorate. (ii) The band required for the play may well have been a wind-band of shawms (traditionally used for dance-music). 'Strike up Pipers' is odd; but 'pipers', the generic term for wind-players, is the operative word. They might also have played recorders for the dirge, the 'solemn hymne'; but perhaps the likeliest explanation is that an unnamed 'lord' or attendant from the 'three or four with tapers' sang the dirge to his own accompaniment.[1]

*As You Like It* seems to have been contrived musically with the special intention of giving the adult singer of Balthasar's role in *Much Ado About Nothing* further opportunities to show his skill and to charm his audience. Amiens sings 'Under the greenwood tree', 'Blow, blow, thou winter winde' and, presumably, as a 'lord' and forester, 'What shall he have that kild the Deare?' But his was not the only opportunity. In the last act two pages enter, without any more warning than 'Here come two of the banish'd Dukes Pages', to sing 'It was a Lover and his lasse'.[2] And, to conclude the play, Hymen

---

[1] Probably 'Balthasar' again; see J. H. Long, *Shakespeare's Use of Music* (1955), p. 134.

[2] The contemporary setting by Thomas Morley (*First Book of Airs*, 1600) is well known. It is not proven, and probably not provable, that he wrote it specifically for the play.

sings a wedlock hymn: 'Wedding is great Junos crowne'.
The stage-direction just before this, *Still Musicke* (probably
recorders),[1] is the only indication at all of instrumentation for
the play ('flourishes' excepted), though J. S. Manifold plaus-
ibly suggests that the wedding requires hautboys. Perhaps
for this play, too, a small professional wind-band sufficed, with
a lutenist and/or a bass-viol player (practising to be Sir Andrew
Aguecheek?) among the company.

Though one of the delightfullest and deepest of the comedies, *As You Like It* is not striking in a musical way. The lyrics
do not really, even as lyrics, greatly extend our knowledge of
the characters; the songs relate more to the *ideas* of the play
(*As You Like It* is a sort of light-hearted enquiry into the
pastoral life, the pastoral convention). Thus, Amiens's
straightforward and extroverted 'Under the greene wood
tree/Who loves to lye with me' receives the expected melancholy, ostentatiously cynical gloss from Jaques: 'If it do come
to passe, that any man turn Asse/Leaving his wealth and ease.
. . . Heere shall he see, grosse fooles as he/And if he will come
to me.' No doubt there was musical mockery here too. A
somewhat deeper mood is sounded by 'Blow, blow, thou
winter winde'; a dimension is added to the pastoral which even
Touchstone, mocking William and Audrey, cannot encompass.
But the tone is not sustained, and in the end we are inclined
to agree with Touchstone, applying his remark to the music
as a whole — 'Truly yong Gentlemen, though there was no
great matter in the dittie, yet the note [*i.e.* the music] was very
untunable'.

The most striking uses of music in the comedies of Shakespeare's maturity are to govern the romantic mood and to
express the inner psychology of the characters. *Twelfth Night*
does both these things. Music is sounding already when the
play begins; Orsino's opening speech characterizes it, but as
music it has already in itself established, as it were, an imaginative *rapport* between the audience and the 'idea' of the play.
As he goes on to develop his reactions, and particularly in the
abrupt, self-indulgent way he breaks it off ('Enough, no more'),
we diagnose his character. 'Orsino is an exotic in search of
a sensation . . . his love affair and his affection for music, so
exquisitely conveyed in the first scene, are much on the same

[1] Manifold, p. 97, quotes *Two Noble Kinsmen*, V. 1, *Still music of record[er]s.*

level.'[1]   Yet such is the art of this opening that we already sense, besides the Duke's self-centred posturing, the evanescent beauty of music and the poignancy of human relationships — 'Man is in love, and loves what vanishes./What more is there to say?'

In *Twelfth Night* Shakespeare returns to the contrast he had found essential in *Henry IV*, and presents it again in musically dramatic terms.   At the one extreme we have the courtly music of Orsino and Olivia; at the other, the bawdy ballads and catches of Sir Toby Belch, Sir Andrew Aguecheek and Maria.   The Clown, Feste, seems to remain a little detached.   In II. 3, which degenerates into a string of catches and scraps of popular songs ('Hold thy Peace, thou Knave', 'Three merry men be wee' and 'There dwelt a man in Babylon, Lady, Lady') Feste inserts 'O mistris mine where are you roming?'[2]   It is, like his song at the end of the play, a timeless comment on the essential human situation, cleared of the blustering jollity of the drunken knights and of the over-ripe sensibility of the Duke.   Viola, as a character, does much to maintain this balance between two different forms of engrossment in an unreal present.   It is, therefore, especially interesting to perceive, with all the editors of the play, that Viola's was originally intended to be a singing role ('I can sing/And speake to him in many sorts of Musicke').   Revision, it has been noted, is especially obvious in the next musical scene. The Duke, still wallowing, asks Cesario-Viola for 'that peece of song/That old and Anticke song we heard last night'.   But, instead of the expected song from Viola, Curio has to go off to find Feste, while the music plays 'the tune the while'. Feste sings 'Come away, come away death', a song that mirrors the Duke's love-morbidity rather than his own mood. The status of a Duke, as well as the needs of the play, suggests that a professional 'broken consort' was employed.

## 6. THE TRAGEDIES

Shakespeare's tragedies, from *Romeo and Juliet* to *Antony and Cleopatra*, show more than any other group of plays the intensely

---

[1] Richmond Noble, *Shakespeare's Use of Song* (1923), p. 83.

[2] The original music has been much discussed.   To the two versions of an Elizabethan tune with this title (in Morley's *Consort Lessons* and in *The Fitzwilliam Virginal Book* respectively) Vincent Duckles has added a third, with words by Campion, from the Gamble MS. (*Renaissance News*, vii, 1954, p. 98).

dramatic use which he could make of comparatively slender musical resources; they show increasingly a mastery of 'the mirror of sound' which lifts Shakespeare high above his contemporaries in this as in all other matters.

*Romeo and Juliet* depends for its power on an ecstatic verbal lyricism; Shakespeare makes no attempt to rival or parallel this lyricism with romantic music or songs. The music needed for this play seems to be exactly what a small band of minstrels, in the late medieval style, could provide. They are named as Simon Catling, Hugh Rebicke and James Sound-Post (IV. 5). One need not take the names too literally (the 'bad Quarto' of the play drops Simon and Hugh and inserts Mathew Mini-kin); it seems likely that a 'broken consort' of lute, rebec (a small fiddle) and pipe-and-tabor would have met the play's needs, and there is some evidence that such was the constitution of a touring band in the early sixteenth century at least.[1] The music in *Romeo and Juliet* represents the world of secular merry-making, festive, high-spirited and mundane (*Musicke plaies: and they dance*, I. 5). The discomfiture of the musicians in IV. 5 ('Faith we may put up our Pipes and be gone') symbolizes the perplexity of the worldly warring Montagues and Capulets in the face of the romantic claims of the lovers. Peter, the serving-man, asks for 'some merie dump' to comfort him, and quotes an old song that emphasizes the poignancy of the situation: 'When griping griefes the heart doth wound'.[1]

It the next romantic tragedy, *Troilus and Cressida* (*c.* 1601), there is even less music than in *Romeo and Juliet*; that is, if we except a lavish number of 'alarums', 'retreats', 'flourishes' of trumpets and the like. There is only one scene (III. 1) in which music figures as one of the soft arts of peace, but there it is central to the dramatic meaning. This scene in the Trojan camp presents the dalliance, in the widest sense, of the Trojan lords, Paris and Pandarus, with Helen. F. W. Sternfeld has well described the way in which 'the sickening softness and

---

[1] John Stevens, *Music and Poetry in the Early Tudor Court* (1961), p. 300. In the Quarto texts the musicians are significantly called Minstrels, the older name. But did they also *all* play 'pipes'?

[2] Music for this song survives in 'The Mulliner Book', ed. Denis Stevens, *Musica Britannica*, vol. i; a fragment of the same song with words has recently been discovered in the binding of a book in Christ's College Library, Cambridge (I thank the Librarian for this information); Dr. Sternfeld draws my attention to a lute accompaniment for the same song in the Nat. Lib. of Wales, Brogyntyn MS. 27.

hotness which is the very fever of Troy' envelops it.[1] Pandarus drools effeminately from the moment he comes in ('faire Queene, faire thoughts be your faire pillow'), and his song 'Love, love, nothing but love' is a fitting climax to his display of erotic affection. An excessive fondness for music was generally reckoned to be a symptom of moral weakness. To this near-Puritan sense of music's dangers, backed up as it is by a true humanist regard for the *ethos* of sounds, one must add a realization of the significant place music traditionally had in medieval romance (its erotic powers were no new discovery) and in the Morality play (music is associated with concupiscence and 'abhomination'). No Elizabethan could have failed to realize the over-ripeness and rottenness of the Trojan dalliance. Pandarus's song sounds a premonitory death-knell to the love of Troilus and Cressida; their first and most important love-scene follows immediately upon it.

The practical details of the scene are of some interest. The musicians are probably within the tiring-house; the drift of Pandarus's enquiries to the Servant early in the scene suggest music that is heard, not seen. They are the standard theatre-band, evidently ('here is good broken music'); and they must be playing in the background for the first part of the scene, representing the household music of King Priam. Pandarus sings his song, accompanying himself probably on a lute ('Come, give me an instrument'). Robert Armin, Kempe's successor, probably took this role.[2]

The play of *Troilus and Cressida* moves most tellingly in the realm of dramatized ideas; the disillusion, the loss of vital motive in love and war, culminate in scenes of meaningless chaos and senseless destruction, a perfect dramatic image. *Othello* is much more deeply personal in its tragic implications. This reflects itself in the music of the play. Pandarus's song is admittedly an expression of his personality; but, more importantly, it reflects as he does himself the whole decaying state of Troy. It is symptomatic rather than expressive. Desdemona's 'willow song' is essentially expressive:

DES.  My Mother had a Maid call'd *Barbarie*;
      She was in love: and he she lov'd prov'd mad,
      And did forsake her. She had a Song of Willough,

[1] In '*Troilus and Cressida*: Music for the play', *English Institute Essays 1952*, ed. A. S. Downer (1954); the article also contains useful practical suggestions as to the best music to replace the lost originals.     [2] Sternfeld, p. 128.

An old thing 'twas : but it express'd her Fortune,
And she dy'd singing it.

(IV. 3)

This recollection of hers is very much to the point, for the 'willow song' is an old genre which can be traced, words and music, back to Henry VIII's time.[1]  It is traditionally associated with unhappy love.  But Shakespeare is not merely borrowing an old song here; he adapts it to Desdemona's tragic situation. The climax of the song, where she breaks off ('If I court mo women, you'le couch with mo men'), reveals 'the acid reproach of promiscuity that rankles in Desdemona and comes to the fore, destroying the lyric integrity of the original'.[2]

There is not much other music in *Othello*.  Iago sings popular ballads in the scene where he is making Cassio drunk : 'And let me the Cannakin clinke, clinke' and 'King Stephen was and-a worthy Peere', and one senses their callow, persuasive heartiness.  Instrumental music is brought in by Cassio as a compliment to Othello (perhaps also to Desdemona) at the beginning of the next scene.  It is to be an *aubade*, an early morning salutation.  But, as the Clown observes : 'the Generall so likes your Musick, that he desires you for loves sake to make no more noise with it'.  Dramatically, this forms part of the rejection of Cassio.  Musically, a wind-band was required ('Are these, I pray you, winde Instruments? — I, marry are they, sir') ; they were probably, then, hautboy-players (shawms, minstrels) representing the waits of this Cyprus sea-port.

The last of the tragedies dealing with a theme of romantic love is *Antony and Cleopatra* : it is richly endowed with the brazen din of trumpets, as befits this most regal of all the plays. The 'flourishes', the 'alarums', the 'noyse' of sea-fights 'afarre off' must have greatly contributed to the sense of sumptuousness and splendour.  Dr. Sternfeld suggests that the exaggerated use of trumpets in *Troilus and Cressida* contributes to our feeling of decadence in the Trojan host; in *Antony and Cleopatra* the dramatic point is a more subtle one still.  The lavish voluptuousness of the Egyptian world is certainly

---

[1] B.M. Add. ms. 15233, words only, attributed to John Heywood.  The most recent musical source to be discovered is also the earliest in date, New York Public Library, Drexel MSS. 4185 (see John Stevens, *Music and Poetry*, p. 426).

[2] Sternfeld, 'Shakespeare's Use of Popular Song' in *Elizabethan and Jacobean Studies . . . presented to F. P. Wilson* (1959), p. 159.  Transcription in Sternfeld, *Music in Shakespearean Tragedy* (1963), pp. 41-4.

presented from the start: *Flourish. Enter Antony, Cleopatra, her Ladies, the Traine, with Eunuchs fanning her*. But there is a paradox: however shallow and ill-founded the military glory or the social parade, we are never allowed to doubt the regality of their love, of their 'immortal longings'. The trumpets do not sound hollow because 'heaven and earth . . . strike their sounds together/Applauding our approach' (IV. 9).

Effects of battle and ceremony apart, *Antony and Cleopatra* has interest for us. It was probably written about 1606–7, but nothing is known of the circumstances of its first production.[1] Money must have been available, since the text demands a consort, 'the loud Musicke' and 'Musicke of the Hoboyes'. The last two directions probably both indicate the same instruments — the hautboys. The first reference, though, is to Cleopatra's music:

> CLEO. Give me some Musicke: Musicke, moody foode of
> us that trade in love.

The standard 'broken consort', capable of delicate as well as robust effects, is probably required; it is dramatically envisaged as being ready to play out-of-doors (as such a consort certainly did for Queen Elizabeth on her 'progresses') while Cleopatra was fishing ('My musicke playing afarre off'). The mood of amorous indulgence, of a wilful, fitful kind, is reminiscent of the opening of *Twelfth Night*, which the text also echoes. Music here extends character; it is a subtle part of the dramatic 'imitation'.

Hautboys are the instruments especially associated with the entertainment of guests — [*Hoboyes Playing lowd Musicke. A great Banquet serv'd in* (*Timon of Athens*, I. 2)]. They must surely have played the banquet music for the meeting of the triumvirate on board Pompey's galley. The text says simply *Musicke playes* (II. 7). Enobarbus, placing the guests to dance the Egyptian bacchanale, tells the musicians: 'Make battery to our eares with the loud Musicke . . .'. A boy, introduced simply for the song, 'Come thou Monarch of the Vine', is accompanied by 'music' (certainly not hautboys), with 'the great Fellowes' roaring out the refrain, 'Cup us till the world go round'. As Richmond Noble has observed, 'The song obviously partakes of the character of a hymn, a Bacchanalian

---

[1] At a later date it was performed at the Blackfriars (New Cambridge edition, introduction, p. xxxvii).

equivalent of *Veni Creator*'.[1]   The choice of a magniloquent, quasi-ceremonial drinking-song for this occasion is masterly. It reflects perhaps not so much Shakespeare's sense of the Roman proprieties, the divinity of wine and so forth, as the outwardly grandiose, and yet inwardly unreal, pomp of the 'big three'.

The music of the hautboys under the stage in IV. 3 has been mentioned before.   It signifies to the soldiers that the God Hercules is forsaking Antony.   Its theatrical interest is as an example of 'disembodied' music — a sort of supernatural intervention one might call it, and hence traditional, but employed, unusually, in a play which (unlike *A Midsummer Night's Dream* or *The Tempest*) contains no supernatural beings.[2]

Among the greater tragedies there remains to consider *Hamlet*, *Macbeth* and *King Lear*.   In *Hamlet* there is a good deal of pomp, and one is tempted to think that the excessive use of cannon by Claudius, to dignify his drinking bouts (I. 4) and the put-up duel between Hamlet and Laertes (V. 2), is an attempt to compensate for the hollowness of his kingly position. Besides their regal use, trumpets with propriety introduce 'the Players' within the play.   A 'Danish March' has already been mentioned;   and the hautboys for the dumbshow. Recorders are the subject of a famous discourse from Hamlet himself ('Why do you thinke, that I am easier to be plaid on than a Pipe?').   Were they actually played during the scene? Hamlet, in his exultation at having unmasked the King, calls for music ('Come the Recorders') and some texts have, later, *Enter the Players with Recorders* (Quarto II);   the Folio stage-directions *Enter one with a Recorder* (which Hamlet may have taken from him) perhaps shows how the scene was presented when the 'players' could not all manage to bear their parts.

The most subtle musical effects, however, are achieved through song, the pathetic snatches of Ophelia 'distracted', and the macabre musings of the Clown.   In associating music with madness Shakespeare was once again adapting a well-worn dramatic *motif*;   Elizabethan drama contains many 'mad songs';   the 'lunatick' is coupled with the lover and the poet in this too.   Dr. Sternfeld in a full analysis of the scene draws

---

[1] Noble, p. 127.

[2] The oboes, *qua* oboes, have no ascertainable symbolism here (though we may ponder similar scenes in *Gorboduc* and *Sophonisba*);   they are used for their well-known penetrative power (Manifold, p. 61).   But see p. 26, above.

attention to the two motives in Ophelia's behaviour (love of Hamlet and her father, and fear of losing her virginity), to the marked social impropriety of a gentlewoman's singing in public at all, and to the traditional popularity of 'Bonny Sweet Robin'.[1] Most of the other fragments are untraced, but 'How should I your true love know?' is customarily sung to the tune 'Walsingham', since Ophelia in her distraction garbles scraps from an old ballad connected with pilgrimages to the shrine.[2]

The Clown's song is a distorted version of an old song, 'I loath that I did love' (words attributed to Lord Vaux).[3] Its crude 'dance of death' flavour and unrefined technique reinforce the contrast between the gravediggers' prosaic acceptance of, and Hamlet's sophisticated, hyper-sensitive playing with, the idea of Death.

The 'bad Quarto' stage-direction is well known: *Enter Ofelia playing on a Lute, and her haire downe singing*. This probably represents faithfully the facts of some early performance. That Shakespeare's company had a boy-lutenist is likely; his services were required later, in *Henry VIII*, as the 'wench' to Queen Katherine — 'Take thy Lute wench'. He sang, then, 'Orpheus with his Lute made Trees . . .' (III. 1).

*King Lear*, so rich and complex in every other respect, does not speak with particular emphasis to the musician. There is, to be brief, a pattern of noise in the play, filling out its dramatic shape; the trumpet signals of Lear are gradually silenced by those of Goneril and Regan; his horns are heard only once (I. 4); after this we hear *Storme and Tempest, Storme stille*, until they are replaced by the drums, alarums and retreats of Act V and the formal combat of Edgar and Edmund, with its three trumpet calls. At the end, *Exeunt with a dead March*. There is one respite (not in all the texts): healing music for Lear's condition in the scene where he and Cordelia are reunited (IV. 7). The Fool's and Edgar's snatches of song are dramatic master-strokes, but they have no truly musical significance. Their elliptical, enigmatic wisdom is all in the words — 'He that has and a little tyne wit/With heigh-ho, the Winde and the Raine'. But it could be said that, character-wise, their music signifies the privileged, impersonal detachment of fools and madmen.

[1] F. W. Sternfeld, *Music in Shakespearean Tragedy* (1963), pp. 53-66.
[2] E. W. Naylor, *Shakespeare Music* (1913, rev. 1928), pp. 35-6, with music.
[3] John Stevens, *Music and Poetry*, p. 441, lists three musical versions.

D

*Macbeth*, on the other hand, makes strong dramatic use of music within a wider scheme of sound-effects (discord, as well as harmony, had its associations — indeed, one might say, its theological meaning — for the Elizabethans). Thunder, drum-rolls, bells and knocking all play a part in the grotesque 'mirror of sound' for Macbeth's swelling evil. When music, as music, is employed, it is with a strict dramatic relevance: one may assume, I think, that when Macbeth feasts his loyal subjects (III. 4), the hautboys played as they had earlier (I. 7): *Hoboyes. Torches. Enter a Sewer, and divers Servants with Dishes and Service over the Stage*. The next time the hautboys sound it is for a more sinister entertainment: *A shew of eight Kings*, following on the three apparitions. It is clearly not just dumb-show music but 'hellish' sound of some kind, from Macbeth's line, 'Why sinkes that caldron? and what noise is this?' *Hoboyes*. The Folio text of this scene, and of an earlier one (III. 5) presents one of the thorniest editorial problems in the whole of Shakespeare. The crux of the controversy is the authenticity of the Hecate scenes. Most scholars seem now to agree that a 'restorer', probably Thomas Middleton, has filled out Shakespeare's perhaps self-abridged version by adding

> three passages (III. 5; IV. 1, 39-43; IV. 1, 125-32) in the witch-scenes, which can be distinguished from the genuine text by the introduction of Hecate, by the use of an iambic instead of a trochaic metre, and by prettiness of lyrical fancy alien to the main conception of the witches.[1]

These additions contain various musical stage-directions: *Musicke, and a Song; Sing within. Come away, come away, etc.* (both III. 5); *Musicke and a Song. Black Spirits, etc.; Musicke. The Witches Dance, and vanish* (both IV. 1). The two songs referred to ('Come away' and 'Black Spirits') are found in Middleton's play *The Witch* (*c.* 1610–11) which itself owes a great deal to Ben Jonson's *Masque of Queens* (Whitehall, 1609), with its anti-masque of witches. It looks as if Middleton, in restoring *Macbeth* for a performance soon after this, incorporated *Hecate, and the other three Witches* (Folio stage-direction, III. 1) together with their songs and dances. This music calls for enlarged resources and seems to have none of that special dramatic point which marks Shakespeare's mature tragic art.

[1] E. K. Chambers, *cit.* New Cambridge edition, introduction, p. xxiv.

## 7. THE LAST PLAYS

In 1608 the King's Men acquired the Blackfriars theatre where for many years their principal rivals in popular favour, the boys' companies, had been acting. The Blackfriars was not the only select indoor theatre, though it has become the best known through Shakespeare's supposed association. 'Supposed', because the scanty *positive* evidence only confirms that *Pericles* and *The Winter's Tale* and *King Henry VIII* were acted at the Globe; the Blackfriars is not mentioned.[1] Yet it hardly seems feasible that the company whose greatest playwright (and an important shareholder) was Shakespeare would take the decisive financial step of acquiring a new theatre unless they expected him, and he had agreed, to make use of it.

Production methods at the Blackfriars (and at the Whitefriars, St. Paul's, the Phoenix and other theatres) have been reconstructed from the texts and stage-directions of plays, and from 'platts' and prompt copies; 'there is no such sharp division between public and private theatre practice as is generally assumed'.[2] Jonson hoped to find 'gracious silence, sweet attention/Quick sight and quicker apprehension'; he certainly did find artificial lighting, a subtler acoustic, and a more sophisticated audience, before whom his players were able to 'Keepe natural unstrayn'd Action in her throne' (Carew).[3]

The influence of the court masque is the most relevant disputed fact about the new theatre. Can we assume that there were rare scenic effects 'impossible of achievement at the Globe . . . and modelled largely on the settings of the contemporary court-masques'? Probably not. 'Scenes', in our modern sense, begin to enter the London theatres in the 1620s and 1630s.[4] What, then, of music and dancing? One thing is clear — no commercial theatre company could have afforded to hire a sumptuous array of musicians like the following; nor, probably, could it have housed them:

The greate hall (wherein the Maske was presented) received this division, and order: The upper part where the cloth and chaire

---

[1] Allardyce Nicoll, 'Shakespeare and the Court Masque', *Shakespeare-Jahrbuch*, xciv (1958).

[2] Isaacs, *Blackfriars Theatre*, p. 5.

[3] W. A. Armstrong, *The Elizabethan Private Theatres, Facts and Problems* (1958), p. 16.        [4] Nicoll, pp. 53-4.

of State were plac't, had scaffoldes and seates on eyther side continued to the skreene; right before it was made a partition for the dauncing place; on the right hand whereon were consorted ten Musitions, with Basse and Meane lutes, a Bandora, a double Sack-boot, and an Harpsichord, with two treble Violins; on the other side somewhat neerer the skreene were plac't 9 Violins and three Lutes, and to answere both the Consorts (as it were in a triangle) sixe Cornets, and sixe Chappell voyces were seated almost right against them, in a place raised higher in respect of the pearcing sound of those Instruments; eighteen foote from the skreen, another Stage was raised higher by a yearde then that which was prepared for dancing.[1]

It is even questionable how much of 'the spirit of the masque' could have been re-created by professional actors to a paying audience; true court or courtly plays, like *A Midsummer Night's Dream*, have this spirit rather more pervasively, perhaps, than the dramatic romances themselves.

What, we should ask, was the chief element in the masque? Ben Jonson said it was poetry; Inigo Jones said it was the scenic designs. They were neither of them right. The dance was the event to which the whole creation of the masque moved. 'The performance of the masque by distinguished amateurs, who mingled freely with the guests, reveals that its goal was the masqued ball; and it was only tenuously related to the drama through the elaboration of the fable, or plot, usually explained by a presenter who introduced the masquers.'[2] The masque from the first was a *divertissement* for the best people, a diversion for aristocrats only, disporting themselves before their peers. It was staged at Christmas or Shrovetide (the three days before Ash Wednesday), by the court, for the court, and normally in a large court building, like the banqueting house at Whitehall. The principal masquers were courtiers, not professional actors. In their dances they acted out an ideal which had possessed the aristocratic mind for centuries. The dance was courtesy in action, the very embodiment of the courtly way of life, symbolizing youth, gaiety, social harmony and sexual union.

*The Winter's Tale* is a play which has sometimes been said to contain a direct borrowing from masque — the 'Dance of twelve Satyres'. Robert Johnson wrote music entitled

---

[1] Thomas Campion, 'The Discription of a Maske . . . in honour of the Lord Hayes, and his bride . . .' (1607), *Works*, ed. Percival Vivian (1909), p. 62.

[2] A. Sabol, *Songs and Dances for the Stuart Masque* (1959), p. 1.

'The Satyres Masque' for Ben Jonson's masque, *Oberon*, which is extant in a manuscript collection of masque music of the early seventeenth century.[1] It may have been used in early performances of Shakespeare's play; or, perhaps with more likelihood, have been interpolated in the court performance of *The Winter's Tale* (5 November 1611), since the episode in which it occurs is only loosely connected with the rest of the scene (IV. 3). In any case the borrowing of one item and putting it in a different context does not go far towards establishing the larger point at issue. The hard basic fact remains that the masque served a decorative and ceremonial purpose; it existed to glorify those who took part in it in their own proper persons; it was essentially non-dramatic, relying on the lightest of illusions, and scarcely 'imitated' anything.

Shakespeare's plays, even the last plays, have the opposite effect; they create a world in which strange creatures move, maybe, but many of them are flesh and blood. There is more drama in Autolycus, the ballad-monger, than in any creature of the masque:

> O Master: if you did but heare the Pedler at the doore, you would never dance againe after a Tabor and Pipe: no, the Bagpipe could not move you: hee singes severall Tunes, faster then you'l tell money: hee utters them as he had eaten ballads, and all mens eares grew to his Tunes.
>
> (IV. 3)

A fair selection of near-contemporary music can be linked with Autolycus's balladry, but not all of it is suitable to the occasion and the singer. 'Lawne as white as driven Snow' appears in John Wilson's 'Cheerful Ayres', 1659 (for voice and *un*figured bass, like all mid-seventeenth-century songs); it is markedly undeclamatory in style and may have been set much earlier. On the other hand, the manuscript settings of 'Get you hence, for I must goe' do not seem to tally at all well with the description in the text of the 'three-part' song of Autolycus, Mopsa and Dorcas (IV. 3). There is no need to take too seriously Autolycus's reference to its tune, 'two maids wooing a man'.

There is no music specified for the first, sombre, half of the play; the Oracle, with its 'eare-deaff'ning Voyce' is offstage (III. 1), else we might have had some 'ceremonious, solemne,

[1] Printed in Sabol, no. 48.

and unearthly' music. The two principal musical effects of
the second, pastoral, part are *a Daunce of Shepheards and Shep-
hearddesses* (IV. 3) and the climactic awakening of Hermione
from her statue-like trance: 'Musick; awake her; strike'
(V. 3). 'Strike' is the verb used on both occasions. This
suggests strings; but anything less accomplished than the professional band would hardly serve in this play. There seems
no need for the musicians to appear on the stage. Autolycus
may have strummed an accompaniment for himself on a lute.

*Cymbeline*, despite its wonderful passages, tends to be disappointing in performance. The air of ceremonious sensationalism reaches a climax in the vision of Posthumus whilst a
prisoner:

> *Solemn Musicke. Enter (as in an Apparation) Sicillius Leonatus . . .*
> *leading in his hand an ancient Matron . . . with Musicke before them.*
> *Then, after other Musicke, followes the two young Leonati . . .*
>
> (V. 4)

This stage-direction suggests two groups of musicians in the
visionary procession itself, with perhaps an organ playing
'solemn' music off-stage.[1] (The evidence of Marston's
*Sophonisba*, a Blackfriars play, is in favour of there being an
organ in that theatre. But an Elizabethan chamber-organ
was not a permanent fixture, and the Globe may have used one
too.) The peak of excitement is reached with

> *Jupiter descends in Thunder and Lightning, sitting uppon an Eagle; hee*
> *throwes a Thunderbolt. The Ghostes fall on their knees.*[2]

In this scene it could be said that the music is simply reinforcing
'atmosphere'; it is not closely related either to character or
to action. The same is true to a lesser degree of the two other
musical 'moments' of the play. Arviragus's entry with Imogen,
supposed dead, in his arms ('a solemn music', again, IV. 2)
is followed by the beautiful dirge 'Feare no more the heate
o' th' Sun'. This can properly be described as a musical occasion, because although the boys 'word it', 'speake it', 'say our
Song', they only do so because their 'voyces/Have got the
mannish cracke'. They (and presumably Shakespeare) would
have preferred singing ('sing him to th' ground/As once to
our Mother'). The other occasion for music is Cloten's *aubade*

---

[1] On the meaning of 'solemn' music (= organ), see Manifold, pp. 95-9.

[2] The authenticity of the 'vision' has, of course, been questioned. The editors
of the New Cambridge text cannot themselves agree on the matter.

to Imogen (II. 3). Cloten is an ignorant, imperious boor, with a strictly pragmatical attitude ('I am advised to give her Musicke a morning, they say it will penetrate'). The dramatic point of the song must lie in the startling contrast between its filagree delicacy ('And winking Mary-buds begin, to ope their Golden eyes') and his unbridled coarseness ('Horse-haires, and Calves-guts . . . the voyce of unpaved Eunuck to boot'). An early setting of 'Hearke, hearke, the Larke' is in a manuscript in the Bodleian Library.[1] The musicians perform on stage; if Cloten's remarks can be relied upon, they were string, not wind, players.

If *The Winter's Tale* and *Cymbeline* lead one to think that Shakespeare has lost his feeling for the organic use of musical effect, *The Tempest* is reassuring. 'Music is the very life of *The Tempest*; without its aid the play would be impossible of presentation.'[2] The baseless fabric of the enchanted island is the music which Ariel can conjure up at will; music is, as it were, the spiritual continuum, perpetually sounding ('Sometimes a thousand twangling Instruments/Will hum about mine eares'), but not always heard or heeded. Nothing could be farther removed from the music of naturalistic 'imitation'; if the 'solemn and strange Musicke' *imitates* anything, it is surely the music of the spheres, the underlying harmonies of the Universe. That is one reason why in this play the musicians do not appear; the music must seem a pervasive presence, rather than a particular reality. This is imaginatively conveyed by its general directionlessness ('Where shold this Musick be? I' th' aire, or th' earth?' I. 2); by its mysterious warning power (GONZALO: 'I heard a humming/(And that a strange one too) which did awake me' II. 1); and by the very elusive quality of its meaning ('This is no mortall business, nor no sound/That the earth owes' I. 2).

Metaphysical speculations apart, the audience sees, and hears, Prospero performing his magic through the medium of music; his last 'performance' is a musical-magical one:

> But this rough Magicke
> I heere abjure: and when I have requir'd

---

[1] Printed in John P. Cutts, *La Musique de scène de la troupe de Shakespeare* (1959), No. 4.
[2] Noble, p. 99. On music in the last plays as a whole, see J. M. Nosworthy, 'Music and its Function in the Romances of Shakespeare', *Shakespeare Survey*, xi (1958).

Some heavenly Musicke (which even now I do)
To work mine end upon their Sences, that
This Ayrie-charme is for, I'le break my staffe,
Bury it certaine fadomes in the earth,
And deeper than did ever Plummet sounde
Ile drowne my booke.

*Solemne musicke.*

*Heere enters* Ariel *before:   Then* Alonso *with a franticke
gesture, attended by* Gonzalo . . . :   *They all enter the
circle which* Prospero *had made, and there stand charm'd:
which* Prospero *observing speakes.*

A solemn Ayre, and the best comforter
To an unsettled fancie, Cure thy braines . . .

(V. 1)

The magical powers of music were enshrined for the Elizabethans in a myth which they were forever quoting or enacting
— the myth of Orpheus; it is the subject of a famous song in
a lesser-known play of the last period, *Henry VIII*, of which no
contemporary setting survives:

Orpheus with his Lute made Trees
And the Mountain tops that freeze
Bow themselves when he did sing . . .
In sweet Musicke is such Art,
Killing care, and griefe of heart,
Fall asleepe, or hearing dye.

(III. 1)

But music in *The Tempest* is not simply an anodyne; it is the
spiritual reality which, like divine grace, haunts men until
they come into harmony with it.

The borderline between the philosophical religious and
the magical-supernatural must be delicately drawn.   We
never quite know how solemn we should be.   Ariel, who at one
moment pronounces 'ling'ring perdition' in his capacity as a
'minister of fate', celebrates his own coming freedom from
servitude in an ethereal, fairy-tale song, 'Where the Bee sucks,
there suck I' (V. 1).   (Both this song and 'Full fadom five
thy Father lies' are extant in musical settings composed by
the King's musician, Robert Johnson.)[1]   The part of Ariel
would, naturally, have been played by a boy — the pure,
unemotional, untrammelled quality of an unbroken treble is

---

[1] Printed by A. Lewis, *William Shakespeare; Two Songs from The Tempest*
(n.d.); see also Cutts, *Musique*, Nos. 12 and 13.

peculiarly fitted for songs of magic and the supernatural. This lack of full humanity may have done something to soften the paradox in Ariel's character.

The musical stage-directions require, variously, 'solemne Musicke' and 'Musicke and Song' in II. 1, 'solemne and strange Musicke' in III. 3, 'soft musick' in IV. 1, 'solemne musicke' in V. 1. These suggest, perhaps, organs and a more substantial body of strings ('soft' music) than the normal playhouse consort would provide. The play was performed at court early in 1613, if not earlier, as part of the marriage celebrations of the King's daughter, Princess Elizabeth. Hence, it may be, the larger resources.

Two other musical features of *The Tempest* speak more or less for themselves — the 'scurvy tunes' of Stephano and Trinculo (II. 2) as they work on Caliban's naïvety (Ariel has to descend to their level with 'Tabor and Pipe' in order to communicate with them); and the 'show' of Iris, Ceres and Juno, which Prospero commands Ariel to fabricate, 'a contract of true Love, to celebrate' (IV. 1).

A less obvious and more Shakespearean touch is the musical contrast in the character of Caliban himself. When corrupted and made drunk by Stephano and Trinculo, he is a howling monster — ''Ban, 'ban, Calyban/Has a new Master, get a new Man' (II. 2). And yet, in his nature, he is imaginatively sensitive, alive to the music of the island:

> Be not affeard, the Isle is full of noyses,
> Sounds, and sweet aires, that give delight and hurt not;
> Sometimes a thousand twangling Instruments
> Will hum about mine eares; and sometime voices
> That if I then had wak'd after long sleepe,
> Will make me sleepe againe . . .

> (III. 2)

## 8. CONCLUSION

*The Tempest* itself could provide a fitting conclusion to this essay. There is no play in which the music is more fully, more integrally, used as part of the dramatic effect: a musical-philosophical idea sustains the play and deepens our sense of Providence. At the same time it provides a sense of dignity and harmony appropriate to the personal occasion, a wedding, and also evokes 'the power of a music propitious to royalty and to peace'.[1]

Shakespeare indeed lived at a fortunate time, when the traditional medieval view of music was held in imaginative equipoise with another — a 'Renaissance' view, one may call it. Reduced to its simplest terms the paradox is this. On the one hand, music is still a *speculum* of the divine Order, a shadowing on this earth, not only in notes but in peoples and states, of the perfect harmony which sustains the universe; on the other, music is more and more a 'rhetoric of the emotions', a language of the heart, in which man can embody his innermost human feelings and communicate them to others. The one is God-centred, symbolic, sacramental; the other is man-centred, symptomatic, expressive. Many of Shakespeare's uses of music draw strength from both these philosophies : what in the plays of the previous century would have been purely symbolic in conception is now consciously used for 'atmosphere'. In the later Jacobean plays, with their 'dismal music' and 'infernal music' and so forth, the playwrights have set the first shots rumbling which will culminate in the emotional bombardment of the modern film, with its full orchestra clamorously titillating the audience's ever more jaded emotions. In such a *milieu* the 'communication' has taken charge and ousted the 'imitation' almost entirely. It is the fascination of the Elizabethan drama that the two elements are for the most part well balanced ; and it is the achievement of Shakespeare to weave them both into the dramatic structure and to make them inseparable from it.

This leads us to a final observation about Shakespeare's use of music : the play creates the meaning of the music as much as the music creates the meaning of the play. No degree of expertise (knowledge of instruments and their symbolism, familiarity with the various philosophies of music, with the customary social attitudes of the Elizabethans — even, one must add, with the idiom of the music itself) — none of this expertise can on its own unravel the knot. Shakespeare's genius has embedded music in his plays so deeply that we must experience them fully to see its meaning.

[1] Sternfeld, 'Le Symbolisme musical dans . . . Shakespeare', *Les Fêtes de la Renaissance* (1956).

# PART TWO

# Song and Part-Song Settings
## of Shakespeare's Lyrics, 1660–1960

BY

CHARLES CUDWORTH

'If music and sweet poetry agree . . .'
*The Passionate Pilgrim*

THIS essay makes no attempt at being exhaustive — indeed, any such attempt would be foredoomed to failure, for Shakespeare's influence on composers in general and song-writers in particular has been immense over the past three centuries. I merely hope to give some indication of the richness of the Shakespearean tradition, especially in English music. And since it is extremely difficult to distinguish rigidly between songs which were written for concert use and those which were primarily intended for the theatre, I shall at times mention incidental music or even opera, though these are more fully dealt with elsewhere. My prime purpose, therefore, is to give some account of the song and part-song settings of Shakespeare's poems, lyrics and passages from his plays, from the Restoration to the present day.

## I. THE RESTORATION PERIOD

After the closing of the public theatres in 1648, drama of a sort went on, mainly in the provinces, and in London efforts were made in the 1650s to re-introduce stage performances in the form of masques and operas. But in general the Commonwealth was a barren period as far as new Shakespearian music was concerned. With the re-establishment of the monarchy, the ban on public performances was lifted, and revivals of Shakespeare's plays were soon drawing audiences to the two newly-established theatres — the King's and the Duke's. Here the forestage and the proscenium arch, which were gradually to merge into the modern 'picture-frame' opening, had replaced the old Elizabethan open platform stage; actresses

were appearing for the first time in women's parts, and there
was an ever-increasing interest in spectacle for its own sake.
In these new theatres the musicians were located in various
places : at the side, over the proscenium arch (in the old
'music room') and, in spite of objections from the audience,
even in front of the stage.  Indeed, this last, under Continental
influence, gradually became the usual place, for it had been
found, particularly in opera, that the only way to secure a
reasonable ensemble was to have singers and instrumentalists
more or less on one level as near as possible to each other,
under the controlling eye and hand of the musical director
seated at his harpsichord.

With the return of Charles II, French influence became
predominant on English music.  The King had spent part of
his exile at the court of Louis XIV, and had acquired a taste
for the French style, as exemplified in the music of Lully, that
'Italian frenchyfied' who set the seal of his domineering
personality on all French music for the better part of a century.
Charles established a royal string orchestra of 'four-and-
twenty fiddlers', modelled on the famous 'Vingt-quatre violons
du Roi' of the French court, invited French musicians and
composers to settle in London, and sent English composers to
study in France, so that they might better understand the
'light, fantasticall French way' of composition.  As the years
passed, this French influence was countered by an even stronger
influence from Italy, for the French style, modelled on the
dance, was limited, and composers saw more opportunity for
future development in the freer Italian style.  The miracle of
Henry Purcell, the greatest English composer of his time, if
not indeed of all time, was that he was able to absorb all such
influences, and yet remain completely and obstinately English,
and up-to-date into the bargain — a paradox which other
English composers have not always been able to resolve.  Yet
one cannot understand Purcell without some knowledge of his
immediate predecessors, and of the circumstances in which
his music came to be written.  This is particularly true of his
Shakespearean music, which in almost every case grew out of
other men's work, and especially out of the astonishing adaptations of the plays considered necessary by Restoration playwrights in order to make them suitable for the contemporary
stage.  Though they paid lip-service to Shakespeare as the
greatest English dramatic poet, this did not prevent them

playing havoc with his work, by wholesale remodelling of the plots, and by the introduction of new songs and instrumental music. Pepys, after witnessing an adaptation of *The Tempest* in which Miranda acquired a sister, Ariel a wife and Caliban a female counterpart, could write : 'Shall be again to see it. It is full of variety', which it certainly was ! Indeed, there was in general rather too much variety in the Restoration versions of Shakespeare, especially in those which received the full musical treatment. One of the most famous examples of this was *Macbeth*, which Davenant produced in the mid-1660s, inserting into it the Hecate scenes from Middleton's *The Witch* and fresh material written by himself. For this production some at least of the music was written by Matthew Locke, the most eminent English composer of the early Restoration period. Very little of it has survived, but Locke seems to have been called in again for an even more spectacular production of the play in 1673, at the Dorset Garden Theatre, where it was produced 'in the nature of an opera', for Downes mentions him in *Roscius Anglicanus* (1708) as the composer of the music used. It may have been so, but the music was not published at the time, and seems to have been more or less lost, for in the 1690s John Eccles composed fresh *Macbeth* music. About a century after Locke's time the eminent Georgian composer and musical antiquary Dr. William Boyce published a score entitled 'The original songs, airs, and chorusses, which were introduced into the tragedy of *Macbeth* . . . composed by Matthew Locke'. What led the usually shrewd Dr. Boyce into accepting this music as the work of Locke is not clear, but in so doing he set a puzzle for posterity. Few reputable musicologists today accept it as Locke's, and other names have been put forward, the most likely being Richard Leveridge, to whom it is ascribed in the fine ms. score preserved in the Fitzwilliam Museum, Cambridge. 'The Music in *Macbeth* . . .' was much admired by eighteenth- and early nineteenth-century critics, including both Burney and Hawkins, and for at least a century and a half no production of *Macbeth* was considered complete without it. Yet few today have heard, or heard of, it.[1]

To return to our Restoration playwrights and composers : *The Tempest* offers an unusually striking example of the arbitrary way in which they dealt with Shakespeare's work. It was performed in a garbled version, with alterations by

[1] See R. Fiske, *Music and Letters*, Vol. 45, No. 2, April 1964.

Davenant and Dryden, as early as 1667. It is not certain whose music was used for this production; some of Robert Johnson's original music may have been retained, and perhaps there was some new music by John Banister the elder, Master of the King's Band of Musick. Pepys, who saw the performance, definitely mentions an 'echo piece' in his Diary, and Banister certainly composed an 'Echo Duet', either for this production, or for the 'operatic' version prepared, probably by Shadwell, for the new Dorset Garden Theatre in 1674. This was a spectacular affair at which the royal orchestra assisted: 'The Band of Twenty-Four Violins, with the Harpsicals and Theorbo's, which accompany the Voices, are placed between the Pit and the Stage . . .' — obviously in what we now think of as the orchestra pit. About thirty 'Voices' were employed, and there were considerable opportunities for music of one kind or another, some of which has survived. Some of the vocal music was printed in a rare and curious publication called 'The Ariels Songs in the Play called the *Tempest*' of *c.* 1675, among it a setting of 'Where the bee sucks' by young Pelham Humfrey, the gifted but short-lived composer whom Charles II sent to Paris to study under Lully, and settings by Banister of 'Come unto these yellow sands', 'Full fathom five', 'Dry those eyes' and 'Go thy way' (the 'Echo Duet') (the words of the last two were not by Shakespeare); there is also a setting by James Hart, a well-known composer and bass-singer of the time, of a song — 'Adieu to the pleasures' — also to words not by Shakespeare.[1] The music which Humfrey provided for an interpolated 'Masque of Neptune and Amphitrite' — again not by Shakespeare — survives in a somewhat abbreviated form in a ms. in the Paris Conservatoire.[2] The play may also have contained a setting of 'Arise, ye subterranean winds' by Pietro Reggio, as well as some dances by G. B. Draghi, two Italian composers then resident in London. Reggio's song was published in 1680 in 'Songs set by Signior Pietro Reggio'; Draghi's dance-tunes were not published.

[1] Banister's 'Echo duet' was reprinted by J. F. Bridge in his *Shakespearean music in the plays and early operas*, London, 1923. He had already reprinted 'Come unto these yellow sands' and 'Full fathom five' in his *Songs from Shakespeare: the earliest known settings*, London [1894], which also contains Pelham Humfrey's 'Where the bee sucks', as well as his setting of the 'Willow' song from *Othello*. Several of the *Tempest* pieces are also included in T. Maskell Hardy's *The Songs from Shakespeare's Plays*, London, Curwen ed. 6335-6.

[2] Reprinted in *The Musical Quarterly*, vol. vii, No. 4, Oct., 1921.

In 1675 Locke published the instrumental music which he composed for this production in a work with the curious title of 'The English Opera, or The Vocal Musick in *Psyche*, with the Instrumental therein intermix'd. To which is adjoyn'd the Instrumental Musick in the *Tempest*, by Matthew Lock . . .'. This publication introduces us to one of the strange features of London theatrical life at the time, the use of what was called 'First' and 'Second Music'. Audiences were admitted to the theatre some time before the performance began, and to keep them quiet the theatre band played music at stated times — the 'First Music' about an hour before the curtain rose, the 'Second Music' at some point between the two. At the rise of the curtain a 'Curtain Tune', or the overture proper, was played. Between the acts the orchestra played the 'act-tunes', as they were called, and managers would commission sets of such 'act-tunes' from composers. Hence the sets of orchestral 'Ayres for the Theatre' by Purcell and his contemporaries.

Locke's music for *The Tempest* [1] opens with 'The First Musick', consisting of an Introduction, a Second Galliard (what happened to the first?) and a Gavot. 'The Second Music' opens with a Saraband, followed by a 'Lilk' (? Lilt). Then comes 'The Curtain Tune', an obvious experiment in atmospheric music, and famous as containing the world's first orchestral crescendo — 'lowder by degrees' — and diminuendo — 'soft and slow by degrees' — and finally 'The Conclusion', an ingenious Canon 4 in 2. Incidentally, we have at least one genuine setting by Locke of Shakespeare's own words, as his 'Orpheus with his lute' from *Henry VIII* was printed in Playford's 'Musical Companion' of 1673.

The name of Henry Purcell has always been linked with the *Tempest* music which is printed in Vol. xix of the Purcell Society's edition of his works, but recently some critics have been troubled by certain rather dubious features in some of the items, and various other composers have been suggested, among them Purcell's pupil, John Weldon.[2] However, nothing definite has been proved. Whoever the composer was, he was a master; the settings which we all know and love of 'Come unto these yellow sands', 'Full fathom five', 'Arise, ye subterranean winds', 'Halcyon days' and so on, are certainly

---

[1] Reprinted in the Oxford Orchestral Series, O.103-4, O.U.P., 1934.
[2] See below, p. 105.

E

worthy of Purcell, and the first two have always held a prominent place in the repertory of Shakespearean music. Unfortunately the text of the play — where it 'improves' upon Shakespeare — is so ludicrous that in spite of the beauty of the music it is almost impossible to sit through it patiently in the theatre.

The music to *The Tempest* may be doubtful Purcell; two other Shakespearean pieces attributed to him — 'The Fairy Queen' and 'Timon of Athens' — are genuine Purcell but very doubtful Shakespeare, for in neither case did Purcell set a single line by the great dramatist. Of 'The Fairy Queen' Westrup has said : 'No one who merely heard the music would have the remotest suspicion that the opera was an adaptation of Shakespeare's *Midsummer Night's Dream*'.[1] It was produced at the Dorset Garden Theatre in 1692, when Purcell was at the height of his powers as a composer, and it contains some magnificent masque-music, but nothing that has much to do with Shakespeare's play. However, its various overtures, act-tunes and dances make agreeable incidental music for amateur performances; indeed, the Germans have published instrumental selections from it under the title of 'Spielmusik zum Sommernachtstraum'.[2] For Shadwell's version of *Timon of Athens* Purcell provided an overture, some dance-tunes and a 'Curtain Tune on a ground' (*i.e.* ground-bass), and the music for an interpolated masque, which contains some delightful music set to typical late seventeenth-century verses — but again, not a line by Shakespeare.[3] The same is true of the song 'Retired from any mortal's sight' which Purcell wrote for Nahum Tate's 1681 adaptation of *Richard II*. And it is thanks to the seventeenth century's mania for rearranging Shakespeare that we owe the preservation of Purcell's greatest operatic masterpiece, 'Dido and Aeneas', which was introduced as a masque into Charles Gildon's adaptation of *Measure for Measure* in 1700.

Before leaving the seventeenth century for the eighteenth there is one curious example of musical Shakespeare which ought not to go unmentioned. That inveterate playgoer Samuel Pepys was not always a whole-hearted admirer of

---

[1] J. A. Westrup, *Purcell*, London, 1937; see also below, p. 115.
[2] In 'Hortus Musicus', Nos. 50 and 58.
[3] The music for *Timon of Athens* is in vol. ii of the Purcell Society's edition. 'The Fairy Queen' occupies vol. xii of the same edition.

Shakespeare, but, as we have seen, he much enjoyed the garbled version of *The Tempest*. He also admired *Hamlet*, or at least Hamlet's famous soliloquy 'To be or not to be'; so much so, indeed, that he seems to have persuaded some unknown composer (possibly Cesare Morelli, an Italian musician who was once in his employment) to make a setting of it for him, which has been preserved and reprinted more than once.[1]

## 2. THE EIGHTEENTH CENTURY

Purcell's premature death at the age of 36 left a great gap in English musical life, for there was no one to succeed him. Some of his younger contemporaries, like John Eccles, who composed some now-forgotten music for *Macbeth* and *Hamlet* soon after Purcell's death (and who has been suggested as the composer of 'Locke's' *Macbeth* music), were able musicians, but none was of outstanding genius, and in spite of the frequent revivals of Shakespeare's plays, few of the suites of overtures and act-tunes in the French style, which Purcell's successors continued to write for use in the theatre, had anything to do with Shakespeare. Among the rare exceptions are the act-tunes for *Titus Andronicus*, written by Jeremiah Clarke, of 'Trumpet Voluntary' fame. These were printed in orchestral parts, as was Paisible's (or Peasable's) incidental music for Betterton's adaptation of *Henry IV* as *The Humours of Sir John Falstaff* (1700) and 'Mr. Corbett's musick in the comedy call'd *Henry the 4th*' of *c.* 1703. But gradually these French-style works began to give ground before the Italian style, which reached its climax with the advent of Handel. Yet, oddly enough, Purcell's older 'Ayres for the Theatre' did not fall out of favour for many years. In his *General History of Music* Burney wrote: 'These airs . . . were played as overtures and act-tunes in my own memory, till they were superceded by Handel's hautbois concertos and these by his overtures, while Boyce's sonatas, and Arne's compositions, served as act-tunes'.[2] But the older custom of commissioning sets of such instrumental airs seems to have died out, musical directors obviously preferring to make use of existing published music, and so

---

[1] In Bridge, for instance, and in Macdonald Emslie's article 'Pepys' Shakespeare Song' in *Shakespeare Quarterly*, vol. vi, No. 2, Spring 1955.

[2] *See* C. Burney, *A General History of Music*, ed. F. Mercer, N.Y., 1935, vol. ii, p. 389, footnote (n).

there are no specially composed 'act-tunes' by Boyce or Arne.
Nevertheless composers were still retained to set lyrics, and to
write music for special effects, such as the 'dirges' — often to
non-Shakespearean words — which were introduced into
*Cymbeline* and *Romeo and Juliet* at various times during the
eighteenth century. The composers were of course limited by
the quality of the instruments and voices at their disposal, and
these varied enormously from one theatre to another, and from
one season to another, ranging from the rough, but no doubt
manly, vigour of those 'singers of Roast Beef' who were the
darlings of 'the Gods' to the startling virtuosity of that gifted
little 'Miss Field' who sang Ariel in the Sheridan-Linley
*Tempest* at Drury Lane in 1777. Nor should it be forgotten
that many of the theatre singers were also favourite performers
at Vauxhall and other public pleasure-gardens.[1]

By the beginning of the eighteenth century the players of
instrumental music in the theatre had finally achieved a
settled position, and in 1740 Grassineau could define 'orchestra' as the space 'between the scenes and the audience,
wherein the musicians are disposed to play the overture, etc.
of a play, be it tragedy or comedy, of the opera, oratorio,
serenata, etc'.[2] The musicians themselves, however, were still
thought of as 'the band' or 'the music', the word orchestra
only gradually being applied to them as well as to the place
in which they performed. Judging by old prints, the normal
eighteenth-century English theatre orchestra was not large,
even in London. For ordinary plays — not operas — it
probably consisted of a small nucleus of string players, with a
pair of oboists who could also play the flute, at least one
bassoonist, and a harpsichord player like that 'little Harry
Burgess' who, according to Burney, presided 'at the harpsichord in Drury-lane, where, for second-music, he often played
concertos, generally of his own, as clean and unmeaning as if
set on a barrel.'[3] Which, apart from being rather severe upon
poor Burgess, tells us that the old seventeenth-century tradition
of 'First' and 'Second Music' was still in evidence as late as
the mid-eighteenth century.

The eighteenth century opened auspiciously for the production of new Shakespearean music with the publication in

[1] Burney lists several of them in his *History*; see vol. ii, p. 1007 of Mercer's
edition.            [2] James Grassineau, *A Musical Dictionary*, London, 1740.
[3] Burney, vol. ii, p. 1008.

*c.* 1702 (in his 'Collection of New Songs') of John Weldon's setting for 'Take, O take those lips away' — one of the best of all settings of a lyric which was destined to prove a favourite with eighteenth-century song-writers. As was perhaps to be expected from one whom we have already met as a pupil of Purcell, it was Purcellian in character, and emphasized the rhetorical quality of the verses. Weldon was one of the most gifted of that talented but half-forgotten generation of English composers which came between the death of Purcell and the advent of Handel. Another was Richard Leveridge, already mentioned as the possible composer of the 'Music in *Macbeth* . . .' attributed to Locke. Leveridge, who was famous as a singer, but was also a good composer in his own right, composed an early setting of 'Who is Sylvia?' good enough to have been falsely attributed to Arne, under whose name it appears in several anthologies. Less well known are his settings of 'Now the hungry lions roar' (Leveridge's plural) and 'When daisies pied'. The latter was published under the title of 'The Cuckoo', and has been completely overshadowed by Arne's later masterpiece. Leveridge also made a setting of the Pyramus and Thisbe scenes from *A Midsummer Night's Dream* [1] which was later eclipsed by Lampe's popular setting.

Henry Carey, who is best remembered today for the lyric of 'Sally in our alley', now sung to a traditional air, and not to his own tune, composed some incidental music for *Hamlet*, as chronicled in the *London Daily Post* of 9 February 1736, which advertises : 'The ceremony of Hamlet's lying-in-state, after the manner of his Grace the late Duke of Buckingham, with new music proper to the occasion set by Mr. Carey'. He also set 'What shall he have that killed the deer?' under the title of 'The huntsmen's song' in *Love in a Forest* (1723), Charles Johnson's garbled version of *As You Like It*, which included, among other oddities, a version of the Pyramus and Thisbe scenes from *A Midsummer Night's Dream*.

One of the most eminent of early Georgian musicians was Maurice Greene, Master of the King's Band of Musick, and one-time friend of Handel, who made one of the earliest settings of 'Orpheus with his lute', published in his collection 'A Cantata and Four English Songs' (*c.* 1745). It is not known whether this was written for a specific performance, but it may

[1] See below, p. 115.

well have been, as *Henry VIII* was surprisingly popular in Greene's lifetime. (Georgian playgoers were apparently not bothered by doubts about the authenticity of this play, unlike those later Higher Critics who went so far as to state categorically that 'Shakespeare wrote only 1168½ of the 2822 lines. The rest are by Fletcher.')[1]

The two most celebrated composers of Shakespearean music in the mid-eighteenth century were Thomas Arne and William Boyce, the leading members of what has sometimes been called 'the generation of 1710', in which year they were both born. Both lived in the shadow of Handel, yet managed to preserve a considerable degree of individuality, Arne by deliberately opposing the great man, Boyce by working in Handel's own idiom — perhaps the harder task. Arne was a progressive, ready to accept the new musical ideas coming from abroad; Boyce a conservative, content to work in what he undoubtedly thought of as the British tradition, handed down from Purcell and strengthened by Handel. Arne was the easier melodist of the two; Boyce the better technician. Arne was perhaps the more prolific Shakespearean, though Boyce has more Shakespeare music to his credit than is generally realized. Both were busy as theatre composers, and, as Burney wrote: 'Mr. Arne and Mr. Boyce were frequently concurrents at the Theatres and in each other's way, particularly at Drury-lane'.[2]

Arne's Shakespeare songs are still well known; the most famous of them were published in 1741, when he was about 30 years of age, and only three years after he had made his first great success with his setting of Milton's *Comus*. They appeared in a volume entitled 'The music in the comedy of *As You Like It*, to which are added The songs in *Twelfth Night*'. Besides 'Come away, death' from *Twelfth Night* and 'Under the Greenwood Tree' and 'Blow, blow, thou winter wind' from *As You Like It*, the collection also contains 'When daisies pied' from *Love's Labour's Lost* and 'Tell me, where is fancy bred?' from *The Merchant of Venice*. It is possible that the last two were interpolated into the Drury Lane production of *As You Like It* in December 1740, when the play was advertised as 'not acted these forty years'. Arne's settings have become classics of Shakespearean song, just as Morley's 'It was a lover and his

---

[1] See *A List of All the Songs and Passages in Shakspere which have been set to music . . .*, London, 1884.          [2] Burney, vol. ii, p. 1010.

lass' has.  As the unfailing Burney tells us: 'The melody of
Arne at this time . . . forms an era in English Music; it was
so easy, natural and agreeable to the whole kingdom, that it
had an effect upon our national taste'.[1]  Arne's 'easy, natural
and agreeable' style is nowhere more in evidence than in such
settings as 'Under the greenwood tree' and 'When daisies
pied', with their easy-going six-eight pastoral rhythms.  'Blow,
blow, thou winter wind' represents a slightly squarer, duple-
time kind of 'English Ayre', and is perhaps a little marred by
the fact that Arne did not set the refrain ('Then, heigh-ho, the
holly' — it is sometimes called 'Shakespeare's Carol').  'Come
away, death' is also in the six-eight pastoral rhythm, but in a
far different mood from Arne's other pastorals; its minor key
and suggestion of tolling bells combine to make it one of the
most poignant and effective of all eighteenth-century Shakespearean songs.[2]  'Tell me, where is fancy bred?' is less English
and more Italianate, with its elaborate vocal line and violin
accompaniment, but singers still enjoy singing it.

Arne's first volume of Shakespeare songs must have been
highly successful, for a year or so later he published another,
a curious collection entitled 'The song and duetts in *The Blind
Beggar of Bethnal Green* . . . With the favourite songs sung by
Mr. Lowe [as Lorenzo, a part he played for at least twenty-five
years] in *The Merchant of Venice*'.[3]  This included the delightful
'The Owl' ('When icicles hang on [by] the wall'), one of those
rare sequels which is as good as its predecessor — in this case
'When daisies pied' — and also two of those naïvely spurious
pieces of bogus Shakespeareana in which the eighteenth
century took such delight, the serenade 'My bliss too long my
bride denies' and 'To keep my gentle Jessie'.  The latter
became exceedingly popular, and was included in productions
of *The Merchant of Venice* until well into the nineteenth century.

Another piece of bogus Shakespeareana was included in a
later song-collection by Arne entitled 'Lyric Harmony'.  This
was a 'dirge' interpolated into *Cymbeline*, beginning 'To fair
Fidele's grassy tomb',[4] which became immensely popular, both
in its original solo form and as a part-song. (Arne's magnificent

[1] *Ibid.* p. 1004.
[2] Arne made two settings of 'Come away, death', both in six-eight time and
in F minor; the alternative version is sadly beautiful but lacks the poignancy of
the more famous setting.
[3] London, W. Smith, *c.* 1742.        [4] Words by Wm. Collins.

setting of the real 'dirge' in *Cymbeline*, 'Fear no more the heat
of the sun', was published in *c.* 1762 in a collection entitled
'The Winter's Amusement', and often reprinted anonymously
in later anthologies.) 'Lyric Harmony' also included Arne's
well-known setting of 'Where the bee sucks' composed for a
Drury Lane revival of *The Tempest* in 1746 (in which his
settings of 'Come unto these yellow sands' and of 'The Masque
of Neptune and Amphitrite' were also used [1]); and one of the
earliest known settings of words from a poem, rather than a
play, by Shakespeare — 'On Chloe sleeping' ('Her lily hand
her rosy cheek lies under' from *Lucrece*).

Arne's delightful setting of 'Sigh no more, ladies' began its
career as a solo song, written for John Beard to sing in a revival
of *Much Ado About Nothing*, and published in Arne's collection
of 'Vocal Melody, Book I'. It was later transformed into a
three-part glee, in which form it long remained the delight
of the catch and glee-club singers, as did his Bacchanalian
glee 'Which is the properest day to drink'. This was such a
general favourite that it was often introduced into *Twelfth
Night*, supplanting the genuine old Shakespearean catches.

The rivalry between Arne and Boyce revealed by Burney's
remark, quoted above, was at no time more apparent than in
the autumn of 1750, when John Rich, the manager of Covent
Garden, commissioned Arne to compose music for an interpolated scene in *Romeo and Juliet*, beginning 'Ah, hapless maid'.
Arne's score, published under the title of 'The solemn dirge in
*Romeo and Juliet*, as performed at the Theatre Royal in Covent
Garden',[2] included trumpets, kettledrums ('muffled') and a
bell, as well as voices, flutes and strings. The inserted scene
was such a success that Garrick, at Drury Lane, felt impelled
to write a similar one himself (beginning 'Rise, rise, rise, heart-
breaking sighs'), and employed Boyce to compose the music
for it.[3] Nor was this the end of the matter; Niccolo Pasquali,
an Italian composer then resident in England, set the same text
as Arne, and Charles Avison, organist, composer and critic,
who lived most of his life at Newcastle-upon-Tyne, set the words
used by Boyce (Garrick's version) for voices and strings; a rare
ms. copy of the score of his setting is preserved in the Marquess
of Exeter's Collection at Burghley House near Stamford.

---

[1] Part of Arne's setting of the 'Masque' has survived in the B.M. Add. MS.
29, 370.
    [2] H. Thorowgood, London, *c.* 1750.    [3] Robert Bremmer, London, *c.* 1771.

Arne's last essay in Shakespearean, or at least semi-Shake-spearean, music seems to have been his setting of '[O] Bid your faithful Ariel fly', sung by his pupil Mrs. Farrell in a 1777 Covent Garden production of *The Tempest* obviously intended to outdo the semi-operatic version produced by Sheridan and the Linleys at Drury Lane a little earlier in that same year. Arne's setting is nothing like as good as Linley's, which has become a classic, whilst Arne's has been forgotten. The latter was published in a collection called 'The Syren', which appeared shortly before the composer's death.

One cannot quit Dr. Arne without mentioning his setting of Garrick's *Ode Upon Dedicating a Building to Shakespeare in the Neighbourhood of Stratford-upon-Avon*, written for the famous Warwickshire Jubilee of 1769,[1] which contains one of the loveliest tunes ever composed, even by Arne, the exquisite air to 'Thou soft-flowing Avon'. On the same occasion there was performed a 'Song in honour of Shakespeare' and a serenade 'Let beauty with the sun arise' with music by Charles Dibdin,[2] playwright, lyric-writer, actor, singer, and a protégé of Garrick. Dibdin was also responsible for the music of Garrick's 'The Jubilee or Shakespeare's Garland', later produced at Drury Lane as a 'dramatic entertainment', and he also published some ballads, country dances, cotillions and minuets which he com-posed in connection with the Jubilee celebrations, and a cantata called 'Queen Mab, or the Fairies' Jubilee'. Some years later he produced a mock-Shakespearean song, 'Tarry here with me and love', sung by Mrs. Kennedy in *The Comedy of Errors* in 1780.

Arne was not the first composer to set an ode to Shake-speare, for his rival Boyce had preceded him in this, setting an *Ode in Commemoration of Shakespeare*, beginning 'Titles and ermine fall behind', written by the actor William Havard. This was performed at Drury Lane in 1757, and survives in an incom-plete autograph full score in the Barber Institute at Birming-ham, and a copyist's set of parts in the Bodleian Library at Oxford. The Bodleian also possesses the autograph score of another Shakespearean 'Ode' by Boyce, of a slightly later date, with words by Garrick, beginning 'Arise, immortal Shake-speare'; one song from this, 'Sweetest Bard', was published

---

[1] For a full account of the Warwickshire Jubilee, see *The Modern Universal British Traveller*, London, *c.* 1780, p. 178.
[2] See Dibdin, *The professional Life of . . . Written by Himself*, London, 1803, vol. i, p. 80.

in a collection called 'Thalia', consisting of songs with words by Garrick, composed by various musicians. Another semi-Shakespearean stage-piece in which both Garrick and Boyce collaborated was *Harlequin's Invasion*, Garrick's 'Christmas Gambol' of 1759, which has achieved immortality with its famous 'national' song 'Heart of Oak', but which also included a song entitled 'Thrice happy the nation that Shakespeare has charm'd'. Among the mss. attributed to Boyce in the Bodleian are 'Music for the Masque in Shakespeare's *Tempest*'; 'The Music for animating the statue in . . . *The Winter's Tale*'; 'A Dirge in *Cymbeline*' (with the opening words reading 'Fear no more the darksome sun'); and 'The Dirge in *Romeo and Juliet*', to Garrick's words 'Rise, rise, rise'. The latter is obviously the music written by Boyce for the 1750 Drury Lane production and is quite different from the setting printed by C. Haywood in his article on the subject.[1] Very little of Boyce's Shakespearean music has appeared in print, or even been heard since it was first written. The handful of somewhat more familiar excerpts from *The Winter's Tale*, including 'Lawn as white as driven snow', which long formed part of the standard repertory of Shakespeare music, and appear under Boyce's name in several anthologies, are of doubtful authenticity, except for the delightful trio in gavotte time, 'Get you hence', which displays the 'original and sterling merit' which Burney said stamped the worthy old doctor's compositions, and which Boyce himself published in his own 'Lyra Britannica'. It was, of course, Boyce who published the celebrated 'Music in *Macbeth* . . .' attributing it to Matthew Locke and dedicating it to his friend Garrick, who had employed him several times to write the music for productions of Shakespeare at Drury Lane.

After Arne and Boyce, the most important native-born Shakespearean composer of the mid-eighteenth century was Thomas Chilcot, organist of Bath Abbey, whose extant settings are gathered together in his 'Twelve English songs, with their symphonies, the words by Shakespeare and other celebrated poets'. Chilcot's settings are notable for their beauty of melodic line, apt instrumentation (with the strings sometimes enriched by wind instruments), and a true feeling for the lyrics them-

---

[1] C. Haywood, 'Boyce's "Solemn Dirge" in Garrick's 1750 production of *Romeo and Juliet* in *Shakespeare Quarterly*, vol. xi, p. 173; also E. Taylor, 'William Boyce and the theatre' in *The Music Review*, Nov. 1953, vol. xiv, No. 4, p. 275.

selves. These include 'On a day, alack the day', 'Take, O take those lips away', 'Wedding is great Juno's crown' and 'Orpheus with his lute'. Especially remarkable are 'Pardon, goddess of the night', 'Come, thou monarch of the vine' (often reprinted) and, above all, 'Hark, hark, the lark'. Whether Chilcot wrote his settings for stage use is not known; but they have a freshness and grace which almost matches those of Arne himself; indeed, several of them have been mistakenly attributed to Arne in more than one collection.

It was unfortunate that Handel, the overwhelming presence in eighteenth-century music in England, never wrote any music for Shakespeare, though his influence can be felt behind the composers of whom we have been speaking. Some unknown admirer, realising that Handel had omitted to set any of Shakespeare's lyrics, decided to remedy the oversight by adapting the words of 'Orpheus with his lute' to Handel's aria 'Caro vieni' from 'Riccardo Primo', under the title of 'The power of music'. No doubt the arranger's motives were of the highest, but the words sit awkwardly on the tune, and the exigencies of the melody resulted in an odd over-emphasis of such phrases as 'he *did* sing' and solitary words like '*that*'. Even so, the result was certainly more dignified than a companion adaptation from 'Rinaldo' in which 'Il tricerbero humiliato' became 'Let the waiter bring clean glasses'!

If Handel himself did not set Shakespeare to music,[1] some of the foreigners who came to London in his wake looked to the plays as a source for musical settings. John Frederick Lampe, an able Saxon composer famous for his burlesque operas, made an amusing 'mock-operatic' setting of the Pyramus and Thisbe scenes (1745),[2] and a song-setting of 'Shall I go mourn' from *The Winter's Tale*. Another German, Johann Ernst Galliard, made a setting of 'Take, O take those lips away' which was printed in *The Musical Miscellany*, c. 1730. But the most successful Shakespearean composer among the immigrant Germans was John Christopher Smith the younger, the son of Johann Christoph Schmidt of Ansbach, Handel's friend and amanuensis. The son, brought to England at an early age, became Handel's pupil, and succeeded in retaining the great

---

[1] For odd lines and passages used in the oratorios, see Winton Dean, *Handel's Dramatic Oratorios and Masques* (1959), pp. 414, 484.

[2] See below, pp. 115-16.

man's friendship even when he was at odds with Smith senior. Smith junior was a fine harpsichordist, and a talented composer, whose musical reputation has suffered from his close proximity to Handel, whose amanuensis he also became, in succession to his father. Among Smith's numerous stage works are two Shakespearean operas, 'The Fairies' (1755) and 'The Tempest' (1756)[1]. The lyrics used in both works were culled from various Shakespeare plays, and even from some non-Shakespearean authors. 'The Fairies' is the better of the two and some of its songs are still reprinted in volumes of Shakespearean music. Like Chilcot's, some of Smith's settings are good enough to have been mistaken for Arne's, and indeed would not have disgraced him. 'Sigh no more, ladies' is gracious and melodious; 'You spotted snakes' is almost Mendelssohnian in its fairy-like delicacy. The music of his 'Tempest' has fared less well, but even there Smith's setting of Caliban's rarely-set song 'No more dams I'll make for fish' is memorable and full of character. But in attempting such lyrics as 'Where the bee sucks', 'Come unto these yellow sands' and 'Full fathom five', Smith was attempting to rival two of England's greatest song-writers, and it is no reflection on him that his work has been forgotten in competition with theirs.

A number of minor Georgian composers made Shakespearean settings, some of them of considerable charm. The little-known Christopher Dixon, 'of York', printed a gentle, minor-key setting of 'Take, O take those lips away' in his 'Two English cantatas and four songs' of c. 1760. It has a wistful charm and, being much easier to sing than the better-known setting by Weldon, deserves to be rescued from oblivion. Dr. James Nares, who held several important posts in London, and whose anthems and harpsichord sonatas are still remembered, made a three-part glee-setting of 'Fear no more the heat of the sun' which became very popular among the catch clubs. Nares knew Boyce, and both knew Philip Hayes, Professor of Music at Oxford, who was a prolific if not always inspired composer; among his numerous works is a three-part glee-setting of 'What shall he have that killed the deer?' Another of this circle of men who were primarily church musicians was Joseph Baildon, lay-vicar of at least two London churches, if not more, who left one song linked with Shakespeare's name, though it is not a setting of his words. This is

[1] For a more detailed analysis of these, see below, pp. 106-7, 116.

'Haste, Lorenzo', an engaging little song for soprano and strings 'sung by Mrs. Chambers in the character of Jessica' in the Covent Garden productions of *The Merchant of Venice* from 1752 to 1757. Her Lorenzo was still the indefatigable Mr. Lowe, who had sung the two pseudo-Shakespeare songs by Arne in the 1741 production of the play.

That most famous of all music-historians, Dr. Charles Burney, whom we have already quoted from several times, also made one or two Shakespearean settings, soon after his return to London from his exile in Norfolk; among them were 'The ousel-cock, so black of hue' and 'Up and down', which were included in that extraordinary de-rangement of *The Midsummer Night's Dream* made by George Colman and Garrick, and staged at Drury Lane in 1763 under the title of *A Fairy Tale*. Much of the music was by Michael Arne, Arne's natural son, a gifted composer who is still remembered for that elegant piece of nonsense 'The lass with the delicate air'. Few of the lyrics he set in *The Fairy Tale* were related to Shakespeare's own words, and it was Garrick who wrote the words of his jovial 'Sheep-shearing song', included in *Florizel and Perdita*, a typical eighteenth-century perversion of *The Winter's Tale*, which Garrick staged in London in 1756. In Dublin, where the incredibly-named Macnamara Morgan was the chief perverter, the play appeared as *The Sheep-Shearing*.

One of Michael Arne's collaborators in the music of *A Fairy Tale* was Jonathan Battishill, better remembered as 'poor Batt', a gifted but eccentric character who features in the ms. memoirs of R. J. S. Stevens (now in the Pendlebury Library, Cambridge). Some of 'poor Batt's' anthems are still performed, but his Shakespearean settings which include 'Be as thou wast wont to be' from *A Midsummer Night's Dream*, have suffered the eclipse which has overtaken most of his secular music.

Few actors seek fame as composers, but an exception was Joseph Vernon, a well-known comedian who was also a trained musician, having been a choir-boy in St. Paul's Cathedral, London. In *c.* 1770 he published a volume entitled 'The new songs in the pantomime of *The Witches*, the celebrated Epilogue in the comedy of *Twelfth Night*, a song in *The Two Gentlemen of Verona* . . . and a favourite French Air sung in the comedy of *Twelfth Night*'. The Epilogue is a setting of 'When that I was and a little tiny boy', which Vernon sang in a production of *Twelfth Night* at Drury Lane on 19 October

1763. His 'song in *The Two Gentlemen of Verona*' was a setting of 'Who is Sylvia?'; his 'French Air' ('D'une manière imparfaite') has little to do with either Shakespeare or *Twelfth Night*.

Another semi-Shakespearean collection of songs was published in London *c.* 1770 by Theodore Aylward, Gresham Professor of Music, under the title 'Six songs in *Harlequin's Invasion, Cymbeline* and *A Midsummer Night's Dream*', but it contains only one genuine Shakespeare song, 'Hark, hark, the lark'. This lacked the distinction of Chilcot's solo setting, and never attained the popularity of the later glee-setting by Dr. Benjamin Cooke. Aylward also made a four-part glee-setting of 'Done to death by slanderous tongues' from *Much Ado About Nothing*, which was published in his 'Elegies and glees', *c.* 1790, and he was one of the composers involved in Garrick's Jubilee celebrations of 1769, for which he set the glee 'Come, nymphs and fawns'.

The four-part glee-setting of 'Hark, hark, the lark', by Benjamin Cooke, referred to above, was one of the most popular of all part-song settings of Shakespeare's words. It survived even in competition with Schubert's later solo setting, and held its place in the repertoire until well into the middle of the nineteenth century, both on the stage and off. Cooke, who was a highly-gifted but nowadays much underrated composer, also composed glee-settings of 'Hand in hand', 'Lawn as white as driven snow' and 'Will you buy any tape?' One of his contemporaries was William Jackson, 'of Exeter', the friend of J. C. Bach and Thomas Gainsborough, now unhappily remembered for one of his weakest works, the church service known as 'Jackson in F'. In his own day he was chiefly celebrated as a composer of carefully-conceived vocal canzonets and part-songs. He left one or two Shakespearean settings, some original, some partly borrowed from other composers. Among the former is his 'Take, O take those lips away', a duet printed in 'Twelve Canzonets, Op. 9'; among the latter, an arrangement of Arne's 'Where the bee sucks' as a four-part glee, with Jackson's own setting of 'Over hill, over dale' by way of a middle section (Op. 11). He also set 'On a day, alack the day' as a glee for three male voices, printed in his 'Elegies' (Op. 3, *c.* 1762).

In 1777 *The Fairy Tale*, mentioned above, was revived at the Haymarket with music by Michael Arne, Charles Dibdin, Charles Burney, James Hook, Theodore Smith and Samue

Arnold, the last named contributing an 'Epilogue song'.
Arnold was an immensely prolific composer, busy in the
church, the public gardens and the theatre. He supplied
incidental music for a production of *Macbeth* at the Haymarket
in September 1778,[1] and also made a setting of Parson Evans's
song 'To shallow rivers' from *The Merry Wives of Windsor*.
Later in his career he wrote the music for yet another perversion of *A Midsummer Night's Dream* called *The Enchanted
Wood* (1792).

One of the composers who supplied music for the 1777
production of *The Fairy Tale* was James Hook, a friend and one-
time employee of Arnold, and if anything an even more
prolific writer. Hook, who was born in Norwich in 1746,
came to London in his teens and made his name first as an
organist and then as a song-writer. He worked for a time
for Arnold at Marylebone Gardens, and was organist and
music-director at Vauxhall 'for upwards of half a century'.
Among his two thousand songs, of which the most celebrated
is 'The lass of Richmond Hill', there is at least one to words by
Shakespeare; this is an odd little setting of the 'Willow' song
in *Othello*, composed in 1798 for Mrs. Jordan, who 'accompanied herself on the lute'. Like most of Hook's songs, it is
eminently tuneful, but perhaps its chief interest today is that
it seems to have provided the model for the 'Tit-Willow' song
in 'The Mikado', which is an obvious parody of it.

Of all the late eighteenth-century composers who wrote
music connected with Shakespeare, none was more gifted than
Thomas Linley the younger. A member of an exceptionally
brilliant family, friend and contemporary of Mozart, Linley
seemed to have had all the favours of the musical and theatrical
gods poured out on him, only to die in a boating accident
at the tragically early age of 22. Into his few short years
he crammed a good deal of work, and at least two of
his major compositions were connected with Shakespeare.
One was a magnificent 'Ode on the Fairies, Aerial Beings, and
Witches of Shakespeare', to words by French Laurence, undoubtedly the finest of the eighteenth-century Shakespearean
odes, involving soloists, chorus and 'a full band'.[2] It received

---

[1] 'The favourite Scotch airs in score . . . As they are performed in *Macbeth*',
Warrell, London, *c.* 1778.

[2] Linley's autograph score is preserved in the Folger Shakespeare Library in
Washington D.C. There is a ms. copy of it in the Royal Music Library in the
B.M.

one performance, at Drury Lane on 20 March 1776, and then, after the manner of those days, was laid aside and forgotten until our own time, when it was performed in an abbreviated version by the B.B.C. Anyone who had the good fortune to hear it then will not quickly have forgotten the impact Linley's music made; it was a revelation of fresh melodic charm and imaginative choral writing, displaying the same kind of incipient romantic feeling which one encounters in the early romantic poets. Besides the 'Ode', astonishing in itself for a young man in what is often described as one of the 'dark ages' of English music, Linley also wrote some splendid incidental music for Sheridan's production of *The Tempest* at Drury Lane in January 1777.[1] It is more elaborate than most eighteenth-century settings, and leans towards the 'operatised' versions of J. C. Smith on the one hand and Sir Henry Bishop on the other. Linley's setting of 'O bid your faithful Ariel fly' (words not by Shakespeare) was one of the few of his works to find its way into print. It was reprinted, often in cut and mangled guise, in most of the standard anthologies of Shakespearean music. It was also used in many subsequent performances of the play, in spite of the immense difficulty of the music, which puts it far beyond the capacities of the average soprano or accompanying oboist.

More obscure than the ill-fated Linley were such men as T. Tremain, W. Tindall and J. Clifton, each of whom made at least one Shakespearean setting, often to unusual words. Tremain set 'Take, O take those lips away' as a duet, and also set the less-familiar 'To shallow rivers', printed in his 'Canzonets for two voices' in 1786. Tindall, who also set 'Take, O take those lips away' as a duet (published in his 'Six Vocal Pieces, Op. 1'), made one of the earliest settings of 'Doubt that the stars are fire' from *Hamlet*, a passage which later became a favourite with composers. Tindall's version appeared in his 'Eight Ancient Ballads, Op. 5'. Clifton broke even stranger ground with a setting of 'If music be the food of love' from *Twelfth Night*[2] which became well known enough to be reprinted as late as 1864.

Although most of the foreign musicians who settled in London in the late eighteenth century kept to instrumental

---

[1] MS. score in the B.M., Egerton, 2493.
[2] Purcell's three songs beginning with this line are not otherwise based on Shakespeare.

music and left vocal music to the natives, a few immigrant Germans and Italians attempted settings of Shakespearean lyrics. Niccolo Pasquali, who has already been mentioned as one of those who set the 'dirges' in *Romeo and Juliet*, included in his 'Twelve English songs' of *c.* 1750 a rather florid setting of 'Where the bee sucks'. The works of the brothers Tommaso and Giuseppe Giordani are rather hard to disentangle, as their title-pages quote them indifferently as 'Signor Giordani' without benefit of initial, so that even now no one is very sure which of them composed that celebrated aria 'Caro mio ben'. But as Giuseppe spent the greater part of his life in Italy, it seems reasonable to suppose that most of the music by 'Signor Giordani' published in London and Dublin was by Tommaso, who made the British Isles his permanent home. Anyhow, one of the Giordanis made a charming four-part glee-setting of 'Take, O take those lips away' which was obviously a great favourite with the catch clubs; it was also adapted as a solo song. 'Signor Giordani' also set the 'Willow' song from *Othello*, and 'Crabbed age and youth' from *The Passionate Pilgrim* as a duet. Then there was that 'Signorina Elisabetta de Gambarini' (one of Handel's singers [1]) who in her 'Two English and Italian Songs', published *c.* 1785, included a setting of 'Honour, riches, marriage-blessing' from *The Tempest* under the title of 'The friendly wish from Shakespeare'. One feels this might repay investigation, particularly by young couples who are tired of the usual wedding hymns!

There were a few other women composers of Shakespearean songs at that time; one such was the eccentric Elizabeth Craven, Margravine of Anspach, who settled in Hammersmith, where she gave some very odd concerts, as R. J. S. Stevens relates in his ms. memoirs. Her setting of 'O mistress mine' as a two-part 'madrigal' achieved a certain popularity in its day.

By far the most important late eighteenth-century settings of Shakespeare were of the glee and part-song type. John Stafford Smith, singer, composer and early musicologist, was interested in Elizabethan poetry and music, and in about 1812 published one of the first anthologies of early music, 'Musica Antiqua'. He also made four-part glee settings of his own of such lyrics as 'Under the greenwood tree' and 'What shall he have that killed the deer?' The latter became a stock piece and was included in many anthologies. It is indeed one of the

---

[1] See Winton Dean, Handel's *Dramatic Oratorios and Masques* (1959), p. 656.

F

best settings of that particular lyric, and highly suitable for stage use, being for men's voices, and an obvious *caccia* in six-eight time, with the voices imitating horn calls. Smith's settings of 'When daisies pied' and 'Take, O take those lips away' were three-part glees.

Luffman Atterbury, who died in 1796, made a popular setting of 'Take, O take those lips away' as a round, and Lord Mornington set 'Orpheus with his lute' and 'As it fell upon a day' as four-part glees or so-called 'madrigals'. Samuel Webbe, senior, one of England's best-known glee-composers, set a number of Shakespearean lyrics, including 'Come away, death', 'To shallow rivers' and 'When shall we three meet again?', but strangely enough they did not achieve the popularity of some of his non-Shakespearean settings. On the other hand, William Shield, violist and composer of numerous operas and some agreeable chamber music, also composed a couple of Shakespeare glees which attained great popularity, both on the stage and off. These were often known as 'Shakespeare's Duel and Loadstars' — the 'Duel' being 'It was a lordling's daughter' from *The Passionate Pilgrim*, and the 'Loadstars' Helena's speech from *A Midsummer Night's Dream*, 'O happy fair! Your eyes are lodestars'. Shield also wrote an instrumental introduction to the 'Willow' song, although not a setting of the song itself, and like a good eighteenth-century theatre composer he set an 'Elegy' for four voices, muffled drums, trumpets, bells *con sordini* and flute, which is directly in the line of those 'dirges' for *Romeo and Juliet* which we noticed earlier in the century. This setting of 'Sweet rose, fair flower' from *The Passionate Pilgrim* was published in *c.* 1790 in Shield's 'Collection of canzonets and an elegy', as 'Shakespeare's *Love's Lost*, an elegy sung at the tomb of a young virgin . . .'.

The busiest composer of late-eighteenth-century Shakespeare glees was probably Richard John Samuel Stevens, whose ms. memoirs have already been referred to in connection with 'poor Batt' and Elizabeth Craven. Stevens, who was Gresham Professor of Music, and organist of the Charterhouse, left behind him a handsome autograph music book, now in the Fitzwilliam Museum, Cambridge, labelled *Shakespeare and Stevens* and devoted to his own Shakespearean settings. Although he composed many glees to words by other poets, Stevens was always at his best when setting his 'favourite

Bard', Shakespeare. Particularly fine are his settings of 'You spotted snakes', 'The cloud-cap't towers' — a rich and noble setting, originally for AATTBB, of Prospero's speech from *The Tempest* — and 'Blow, blow, thou winter wind', a four-part setting not unworthy of being placed beside Arne's solo-song version, and having the merit of including the refrain which Arne omitted. Other settings by Stevens include 'Now the hungry lion roars'; 'Come away, death'; 'Sigh no more, ladies'; 'Who is Sylvia?'; 'Crabbed age and youth'; 'It was a lover and his lass' — with 'rustic accompaniment' for the fortepiano; 'Doubt thou the stars are fire' as a solo and as a glee; 'Orpheus with his lute'; and 'Tell me, where is fancy bred?' At their best, Stevens's Shakespearean glees have a charm all their own, and a special romantic quality which is quite inimitable and can still cast a spell over a modern audience. Christopher Wilson, in his interesting but somewhat prejudiced book *Shakespeare and Music* (1922), expressed amazement that Stevens should have set Prospero's speech, but since then it has been set by another and greater composer, Vaughan Williams. In any case Wilson, who accepted without demur Haydn's setting of similarly fugitive lines from *Twelfth Night* ('She never told her love') seems to have known only Horsley's 'mixed-voice' arrangement of Stevens's exquisite glee, and not the original male-voice version.

Stevens's lifelong friend, John Percy, also set several Shakespeare lyrics, including 'When icicles hang by the wall' as a glee, and 'I know a bank' as a soprano solo with flute obbligato. He even forestalled Hector Berlioz with his 'garden scene' from *Romeo and Juliet*, and Vaughan Williams with his 'How sweet the moonlight sleeps upon this bank'. His four-part glee setting of 'Say not so, friar' was composed 'in answer to Mr. Stevens's "Sigh no more, ladies"'. But all Percy's Shakespearean settings are now forgotten, and he is remembered, if at all, only as the composer of the once-popular 'Wapping Old Stairs'.

Among the many late-eighteenth-century glee-composers who made settings of Shakespeare were Dr. Harington of Bath, who set 'She never told her love' as a trio; W. Russell, who set 'Doubt thou the stars are fire' as 'Hamlet's Letter to Ophelia'; W. B. Earle, who vainly attempted to rival Stevens with a setting of 'You spotted snakes'; J. W. Callcott, a prolific glee-composer who set the popular 'Take, O take those

lips away' as well as 'Fear no more the heat of the sun'; Sir
William Herschel, the famous astronomer-musician, who set
'When shall we three meet again?' as a male-voice trio; the
Irish 'musical knight', Sir John Stevenson, best remembered as
Thomas Moore's collaborator, whose settings include a number of lyrics from *Hamlet*, and 'Come unto these yellow sands',
set as one of those odd glees with piano-duet accompaniment
which were popular at the time. He also set 'Take, O take
those lips away' yet again, and 'If music be the food of love',
'Tell me, where is fancy bred?' and 'When that I was and a
little tiny boy'.

Before taking leave of the eighteenth century, which added
so richly to the corpus of Shakespearean music, we should
perhaps take a brief glance at one or two of the German com-
posers of the period who wrote incidental music for Shakespeare's plays, which were already beginning to be popular in
Germany in translation. Haydn, who during his residence in
England set the lines from *Twelfth Night* referred to above,
also wrote incidental music for German productions of *King
Lear* and *Hamlet*. Johann André the elder, music-publisher of
Offenbach, wrote incidental music for a production of *King
Lear* in Berlin in 1778. J. F. Reichardt, the well-known Berlin
*Kapellmeister* and literary man, composed music for the Witches'
scenes in *Macbeth*, and the Abbé Vogler, chiefly remembered
now as the subject of a poem by Browning, but a famous
musical figure in his own day, composed music for a production
of *Hamlet* at Mannheim in 1779.

### 3. THE NINETEENTH CENTURY

The Georgian style of composition, especially in the setting
of Shakespearean material, continued well into the nineteenth
century, for many of the late Georgian glee composers lived on,
among them Dr. Joseph Kemp, whose *Illustrations of Shakespeare*
(1814) included song settings of such unusual lyrics and
passages as 'Oh, for my beads' from *The Comedy of Errors* and
'A lover's eyes' from *Love's Labour's Lost*, as well as the more
usual 'Doubt thou the stars are fire' and the 'Willow' song.
In these and in the numerous Shakespeare settings of William
Linley, the last of the brilliant Linley clan, one can still feel
the influence of Arne's settings of the 1740s. In 1815–16

Linley produced a two-volume anthology of Shakespeare music, under the title of 'Shakespeare's Dramatic Songs', which more or less sums up the Georgian style, including as it does many of the standard classics by Purcell(?), Arne, Boyce, Thomas Linley, J. C. and J. S. Smith, R. J. S. Stevens, Dr. Cooke and William Linley himself, for whenever he could not find a setting for a particular lyric, he wrote one. The results were sometimes rather ludicrous, but occasionally he struck gold; his setting of 'Now the hungry lion roars' was included in several subsequent anthologies, and he did yeoman service in preserving many settings by his predecessors which might otherwise have been lost.

It was in the year which saw the publication of Linley's anthology that the most fearsome despoiler of Shakespeare began his work. This was Henry Rowley Bishop, a highly-gifted musician, composer, musical director and general deranger of other men's work, whether literary or musical. Bishop had already acquired some celebrity as a purveyor of so-called 'operas' for the British public when in 1816 he pro-duced his first Shakespearean effort: *Antony and Cleopatra*. Later he produced a number of other similar pastiches of Shakespeare and music. Some of these were called 'operas', some left as plays, though with an unusual amount of music in them. Bishop has been much abused for his 'operatised' versions of Shakespeare, but in truth one must admit that he was only carrying on the tradition begun with Davenant and Dryden and continued through Garrick, Sheridan and Thomas Linley. Unfortunately Bishop came at a period when or-chestras were much larger and taste at a rather low ebb, and he consequently made a much louder and sometimes more vulgar noise than his predecessors. Oddly enough, almost the only music which has survived from his 'operatised' versions is of a rather sweet and sentimental kind: 'Lo, here the gentle lark', which he took from *Venus and Adonis* and introduced into his *Comedy of Errors*. With its brilliant colora-tura solo and matching flute obbligato it is still brought forward when any soprano wishes to show off her technique. Other famous Bishop settings, not so often heard nowadays, unfortunately, are 'Bid me discourse', also from *Venus and Adonis*, but introduced by Bishop into *Twelfth Night*; 'By the simplicity of Venus' doves' from *A Midsummer Night's Dream*; and 'Should he upbraid' based on the passage 'Say that she rail' from *The Taming of the Shrew*, but transferred to *The Two Gentlemen of Verona*. These were all florid songs of the Italian-opera type, first cousin to Rossini's arias, but they found their way into the mid-Victorian anthologies of Shakespearean song in spite of their technical difficulties. Other settings by Bishop which appear in anthologies are some of his part-songs and ensemble numbers, such as 'Come, thou monarch of the vine' from *Antony and Cleopatra*, but used in *The Comedy of Errors*; 'What shall he have that killed the deer?' modelled on, but not as good as, Stafford Smith's earlier version; and yet another of the spurious 'dirges' in *Romeo and Juliet*, 'Hark! How with awful pause . . .'.

Bishop was the leading member of a group of astute and often able music-directors who misused Shakespeare to their own ends in the early decades of the nineteenth century. Another such was John Davy, now chiefly remembered for his sea-song 'The Bay of Biscay', who towards the end of his life arranged the music for a production of *The Tempest* (1821) in which he brought together the work of many of his predecessors from Purcell onwards, with an overture which is a late example of the old three-movement *sinfonia* type, and includes orchestral arrangements of Purcell's 'Come unto these yellow sands' (for the slow movement) and the Arne-Jackson 'Where the bee sucks' (for the finale). Another member of the group was C. E. Horn, the composer of 'Cherry Ripe'. He too was concerned with the music for the 1821 *Tempest*, as well as for *The Merry Wives of Windsor* at Drury Lane in 1823. His best-known setting of Shakespeare is his duet 'I know a bank', which long held a place in productions of *A Midsummer Night's Dream*, and was even used in conjunction with Mendelssohn's famous incidental music. Another member of the same circle was M. P. King, whose 'Witches' glee' ('When shall we three meet again?') became a recognized part of the Shakespearean repertory, though it had to withstand the competition of the pseudo-Locke *Macbeth* music, still in use in the theatre. King also set 'How sweet the moonlight sleeps upon this bank' as a trio and, more unusually, 'O heart, O heavy heart' from *Troilus and Cressida*, a play not distinguished for musical settings. Other unusual choices by King were 'O never say that I was false of heart' (Sonnet 109) and 'Why, let the stricken deer go weep' from *Hamlet*. But these, and all his other works, are neglected now.

T. S. Cooke was another composer of the time whose Shakespearean settings long remained in the repertory, particularly his charming 'Over hill, over dale', which deserves to be rescued from oblivion. The famous tenor, John Braham, who was something of a composer, introduced some of his own settings into an 'operatised' version of *The Taming of the Shrew* [1] in which he appeared in 1828, among them 'Make me a willow cabin at thy gate' from *Twelfth Night*, 'If music and sweet poetry agree' from *The Passionate Pilgrim*, and 'Let me not to the marriage of true minds' (Sonnet 116).

It might perhaps be as well to pause here for a moment to consider those Continental composers who, as befitted good early Romanticists, were influenced by Shakespeare and set his words to music. Weber, whose fairy opera, 'Oberon', owes nothing to Shakespeare but the names of some of the characters, set 'Tell me, where is fancy bred?' as a trio under the title of 'Sagt, woher stammt Liebeslust?' In the accounts of the Stratford-upon-Avon Tercentenary Festival of 1864 it is stated that 'Madame Parepa contributed Weber's grand *scena* "Portia"', but so far I have not been able to identify this. Schubert contributed only a few pieces to the Shakespeare repertory, but two of them, though set to German translations, are among its choicest gems — 'Hark, hark the lark' (D. 889) and 'Who is Sylvia?' (D. 891). His 'Come, thou monarch of the vine' ('Trinklied: Bacchus feister Fürst') (D. 888) is less well known, and, for Schubert, rather disappointingly ordinary.

To Berlioz, the greatest of all the French Romanticists, Shakespeare was a leading source of inspiration, but surprisingly enough he does not seem to have set any of the lyrics. His 'Shakespearean ballad' for two female voices, 'La Mort d'Ophélie', is a setting of the Queen's speech from *Hamlet*, 'There is a willow grows aslant a brook'. He also wrote a cantata on Antony and Cleopatra, based on a French play, which he headed with a Shakespearean quotation and drew on later for that strange gallimaufry 'Lélio, ou le retour à la vie' which also includes his superb choral fantasia on *The Tempest*.[2] But his main Shakespearean works were operatic [3] and orchestral.[4]

Carl Loewe, famous as a composer of *lieder*, and much

---

[1] See below, p. 127.       [2] See below, p. 182.
[3] See below, pp. 133-5.      [4] See below, p. 184.

influenced by such English ballads as 'Edward', also set some Shakespeare songs, from *Hamlet*, *Othello* and *Twelfth Night*; but they have never become well known in England. Nor has the setting by Schumann of 'When that I was and a little tiny boy' (Op. 127).

The finest of all German Shakespearean settings was without doubt the work of Mendelssohn, whose incidental music to *A Midsummer Night's Dream* was so congenial to English taste that for many years no production of the play was considered complete without at least some of it; much of it was reprinted in anthologies.[1] Typically enough, nineteenth-century music-directors promptly proceeded to gild the lily by adding arrangements of Mendelssohn's 'Spring Song' and 'Bee's Wedding' to his score for *A Midsummer Night's Dream* to provide dances for the fairies.

As the eighteenth century had been noteworthy for its Shakespearean song-settings, so the nineteenth was to become remarkable for the amount of new incidental music specially composed for productions of the plays, mainly because the growing elaboration of scenery called for music to cover the scene-changes as well as to provide 'atmosphere'. Mendelssohn, though the greatest, was only one of the many musicians engaged to provide incidental music in the theatre. Among his English contemporaries was J. L. Hatton, who in his capacity as music-director of such theatres as Drury Lane and the Princes composed incidental music for a number of the plays, much of which is now in the Folger Shakespeare Library, Washington, D.C. His settings seem to have fallen into oblivion, perhaps because, as Christopher Wilson said of his 'When that I was and a little tiny boy', 'Hatton's setting is quite pretty, but he plays the deuce with the words!' A humble contemporary of Hatton's was Edward Fitzwilliam, who composed a setting of 'Over hill, over dale' as a solo song with clarinet obbligato, published as No. 3 of his 'Songs for a Winter Night'.

One devoted Victorian amateur, Richard Simpson, broke new ground by setting all Shakespeare's sonnets. In 1878, two years after his death, thirteen of these were published, together with five of his other settings of Shakespeare; the selection was made by 'Mrs. Macfarren' — presumably Natalia, wife of George Macfarren, who with his brother

---

[1] For a full description, see below, pp. 178-82, 225-7.

Walter was much concerned with the writing of Shakespearean music. George's overtures to *Romeo and Juliet*, *The Merchant of Venice* and *Hamlet* were stock pieces in the Victorian theatres, and he also wrote a number of popular Shakespearean part-songs, published by Novello in their Part-Song Series. Walter also wrote some Shakespearean part-songs and composed overtures to *The Winter's Tale*, *The Taming of the Shrew*, *Henry V* and *Othello*.

Sullivan, who was probably the most gifted English composer of Shakespearean music in Victorian times, first came into prominence with his incidental music for *The Tempest*. Soon after its first English performance at the Crystal Palace in 1862 (it had been given in Leipzig in 1861) Sullivan was commissioned by Metzler the publisher to compose a group of Shakespeare songs at 'five guineas apiece'; they were 'Orpheus with his lute'; 'O mistress mine'; 'Sigh no more, ladies'; the 'Willow' song; and 'Rosalind' (a setting of the lines beginning 'From the east to western Ind' from *As You Like It*). The first is one of the classic settings, but 'O mistress mine', though full of the inimitable Sullivan sparkle, is sadly neglected. In 1865 Sullivan produced his cantata 'Kenilworth' at the Birmingham Festival; it contains settings of 'How sweet the moonlight sleeps upon this bank' and 'In such a night as this', both from *The Merchant of Venice*, and also of 'It was a lover and his lass'. In later years Sullivan was in great demand as a composer of incidental music for Shakespeare productions.

In 1816, for the bicentenary of Shakespeare's death, Kemble tried to revive the stage version of the 'Jubilee; or Shakespeare's Garland', but with little success; in 1827 and 1830 two 'Commemoration Festivals' were held in Stratford-upon-Avon with some musical performances which included the inevitable pseudo-Locke 'Music in *Macbeth* . . .' as well as an unspecified setting of 'Shakespeare's Epitaph' and an ode specially written by Isaac Cowen and set to music by his nephew, Charles Salaman. These, however, were local affairs. In 1864 the Tercentenary of Shakespeare's birth was celebrated nationally. In London there was, among other things, a three-day 'Grand Bardic Jubilee' which took place at the Royal Agricultural Hall, where two concerts of Shakespearean music were given, with a 'Band and chorus of 2,000' conducted by 'Mr. Benedict' and a galaxy of soloists and

actors which included such celebrities as Sims Reeves, the
famous tenor, and Phelps, the tragedian. It is interesting to
see what was then considered to be typical Shakespearean
music — the 'Music in *Macbeth* . . .', of course; Arne's
classic song-settings, such as 'Blow, blow, thou winter wind'
and 'Under the greenwood tree'; Linley's 'O bid your faithful
Ariel fly'; Haydn's 'She never told her love'; Bishop's 'Bid
me discourse' and 'What shall he have that killed the deer?';
Schubert's 'Hark, hark, the lark' and 'Who is Sylvia?';
Horn's 'I know a bank'; Stevens's 'Cloud-cap't towers';
Macfarren's overture to *Romeo and Juliet*, Nicolai's to *The
Merry Wives of Windsor*, and Sullivan's settings from his epoch-
making *Tempest* music, still only a few years old. All in all, a
fine programme, which I for one would love to hear repeated.

Stratford's Tercentenary Festival included Mendelssohn's
music for *A Midsummer Night's Dream*; an overture to *As You
Like It* by Harold Thomas; a 'medley-overture' by one
Allridge; the usual Arne, Bishop, Stevens and Horn items, as
well as the mysterious 'Portia' by Weber referred to above.
One intriguing item was an 'Instrumental Fantasia on Shakespearian Airs, with solos for Pianoforte, Flute, Clarionet, Cornet-
à-Pistons, Violin, Violoncello, Contra-Basso and Euphonium,
arranged expressly for this occasion by C. Coote'. Coote was
a well-known purveyor of dance-music; his curious chamber-
ensemble looks suspiciously like the dance-band which played
his 'Shakespeare Quadrilles and Lancers' at the 'grand fancy
ball' a night or two later.

The 1864 Tercentenary seems to have occasioned the re-
issue of one of the classic Shakespearean anthologies, John
Caulfield's *Collection of the vocal music in Shakespeare's plays*, first
issued in the 1820s by Caulfield himself, then reprinted by
various publishers, including the well-known theatrical publisher, Thomas Hailes Lacy, at about the time of the Tercentenary, and finally reprinted yet again in a larger format by
his successor, the even more celebrated Samuel French. Caulfield and his musical co-editor, John Addison, collected a great
deal of material by dint of diligent enquiry in green-rooms
and orchestra-pits, but they were not very scholarly, and a
great many misattributions stem from their pages, which were
all faithfully perpetuated in the later editions. Another
Tercentenary publication was the handsome *Shakespeare Vocal
Album* with its attendant 'Magazine', which contained the

same material issued in separate numbers. Between them Caulfield and the *Vocal Album* amount to nearly 600 pages, and give a fair idea of the corpus of Shakespearean song which had grown up during the eighteenth and nineteenth centuries. They even included one or two 'ancient melodies' and catches from the seventeenth century, but very little of the music composed before Purcell, not even Morley's 'It was a lover and his lass'. Even that good musical antiquarian E. F. Rimbault, who issued a collection of 'Thirteen Standard Songs of Shakespeare', [1] confined his choice to the normal repertory from Purcell to Bishop and Schubert; it was left to a later age to resurrect the music and instruments of Shakespeare's own time. There were, however, two further events which had some musical repercussions, one of some importance. In 1878 Alfred Roffe compiled a useful *Handbook of Shakespeare Music*, and in May 1883 a meeting of the New Shakspere Society gave rise to an even more useful catalogue, *A List of all the songs and passages in Shakspere* which have been set to music, compiled by the Society's 'conductor', J. Greenhill, in collaboration with F. J. Furnival and the Rev. W. A. Harrison. The editors were a trifle precious in their methods, insisting on First Folio spelling, sometimes with ludicrous results, as it was often wildly at variance with the eighteenth- and nineteenth-century settings; but on the whole the compilers were enviably accurate in their lists, and all later researchers into Shakespearean music must be grateful to them. In the last decade of the century Messrs. Novello published some 'Catalogues of Shakespeare Music' which are also of great interest.

Part-songs were still very much in fashion and many minor composers contributed examples to the repertory. Little of their Shakespearean work is known today, or even of that of their more eminent contemporaries, Parry and Stanford, the joint leaders of what is often called the English Music Renaissance, though Stanford wrote an opera based on *Much Ado About Nothing* as well as 'The Clown's Songs' in *Twelfth Night*, and Parry made a solo setting of 'Crabbed age and youth' which is still sometimes sung. Charles Wood, who succeeded Stanford as Professor of Music at Cambridge, set the lyrics in *As You Like It* as songs or part-songs, and another Cambridge musical don, Alan Gray, left a charming setting of 'O mistress mine' which would be worth reviving. And one little setting

[1] No. 47 of Chappell's *Musical Magazine*, London, 1866.

of 'Sigh no more, ladies' by W. A. Aikin, a medical man by
profession but a gifted amateur composer and musical theorist,
has a touch of immortality about it, and still gives pleasure
wherever it is sung.   How much more obscure the 'Twelve
songs from Shakespeare' by the Liverpool composer William
Faulkes, almost unbelievably labelled Op. 204, which are still
to be seen in the Liverpool Public Library!

Returning to the Continent for a moment, Peter Cornelius,
composer of 'The Barber of Baghdad' and some charming
Christmas songs, also made no fewer than four settings of
'Come away, death', but these have been discarded in favour
of the setting of the same lyric by Brahms, who made a magic
part-song version of it for female voices, two horns and harp.
Brahms also left us 'Five songs of Ophelia' for solo voice and
piano.   The vocal works of Richard Strauss also include
'Three Ophelia songs', while the great conductor Felix
Weingartner wrote some exquisite incidental music for *The
Tempest* and a symphonic poem on *King Lear*.   C. M. Widor
wrote some incidental music for a French version of *Twelfth
Night* with the intriguing title of *Conte d'avril*; Hugo Wolf set
some of the lyrics from *A Midsummer Night's Dream*.   *The
Tempest* has inspired many composers; Ernest Chausson
wrote songs and incidental music for it, Honegger an orchestral
prelude to it and two songs, and Frank Martin wrote five
'Ariel' songs for chorus later incorporated into his opera
'Der Sturm'.[1]   He also wrote some incidental music for *Romeo
and Juliet*.   Erich Korngold achieved fame with his incidental
music for *Much Ado About Nothing*, and also set the Clown's
songs in *Twelfth Night*.   But all these composers pale into
insignificance when compared with the Italian Mario Castelnuovo-Tedesco, who has set practically all Shakespeare's
lyrics, written overtures to many of the plays, and made operas
out of two of them, so far.[1]

Although Castelnuovo-Tedesco was born in Florence, he
has lived in the United States since 1939, where, in view of the
great interest taken in Shakespeare and in the production of
his plays, not only at Stratford-upon-Avon but at Stratford,
Connecticut, one would expect to find a vast amount of
Shakespearean music.   Oddly enough, this does not seem to

[1] For a full description, see below, pp. 114-15.
[2] For incidental music by Balakirev, Fauré, Kabalevsky, Sibelius, Tchaikovsky,
etc., see below, pp. 225-235.

be the case, though there has been a gentle trickle of American music for Shakespeare ever since the early nineteenth century. John Knowles Paine composed a symphonic poem on *The Tempest*, and an overture to *As You Like It*; William Fry an overture to *Macbeth*; Edward MacDowell composed a symphonic poem on Hamlet and Ophelia (1885). These were all orchestral pieces, but that American composers did set Shakespearean lyrics is evident from the anthology 'Fifty Songs of Shakespeare' published in Ditson's *Musicians' Library* in 1906. Besides some old friends from earlier anthologies, this collection includes 'Who is Sylvia?' by Monk Gould; 'Blow, blow, thou winter wind' and 'Sigh no more, ladies' by William Arms Fisher; 'Orpheus with his lute' and 'Under the greenwood tree' by Carl Busch; 'Let me the canakin clink' and 'Crabbed age and youth' by Harvey Worthington Loomis; and another setting of 'Orpheus with his lute' by Charles Fonteyn Manney. Grace Wassall's *Shakespeare Song Cycle* of 1904 contained twelve pieces, including solo songs, duets, trios and quartets. Franklin Hopkins published a *Shakespeare Album* of songs in 1913, and in 1927 Mrs. Alice Riley published in Chicago her *Shakespeare's lovers in a garden . . . a flower masque*. Among more recent American composers who have interested themselves in Shakespeare are Aaron Copland, who wrote incidental music for *The Five Kings*, an entertainment 'after Shakespeare' by Orson Welles, and Otto Luening, who has released a 'Suite' from *King Lear* for tape-recorder. Quincy Porter and Virgil Thomson have both written incidental music for *Antony and Cleopatra*; the latter has also published five Shakespeare songs, 'Was this fair face the cause?' (from *All's Well That Ends Well*); 'Take, O take those lips away'; 'Tell me, where is fancy bred?'; 'Pardon, goddess of the night'; 'Sigh no more, ladies'. Samuel Barber has written incidental music for *As You Like It*; Paul Bowles for *Twelfth Night*; and David Diamond has composed music for *Romeo and Juliet* and a 'Timon of Athens' subtitled 'Portrait after Shakespeare'.

## 4. THE TWENTIETH CENTURY

To return to Great Britain at the turn of the century. It seems strange that Elgar, the greatest composer of the Victorian and Edwardian eras, should have left so little Shakespeare music.[1] The tantalising 'Shakespeare's Kingdom' is on a text by Alfred Noyes, not Shakespeare. If Elgar did set any of the lyrics they have never been published, and he seems to have taken the words for his songs from among his own contemporaries. But theatre-composers were as busy as ever turning out incidental music for the actor-managers of the day. Apart from Edward German, whose highly successful Shakespeare music is now forgotten except for the dances from *Henry VIII*, there was Alexander Campbell Mackenzie with his *Coriolanus*; George Henschel with *Hamlet*; Coleridge-Taylor with *Othello*; and Frederick Rosse with *The Merchant of Venice*. Two extracts for this last, the 'Portia' intermezzo and the 'Doge's March', achieved an extraordinary popularity and still figure in military band programmes. One eminent music-director of those days was Michael Balling, who wrote music for Frank Benson's productions; others were Norman O'Neill and that Christopher Wilson who has already been mentioned as the author of *Shakespeare and Music*, and who also wrote much incidental music to Shakespeare in the course of his work; little of it was printed, and it is difficult to know how good a composer he was, though like Sullivan before him he was a Mendelssohn Scholar.

It was in Wilson's time that the first signs of a new approach to Shakespearean theatre music became apparent, with the lectures and books of J. F. Bridge and the publication in 1913 of E. W. Naylor's *Shakespeare Music* (music of the period). This gradually led to the abandonment of the old repertory of Shakespearean music and the substitution for it either of more or less musicological reconstructions of the original music of Shakespeare's own time,[2] or of the very much scaled-down modern incidental music such as we still hear at Stratford-upon-Avon and elsewhere. There were, however, still some notable Shakespearean song-writers — Roger Quilter, for instance, who occupies much the same place among twentieth-century Shakespearean composers as Arne did in the eighteenth century. Quilter made his name with his 'Three Shakespeare songs' ('Come away, death'; 'O mistress mine'; 'Blow, blow, thou winter wind') (Op. 6) published

---

[1] For 'Falstaff', see below, pp. 218-21.
[2] Such as Denis Stevens's 'made-up' versions of the five songs in *As You Like It*, prepared for the Mermaid Theatre production in 1951, and later published by Hinrichsen.

in 1906, which added three more classics to the Shakespearean repertory.   Three more sets of songs (Op. 23, Op. 30 and Op. 32) and one or two isolated numbers practically covered the more famous Shakespearean lyrics, but without approaching the heights of Op. 6, by which he is best remembered.   But the greatest of all modern English composers of Shakespeare music was Ralph Vaughan Williams, who died in 1958. Shakespeare was always one of his great loves, and he often turned to him when in search of 'words for music'.   He made settings of 'O mistress mine' and the 'Willow' song as early as 1890, when he was only eighteen, but they were not published until 1913, by which time he had become the acknowledged leader of the new folk-song school of English music.   He also made two solo settings of 'Orpheus with his lute', one as early as 1903, the other in 1925.   Between them, in 1922, appeared his part-song settings of 'It was a lover and his lass' (for SA) and the true 'dirge' from *Cymbeline* (for SATB).   His 'Three Songs from Shakespeare' of 1926 included the second 'Orpheus with his lute' mentioned above, together with 'Take, O take those lips away' and 'When icicles hang by the wall'. In 1929 came his rollicking opera, 'Sir John in Love'.[1]   This has never had the stage success it deserves, but some of its tunes are familiar to concert-goers in the form of a cantata taken from the opera, called 'In Windsor Forest'.   In 1938 Vaughan Williams composed a 'Serenade to Music' in honour of the Golden Jubilee of his friend Sir Henry Wood as a conductor.   He took his text from the 'garden scene' in *The Merchant of Venice* — 'How sweet the moonlight sleeps upon this bank'.   The resultant work, scored for sixteen solo voices and orchestra, contains some of the loveliest and most evocative of all the music composed to Shakespeare's words.[2]   Last of Vaughan Williams's tributes to Shakespeare were the three songs (for SATB) composed for the British Federation of Music Festivals in 1951 — 'Full fathom five' ,'The cloud-cap't towers' and 'Over hill, over dale' — pieces of the rarest imagination.   The first, in particular, is almost eerie in its suggestion of shifting images refracted through sunlit water and the sound of far-off bells heard over the waves.

One of Vaughan Williams's colleagues in the folk-song movement was Cecil Sharp, who in 1914 wrote some incidental music for *A Midsummer Night's Dream*.   For the Tercentenary

---

[1] See below, pp. 126-7.          [2] See below, p. 218.

Celebrations of 1916, overshadowed by the tragedy of the First World War, J. F. Bridge composed a Shakespearean motet to words taken from *2 Henry VI* ('God's goodness hath been great to thee . . .').[1]

It would be impossible to enumerate all the gifted British composers of that generation and the one immediately following who found inspiration in Shakespeare — men as diverse as Walford Davies, Frederick Delius, Martin Shaw, John Ireland, E. J. Moeran and many more. One famous songwriter, Peter Warlock, whose real name was Philip Heseltine, was inevitably led by his love of all things 'Jacobethan' to the Elizabethan lyric-writers, though not often to Shakespeare. And when he did set Shakespeare, he was apt to trick him out with fanciful titles — 'Pretty ring time' for 'It was a lover and his lass'; 'Sweet and twenty' for 'O mistress mine'; 'Mockery' for 'When daisies pied'; and 'The sweet of the year' for 'When daffodils begin to peer'. It must, however, be admitted that all these titles were derived from the verses themselves, and perhaps Warlock just wanted to differentiate his settings from all those that had gone before and the others which were bound to follow after.

Among the host of recent composers who have set Shakespeare's words, none showed greater sensitivity than Gerald Finzi, whose premature death in 1956 robbed England of one of her most gifted song-writers. His Shakespearean song-cycle 'Let us garlands bring' dates from 1942, and includes fine settings of 'Come away, death'; 'Who is Sylvia?'; 'O mistress mine'; 'Fear no more the heat of the sun'; and 'It was a lover and his lass'. He also wrote some enchanting incidental music for a B.B.C. production of *Love's Labour's Lost*, of which the song-settings only were published. Another admirable work of the same kind is Lennox Berkeley's music for *The Winter's Tale*, published in 1960 as his Op. 54. A busy writer of Shakespearean music is Leslie Bridgewater. In his capacity of music-director to various theatres, including the Royal Shakespeare at Stratford-upon-Avon, he has written about twenty sets of incidental music and set all Shakespeare's lyrics, many of which were published in 1964. There is also a long-playing record devoted to his Shakespearean song-settings.[2]

---

[1] Another result of the 1916 Tercentenary was the publication of A. H. Moncur-Sime's *Shakespeare: his music and song*, in which he lists many settings by contemporary composers.    [2] Westminster XWN 18742.

Shakespearean music, in the form of songs and part-songs, continues to pour off the printing-presses; part-song writers, in particular, seem to turn automatically to Shakespeare when they want a rhyme to set to music. Some of them are eminent, some are almost unknown, yet the interesting thing is that, now as always, when composers set Shakespeare's lyrics, the results are usually tuneful and often memorable. Of unusual interest are Geoffrey Bush's 'Twelfth Night', an entertainment for tenor, chorus and orchestra; John Gardner's 'Seven Songs' for mixed chorus and small orchestra, Op. 36, which includes four Shakespeare lyrics; Arthur Young's 'Four Shakespearean Songs in Swing' and 'Six Shakespeare songs' (of which actually only three are by Shakespeare) 'set to music in the modern manner'; Stravinsky's notable 'Three songs from William Shakespeare' of 1953, scored for mezzo-soprano, flute, clarinet and viola, and including 'Full fathom five', 'When daisies pied' and the unusual 'Music to hear, why hear'st thou music sadly?' (Sonnet 8). Dmitri Kabalevsky has set ten of the Sonnets, and Britten's 'Nocturne' (Op. 60) ends with a most memorable setting of Sonnet 43, 'When most I wink'. We might also mention Thea Musgrave's 'The Phoenix and [the] Turtle' for chorus and orchestra. Nor should we forget Salvatore Martirano's 'O, O, O, That Shakespeherian rag', for chorus and instrumental ensemble, if only to show that an interest in Shakespeare is not confined to squares; perhaps the composer believes, with Samuel Butler, that the one thing Shakespeare might really have enjoyed would have been a good burlesque of *Hamlet*. Johnny Dankworth, too, has added to the repertory of Shakespearean jazz with various settings, including a very attractive 'If music be the food of love', as well as a vocal version of part of Duke Ellington's 'Such Sweet Thunder'. And finally, peering very much into the future, we come to Roman Haubenstock-Ramati's odd-looking 'Mobile for Shakespeare' (Sonnets 53 and 54 for voice and 6 players). It seems that Shakespeare's words can inspire even the *avant-garde*!

# Shakespeare and Opera

BY

WINTON DEAN

## I. AESTHETIC

IN surveying the field of Shakespearean opera it is necessary
to fly in the face of aesthetic convention and apply a double
standard. We must judge how far an opera takes the measure
of the play on which it is based. This is the first and last test,
but if it is the only one it means reducing the field to two or
three masterpieces and a handful of interesting failures and
dismissing the rest out of hand. Public opinion does in fact
produce a result of this kind. But a rigorous and exclusive
criterion has disadvantages. It planes away the contours of
history by burying much interesting material and diminish-
ing the perspective in which the masterpieces appear. It
ignores the fact that until a century ago very few composers
and librettists, in dealing with a Shakespearean subject, were
conscious of any literary challenge; by setting them against
Shakespeare we are misinterpreting their aims. And it takes
no account of the possibility that taste may change. Until
very recently no one thought of reviving the operas of Monteverdi and Handel. Verdi's 'Macbeth' had its London
première as recently as 1960. Who knows what our grand-
children may not choose to uncover from the past?

An opera needs to be considered as an entertainment in
its own right, quite apart from its relationship to any literary
original. There is no *a priori* reason why Shakespeare should
not have inspired popular and enjoyable operas whose artistic
content cannot bear comparison with the plays. The shade
of Goethe, however affronted, has not killed Gounod's 'Faust'.
In fact, a good deal of aesthetic pleasure, historical revelation
and sheer entertainment can be derived not only from the few
respectable failures but from the totally forgotten operas.
Some are very poor indeed, but the majority throw light on
the tastes of their period; in this respect the librettos are
often more instructive than the music. There is after all a

perennial fascination in observing how the plays of Shakespeare have worked upon the intelligence of men of different
countries and different ages.

A first glance at the canon does suggest one halfpennyworth
of bread to an intolerable deal of sack. The opera composers
who have tried their hands at Shakespeare include, besides
many nonentities, at least seven acknowledged masters —
Purcell, Rossini, Bellini, Berlioz, Verdi, Wagner and Britten —
several others, such as Gounod and Smetana, with works in
the regular repertory, and many lesser figures of distinction,
among them Holst, Vaughan Williams, Bloch and Malipiero.
The librettists include some of the most admired — Da Ponte,
Scribe, Romani and Boito. Yet the product is disappointing.
To a certain extent mischance seems to have played a part.
Purcell wrote at a time and place when, if it were not for the
miracle of his own 'Dido and Aeneas', a satisfactory operatic
balance might be dismissed as impossible. Rossini and Bellini
were also handicapped by the *Zeitgeist*, though less fatally than
subsequent neglect might indicate. Wagner attacked Shakespeare before his style was formed (so did Verdi, but he
returned later), while Berlioz, whose literary and musical
imagination were uniquely equal to the task, allowed himself
to be side-tracked at a crucial point. There remain Verdi's
two late masterpieces and Britten's 'Midsummer Night's
Dream'. Of the other composers mentioned, only Bloch came
within measurable distance of producing a great Shakespeare
opera.

If projected operas are added, the impression of what we
have missed grows more tantalizing. A *Tempest* libretto was
actually written for Mozart, and at least two for Mendelssohn.
Beethoven began an opera on *Macbeth*, Tchaikovsky one on
*Romeo and Juliet*. Berlioz's Shakespearean preoccupations
might have yielded several more operas, and Verdi, apart
from his lifelong concern with *King Lear*, considered an 'Antony
and Cleopatra', with libretto by Boito, after 'Falstaff'.
Whether Debussy could have made a success of *As You Like It*,
or Puccini of *King Lear*, is more problematic. Of the greatest
dramatic composers Handel alone seems never to have considered a Shakespeare opera; but even he set a number of
lines from the plays, perhaps without knowing it, in his
oratorios.[1] Explorers of nineteenth-century operatic by-ways

[1] See Winton Dean, *Handel's Dramatic Oratorios and Masques* (1959), pp. 414, 484.

may unearth a 'Love's Labour's Lost' by Mozart (Paris 1863) and a 'Twelfth Night' by Schubert (Hamburg 1885); these are quaint attempts to fit new librettos to the music of 'Cosi fan tutte' and 'Die Zauberharfe'.

Judged by the strict standard, the scarcity of masterpieces is not surprising. Opera is the one field in which composer meets dramatist on equal terms, both working on the largest scale. Therefore a composer turning a play into an opera of comparable stature requires a quality of imagination and technique equal to that of the dramatist. This condition alone must disqualify all but a handful of Shakespeare operas from the highest honours. The situation of course varies from play to play. The great tragedies are bound to overthrow most of their antagonists, whereas a composer of comparatively modest gifts might create a satisfactory opera out of *The Taming of the Shrew*. But Shakespeare presents so many different challenges to the composer, who must come to terms, separately and together, with the plot, the characters, the poetry and the spiritual climate of the play he chooses to set.

The plot may well be the least of his difficulties. It is true that the different time-scale of opera enforces compression: music, even when it is as succinct and swift as in Verdi's 'Falstaff' (and it practically never is), requires more time for the development of character, atmosphere and action than the spoken word. But Shakespeare's plots are not uniformly complex; in some plays, such as *The Tempest* and *The Winter's Tale*, very little need be sacrificed. Subplots and minor characters may have to go. *The Merchant of Venice* without the Gobbos makes an admirable libretto with very few changes of scene, as Castelnuovo-Tedesco has demonstrated. Boito removed two of Anne Page's suitors and the Fat Woman of Brentford episode from *The Merry Wives of Windsor* without impairing the design, and he compressed *Othello* by beginning with Shakespeare's second act. *Macbeth*, a short play, is not unmanageable, though Verdi's libretto cuts some of the corners too fine. *Hamlet* and *King Lear* are much more intransigent owing to the greater complexity of the action; but there are other reasons for the universal failure here.

In fact, many composers, especially in the present century, have hampered their operas as much by what they left in as by what they cut out. In this respect some of their predecessors were wiser: Romani, in reducing *Romeo and Juliet* to its bare bones, allowed the composer room to expand and speak his own language.  It is possible to carry respect for Shakespeare to excessive lengths, to have too strong a literary sense.  A setting of a play as it stands is bound to alter its values; the over-all application of a musical sugar-coating is all too likely to suffocate the drama without creating an opera.  Bellini's 'I Capuleti e i Montecchi' is a better opera than Frank Martin's 'Der Sturm' partly because the latter preserves so much of the original dialogue that the music has no room to flex its wings.  A parallel fault, the retention of far too many minor characters, hangs a millstone round the neck of Barkworth's 'Romeo and Juliet' and Vaughan Williams's 'Sir John in Love'.  Britten solved a problem of this kind brilliantly in 'A Midsummer Night's Dream'; but he needed all the nimbleness of genius as well as a very skilfully compiled libretto.  A few composers have tried to have the best of both worlds.  The librettist of Hahn's 'Le Marchand de Venise' not only included almost every scene and character in the play, apart from the two Gobbos, but expanded it at the points where a composer might be expected to fill his sails.  Some of these episodes (by no means all) are cleverly contrived; but the result is an opera nearly as long as 'Les Troyens' or 'Parsifal'.

The question how much of the original plot a composer ought to preserve must be answered empirically; the gap between the two arts can be bridged at different levels.  Suppression or modification of details is no more automatically to be condemned than literal fidelity is to be applauded.  A modern audience would doubtless reject an extreme upheaval of the story, if only because the plays are so familiar; it is difficult today to imagine a 'Romeo and Juliet' with a happy ending, though there were several in the eighteenth century, or a 'Hamlet' in which the hero survives to mount the throne, as he does in more than one nineteenth-century opera.  But the English straight theatre, right into the nineteenth century, allowed perversions of Shakespeare quite as grotesque as these.

By common consent the best Shakespeare librettos are those of Boito, which include the 'Hamlet' he wrote for Faccio. His method involves both contraction and expansion: the former to remove inessentials and episodes not easily soluble in music, the latter to allow for the different distribution of weight that an opera requires in comparison with a play. Having settled the structural framework, he was able to incorporate much of Shakespeare's language. One reason for his success is his exploitation, whether conscious or not, of a significant feature of the plays. Their design, while equally repugnant to the old eighteenth-century aria opera and the Wagnerian music-drama, is actively suited to the aria-ensemble plan common to all opera, comic or serious, from Mozart to Verdi. The soliloquies give obvious openings for arias. Some of them do more : Lady Macbeth's first scene, for example, beginning with her reading of the letter and followed by two speeches, the first pensive ('Glamis thou art, and Cawdor'), the second — after the messenger has brought news of Duncan's approach — a passionate invocation ('Come, you spirits that tend on mortal thoughts!'), exactly anticipates the cavatina-cabaletta pattern of romantic opera, down to the external interruption that changes the mood in the middle. Shakespeare's technique of developing tension and conflict within the scene, whether between two or more characters, lends itself to the close forms of duet, trio and quartet. Equally prominent are the episodes that call for choral and ensemble treatment, such as the council and battle scenes, the street fights in *Romeo and Juliet*, the trial in *The Merchant of Venice*, the forum scenes in *Julius Caesar* and many more. These are not commenting choruses in the manner of Greek tragedy, but incidents that advance and illustrate the action. They are the very stuff of opera.

Nor is this all. Some of the comedies, such as *The Taming of the Shrew*, *Twelfth Night* and *The Merry Wives of Windsor*, are virtually a string of potential *buffo* ensembles ; and they show clear parallels, in their treatment of intrigue and comic imbroglio, their carnival spirit and some of their characters, with the operatic world of Cimarosa and Rossini. There may be a genuine if remote blood relationship here. Most of Shakespeare's comedy plots came from Italy, stemming from the tradition that ultimately developed through the *commedia dell'arte* into *opera buffa*.[1] His clowns in particular, though anglicized, still bear traces of a family resemblance ; indeed, his habit of relieving the mood of a tragedy by interspersing a few comic scenes was shared by many Italian composers of serious opera from Monteverdi and Landi to Scarlatti, and became almost universal in the early romantic period. It is

---

[1] The birth of opera itself was of course contemporary with Shakespeare, though the ensemble was a later development.

no accident that the enormous increase of Shakespeare's operatic popularity dates from just that period when the *buffo* tradition reached its full development and fertilized the evolving forms of romantic opera.

There is thus an operatic element in Shakespeare, absent from much later drama (such as French classical tragedy), which corresponds to Verdi's structural method. The point had been dimly grasped long before in the ensembles of Steibelt's 'Roméo et Juliette' (1793), which are vigorous enough to suggest the masterpiece that might have resulted had Mozart received a Shakespeare libretto from Da Ponte. This is not too fanciful a conjecture : Da Ponte's 'Gli equivoci', based on *The Comedy of Errors*, was set by Mozart's pupil Storace for Vienna in the year of 'The Marriage of Figaro'. This was perhaps the earliest period at which a great Shakespeare opera was a real possibility. It may be too much to suggest that composers who avoid the ensemble, like Martin and Malipiero, are working against the grain ; but they impose an enormous strain on their musical invention.

Shakespeare's characters constitute a more formidable obstacle to a composer than his plots. In modern times (though this has not always been the case) a Shakespeare opera whose characters are poor walking shadows of their original selves is not likely to hold the stage for long. Bernard Shaw's dictum that no dramatist can create a character greater than himself is equally true of the opera composer. The difficulty is not confined to the great tragedies. Many of the comedies contain powerful and idiosyncratic figures like Shylock, Falstaff, Prospero, Leontes and Malvolio, not to mention Caliban and Oberon, who are likely to tax all but the most flexible musical imagination. A hollow central figure will bring down the opera it ought to support. Balfe's 'Falstaff' might be worth reviving as a period piece if its characterization, especially that of Falstaff himself, were not wholly stereotyped ; and many 'Tempest' operas, especially in Germany, have destroyed themselves by reducing Prospero to a platitudinous imitation of Sarastro.

Shakespeare's language raises a different set of problems. The plays are created by a counterpoint of words, whose arrangement in poetry or prose is responsible for their impact on an audience. Opera, while employing words, speaks principally through the music. To separate the skeleton of plot from the flesh of language is to pull apart a living organism; but it may prove a less damaging operation for a composer than to pit his strength against Shakespeare's own words. Great poetry, which already has its intricate rhythms and overtones, is far harder to set to music than plain pedestrian verse. It can be done, as Britten has shown, but only by a composer who is not afraid to impose his own personality on the text. The fact that most foreign composers have set Shakespeare in translation must have been a help rather than a hindrance, though the translations themselves, especially those of Schlegel in Germany, have gathered their own overtones. Whether the composer sets Shakespeare's own words, or a translation, or a paraphrase, or attempts to reproduce nothing beyond the principal situations — and all have been tried — he must rethink everything from the beginning, and spin a new element from his entrails.

Finally, how can an opera suggest the spiritual climate of a Shakespeare play? This is scarcely the place to attempt a definition of Shakespeare's genius; but it is plain that the universal quality of the great tragedies, their profound cultivation of the individual, the generic and the symbolic, must present an almost insuperable problem of adaptation to a more deliberate time-scale. It is just possible to imagine a Wagnerian 'Hamlet', but hardly on a scale much shorter than that of 'The Ring'. In fact, there has been only one approach to a satisfactory solution, Verdi's 'Otello', the work of a very experienced operatic composer and a librettist of genius, who exploited to the full the one major advantage an opera has over a spoken play: its ability to express conflicting emotions, hidden thoughts and ironical overtones simultaneously, while continuing to expound the story. 'Otello' is not a particularly long opera, but in spiritual stature it ranks little if at all below the play.

Even when dealing with the comedies and less titanic tragedies a composer cannot easily present the full range of Shakespeare's world, whose perimeter comprehends so much of human experience. *Romeo and Juliet* has inspired more than two dozen operas, mostly in Latin countries, but instead of an immortal love story they have too often presented a novelettish melodrama. An even worse fate has befallen the late comedies in German countries, where their gnomic content has made a natural appeal. *The Tempest* emerges as a mixture of moral

homily and coarse-grained farce, *The Winter's Tale* as a sentimental romance with no humour at all; the characters cease
to breathe and the operas collapse under their own weight.
The peculiar mixture of astringency and sentiment in Shakespeare's style has been a constant stumbling-block to composers, especially in Germany and France, since the Age of
Enlightenment. Nearly all — with Berlioz a conspicuous
exception — have overplayed the sentiment and produced a
sugary, if not sickly, confection utterly remote from the bracing
original.

## 2. HISTORICAL

No one knows the total number of operas based on Shakespeare's plays. Those listed in the catalogue on pp. 243-90,
apparently the first serious attempt to map the field, amount
to about 180, of which nearly eighty (and probably more)
have been published in full or vocal scores, not always in their
entirety, and others are represented by printed librettos.
This total is undoubtedly incomplete, and it may include a
few works whose connection with Shakespeare is tenuous or
even imaginary. The evidence, where an opera has not been
published, is often elusive and sometimes contradictory.[1] Of
the tragedies and comedies, all but two (*Titus Andronicus* and
*The Two Gentlemen of Verona*) have sired at least one opera;
the histories for obvious reasons have proved less fertile. Most
European countries outside the Balkans, and at least two in
the New World, have made their contributions, in some
twelve languages. Italy and Germany (including Austria)
head the list with forty-five operas apiece, followed by Britain

---

[1] A number of works which sound Shakespearean are in fact based on quite
different sources. This applies to most of the operas about Julius Caesar, Cleopatra, Coriolanus, Pyramus and Thisbe, and the youth of Henry V; also to a
few others with titles suggesting Shakespeare's characters (Henry VIII, Richard
III, Beatrice, Juliet, Rosalind). Nearly all eighteenth-century 'Hamlet' operas
are based on the libretto by Zeno and Pariati, taken from Saxo Grammaticus;
a number of 'Tempest' operas derive from Ostrovsky's play *The Storm*; Walton's
'Troilus and Cressida' from Chaucer's epic poem. Hüe's 'Titania' (1903), like
Weber's 'Oberon', has no closer link with Shakespeare than a quarrel between
Oberon and Titania. Offenbach and Ambroise Thomas both borrowed the title
of *A Midsummer Night's Dream*. Thomas's opera brings Shakespeare on the stage
together with Falstaff and Queen Elizabeth I. Falstaff makes an assignation with
the disguised Queen in a tavern, and Shakespeare gets drunk in her presence and
is conveyed incapable to Windsor Park. Serpette also wrote an opera on
Shakespeare's life (1899).

and France with about twenty-five. These proportions were to be expected, but it is odd that Czechoslovakia should have produced three times as many Shakespeare operas as Russia. The Russian total is four, of which two are very recent and one has never been staged.[1] The average of failures in all groups is naturally high; the most unexpected fact is the almost complete absence of success among German operas. Only one, Nicolai's 'Die lustigen Weiber von Windsor', has an international reputation; very few of the others have ever been produced outside Germany.

There have always been two variables in the history of Shakespearean opera: the differing attitude of each period, and sometimes of each country, towards Shakespeare as a dramatist and towards opera as an art. To the later seventeenth century Shakespeare was out of date: he needed verbal refinement and the addition of spectacle if he was to be made presentable. Eighteenth-century England found him wild and Gothick, but enjoyed his plays in the domestic adaptations of Cibber, Garrick and others. His popularity on the Continent dates from the later decades of the century, when the plays were first widely translated — another factor in their operatic career. The early nineteenth century, especially on the Continent, saw him in its own romantic image as a precursor of Goethe and Schiller, Byron, Dumas and Hugo, the creator of vast poetic dramas still capable of liberating intense emotion and inflammatory ideas, moral, social and political. Later generations turned to his philosophical and psychological implications. To the twentieth century he is at once a classic, a subject for theatrical experiment, a symbolist and a source of moral and semantic disputation. As with all great artists, each age has discovered in Shakespeare what it wished or needed to find.

But it has not always been practicable to give these discoveries operatic expression. Opera is essentially a social art, and social influences have always exercised a powerful control — sometimes a stranglehold — over its behaviour. Until the French Revolution serious opera, apart from a few local deviations, was exclusively aristocratic, the amusement of

---

[1] As a curiosity it may be noted that the first Russian opera published in full score (1791), a pasticcio entitled 'The Early Reign of Oleg' with libretto by the reigning sovereign Catherine the Great, is stated to have been written 'in imitation of Shakespeare, not observing the traditional rules of the stage'.

princes, courts and persons of wealth and leisure. After the revolutionary wars its main basis was no longer the glorification of a settled order but the projection of popular entertainment, often accompanied by political and social propaganda. The typical romantic opera (though to a lesser degree in Italy than elsewhere) is a hotchpotch combining high and low life, comedy and pathos, homily and hedonism, the religious and the pagan, the natural and the supernatural. But since the audience was to be the widest possible, its intellectual content was almost invariably low; the dramatic situations were multifarious and often spectacular, but never psychologically complex. While it welcomed the teeming world of Shakespeare, it could not penetrate the depths beneath its surface.

Wagner's reaction against this tradition led to its antithesis, a music-drama based on psychological and philosophical (and of course musical) development of the utmost intricacy, with very little outer action. While in Wagner the romantic love of sensation gave way to conceptual thought, in the *verismo* opera of Italy and France it led to an exaggerated sensationalism, which took as its theme the basic emotions of ordinary men and women and exploited them in as realistic a spirit as possible. The last quarter of the century also saw the rise of nationalist opera in the countries that had hitherto possessed no strong native tradition, that is to say all except Italy, France and Austro-Germany. Twentieth-century opera has been markedly eclectic, using every modern technique of composition and every musico-dramatic method evolved over the last three centuries, and testing them in every imaginable combination.

This complex story is reflected in Shakespearean opera, which — at least since the late eighteenth century — offers a history of the art in miniature, and all the more clearly for the scarcity of masterpieces. We find everything from the *castrato* to serialism, from *bel canto* to *musique concrète*. There are some gaps in the early years, but none of significance after about 1775, when a sudden spurt of Shakespearean operas, especially in Germany, coincided with the literary revival that initiated the main romantic movement. The most popular plays were *The Merry Wives of Windsor* (set by Ritter, Dittersdorf and Salieri within five years, apart from two forgotten French works a generation earlier), *Romeo and Juliet* (eight settings between 1773 and 1796) and especially *The Tempest*, which inspired no fewer than eight operas in the two years 1798–9, four of them in 1798 on the same libretto.[1] This was 'Die Geisterinsel', by the dramatist F. W. Gotter, who had also written the libretto of Georg Benda's 'Romeo und Julie' (1776), one of the most successful operas of its day. These German operas belong to the *Singspiel* type; that is, they include much spoken dialogue, interspersed with songs, duets and occasional ensembles of simple construction. Like all the innumerable works of their kind before 1820, except Mozart's two examples and Beethoven's 'Fidelio', they were too rudimentary in organization, dramatic and musical, to stand the test of time.

The revolutionary years in France and the early decades of the nineteenth century saw several other popular operas on *Romeo and Juliet* and the first serious attempts to grapple with the great tragedies. Almost all these operas were French or Italian. The Germans, despite their activity a generation earlier and the stimulus of Schlegel's excellent translations, produced very few Shakespeare operas in the first half of the century. German romantic opera was so preoccupied with fantastic, supernatural, exotic and medieval subjects, of which it poured forth examples by the score, that it had little time for great dramatists, even those of its own age and country.

Hitherto each generation had forced Shakespeare into the mould of current convention. Purcell's operas are more concerned with spectacle, whether scenic, choreographic or mechanical, than with plot or even music. Rolli's 'Rosalinda' libretto paraphrases a few passages from *As You Like It* in the recitative of the first two acts, and even uses 'Blow, blow, thou winter wind' as an aria for the exiled Duke, but its pattern is that of Handel's Italian librettos; each aria — and there are no ensembles apart from the conventional final *coro* — expresses a single emotion and is followed by an exit, and an astonishing amount of violent action is sometimes crammed into a bar or two or recitative. The earliest librettos based on *Romeo and Juliet*, those of Sanseverino and Gotter, turn the tragedy into a fashionable *comédie larmoyante*. Zingarelli's opera (1796) admits the death of Romeo (though not of Juliet), but the libretto is a ramshackle piece of work typical of the debased

---

[1] Multiple settings of the same libretto were common in the eighteenth century and the early years of the nineteenth, but this seems to be the only Shakespearean example.

*opera seria* of its period. Steibelt's is more interesting — though hardly more Shakespearean — for its affinities with the strenuous and ethical *opéra-comique* evolved by Cherubini and immortalized by Beethoven. 'Die Geisterinsel' translates the mixture of tenderness, sententiousness and grotesquerie inherent in *The Tempest* into the inconsequent terms of Schikaneder, with an amorous page after the model of Cherubino thrown in for good measure. Da Ponte's adaptation of *The Comedy of Errors* is by far the most skilful of these librettos and the most faithful to the spirit of the play. This was not too formidable a task, for the plot, taken from a Plautus farce, was almost an archetype of the *opera buffa* at which Da Ponte was so adept. But the brilliant opening scene — a shipwreck that lands the Syracusan master and servant near the home of their identical twins at Ephesus — and the smooth contrivance of the ensembles proclaim the master librettist.

Felice Romani's four Shakespeare librettos (1822–34), on *Hamlet*, *Henry IV* and *Romeo and Juliet* (2), show another clever craftsman at work. They do end more or less in key with Shakespeare — the tragic finale was returning to favour, and Romani was not afraid to close *Henry IV* with the rejection of Falstaff — but they alter relationships and situations wholesale in order to provide the strong but far from silent conflicts that the audiences of Mercadante, Vaccai and Bellini expected, and they make no attempt to retain the language or the temper of the plays. Even the best romantic librettists treat Shakespeare in exactly the same way as the *mélodrames* of Pixérécourt and the tragedies of Lemierre and Voltaire : it is as if a modern author were to boil down the works of Ibsen, Shaw, Agatha Christie and Samuel Beckett to their highest common factor. Romani effected this with considerably greater skill than most of his fellows. Wagner's libretto for 'Das Liebesverbot' belongs to this class ; so (until the last act) does that of Rossini's 'Otello'. Some of the results are ludicrous : Rouget de Lisle's version of *Macbeth* and Scribe's of *The Tempest* are monuments of unconscious humour.

Towards the middle of the century this approach changed. Librettists began to abandon the methods of Procrustes and treat Shakespeare's plots and language with a measure of respect. While Romani confessed to finding *Hamlet* too fantastic for current taste, S. M. Maggioni in his preface to the libretto of Balfe's 'Falstaff' (1838) apologized for not following

the play more strictly.    In fact, he was reasonably faithful by
the standards of his day, most of his changes being cuts.    This
was the time when the English stage finally rejected the additions of Garrick and Cibber, and 'Falstaff', though set in
Italian, was written for a London audience.    But the same
spirit was abroad on the Continent.    Nicolai's 'Lustigen
Weiber von Windsor' (1849) is even closer to Shakespeare.
The two 'Macbeth' operas of this period show a vast change from
Rouget de Lisle.    Verdi's (1847), for all its comic choruses of
witches and murderers, is for the most part a literal if shortened
translation of the play.    Taubert's (1857) follows Shakespeare in
detail—until the last scene, when it topples into hopeless bathos
in order to keep the prima donna on stage during the battle.

The tendency hardened during the 1860s.    Berlioz in
'Béatrice et Bénédict' not only retained much of Shakespeare's
dialogue — which was not difficult, since it was spoken —
but distilled the essence of the two central characters in words
and music.    Faccio's 'Amleto' had the inestimable advantage
of a libretto by Boito, which is scarcely less successful at repro-
ducing the spirit of the play than his later work for Verdi.
The printed libretto of Marchetti's 'Romeo e Giulietta' has an
interesting preface in which the author and composer declare
that, in reaction against the free versions of Zingarelli, Vaccai
and Bellini, they have endeavoured to 'photograph' Shakespeare.    A modern audience might find this a surprising claim;
but the authors, like Boito, have clearly tried to translate one
medium into another without losing more than they could
help, and several scenes retain Shakespeare's dialogue.    Gounod's 'Roméo et Juliette' and Ambroise Thomas's 'Hamlet',
both with librettos by the hack firm of Barbier and Carré, are
more standardized productions with the usual titivations
demanded by Parisian taste; even so, they included a good
deal of Shakespeare, and in 'Hamlet' were soundly rated by
contemporary critics for doing so.    By an odd coincidence two
minor French composers had just completed operas on the
same two tragedies when those of Gounod and Thomas were
produced.    Their work was temporarily held back and proved
to be still-born; but Pierre de Garal's text for Hignard's
'Hamlet' is more faithful than any other.

Not everyone was as respectful as this.    The romantic
period had an unquenchable appetite for religious scenes in
opera, especially weddings, prayers and funerals.    Where

Shakespeare supplies these, as in *Romeo and Juliet* and *Hamlet*, we are sure to find organ or harmonium (or both) and the fruitier aspects of sacred harmony. Where he does not, they can generally be worked in. Berlioz turned his back on fashion by omitting the church scene in *Much Ado About Nothing*, but Pinsuti and Taubert added gratuitous and extensive wedding sequences to *The Merchant of Venice* and *Twelfth Night*, and the former ended his opera with a religious *tour de force*, the prayers of the Christians assembled at Belmont competing with those of the Jews accompanying Shylock into exile on board ship off the coast.

All these operas, together with a renewed spate from Germany during the seventies, are based on the aria-ensemble plan. The Italian works, even at their most derivative, seldom expire without a kick; those of Buzzolla ('Amleto', 1847) and Pinsuti are little more than imitations of Verdi, but their bounding energy keeps the ear amused. The French operas are subject to bouts of pretentious triviality; the German are duller and heavier, their lyrical impulse clogged by the more sophisticated heritage of Mendelssohn and Schumann. (Nicolai, who spent much of his career in Italy and who alone preserved some of the woodland magic of Weber, provides the one exception.) Verdi's collaboration with Boito is the climax not only of the Shakespearean story but of the ensemble opera itself. The design is refined and subtilized by the enrichment of the recitative and the relaxation of the boundaries between the set numbers (not their abandonment), so that the musical and dramatic flow are all but synchronized. Not the least remarkable feature is the manner in which Verdi's overwhelming personality masters the material without distorting it. Differences of emphasis there must be, but on this level of genius they become irrelevant. For once the *Zeitgeist* was favourable to a union of minds across the centuries.

The massive shadow of Wagner was slow to envelop Shakespearean opera, and when it did so its influence was fitful. There have been several attempts at music-drama based on a symphonic leitmotive technique, but this was grafted on to about as many different idioms. Fibich, Bloch, Hale, Zillig and Castelnuovo-Tedesco have tried it with varying success; each set his libretto in a different language, but only on Fibich and Zillig is Wagner's musical influence decisive. Most of these composers fail because they lack Wagner's power of developing, transforming and regenerating their motives so as to spin a continuous living texture. Only Bloch has shown that a Shakespearean opera on Wagnerian principles is not a chimera. Others, like Goldmark in 'Das Wintermärchen', fall heavily between the two stools of Wagnerian arioso and formal grand opera. The general coarsening of the grain in late romantic opera is even more apparent in the Italian *verismo* school. Whereas Puccini was largely successful in combining realism with music-drama, many of his contemporaries and imitators reproduced the more depressing characteristics of both. Zandonai's 'Giulietta e Romeo' debased Shakespeare to the level of D'Annunzio, and Mancinelli applied an equally heavy hand (reinforced by a backstage battery of eight horns and eight trumpets) to *A Midsummer Night's Dream*, of all plays.

The use of recurring motives in some form or other is common to all twentieth-century Shakespeare operas except one or two, like Blacher's 'Romeo und Julia' which adopt a selfconsciously neo-classical posture. Even composers reacting most strongly against earlier conventions, like Martin and Malipiero, retain it for dramatic purposes. Its history goes back long before Wagner, and it has such obvious advantages as a dramatic tool that there is no reason to suppose it played out. But it is no substitute for organic musical design; and if the motives themselves are not memorable it defeats its own purpose. Silver in 'La Mégère apprivoisée' has leading themes for Petruchio and Katharina that actually begin the opera, but they are so insignificant that they can easily escape notice altogether.

It is difficult to imagine Shakespeare serving the cause of nationalism outside England, and only the Falstaff operas of Holst and Vaughan Williams, based on folk idiom, can be placed in this class. Nearly all the twentieth-century English librettos on both sides of the Atlantic, through a natural reluctance to depart from Shakespeare's language, confront the composers with serious problems of form. (Continental composers who have set literal translations, such as Malipiero, Castelnuovo-Tedesco, Martin, Blacher and Klebe, have run up against similar obstacles.) A few — Stanford's 'Much Ado About Nothing', Gatty's and Hale's 'Tempest', Adrian Beecham's 'Merchant of Venice' — make things worse by filling gaps or replacing prose passages with deplorable gobbets of rhymed pseudo-Elizabethan doggerel. Several enlist the

H

support of other works of Shakespeare (principally the sonnets), contemporary dramatists and poets, and occasionally authors farther afield. Giannini's 'Taming of the Shrew' is something of a Shakespearean acrostic with insertions from more than a dozen works. Holst, Castelnuovo-Tedesco and Sutermeister ('Romeo und Julia') also incorporate sonnets; Vaughan Williams, Holst, Barkworth and Hale, as well as Smith in the eighteenth century, use Elizabethan or traditional lyrics of various kinds; Malipiero goes to Horace for two choruses in 'Giulio Cesare'.[1] It cannot be denied that most recent English composers have found Shakespeare too formidable a collaborator; all too often respect for the poetry has stifled a none too lively muse. Only Britten and perhaps Holst survive the test : the former is the only composer of a successful full-length opera based entirely on Shakespeare's own words.

Modern composers show no signs of losing interest in Shakespeare; nearly seventy of the operas in the catalogue have been composed or first produced since 1900, an average of more than one a year. On the whole, despite improvements in general and literary taste, their artistic standard scarcely reaches that of their nineteenth-century predecessors. No doubt there is a flux in such matters; and good operas — not to mention great ones — are scarce on the ground in any age. Whether the present condition of music is favourable to Shakespearean opera may be doubted; certainly the advanced techniques have contributed almost nothing so far. But this state of affairs is unlikely to be permanent. The possibilities of Shakespeare as an operatic source are far from exhausted. We have no satisfactory opera on *The Tempest* or *Twelfth Night*, and very few at all on *As You Like It*; yet all these plays — and several others — seem positively to invite operatic setting. One day there may even arise a composer capable of challenging *Hamlet* or *King Lear*.

## 3. THE COMEDIES

The most popular of the comedies, and indeed of all the plays, has been *The Tempest*, with a brood of at least thirty operas,

---

[1] A number of foreign composers, including Veracini, Chélard, Halévy, Salvayre and Sutermeister ('Die Zauberinsel'), have introduced English or Scottish tunes for purposes of local colour, sometimes in the oddest contexts.

more than half of them by German composers. It is easy to
see why. The plot is simple and has few changes of scene; it
offers human intrigue on two levels (courtly conspiracy and
low comedy), a romantic thread of shipwreck, love and
adventure, and a spectacular manifestation of the natural and
supernatural worlds in operatically attractive proportions.
Above all, the play is a clear allegory of good and evil. Ger-
man-speaking countries have pounced on this and emphasized
the superficial resemblance to 'Die Zauberflöte'. There is no
Queen of Night (unless Sycorax is enlisted — and she does
appear in more than one opera), but Prospero, Ferdinand,
Miranda and Caliban will stand for Sarastro, Tamino, Pamina
and Monostatos, and a little juggling can conjure Stephano
or Trinculo into the posture of Papageno and Ariel into that
of the three genii; indeed Frank Martin has set Ariel's music
for a small vocal ensemble. But there are traps for the unwary.
While the two intrigues and the supernatural element, including
Ariel, do not call for exceptional qualities, it is otherwise with
the weighty pronouncements of Prospero, the mixture of the
grotesque and the poetic in Caliban, and the unique quality
in Miranda, the girl who has seen no man except her father.
If the opera is to be worthy of the play, her music must convey
a sense of wonder, a vision of her 'brave new world', quite
different in kind from the love-music of Ferdinand. No
composer has yet solved any of these difficulties.

No doubt Purcell might have done so had his contact with
the play been less tangential; but his music, written for Shadwell's arrangement of the Dryden-Davenant adaptation of
*The Tempest*, is an opera only in a limited sense.[1] With one or
two exceptions the speaking characters do not sing, and the
singers are chiefly confined to the two masque sections, where
they represent mythological figures extraneous to the action.
Shakespeare provided a model for this in the scene for the three
goddesses in Act IV of the play, though Shadwell omitted to
take advantage of it, perhaps because it was insufficiently
spectacular. The Restoration dramatists embroidered the
plot with an absurdly symmetrical pattern, and the dialogue
with their age's own brand of sexual innuendo. Miranda is
balanced by a man (Hippolito) who has never seen a woman,

---

[1] There has recently been a suggestion that the music is not by Purcell (see
p. 55). If so, it becomes necessary to postulate an obscure contemporary with the
same resplendent genius.

and to provide a mate for him she has a sister Dorinda.
Caliban too has a sister, Sycorax, who makes indecent advances
to Trinculo, and even Ariel has a mate of his own species.[1]
Purcell's music, which employs the latest Italian conventions
of the day, including the *da capo* aria, is of superb quality.  Only
two of Ariel's songs ('Come unto these yellow sands' and 'Full
fathom five') use Shakespeare's words; they and the touching
air 'Dear pretty youth', sung by Dorinda over the unconscious Hippolito, are just enough to indicate what an opera
Purcell might have written had he been able to bring the
music into full contact with the action.

J. C. Smith's[2] opera also fails to come to grips with the
play, though its aim seems to have been mild diversion rather
than spectacle.  The libretto has been attributed to Garrick,
but may be the work of Smith himself.  It reads very curiously,
since most of the dialogue is condensed from Shakespeare,
whereas the words of the airs (with some half a dozen exceptions) are borrowed from other sources, covering a period of a
century and a half.  They include Ben Jonson ('Have you seen
but a bright lily grow?'), the Dryden-Shadwell version ('Dry
those eyes') and minor poetasters of the eighteenth century.
Little thought was spared for dramatic aptness: Ariel refers
to himself as 'half tippled at a rainbow feast', and shortly after
an ambitious setting of Prospero's speech 'Ye elves of hills,
brooks, standing lakes and groves' in the grand Handelian
manner Ferdinand opines that 'life resembles April weather'.
A note in the libretto asks the reader 'to excuse the omission
of many passages of the first merit, as they stand in the said
play; it being impossible to introduce them in the plan of
this opera'.  The plan is less odd than Dryden's but it dis-
locates the plot by cutting out Caliban's conspiracy and substituting an irrelevant subplot.  Caliban was evidently too
uncouth for Augustan taste: Prospero disdains even to mention
him, and he appears in a single scene in order to get drunk.
Stephano and Trinculo are identified with Shakespeare's
Master and Boatswain and reinforced by two more nautical
figures — taken over from Dryden — Ventoso (mate) and
Mustacho (mariner), with whom they indulge in a prolonged

---

[1] This was not meant to be a parody; the authors were convinced that they
were improving Shakespeare.  As late as 1845 Dorinda and Hippolito appeared
in 'straight' productions of *The Tempest*, along with two spirits called Rosebud
and Bluebell.                    [2] See above, p. 66.

alcoholic dispute about the government of the island.

Limitations in the original company seem to have helped to unbalance the opera. Alonso, Antonio and Gonzalo are reduced to ciphers, with nothing to sing and only a few lines to speak. The reader of the printed score, which in the manner of its day names the singers and not the characters, might be forgiven for supposing that at the end of Act II Prospero joins Stephano and Ventoso in a drinking song. It appears that Beard doubled the parts of Prospero and Trinculo, and Champness those of Caliban and Mustacho (though at one point, according to the libretto, both are on stage at once). The weight of the music is carried by Ferdinand, Miranda and Ariel, all mezzo-soprano parts; Ferdinand was played by a woman — Rosa Curioni. Ariel sings more Shakespeare than the others — but not 'Where the bee sucks', which Smith had appropriated to *A Midsummer Night's Dream* the previous year. His first air, one of the best in the opera, combines the opening of Dryden's 'Arise, ye subterranean winds' with the speech 'I boarded the king's ship' in Scene 2 of the play, transposed to the future tense.

The music consists mostly of solo airs, with three duets, a comic trio and a brief final 'chorus'. The style varies between Handelian gesture and rhetoric, slight ballad tunes, and the rococo manner of Arne with plenty of Scotch snaps and *affettuoso* ariosos in 3/8 time. Smith seems most vital when closest to Handel, as in the music he wrote for Beard. There is an angry duet for Trinculo and Mustacho in which words and music both echo the duet 'Go, baffled coward' in 'Samson', which the same singers sang at Covent Garden in the same year.

The libretto of 'Die Geisterinsel', originally written by F. H. von Einsiedel in 1778, reconstructed by F. W. Gotter early in 1791, and eventually set (after further alterations) by four composers in 1798, is a strange work with a stranger history, which cannot be related here.[1] The two authors were enormously proud of their achievement (Goethe called it a masterpiece) and at various times considered bestowing it on most of Europe's leading composers, including Mozart, Haydn, Grétry, Dittersdorf, Wranitzky and Himmel. Their settled

---

[1] See W. Deetjen, '*Der Sturm* als Operntext', *Shakespeare-Jahrbuch*, vol. 64, 1928, for the correspondence of the two librettists, and A. Einstein, 'Mozart und Shakespeare's *Tempest*', *Monatshefte für Deutschen Unterricht*, 1941.

choice was Mozart, who was reported to have accepted it in
the autumn of 1791, just before his death. Dittersdorf later
rejected it. The libretto as it stands is singularly remote from
Shakespeare in language and spirit. Alonso, Antonio and the
other lords do not appear (Prospero is said merely to have been
rejected by his country); Ferdinand's only companion apart
from the crew is his skittish page Fabio. The main action is a
struggle between black and white magic. The balance of
power veers between Prospero, who rules by day, and Sycorax,
who rules by night. Prospero has to ensure that Ferdinand
and Miranda do not fall asleep (and so into the enemy's power)
by keeping them up all night counting corals. The storm,
which does not occur until the finale of Act I, is the work of
Sycorax. The opera begins with Miranda laying flowers on
the grave of Maja, a deceased good spirit; and it is Maja,
brought back to life by Ariel, who overcomes Sycorax in a
mimed sequence in Act III, and ensures the happy ending.
After some vigorous cursing Caliban dives into the sea to join
his mother and the entire company sings a hymn in honour of
the fatherland.

This mixture is typical of the contemporary *Singspiel*. 'Die
Zauberflöte' is only the most famous of many operas that
combine magic (good and evil), spectacle, ethical humanism
and low buffoonery. There are several supernatural demon-
strations: Prospero, for the edification of Ferdinand, causes
a volcano to erupt and then put forth a blooming rose. The
struggle between Sycorax and Maja (both played by dancers,
though the original plan was to use singers) is accompanied by
similar effects. If Prospero is inclined to talk like Sarastro,
Ariel is still more sententious. He is always telling Prospero
what to do, even to the disposal of his own daughter, and is
addicted to such resonant utterances as 'The gate of the realm
of shadows rests under a sevenfold seal'.

Of the two published scores, Zumsteeg's is by far the more
accomplished. Reichardt's is a pastiche of Mozartian mannerisms without any of the structural power or thematic
pregnancy that underlies them; his ensembles and finales
are particularly feeble. The measured nobility of 'Die Zauberflöte' declines into a mixture of short-winded little tunes, square
rhythms and sudden spurts of extraneous coloratura, supported by a very narrow harmonic range. It is easy to see how
Brahms came to include a tune by Reichardt in a collection

of German folksongs. But Reichardt does attempt to distinguish the characters, using wind instruments, for example, to accompany Ariel and the spirits, and his Caliban is evidently meant to be comic; in the first finale he bursts suddenly into a polacca marked *Mit affektirten modischem Vortrag* — a passage that Zumsteeg set quite seriously. The polacca may be intended as a parody of the latest operatic fashion, introduced by Cherubini in 'Lodoïska'. The most interesting feature of Reichardt's opera is the overture, based entirely on four themes from Act I, into which it leads without a break.

Zumsteeg's overture is also striking: one theme all but anticipates Beethoven's third piano concerto, and the whole style, though not very individual, has a sense of purpose and direction. His ensembles are more solidly constructed, his technique more flexible and free from the drag of the North German choral society; but the characterization is if anything flatter than Reichardt's. He scarcely attempts to differentiate spirits from mortals, and Ariel, Caliban and Prospero have a strong family likeness.

At least three other *Tempest* librettos survive from the years 1798–9. Müller's opera is described as 'heroisch-komisch', which means that everything is subordinated to spectacle and farce of a coarse and corny type then popular in Vienna. Besides Shakespeare's comic figures (whose role is much expanded) Stephano has a sister, Rosine, who defeats Caliban's advances by a deft use of judo and finally consents to marry Trinculo and establish a 'Narrenfabrik' to keep the court supplied with jesters. Bianka (Miranda) is so excited by her father's promise of a young man that she casts herself into the astonished arms first of Trinculo, then of Rosine, and greatly embarrasses Ferdinand when his turn comes by making all the running. Ariel teases the comics by conjuring up three seductive female shapes, which at the decisive moment change into three bears. There is a great deal of this buffoonery, including a scene in which the comics are buried up to their necks. The opera begins with a spectacular storm and shipwreck, and the finales are full of the most elaborate magic transformations. It comes as a surprise to find a few passages translated directly from the play; Caliban's 'Be not afeard' speech, however, emerges as 'Die ganze Luft ist voll von Waldhornisten, Geigern und Trommelschlägern'.

Ritter's libretto (by J. W. Doering) is a less extravagant

example of the same type, and indeed cribs two or three scenes from Müller's. Stephano does not appear, but Trinculo has a large part, very much after the style of Papageno. He steals Prospero's magic robe and convinces Caliban that he is a great magician named Magnus Pumphius Karpunkulus, a descendant of Dr. Faustus, and that Prospero is an incompetent pupil whom he was compelled to dismiss. Ariel spends much of the opera in the guise of a woman tormenting Antonio and Trinculo; when the latter tries to kiss 'her' he finds a tree in his arms. Hensel compiled his own libretto from those of Gotter and Doering, and added a preface in which he opted for simplicity and harmonic expressiveness as opposed to the affectations of Mozart and his school, with which he thought the public had been surfeited.

Mendelssohn considered and rejected two librettos on *The Tempest*, one by Carl Immermann in 1831–2, the other by Scribe in 1846.[1] The latter was subsequently set by Halévy and translated into Italian for performance in London, the regular procedure in those days. Scribe wrote in a letter to the impresario Lumley: 'I have done the utmost to respect the inspirations of your immortal Author. All the musical situations I have created are but suggestions taken from Shakespeare's ideas.' If so, they are taken a very long way. Apart from the storm and the drinking scene, whose principal feature is a song by Stephano praising the virtues of 'Rhum', the single feature of the play that Scribe deemed fit for operatic treatment is contained in Prospero's rebuke to Caliban: 'Thou didst seek to violate/The honour of my child'. At least one English composer has suppressed this; the only Frenchman concerned with *The Tempest* makes it the fulcrum of the plot. Caliban's part, written for the great bass Lablache, is the largest in the opera. He and Ferdinand are rivals for Miranda's favours, and it is Caliban who takes the lead. Prospero is a none-too-efficient magician who scarcely appears after Act I and (like Antonio and Alonso) is left out of the finale of the opera. Ariel is locked into a tree by Caliban early in Act II and apparently never released; since the part was taken by a dancer (Carlotta Grisi), this does not impair the vocal resources. Sycorax also is held prisoner throughout, in the cleft

---

[1] Romani too was approached in the same year. Mendelssohn's opera was to have been produced in London with Jenny Lind as Miranda and Lablache as Prospero.

of a rock behind the scenes, but she has a good deal to say for herself.

Scribe's half-comic, half-cynical treatment of the super- natural — like his failure to tie up the strands at the end — is characteristic. Sycorax from her coign of disadvantage tells Caliban that if he picks three flowers from the rock where she is imprisoned, three of his wishes will be granted. To her intense digust he does not use his first wish to release her, but spends most of Act II dragging Miranda unconscious round the island till he falls in with Stephano and Trinculo and gets drunk. At the climax of their Bacchanal Miranda smartly snatches the flowers and charms Caliban and the sailors into immobility. Later she falls a victim to Sycorax's insinuations about Ferdinand and tries to kill him. When Caliban re- covers the flowers he discovers that the three wishes have been exhausted, and the voice of Sycorax is heard cursing him for ever for his ingratitude.

Halévy's music, a compound of Rossini, Meyerbeer, Weber and Auber, is insipid and conventional, but sometimes un- intentionally funny. The maximum of vocal embellishment is superimposed upon a minimum of melodic impulse. Several motives recur, including three associated with Caliban, but their treatment is not systematic or even consistent. The best scene is the stormy Prologue on board ship, which begins with a chorus of invisible spirits and ends with a massive choral prayer in eight parts, *Andante religioso, dolcissimo con molta espressione*; the tune seems to be an unconscious recollection of 'O come, all ye faithful'. A more deliberate quotation occurs in the ballet music: described in the score as an ancient Eng- lish air taken from the original tragedy [sic] of *The Tempest*, it turns out to be Arne's setting of 'Where the bee sucks' harmonized in the style of Auber.

Urspruch's opera is closer to Shakespeare. He transfers Prospero's dukedom to Palermo, apparently to justify a vision of a bay with golden cupolas, columns and marine gardens in the first scene, and in Act II introduces a chorus of voluptuous huntresses, dressed in mythological costume with bows and arrows. They claim equal skill in love and hunting — which is scarcely consistent with their supposed office as attendants of Diana — and at once pair off with the courtiers. Ariel explains that they are only phantoms, but they enable the composer to combine two favourite gambits of German

romanticism, the huntsmen of 'Der Freischütz' and the
flower-maidens of 'Parsifal'. The long masque in Act III has
a model in the play, though the librettist prefaces it with most
of Prospero's 'Our revels now are ended' speech before the
revels have begun. He devoutly fathers Caliban upon Satan
and does not allow much play to Ariel, but — remarkably for
a German romantic — is quite free from pretentious symbolism
and hollow rhetoric. This is also true of the music, which is
otherwise deeply rooted in its period, reflecting the influence
of Schumann, Mendelssohn, Brahms and the more lyrical
parts of 'The Ring'. Caliban, who habitually refers to himself
with a wistful self-pity, is comic rather than grotesque; but
his musical motive is suitably ungainly, and its various forms
are skilfully woven into the orchestral texture. This is a
competent and well-organized if second-rate opera.

Fibich's 'Bouře', though both its authors were Czech,
suffers far more seriously from the Teutonic virus. The
libretto begins like the play, but deviates more and more into a
Wagnerian morality, and has almost finished with Shakespeare
by the end of Act II. Prospero assumes the more sesquipedalian
aspects of Wotan and Gurnemanz, especially in Act III. The
symbolism often verges on the ludicrous. In the second finale
Prospero comes on in a chariot drawn by Caliban and three
dragons, lectures Alonso, Antonio and the courtiers, and
points to Caliban's posture as an illustration of the triumph of
truth over falsehood : 'he is matter and I am ideal'. In Act
III the game of chess between Miranda and Ferdinand is
expanded into a long and rather obscure allegory of married
life. Spirits whisper thoughts of desire into their ears, but
when they are on the point of kissing Ariel knocks their heads
together and the spirits laugh. They have a mild tiff, and
Miranda refuses to finish the game. Ariel says this is a healthy
sign and calls Prospero, who at once gives Miranda to
Ferdinand.

The score owes a great deal to Wagner (of all periods) and
a little to the Smetana of 'Dalibor'. Only in the music of Caliban, Stephano and Trinculo, which is very heavy-handed, is
there a trace of the Czech peasant idiom. The numerous
leitmotives have little character or flexibility. Despite a few
lively passages, mostly connected with Ariel — one of them
curiously reminiscent of Widor's organ Toccata in F — the flow
of the music is sluggish and turgid. The excessive use of

outworn formulae like the diminished seventh does not help to keep it alive.

Little need be said of the two twentieth-century English operas on *The Tempest*. Hale's is chaotic in style and remarkable for some extraordinary aberrations of language. Stephano says of Caliban 'He's still in a funk' — apparently to supply a rhyme for 'drunk' — and Caliban addresses his companions thus about Prospero: 'Then you must remember to first possess his books; For once he is without them quite stupid he becomes.' Gatty's libretto also dilutes the language (the action of both operas deviates little from the play), but the music is at least competent. Its idiom falls between two stools, lacking the melodic invention needed for a number opera and the symphonic development for a music-drama, though many short motives are worked into the texture. The constant arioso at a tempo neither fast nor slow makes a pale, anonymous effect. The word-setting, however, is sensitive, especially in the great poetic speeches; a less fastidious musical taste — a touch of Puccini, in fact — might have brought them to life.

Fastidiousness is the last reproach that can be levelled against Sutermeister's 'Die Zauberinsel', which debases the play into a ponderous German pantomime, at once spectacular and sentimental, and buries the characters beneath a mountain of synthetic philosophizing. 'Die Zuberflöte' and 'Die Frau ohne Schatten' seem to have been among the models; the lovers are put through tests, the courtiers blindfolded by spirits and made to dance like Monostatos, and Prospero becomes a limp and almost maudlin version of Sarastro. Worst of all is the vulgarization of Ariel, who plays the part of Pandarus for the benefit of the lovers and enlists the aid of various supernatural agencies, including the planet Venus, since 'we are all attached to love'. Prospero, equating the sea with life and the magic island with fantasy, has already summoned Ferdinand to play 'the most beautiful game in life, the game of love' (before putting various obstacles in his way); at length he performs a marriage ceremony on stage and sends the lovers into a wood, whence they reappear transfigured at the end of the opera. The final hymn to love as the motive power of eternity and the solar system, addressed to the audience, no doubt had a topical reference in 1942.

As in Fibich's opera, Miranda dreams of Ferdinand before she sees him and the treatment of the comics is clumsy. But there is nothing Wagnerian about the design, and the style is highly eclectic, with echoes of Strauss, Debussy and many late romantic composers. The fairy choruses suggest a mixture of 'Hänsel und Gretel' and 'The Immortal Hour'. Ferdinand's love theme is almost identical with the Hermione motive in Goldmark's 'Wintermärchen'; both derive from a favourite melodic fingerprint of Bizet. Sutermeister uses an English morris dance for 'Full fathom five' and an old Swiss war song as the refrain of Alonso's dirge for Ferdinand. The whole opera (despite much irregular barring) is founded on square diatonic little tunes, harmonized sometimes with the utmost succulence, sometimes in the off-beat manner of Orff with a liberal outlay of obbligatos, pedals, percussive punctuation and 'wrong' notes. Extra-musical effects — wind, thunder and lightning machines, spoken dialogue, *Sprechgesang* — play a conspicuous part, and so do supernumerary choruses of nymphs, genii and inanimate voices (the wind, time, dusk), whose offstage humming becomes a tiresome mannerism.

Frank Martin's 'Der Sturm' could scarcely show a greater contrast. The libretto is a slightly shortened version of the play in Schlegel's translation. The music, which employs various modern techniques — neoclassicism, serialism and *Sprechgesang* besides the spoken word — is austere to a fault. The voice parts are set almost entirely in angular recitative, drily supported by a large force of percussion and wind (with prominent saxophone) but few strings. Ariel's music is an exception; it is mimed by a dancer and sung by an invisible chorus with its own small offstage orchestra containing a harpsichord and a jazz percussion outfit. Apart from this and the pastiche dances (after Lully) for the masque in Act III, the opera is almost devoid of contrast; there are no ensembles in the ordinary sense of the term. Ariel has several related motives, and Prospero is characterized by side-slipping chord progressions in a trampling (generally crotchet) rhythm but they do not create a symphonic texture. The use of a twelve-note row on the saxophone when Caliban enters carrying logs, and another of eleven notes on solo viola when Ferdinand is similarly employed in the next scene, has a certain aptness.

The opera fails because it attempts the impossible. Such a literal and unadorned setting, apart from reducing the pace to a crawl, sets up an impossible challenge to the poetry.

*Sprechgesang* and a *parlando* delivery, so far from adding anything to 'Be not afeard' and 'Our revels now are ended', only
confirm that music is superfluous.  Nor does Martin recreate
the lyrical and magic elements of the plot in musical terms;
the love of Ferdinand and Miranda remains cold and Prospero
becomes a droning bore.  The best music occurs in Ariel's
songs, especially 'Full fathom five' with its rhythmically varied
refrain.

The first operatic version of *A Midsummer Night's Dream*
is again by Purcell.[1]  The music of 'The Fairy Queen' consists
almost entirely of a spectacular series of masques, one in each
act, designed for the entertainment of Titania;  the play was
severely truncated to make room for them.  Most of the singing
characters are mythological, but they include a drunken poet
and a Chinese man and woman, the final masque taking place
in a Chinese garden with a chorus of 'Chineses'.  Among the
dancers are swans, savages, Chinese children, monkeys, green
men and other fauna.  Delightful as the music is, it scarcely
makes contact with Shakespeare's plot, except perhaps in the
Masque of Night, which takes the place of 'Ye spotted snakes'
and ends with a beautiful chorus as the fairies steal away and
leave Titania asleep.  Although Purcell set none of Shakespeare's words, he clearly possessed that instinct for the fresh
innocence of fairyland that was to be reborn in Mendelssohn
and Britten.

In 1716 Richard Leveridge produced 'The Comick Masque
of Pyramus and Thisbe', based on Shakespeare's clown scenes,
and himself played the Prologue and Pyramus.  He anticipated
Sheridan's method in *The Critic* by presenting the show as a
parody of the newly fashionable Italian opera, with the supposed composer, Mr. Semibreve, and his friends Crotchet and
Gamut commenting on the performance.  The prose passages
were evidently spoken and the blank verse sung as recitative,
for at one point Semibreve interrupts the latter to correct a
cadence.  The operatic jokes are quite amusing, but Leveridge's
additional verses are the sorriest drivel and he missed some
obvious points in the original;  Quince's mispunctuated prologue is corrected, and 'I see a voice' altered to 'I hear a
voice'.  Lampe's similarly-titled work of 1745 ('A Mock-
Opera') is partly based on Leveridge's libretto.  The music,
which includes a four-movement overture with horns, is a

---

[1] See above, p. 56.

pleasant enough example of the ballad style, influenced by Arne and 'Acis and Galatea'; but apart from exaggerated tempo marks (*Presto e Furioso, Lamentevole*) and the frequent repetition of absurd words, there is little in it to suggest a parody. The singers included Handel's leading tenor and bass, Beard and Reinhold; Thisbe was not sung by a man, as in Leveridge's masque, but by the composer's wife.

Smith's first Shakespeare opera, 'The Fairies' (1755), is based on the same plan as his 'Tempest'. The libretto is superior; instead of vulgarizing the comic subplot he omits it altogether, apart from a bare reference to Titania falling in love with a clown, and with it the whole of Shakespeare's Act V. The lovers fall easily into the framework of *opera seria*, though the balance is upset by the fact that Demetrius, presumably played by a straight actor, has no arias. The dialogue was set in recitative: the libretto gives this fact as a reason for its abbreviation. It is nearly all taken from the play, and so are seven of the arias: three more ('Where the bee sucks', 'Sigh no more, ladies' and 'Orpheus with his lute') come from other Shakespeare plays. The rest, according to the libretto, are from 'Milton, Waller, Dryden, Lansdown, Hammond, etc.' The two Milton arias, rather oddly, are corruptions of passages from *L'Allegro* which Handel had already set with the finality of genius. The Prologue, written and spoken by Garrick, interrupts 'the Band of Music', and apologizes for presenting an opera in a language the audience can understand:

> This awkward Drama — (I confess th'Offence)
> Is guilty too of Poetry and Sense.

The music, like that of 'The Tempest', is a mixture of the baroque (Handel) and rococo (Arne) — the march in the overture is an obvious echo of the famous one in Handel's 'Scipione' — but less dramatic and less interesting, with little feeling for the niceties of character. It was, however, very successful. The famous castrato Guadagni, who sang in the first performances of Handel's 'Theodora' and Gluck's 'Orfeo', distinguished himself as Lysander — a part written for Rosa Curioni. Oberon, Puck and another Fairy were all played by boys, one of whom, the younger Reinhold, became a famous bass.

*A Midsummer Night's Dream* made little appeal to nineteenth-century opera composers,[1] but has returned to favour in the twentieth. Mancinelli's libretto is a crude mixture of literalism, lushness and physical violence. The fairy scenes are much contracted, the ceremonies of Theseus's court expanded with fleshly ballets and substantial choruses. The love story is simplified in outline, since Puck does not anoint the wrong man's eyes and there is consequently no quarrel in the forest; but text and stage directions alike are encrusted with sensual imagery (Demetrius advances on Hermia 'avido della sua bianchezza'). The rustics have a thin time. The chorus ridicule their offer of a play; their first rehearsal is broken up by an irate Demetrius, who mistakes Bottom's remarks about Thisbe for a reference to Hermia and gives him a violent beating; when they resume in the forest, Puck terrifies them with neighing and stamping noises which they attribute to a herd of centaurs; in the last scene they are not even allowed to finish the play, which Theseus and the chorus interrupt at the Lion's speech. The centaurs are part of the realist background : the librettist takes the Athenian locale seriously and introduces frequent allusions (and sacrifices) to pagan deities. Puck — a spoken part, as in Britten's opera — is a cruel spirit who spends his time puncturing Bottom with wasp-stings and nettles and indulging in other forms of horse-play. Bottom's reaction to the removal of the ass-head, which he wears for a very short time, is to go in search of a barber. Nothing remains of Shakespeare's spirit, and the surviving details of the plot are distorted almost beyond recognition.

The music emphasizes the carnal flavour. It combines the coarser aspects of Puccini and Strauss with a fidgety and selfconscious harmonic idiom; the melodic impetus which alone could leaven such a lump is wholly lacking. The fairy scenes, more spontaneous than the rest, are squeezed into one sequence in the second act. The treatment of Theseus's court and the rustics, who are not used for parody, is equally ponderous, and the scoring is formidable. The opera ends with a huge ensemble for eight soloists and eight-part chorus (in addition to the six rustics in unison), supported on the stage by eight trumpets.

---

[1] The earliest German setting, E. W. Wolf's 'Die Zauberirrungen' (1785), survives only in a playbill; music and libretto perished when the Weimar theatre was burned down in 1825. The librettist retained nearly all Shakespeare's characters, but transferred the action from Athens to a German court. 'Puck' was played by a man.

Carl Orff has twice written music for *A Midsummer Night's Dream*, in 1939 and 1952. Neither score is strictly an opera, though the second is something more than incidental music. It contains the full Schlegel text of the play with a note that words, music and stage-directions are conceived as an organic whole, to be played without an interval. Besides the pit orchestra and a backstage force which between them include mandolines, harmonicas, cimbalom and two large stands of percussion, two bodies of instrumentalists sit on the stage throughout, three trumpets to provide fanfares, and a small group (mostly wind and percussion) to accompany the rustics' scenes and to fall ostentatiously asleep, except for a solo double bass, while Bottom sings 'The ousel cock'. Not much of the text is sung, but many speeches are punctuated by single chords, patches of multiple rhythm from the percussion, and other background effects. There are a few longer episodes, mostly instrumental; they include a catchy tune for the rustics borrowed from Orff's opera 'Die Kluge', and a backstage final chorus with nonsense words.

Benjamin Britten's is the most successful Shakespeare opera since Verdi. The libretto reduces a play of no little complexity and luxuriance to manageable proportions without sacrificing anything vital. Most of the big set speeches are wisely omitted or shortened, and there is some redistribution. The most important change affects the balance between the four constituent elements, Theseus and his court, the lovers, the rustics and the fairies. Shakespeare introduces them in that order, presenting all the mortals before they are touched by magic. Britten begins with the fairies; the opening bars of the opera weave the spell of the enchanted wood, and this is reaffirmed at the start of each subsequent act. All three acts end with the fairies in command. This alters the perspective: we never see the mortals except through the magic that envelops them and us. There is some slight awkwardness of detail. Hermia and Lysander arrange their assignation, lose themselves and lie down to sleep, all at the same spot. Act III begins before dawn and ends at midnight, with little allowance for the day in between; a break between the two scenes could have remedied this but might have snapped the spell of the music.

Britten took other risks, but in nearly every case showed the capacity of genius to invest a little on the roundabouts and make a handsome profit on the swings. He omitted Theseus and Hippolyta until the last scene, which begins with the opening lines of the play, and justified the move in advance by introducing Theseus's hunting horns after the reconciliation of Titania and Oberon and the latter's reference to Theseus's marriage (where Shakespeare in Act IV has the directions 'horns winded within') and developing the same music between the departure of the rustics from the wood and the palace scene. He achieved a brilliant short-circuit by giving the four lovers a kind of group characterization based on a single theme (set to the key-line 'The course of true love never did run smooth') together with certain associated rhythms — a solution only possible for a composer with a style at once terse and inventive. His choice of a countertenor voice for Oberon preserves the high tessitura of the immortals and brings out the feline quality of the character. The boys' voices of the fairies pick up a certain tartness in Shakespeare's originals (also played by boys), but they are apt to seem all too mortal in the theatre. Puck is an acrobat who speaks his lines — not too many of them; Britten has discreetly transferred some of his part to the chorus of fairies.

The music, though light in texture even in the fuller version made when the opera was transferred from Aldeburgh to Covent Garden, is essentially symphonic rather than impressionist. Only a high degree of motivic organization could have united so many diverse dramatic elements in a satisfactory whole of moderate length. Significantly the weakest part of the opera is the loosest in design, the play of Pyramus and Thisbe in Act III; the parodies of Verdi and Donizetti, though very funny, are not quite in scale with the rest. Britten combines a dramatically allusive framework of motives with a self-generating development based on variation, inversion, canon, ostinato and intense rhythmic momentum. If these methods are common property, the use of tonality as a unifying factor and a means of emotional expression is as old as the hills. Yet Britten can still move us by a mere alternation of major and minor, as in some of the lovers' music, and by long passages in a single key, as in the scene for Titania, Bottom and the fairies in Act II or the introduction to Act III. He can construct the whole of Act II as a kind of passacaglia based on four triadic chords (each scored for a different group of instruments), which together contain the twelve semitones of the

I

chromatic scale. This tonal serialism expands and renovates the tradition without sacrificing its advantages. It also shows up the fashionable idea of the necessity of atonality today for the nonsense it is.

The opera can be analysed in other ways. Each group of characters has its own instrumental colour, harps and percussion for the fairies, strings and upper woodwind for the lovers, brass and bassoon for the rustics. Instruments as well as motives are linked with individuals, the celesta with Oberon, high trumpet and side-drum with Puck. The wood in Act I and the idea of sleep that enfolds Act II are expressed by remotely related or contrasted diatonic chords. But the primary impression is one of fresh lyrical invention, especially in the fairy music. The longer solos of Oberon and Titania use a kind of Purcellian melisma with moving effect, and the exquisite finales of the last two acts add new magic to that of the words. Britten can combine sensuous beauty with humour and irony, as in the long woodwind phrases of the scene for Bottom and the fairies in Act II, without the one curdling the other. It is clear that the compound of poetic language, rude humour, sleep and magic in the play made a special appeal to his imagination. Perhaps a wider sympathy with Shakespeare may yet be revealed.

The first opera on *The Merry Wives of Windsor*, 'Le Vieux Coquet', by a French violinist named Papavoine, is said to have been killed by its libretto after one performance. The operas of Ritter and Dittersdorf, both on the same libretto, were failures; of the former only Falstaff's part survives. According to F. Erckmann [1] neither possesses much character. Salieri's [2] is a superficial work in the flimsy Neapolitan style that Mozart's genius has now rendered intolerable, but the libretto has points of interest. Mistress Ford, not her husband, visits Falstaff in disguise — as a German servant with very little Italian. Since Falstaff's German is equally limited, they converse in a mixture of languages aided by gesture: as Falstaff puts it, 'Ich bissel deutsch, tu bissel nostra lingua: a bissel pantomime, a bissel discretion'. Needless to say he offers her consolation and is indignantly repulsed. The opera begins with a dance in the house of Slender (who takes the

---

[1] 'Sir John Falstaff in Opera', *The Chesterian*, Sept. 1923.
[2] Revived at Siena in 1961 in an edition by Vito Frazzi that seems to have allowed it little chance.

place of Page), and the overture consists of a series of *contre-danses*; when the curtain rises, refreshments are being handed round — a situation copied from the ballroom scene in 'Don Giovanni'.

Balfe's 'Falstaff' was another failure. The critic of *The Athenaeum* said the music was not sufficiently popular in style or grateful to the singers (a preposterous charge, since it was obviously conceived for a star cast that included Grisi, Rubini, Tamburini and Lablache) and added the singular complaint that the composer did not exhaust the possibilities of the orchestra. As in Nicolai's opera, all three of the wives' tricks on Falstaff are retained, the Fat Woman of Brentford scene forming the finale of Act II. On the other hand Anne Page's only suitor is Fenton, who is engaged to her and enjoys her father's favour from the start. This side of the plot is conventionally handled. Falstaff delivers a third identical letter to Anne, which makes Fenton very jealous — not surprisingly, in view of her pert behaviour. Mistress Quickly plays only a mechanical part in the recitative.

Although Balfe called his work a grand opera,[1] he imitated the style of Rossini's Italian farces with all their period clichés — double crescendos, modulations to the submediant, resounding thumps on off-beats in *dolce moderato* passages, triplet rhythms, pattering repeated notes and a brilliant coloratura aria for Grisi (Mistress Ford) to bring down the final curtain. This suits the story well enough, but Balfe has too little of his own to add and no feeling whatever for character; in the duet for Falstaff and the disguised Ford the music would not suffer if the parts were interchanged. Ford vents his jealous fury in a gay polacca, and there is a copious supply of waltzes and galops (one of them at the end of the duet just mentioned). The Windsor Park scene begins with a trombone solo and contains no fairy music. The best thing in the opera is the short 12/8 love duet for Falstaff and Mistress Ford just before his second exposure; it has the delicate charm of a Field nocturne.

It says much for Nicolai's opera (1849, though begun as early as 1845) that it has not been killed by Verdi's masterpiece. Certain episodes, notably the garden and Windsor

---

[1] It was the first opera written for the Haymarket Theatre by a British composer since Arne's 'Olimpiade' (1764), though Lord Mount Edgcumbe's 'Zenobia' had one performance there in 1800. It is not true, as Erckmann says, that only portions of Balfe's score were published.

Park scenes, are almost worthy of Verdi and a great deal better than most of his music at this period. Nicolai hesitated before tackling the subject — he said that only Mozart was a fit companion for Shakespeare — and then sketched the libretto himself. Mosenthal, who versified it, was no Boito, but he was not insensitive to Shakespeare and borrowed hints from three other plays, *2 Henry IV*, *Twelfth Night* and *A Midsummer Night's Dream*. The drinking scene and Mistress Page's [1] ballad of Herne the Hunter are stock devices of romantic opera, but they fit in well, and some of the modifications — the simultaneous presence of Anne's three suitors in Page's garden, the chorus to the rising moon (on the beautiful introduction of the overture), Page's appearance as Herne the Hunter and his arrest of Falstaff for impersonation — are remarkably happy. But it was a mistake to begin with the wives rather than Falstaff; neither the latter nor Ford appears before the linen-basket scene, which thus loses much of its impact. Moreover the design of the second finale (Falstaff as the Fat Woman of Brentford, Ford and his friends again searching the house) is too close a copy of the first. Many of Shakespeare's characters, including Mistress Quickly (though she was in the original plan), Sir Hugh Evans, Shallow, Pistol, Bardolph and Nym, are discarded, and Page's case against Fenton is based on his poverty, not his noble birth.

The score is derivative but neither stale nor synthetic; where Nicolai learned from Mozart, Weber, Rossini and Mendelssohn he somehow contrived to keep the ingredients fresh. The fairy music is not far below its Mendelssohnian model; there are several parallels with 'Abu Hassan', which may have inspired Mistress Ford's caricature lament in the first finale; the 'quartettino' in the garden scene, with the two hidden suitors forced to witness the success of their rival, has something of the ironic wit of 'Le Comte Ory'. Unlike most German composers of comic opera since Mozart, Nicolai had a genuinely light touch; his wit is pointed, his humour never degenerates into coarse farce. (His use of dance rhythms, including a waltz and a polka in the opening duet of the wives, was not lost on Johann Strauss; the final section of the duet for Falstaff and the disguised Ford might come from 'Die Fledermaus'.) The compound of lyrical beauty and

---

[1] Frau Reich in the opera; I have, as elsewhere in this essay, used the original names of the characters.

delicate irony in his orchestral accompaniments is sometimes
almost Mozartian; the composer who could write the duet
for Ford and his wife in Act II might have gone far had he
lived. The whole opera shows a nice feeling for theatrical
effect, atmosphere and instrumental colour (the garden scene
in particular is beautifully scored). The characterization is
neat if never profound. Falstaff makes an effective first
entrance like some village Sarastro in his cups, but comparison
with the humanity of Verdi's portrait inevitably reduces him
to a conventional *buffo* bass, and the tragic undertones of Ford's
jealousy remain unplumbed. The overture is a masterpiece
by any standard. Most of its themes come from the Windsor
Park scene, which is admirably sustained until the very end,
where the action collapses into spoken dialogue and a per-
functory final trio just at the point where music should assume
complete command.

Verdi's 'Falstaff', the climax of two centuries of *opera buffa*,
is at once an historical and an artistic landmark. Boito's
libretto is a masterpiece in its own right, distinguished in
style and superior to the play both in tautness of design and
in the characterization of the principal figure. His recon-
stitution of the great Falstaff of *Henry IV* within the framework
of *The Merry Wives of Windsor* has often been acclaimed. The
attempt itself was an imaginative stroke; its entire success is
the product of superlative craftsmanship. *The Merry Wives of*
*Windsor* contains one or two echoes of the greater Falstaff, such
as the short soliloquy 'Sayst thou so, old Jack? Go thy ways'
(II. 2). Significantly Boito uses this twice, and he incorporates
at least eight passages from *Henry IV*, five from the First Part,
three from the Second. Two episodes in the opera, the brief
aria 'Quand' ero paggio' and the monologue at the beginning
of Act III, combine lines from both parts. The insertions come
in quite naturally and with marvellous aptness. The famous
soliloquy about honour is deftly attached to Falstaff's dismissal
of Pistol and Bardolph for refusing to play the pander (I. 3 of
the play) by means of his rebuke to Pistol in a later scene
('You stand upon your honour.' II. 2). Boito doubly justified
his introduction, near the end of the opera, of Falstaff's claim
to be 'not only witty in myself, but the cause that wit is in
other men' (*2 Henry IV*, I. 2). The words of the fugal finale,
which appear to have been dubbed on the music,[1] are a neat

---

[1] Frank Walker, *The Man Verdi*, p. 498.

abstraction from Jaques's 'All the world's a stage' speech in *As You Like It* (II. 7).

Boito simplifies the plot in outline, but sometimes embroiders it in detail. His Dr. Caius, Anne's only suitor apart from Fenton, and the target of all the assaults by Falstaff and his henchmen described in the first scene, is a conflation of Caius, Shallow, Slender and Sir Hugh Evans. Page is omitted, his daughter being transferred to Ford, but as compensation we have Bardolph, Pistol and a rich portrait of Mistress Quickly, who is more prominent than in the play. The Fat Woman of Brentford episode disappears, apart from Ford's rummaging in the basket, which is transferred to Falstaff's first discomfiture and occurs before he enters that receptacle. The alternating (and eventually simultaneous) ensembles of women and men in the garden scene are a virtuoso elaboration of an idea faintly suggested in Shakespeare's II. 1. Another such improvisation is the treatment of the love of Fenton and Anne in brief furtive snatches, about which Boito wrote to Verdi: 'I should like, as one sprinkles sugar on a tart, to sprinkle the whole comedy with that gay love, without collecting it together at any one point' — an idea as original as it is appropriate.

Boito's most brilliant inventions occur in Act II. The hilarious exit of Falstaff, dressed for seduction, and the disguised Ford after the latter's jealous monologue (compounded of two such scenes in the play) restores the comic Muse to her throne just in time. The finale is in the pure tradition of *opera buffa*, refined to the uttermost without losing any of its gusto. The ejection of Falstaff and the basket into the Thames, which in Shakespeare precedes Ford's search, is reserved for the very end. The episode where the young lovers are heard kissing behind a screen and are stalked by Ford and his minions under the impression that they are Falstaff and Mistress Ford — who are struggling with the dirty linen on the other side of the stage — is all Boito's. When Verdi received Boito's first sketch, he saw this as the culminating point of the opera and was afraid that Act III might prove an anticlimax, a danger he evaded with consummate skill. Boito's refinements in the last act include Mistress Quickly's overhearing of Ford's instructions to Dr. Caius about recognizing Anne in disguise — which short-circuits a lot of explanation — her own disguise as a Witch, the substitution of Bardolph for the 'great lubberly boy' in the mock-marriage, the insertion from *2 Henry IV* about

Falstaff's wit, and the final fugue. Neither Bardolph nor Pistol appears in this scene in Shakespeare; the addition of Pistol was Verdi's suggestion.[1] The one dubious change is the uncanonical marriage performed by Ford; but the music is so delightful that this raises no query in performance.

If the libretto is basically true to Shakespeare, so is the music. Boito wrote after the first performance: 'Shakespeare's sparkling farce is led back by the miracle of sound to its clear Tuscan source' in Boccaccio. The seeds that Shakespeare found in Italy attain their richest musical flowering here in comedy, as their tragic counterpart had done six years earlier in 'Otello'. There are many correspondences between the two operas, especially in their definition of the hilarious and the sinister aspects of human rascality; Falstaff's monologue on honour, as Stanford remarked in 1893, is the comic sister of Iago's Credo. Ford in his jealous outburst speaks the very language of Othello. This is certainly not to be taken for parody. 'Falstaff', like another great comic opera, Mozart's 'Marriage of Figaro', comprehends a wealth of potentially tragic experience within a genial frame without losing its proportions. The simultaneous exit of Ford and Falstaff through the same door comes not as an anticlimax but as an immensely satisfying restoration of the balance. The sense of pity which, as Francis Toye remarks, is raised by Falstaff's 'Quand' ero paggio' is surely governed by our recollection of 2 Henry IV — a recollection deliberately stimulated by Boito. The prime characteristic of the opera is its mellow humanity, an emotional warmth that is all the more satisfying for not being squandered.

Music and drama play into each other's hands with a marvellous economy of effort. The recurring motives are neither numerous nor symphonically employed (only that of Falstaff's assignation with Mistress Ford, 'Dalle due alle tre', shows any tendency to independent life in the orchestra); they are reminiscence motives of the simplest kind. Yet so astute is their placing, dramatic and musical, that they set up a myriad associations. It would be fascinating to trace the ironical reverberations of Mistress Quickly's immortal curtsey ('Reverenza!') or her 'Povera donna', applied to both wives in all manner of contexts, whether as victims of Falstaff or of

---

[1] So was the transference of Ford's monologue from the second to the first scene of Act II (Walker, pp. 495, 497).

their husbands. Falstaff's greeting to the disguised Ford in Act II ('Caro Signor Fontana') recurs with totally different ironical connotations in the last scene, first when Falstaff greets Ford still under the impression that he is Brook, and again when, after Ford has unwittingly married Anne to Fenton, he asks which of them is the dupe now.

There is a special musical reason for Verdi's triumph here, quite apart from the expressive quality of the material. In 'Falstaff' the set numbers and regular periods of his early operas have developed into a fluid style that can comprehend the extremes of *parlando* dialogue on the one hand and elaborately organized ensemble on the other. The motives are all cadence figures or at least have a cadential tendency. By applying a touch of finality to the music they take on a variety of nuance and emphasis; and since the ear, not being indulged with regular periods, never knows when to expect this, the opportunities for surprise are endless. (Wagner, with his very different form of arioso, more often used leitmotives to postpone an expected cadence.) Falstaff himself has no motive, apart from a tendency to lean his weight on the key of C major, in which the opera begins and ends. This itself is a telling stroke : so multifarious a figure would be impeded by a prop.

Verdi solved the problem of the last act by curbing the breathless pace of the opera and expanding the melodic span. Anything like the lovely Minuet of the wedding scene would have been stylistically out of place in the earlier acts. As a result 'Falstaff' is almost unique among comic operas in having its richest act at the end. The appearance of the 'fairies', who evoke some of the most enchanting music ever written, assists this result. Verdi may have been inspired here, as Nicolai explicitly was, by memories of *A Midsummer Night's Dream*. We know that for fifty years his mind had been impregnated with Shakespeare. It may well be that two of the most striking features of his last operas, the purity and innocence of the love music and the superb detachment that allows equal play to romantic impulse and classical restraint, reflect the influence of the dramatist. 'Falstaff' could never have been created without Boito's equal sensitivity to music and letters, or the profound and instinctive response of both authors to Shakespeare.

Since Verdi, only Vaughan Williams has set *The Merry Wives of Windsor*. 'Sir John in Love' is a disappointing opera, partly owing to the clumsiness of the libretto, partly because it treats the plot as a slow comedy of rustic life instead of a sophisticated farce. Vaughan Williams himself interleaved the play with additional lyrics from other plays by Shakespeare and contemporary sources, including Jonson, Middleton, Campion and *Gammer Gurton's Needle*. Apart from the Fat Woman of Brentford, he omitted very little. Every one of the play's twenty characters appears, and they crowd each other out; the composer, whose gifts in any case were expansive and lyrical rather than dramatic, has no space to develop or differentiate them. Slender and Caius are nicely indicated, but Falstaff receives too little attention and the lovers too much, and the abortive duel between Caius and Sir Hugh Evans would have been better cut. There is too much communal clodhopping, sometimes dragged in at the expense of the plot.

Nor is the folky idiom of the music — twelve genuine folk-tunes are identified in the score, and the rest is in the same vein — really suited to the play, which needs a quicksilver deftness if it is not to become tedious. The style seems ponderous by comparison with Verdi and Nicolai. No doubt the 'fairies' of the last scene are yokels dressed up, but it was a mistake to deprive them of their magic. There are other dramatic miscalculations. Falstaff is carried out in the basket too soon, before the natural climax of the scene, and he is too long out of the limelight in the last act, in which the love music for Fenton and Anne, though beautiful in itself, is so prolonged as to assume the proportions of a cantata — into which the composer subsequently converted it.

The remaining comedies, with rare exceptions, attracted no operatic settings before the romantic period. Like *The Merry Wives of Windsor*, *The Taming of the Shrew* is one of the more accessible plays. It offers simple but effective contrasts, contains little great poetry, and demands vitality rather than profundity of characterization. Moreover Shakespeare gave it a brilliantly theatrical final scene, which composers as a rule have chosen to ignore. The first setting, a pasticcio by Braham and Cooke, is scarcely more of an opera than the contemporary confections of Sir Henry Bishop.[1] The words are cobbled together from many Shakespearean sources with no feeling for uniformity; the music borrows from Rossini, Mercadante and Sir John Stevenson. If the vocal score is

[1] See above, p. 75.

correct, Katharina takes the place of Bianca in the music lesson and ultimately pairs off with Hortensio.

The later versions generally simplify the plot by reducing the number of Bianca's suitors and the complex series of disguises that confuse the action. All introduce modifications of their own and soften the bite of the story, which calls for something like the exuberant artificiality of the young Rossini. In Goetz's opera Petruchio has tried conclusions with Katharina once before, and his objective is not a rich wife but the satisfaction of a jaded palate; he wants a woman who will stand up to him. Grumio is cut out, but Hortensio takes his place as Bianca's absurd elderly admirer. The libretto, though neatly constructed, emasculates Petruchio and Katharina, especially in the big wooing scene; he repeatedly declares his love in conventional terms, while she is eager to surrender almost from the start. The music suffers from a parallel weakness. Although Katharina's part in the last act, after her pride has been subdued, has a touching pathos, she never comes to life as the shrew. Her song of hatred for men, accompanied by Bianca on the guitar, is the utterance of a domestic cat rather than a tigress and indistinguishable in temper from the music of her sister. The wooing scene is as tender as any romantic love-duet. This throws the whole opera out of balance. It was the wrong subject for Goetz, who lacked animal spirits and could manage nothing more passionate than a faint agitation. Nevertheless he had a charming lyrical gift, influenced by Weber and especially Schumann, and wrote attractively for the orchestra; the voice parts are marred by an obsessive squareness of rhythm, even in recitative. Some of the comedy, when not too overlaid by sentiment, is delightful, notably the double serenade in Act I to which Hortensio (supported by a stage band) brings a faint aura of Beckmesser, the double wooing of Bianca by Hortensio disguised as a musician and Lucentio as a teacher of languages (as in Shakespeare's III. 1), and the Act IV quartet with the Tailor, who is represented as a mincing Frenchman and accompanied by a solo violin.

The librettists of Silver's 'La Mégère apprivoisée' weaken the plot by making Katharina accept Petruchio under duress: her father will send her to a convent if she does not. Her character is, however, established at the outset by the entry of a tailor under a heavy bombardment of household projectiles; and so is Petruchio's, that of a man seeking the challenge of the impossible. The climax is sentimentally contrived : Katharina, exhausted by her rough reception in Petruchio's house, falls asleep in an armchair, but overhears Petruchio soliloquising on the painful but necessary task of hardening his heart in order to rouse the divine fire of love in her response. The musical style, long obsolete by 1922, might be described as sub-Massenet with touches of Fauré and Chabrier (for example in the habanera played by a stage band in Act II) ; it is amiably insipid, weak in thematic invention and characterization. The wedding scene contains a suite of pastiche dances in the manner of Delibes, designed for the ballet of the Paris Opéra. Act III begins with a Symphonic Entr'acte, representing the ride of the bridal couple through the storm and obviously suggested by the intermezzos of the Italian *verismo* school.

The American composer Giannini uses more of Shakespeare's plot than anyone else, including all three of Bianca's suitors and the disguising of the Pedant as Lucentio's father. His libretto makes ingenious use of at least four other Shakespeare plays and ten of the Sonnets, chiefly for additional love-scenes, but (like those of Goetz and Silver) rejects Shakespeare's final scene in favour of a conventional love-duet for Katharina and Petruchio. The finales of both scenes in Act II, a love-duet for Bianca and Lucentio largely based on *Romeo and Juliet* and a *buffo* ensemble before Katharina's marriage, are also insertions. This act is considerably changed in order to bring the wedding to the end; Petruchio and Grumio make their entry in old clothes on the previous day. In Act III it is Katharina's action in hiding the eloping Bianca and Lucentio ('Love . . . taught me this device') that convinces Petruchio of his victory.

Giannini's artificially bright and synthetic style suggests a grittier Menotti. The basic idiom is much indebted to Puccini, with a top-dressing of bitonality and other modern devices. The instrumental texture is congested and heavy for a light comedy. Leitmotives are used extensively, sometimes in combination. The fugal trio in Act I, when Tranio and Lucentio change clothes, makes a clever disguise motive, but those of the principal characters are too obviously derivative. Petruchio's, which begins the opera, is almost identical with the opening of Schumann's Rhenish Symphony; Katharina's

was used by Bizet for Glover in 'La Jolie Fille de Perth';
those of Lucentio and Bianca are strongly impregnated with
Puccini, as is the theme associated with Petruchio's taming,
which becomes the foundation of the final duet.  The love
music of both couples suffers from a basic similarity.

Shebalin's opera, though traditional if not reactionary in
idiom, is unquestionably the best setting of *The Taming of the
Shrew*.  It has humour and high spirits, a light touch and tunes
that haunt the ear.  The libretto is well knit, and where it
diverges from the play generally preserves its spirit.  Petruchio
makes Katharina change her wedding-dress for that in which
his great-grandmother was married.  When he gets her home,
he points to his drunken old servant Curtis, says he is a beautiful young girl, and orders Katharina to kiss him, rebuking her
when she does so (compare their argument about the sun and
moon in IV. 5 of the play).  The dénouement is differently
approached.  Upset by Petruchio's wooing, Katharina rushes
into the stormy night and is brought back unconscious.  He
begins to feel he has gone too far and forfeited her love; when
her obedience wins him his bet in the last scene (as in the play)
he concedes her the victory.  But Shebalin varies the wager
(V. 2, 65 ff.) and backdates it to Act I, where Petruchio bets
Lucentio and Hortensio a thousand ducats that he will marry
Katharina tomorrow and tame her in a month (the servants
have their own bet on the side), thus neatly tying up the plot.

The music is deeply rooted in Tchaikovsky's ballet style —
there are several polonaises and waltzes with a 'Nutcracker'
flavour — and also indebted to Borodin (for example, Bianca's
charming air in Act I, beginning with her leitmotive) and
Prokofiev (the swaggering *Alla marcia* with falling sevenths to
which Petruchio enters in Act II).  There are reminiscences of
the *opera buffa* tradition as far back as Rossini and Boieldieu;
the main theme of the taming duet in Act II, used for the
second subject of the overture, echoes 'La Dame blanche'.
The motival structure is quite elaborate (and appears to have
been tightened up by the composer since the publication of
the vocal score, to judge from the Russian recording).
Petruchio's falling seventh, which begins the overture, per-
vades the opera in many moods and contexts.  Most of the
motives are distinctive and the characters well drawn, especially Petruchio, though Katharina is hardly shrewish enough
in the early acts.  The tone of the music is a trifle sweet for the

subject, but its lyricism is singularly fresh and attractive.

*The Merchant of Venice* has inspired no masterpieces, but a good deal of more or less entertaining pastiche — of Verdi in Pinsuti's opera, Sullivan in Adrian Beecham's, Massenet in Hahn's and Puccini in Castelnuovo-Tedesco's. Pinsuti's score contains another element, a mixture of Mendelssohn, Gounod and 'The Lost Chord' manner of Sullivan which has a distinctly Anglican flavour and no doubt derives from the composer's residence in England. He employs it for prayers and sacred ceremonies, of which there are a startling number. Christians and Jews are served alike, generally with organ or harmonium accompaniment marked *Andante religioso*. The Wedding March in Act II would be worth revival in a Hoffnung concert as the missing link between Mendelssohn and Wagner. The chief model, however, is the Verdi of 'Il Trovatore', and the libretto is built to this specification, with big ensembles of perplexity in the trial scene and cabalettas of exasperation and revenge. Lorenzo, Jessica, Gratiano and the clowns do not appear, though Jessica's elopement is built up, together with the crowd's taunting of Shylock as a mad dog, as a motive for the latter's baleful bargain with Antonio. While the three casket scenes are polished off in a single ceremony lasting a matter of seconds, much time is devoted to Portia's wedding, with a religious service, a ballet and a sinister appearance of Shylock threatening woe; and the interrupted festivities are resumed at considerable length after the trial. The characterization is weak, and the music nowhere original, but it does not lack energy. The principal love theme of Bassanio and Portia, with its springy triplet rhythm, is an endearing imitation of Verdian panache.

Adrian Beecham's opera suggests a cross between 'Trial by Jury' and Edwardian balladry, with some grotesque word-setting, inconsequent harmony and a total inability to construct ensembles. If Beecham takes the play into the realm of operetta, Hahn inflates it into a grand opera. The librettist seems to have been seized with Hofmannsthal's habit of over-elaboration. Jessica's elopement is delayed by a long carnival scene, an intervention from Tubal (who is gagged and removed) and a most undramatic love duet which reproduces the melody of 'Never mind the why and wherefore' in 'H.M.S. Pinafore', soulfully harmonized in slow tempo. Tubal is more prominent than in the play, and groups of disputing Jews

and Venetians interrupt the trial in a manner recalling
'Salome'. Portia has superfluous airs in both parts of Act III,
and Shylock an extra scene after the trial. This is a pity, for
some of the music is impressive. The quartet for low voices
(a baritone and three basses) when the contract is signed
expresses character and atmosphere most vividly with the aid
of a rhythmic ostinato. Shylock's hate monologue has considerable power, and so has the end of Act I where, just after
Jessica's elopement, he learns from Tubal that four of Antonio's
ships have been sunk. Leitmotives are used copiously but not
always dissolved in the fabric of the score, which contains much
flat recitative. Shylock's (an insinuating upward chromatic
run) and Portia's (an exuberant melody with falling sixth
and seventh reminiscent of Chabrier) are strikingly apt.
There is one brilliant *coup* at Shylock's exit after the trial,
when his regular motive is suddenly surcharged with the theme
of his hate-monologue as he turns to look at Antonio and his
friends for the last time. Hahn's idiom recalls every prominent
French composer from Meyerbeer to Fauré, not to mention
an occasional touch of 'Tristan und Isolde' and Puccini, but
it has the courage of its convictions and a certain colour of its
own. The only comic touches are supplied by Morocco and
Aragon. The former enters with a great display of barbaric
rhythms, attended by his suite singing in Arabic, but drops
into honeyed Massenet when he makes love ; the latter, with a
retinue of eight grandees of Spain, a habanera rhythm and a
song about his lineage, might be the blood-brother of the Duke
of Plaza Toro.

The latest opera on *The Merchant of Venice*, Castelnuovo-
Tedesco's, has an excellent libretto based verbatim on the
play with surprisingly few cuts and only two additions, an
effective scene at the end of Act I when Shylock, searching
frantically for Jessica and his ducats, is mocked by the crowd,
and Sonnet 105 as a final ensemble addressed to the audience.
The composer says in a note that he would prefer to omit the
ring intrigue and end the opera with the trial, but he includes
the equivalent of Shakespeare's Act V in an appendix. Otherwise he cuts only the Gobbos, and saves time by using dancers
for Morocco and Aragon, who again furnish an opportunity
for exotic colour. The music combines a Wagnerian leitmotive system with a lyrical romantic style based on Puccini
and late Verdi. It is eminently theatrical, richly scored, un-

afraid of dance rhythms, catchy tunes and romantic harmony, and adept at creating atmosphere, especially in the Belmont and trial scenes. Shylock's music shows an attempt at racial characterization; his motives are distinguished from the others by a suggestion of oriental scales, not unlike the more barbaric passages in Borodin, who is all but quoted in one of them. This leaning towards the second-hand, together with a serious structural weakness, prevents the music rising to the level of the subject. Although the motives are often superimposed (four of them in the final bars of the opera), they never grow into anything new. Shylock's are repeated in almost every bar for pages on end until they become wearisome, but they do not bring him to life. He remains a ranting melodramatic villain, a *verismo* Iago; like the whole opera, he lacks that touch of grandeur that only a strong creative imagination can supply.

Berlioz's 'Béatrice et Bénédict' is a tantalizing work, for its defects seem almost the result of wilfulness. Of all composers he was the most naturally adapted to produce a great Shakespeare opera, not only on account of his genius, literary as well as musical, but through some affinity of temperament. Whenever he touched Shakespeare — and he was concerned at different times with five other plays besides *Much Ado About Nothing* [1] — he created something of outstanding quality; and this was clearly released by actual contact with Shakespeare's words and characters. Yet in turning *Much Ado About Nothing* into a short two-act opera he devoted a disproportionate amount of space to a character of his own invention, a musical pedant named Somarone, in whom he caricatured the type of contemporary professional musician he most disliked.

He reduced the play to a single strain, the sex-war between the two central characters. Don John's conspiracy, the Dogberry-Verges episodes, the church scene, all vanish; Hero and Claudio become little more than spectators. Claudio has no solo music and less to sing than Ursula. The disappearance of his rejection of Hero compels Berlioz to approach the climax by a different route, but he solves this problem brilliantly. Although Somarone may be said to take his cue from Shakespeare's Balthasar, his 'épithalame grotesque', heard first in rehearsal and again later with an added oboe part, his disquisition on the nature of fugue, and his ponderous failure to

[1] See below, pp. 182-97.

remember the words of the drinking song are no more than journalistic padding. Yet Berlioz's additions in the two duet-finales, the first of which has no counterpart in the play, Beatrice's air (expanded from the last speech in III. 1) and the trio of women (entirely new and including a quotation from *Othello*) are not only admirable but positively Shakespearean.

It is much the same with the music. Somarone's scenes are not bad ; they are merely alien. The rest of the score is all of a piece, and almost all first-rate. It is worth trying to account for its Shakespearean quality. For one thing the orchestration, which sparkles like a diamond, combines virtuosity and delicacy in a dazzling equivalent for the play's verbal wit. Then the tone is just right. The extraordinary refinement of Berlioz's imagination could convey irony and intense emotion in the same breath and invest a commonplace formula like the simple thirds of the duet for Hero and Ursula with a piercing beauty. Shakespeare did the same in such lines as Lear's 'I am a very foolish fond old man' (IV. 7). Here we approach the heart of Berlioz ; a compound of energy, melancholy and serene detachment, an unfathomable sadness beneath a shimmering surface of high spirits. Again and again in ostensibly cheerful movements like the airs of Hero and Beatrice or the haunting Sicilienne with its equivocal tonality and irregular phrase-lengths he conveys a unique sense of the transitoriness — even the ambivalence — of all human experience. This mood he undoubtedly associated with Shakespeare.[1] Its fullest expression in 'Béatrice et Bénédict', the magical nocturne for Hero and Ursula, inevitably recalls the still greater duet in Act IV of 'Les Troyens', which is a setting of the moonlight scene for Lorenzo and Jessica in Act V of *The Merchant of Venice*.

For all this one can see why 'Béatrice et Bénédict' has never been popular. It has the air of a *divertissement*, of never quite getting to grips with the subject. Somarone and the drinking scene are not the only irrelevances in a very short opera ; the first finale, for all its beauty, does not touch the main action at all. Yet Berlioz left in spoken dialogue the climactic scene in which Benedick is made to overhear the other three men discussing Beatrice's love for him, although in the female trio he showed himself supremely capable of setting such a psycho-

[1] He closed his Memoirs with the $4\frac{1}{2}$ lines from *Macbeth* beginning 'Life's but a walking shadow'.

logical action-piece to music. The second finale, marvellously apt and vivacious as it is, is musically too short. Berlioz's imagination had a strong literary tinge (it extends even to such details as the scoring of the drinking scene for guitars, tambourine, two trumpets, cornet and glasses banged on the table). This fact may, at one and the same time, have strengthened his sympathy with Shakespeare, weakened his opera, and ensured that, when we are under its spell, its weaknesses scarcely seem to matter.

After Berlioz, Stanford's 'Much Ado About Nothing', though a thoroughly competent piece of work, seems pedestrian. Sturgis's libretto tidies up the play and tones down the language, sometimes into sheer Wardour Street. It follows the plot faithfully, but alters the balance and increases the sugar content by introducing several love-passages for Hero and Claudio. The masque at Leonato's party in Act I and the religious chanting in the church scene are legitimate decorations, and so perhaps is the use of 'Sigh no more, ladies' as a choral framework for Act I and the whole opera. The music suggests a mixture of Brahms and Sullivan and is best when most lyrical: the exchanges between Beatrice and Benedick could do with more Latin sparkle, and the strong drama of the church scene falls into staginess. The use of the spoken voice for the two words 'Kill Claudio' is a good touch. The Dogberry-Verges scenes are genuinely funny, especially the treatment of Verges, who whenever he wishes to speak comes forward to a motive comprising a fat Handelian cadence followed by a 'till ready' accompaniment, only to be silenced by Dogberry. He never utters a syllable. Dogberry's 'written down an ass' has a remote foretaste of Britten's Bottom. By far the best single item is the beautiful setting in 5/4 time of the dirge 'Done to death by slanderous tongues'. The motives, neatly used but a trifle colourless, are less Wagnerian in style and treatment than might have been expected in 1901.

There appear to have been no more than two settings of *As You Like It*, separated by two centuries: the first by an Italian contemporary of Handel, the second by a modern American contralto singer with the double distinction of being the only female composer of a Shakespeare opera and perhaps the only operatic composer whose legs have been insured for ten thousand dollars. Something has been said about the libretto of Veracini's 'Rosalinda', which links the Forest of

K

Arden with the eighteenth-century pastoral convention of aristocratic swains maskerading as shepherds (Celia buys a farm in Act II and settles down 'in rural liberty'), but makes the plot sound very silly in the process. The last act, which includes a prison scene and a spectacular siege, bears no relation whatever to the play. Three of the male parts were sung by sopranos, the usurping Duke and the second man (built up into a suitable mate for Celia) by women, Orlando (renamed Costante) by a castrato. Six of the arias were published, and described by Burney as 'wild, aukward, and unpleasant; manifestly produced by a man unaccustomed to write for the voice'. The divisions certainly resemble violin exercises, and there is little remarkable about the music, though one of Costante's arias contains a surprising number of changes in tempo and metre. Another is based on a Scots tune, 'The lass of Patie's mill'; Burney dismissed this as a contemptible idea, since 'few of the North Britons', even if they frequented the opera, would squander half a guinea on a tune 'which perhaps their cook-maid Peggy can sing better than any foreigner'.

Taubert's 'Cesario' follows *Twelfth Night* for the greater part of two acts, enlivened by such titbits of romantic opera as choruses of sailors, street-vendors, jugglers, watchmen, gondoliers, huntsmen (in Olivia's garden) and wedding guests. The second finale, in which Sebastian falls in love with Olivia's portrait, Junker Christoph von Bleichenwang (Aguecheek) serenades Olivia and is answered by Maria in disguise, and the hunt comes galloping back just as Malvolio breaks out of the cellar with straws in his hair, owes nothing to Shakespeare. Nor does most of Act III, whose framework is a naval wedding (with a ballet of Tritons and sea-spirits); this allows Olivia and Sebastian and the other two couples to join the queue for the services of the priest. Shakespeare's comedy is both sweetened and coarsened; Feste is omitted, and the relationship between Orsino and the disguised Viola (Cesario) grossly sentimentalized. The music reflects the more commonplace attributes of Weber, Mendelssohn, Schumann and Spohr without their virtues; its blend of succulence and primness inhibits character and vitality even where Taubert shows some technical enterprise, as in the solos for the two knights and Fabian in Act I, a drinking song, a love song and a song ridiculing drink and love, which are presented first in turn and then simultaneously. Orsino's love song in Olivia's garden betrays the demure agitation of a governess dropping a stitch; the chorus of the watch is a debased Teutonic counterpart of the similar scene in Bizet's 'La Jolie Fille de Perth'.

It is difficult to form an impression of Smetana's 'Viola', the product of his last years, of which less than an act was completed. The bold chromatic style, indebted to Liszt and Wagner, recalls 'Dalibor' rather than 'The Bartered Bride'. The interlude between the second and third scenes has a flavour of the whole-tone scale, picked up perhaps from the Russians. Viola, Sebastian and Olivia were all to be mezzosopranos, though none of Olivia's music was written.

*The Winter's Tale* made a predictable appeal to the romantics of Central Europe. The German librettos set by Barbieri, Bruch and Goldmark each convert the play into a grand opera, expunging Autolycus, the Clown and every vestige of comedy, apart from a single *buffo* air sung by Goldmark's Old Shepherd. In all three operas the main plot adheres only too easily to the melodramatic model of the period, while the pastoral act loses its freshness and becomes a sentimental charade. Barbieri's librettist Gross completely transforms the character of Camillo; he becomes Bassianus, a rejected lover of Hermione, who stimulates Leontes's jealousy to further his own revenge and himself exposes Perdita. Years later his conscience begins to prick, and he helps to sort out the tangle after overhearing the Old Shepherd describe the discovery of the child. Hopffer (the author of a five-act comedy called *Der Wildschütz von Avon*) seems to have based his libretto partly on Gross. Both make Polixenes king of Arcadia and call the Old Shepherd Tityrus; both introduce spectacular portents — earthquake, thunder and lightning — when Leontes repudiates the oracle. In Hopffer's version Hermione, in prison before her trial, sees a vision (*Traumbild*) in which the ship carrying Perdita is wrecked but the child is rescued by sea-goddesses and adopted by Tityrus. This may have been suggested by Paulina's dream in Gross's Act IV, where she describes to Leontes how she saw Hermione and Perdita rise like Aphrodite from the sea. Hopffer's Paulina becomes Irene, the widow of a banished king, who with singular tactlessness sends the infant Perdita on her own initiative to Polixenes. Goldmark's librettist falsifies Leontes; after ordering Camillo to poison Hermione he bursts into tears, explaining

that he could not love her half so much, loved he not honour
more. Several favoured devices of romantic opera, a sailors'
chorus (barcarolle), a cradle song for Hermione, and a melodramatic scene in which Antigonus and four men in armour
kidnap Perdita from her cradle, are introduced in Act I.
Mamilius dies of fright when his mother faints.

Both Bruch and Goldmark employ a second-hand and
rather saccharine idiom that sorely needs a touch of bitters,
and both are weak in characterization, making too little
distinction between the Sicilian and the pastoral acts. Bruch's
style has much the same ingredients as Taubert's. The choral
writing is painfully square, with an almost total absence of
counterpoint. The *Traumbild*, which foreshadows the Dream
Pantomime in 'Hänsel und Gretel', is picturesquely scored,
with three solo cellos, triangle and harp to the fore. Its themes
recur elsewhere in the opera, notably the slow alternating
major and minor triads (a Hermione motive) which begin
the overture and accompany the unveiling of the statue in
Act IV.

Goldmark's score, the work of his old age, is even more
eclectic and as over-ripe as a fallen peach. It bears traces of
all the German romantics from Mendelssohn and Schumann
to Humperdinck, Reger and Strauss, with a dash of French
and Italian (Puccini) to boot. The motives, though not
structurally employed, are sometimes very effective; for
example, the orchestra's reference to Hermione when Camillo's
first sight of the grown Perdita reminds him of something he
cannot recall. The pastoral scenes have a strong scent of
'Hänsel und Gretel'. The principal weakness of the score,
apart from its incompatibility with the temper of the play, is
the subjugation of a weak melodic and rhythmic invention to
a luxuriant chromatic harmony. This produces an intolerable
sickliness as of some latter-day Spohr, especially in Perdita's
Act II lament and the opening of Act III, both in E flat minor.
The statue scene releases a backstage organ and harmonium,
with results that can be imagined.

The one opera on *Measure for Measure* has the distinction
of being the work of Richard Wagner, though a first glance
at the score suggests a mixture of 'Zampa' and 'The Pirates
of Penzance'. The former may have been one of Wagner's
models, as Auber's 'La Muette de Portici' certainly was.
Rossini, Weber and Marschner also left their mark. The

titanic ensembles are full of verbal and musical repetition; Act I has a finale to end all finales, *stretto* piled on *stretto* and climax on climax; the conclusion of Act II with its processions, stage band, bells and salvos of artillery derives straight from Spontini. Wagner composed the opera at a time (1834–6) when he was reacting against Beethoven in favour of French and Italian music, and he had no subsequent illusions about its quality.

He interpreted the play as an attack on Puritanism and hypocrisy and a glorification of the sensual instinct; there is no 'measure' of any kind in the libretto. All the characters are unpleasant, and some scarcely consistent. The action is transferred from Vienna to Palermo, and Angelo becomes the German Viceroy Friedrich (was this a Beckmesserish dig at some adversary?), a character with forebodings of Scarpia; his ban on fornication is pure hypocrisy, since the slightest provocation rouses his lust. Mariana, already married to him but discarded for social reasons, enters the convent with Isabella early in the opera, and so supplies the solution to the latter's problem before it arises. Isabella herself is a forward wench who needs little persuasion to plead with Friedrich. Lucio makes love to her in the convent and she marries him in the end, despite his shameless pursuit of her ex-maid. Her scene with Claudio in prison loses all its force, since she has already planned the substitution and is merely testing his character. Pompey emerges as Pontius Pilate, a *buffo* tenor concerned to redeem the name his parents tactlessly bestowed on him. Most of the comic scenes and characters are new, as is the second (and last) finale, a typical Italian imbroglio of disguises and mistaken identities, at the climax of which the King (Shakespeare's Duke) makes his single and silent entry.

The music is excitable but rhythmically impoverished, and full of Italianisms vocal and instrumental — honeyed thirds, extraneous cadenzas and top notes (effects without causes!), polkas and polaccas, and all the Rossini tricks mentioned above in connection with Balfe's 'Falstaff'. Friedrich even has a cavatina and cabaletta, separated by the delivery of a letter. The future Wagner is remotely discernible in the hectic chromatic scales, long sequences, sudden interrupted cadences and a tendency to modulate sooner and more radically than his models. The first hesitant steps towards symphonic leit-motive (four themes recur in the recitative of Friedrich's Act

II scena) show no advance on Wagner's predecessors. The
chromatic intervals of the Liebesverbot motive itself are faintly
prophetic, though it is scarcely developed beyond simple
diminution. The phrase associated with the convent in the
second scene reappears in 'Tannhäuser' as the motive of grace
or repentance.

Some of the lesser comedies have made occasional contributions to operetta — Beecham's 'Love's Labour's Lost' (published only in French), Audran's 'Gillette de Narbonne' and
Missa's 'Dinah'. The last two are versions of *All's Well That
Ends Well* and *Cymbeline*, with the sexual kernel extracted and
polished up for the Paris market. Audran retains the barest
skeleton of the plot in so far as it concerns Bertram and Helena,
but reduces all the characters to puppets: Gillette (Helena)
becomes a perky soubrette, Olivier (Parolles) a conventional
comic servant, Rosita (Diana) a promiscuous married gipsy
who can never preserve her virtue when an admirer whispers
'Turlututu' in her ear (so much for Shakespeare's virtuous
Florentine !). The scene is the court of King René of Provence,
the intellectual content nil, the score a string of strophic numbers with the simplest rhythmic and harmonic basis, nearly all
in polka or waltz rhythm. On its own level, that of Offenbach's
flippant wit, it is not bad entertainment. The tunes are chirpy
and prehensile, and there is a charming arrangement of an old
French cradle song also used by Couperin, Bizet, Fauré and
Debussy.

'Dinah' is more pretentious — it is a 'comédie lyrique' set
to continuous music — and less easy to swallow. The plot
derives from the Imogen-Posthumus-Iachimo intrigue in
*Cymbeline*, coarsened almost beyond recognition.[1] The scene
is Venice, complete with gondoliers, barcarolles and courtesans
by the dozen. Dinah (Imogen) is the adopted daughter of the
Doge and not yet married to Mentano (Posthumus), who is
subjected to continual molestation by all the women of the
town, headed by one Flora. Iachimo steals the necklace during
an attempted rape, and mutual suspicions are only allayed
after an obscure and melodramatic fourth act during which
Mentano enlists in the army and Philario kills Iachimo in a
duel. The music is an insipid mixture of Gounod and Offen-

---

[1] The first 'Cymbeline' opera, composed by Rodolphe Kreutzer during the
French Revolution, was dismissed by Félix Clément with the words: 'Il fallait
laisser cette scabreuse intrigue dans les contes de Boccace'.

bach, varied by crude attempts at boldness, such as the ending
of the first two acts on inconclusive chords.

Zillig's formidable 'Troilus und Cressida' is two works in
one, a choral symphony in seven movements superimposed on
a music-drama in six scenes. The choruses are gnomic utterances in the manner of Greek tragedy, which was evidently
the model for the whole composition. The high-flown libretto
retains a little of the play's flavour in Pandarus and Thersites,
but cuts the political scenes and alters the emphasis by raising
the moral stature of the two principals. Troilus is a heroic
lover, Cressida almost a romantic heroine. She yields half-
reluctantly to Achilles, who combines his own role with those
of Diomed and Ajax. He kills Troilus when he is defenceless
(as he kills Hector in the play), and Cressida dies penitent on
the funeral pyre. Although the opera ends with Cassandra,
its final message is one of hope, of a new world to rise from
Troy's ashes. A not very happy insertion is Pandarus's
attempt to procure Troilus for Helen when Paris is laid up
with a wound; Troilus, who has been led to expect Cressida,
recoils with horror.

Despite the composer's reference to twelve-note technique,
the basic idiom is a highly spiced and sometimes curdled
romanticism depending from 'Parsifal' and the Schoenberg of
the second quartet, with various other elements superimposed,
including polytonal chord-clusters and (in Helen's music) a
hint of Debussy and the whole-tone scale. The love scenes are
full of Tristanesque yearning, and the leitmotive scheme under-
lines the Wagnerian reference. Each character is haunted by
a motive (though mostly unvocal — Pandarus's is a kind of
squawk — they are frequently announced by the voice), and
others are associated with abstract ideas. The instrumental
texture is solid to a fault and threatens to overwhelm the solo
voice in the dramatic scenes, which have no ensembles apart
from short canonic passages. The best music occurs in the
choruses, which are better balanced and chew the philosophical
cud in a solemn and sometimes impressive manner.

## 4. THE HISTORIES

The romantics' search for operatic material led them inevitably
to the wild oats of Henry V, and at least eight operas with the

title 'La gioventù di Enrico V' appeared within twenty years.
Only the last of these, by Mercadante, appears to have any
foundation in Shakespeare, who failed to give the Prince's
misdemeanours a sufficient sexual basis. Even Romani,
Mercadante's librettist, took care to involve him in an amorous
and a political intrigue. One of the Prince's reprobate companions, Lord Arcourt, wants to make his sister Queen by
marrying her to the Prince, who without at first knowing her
identity is keen to abduct her. But she loves Arturo di North-
umberland, an enemy of the Lancastrian dynasty disguised as
a coachman. After a complex series of adventures involving
such dignitaries as the Garter King of Arms, Lord Wervich,
the Lord Mayor of London and the Lord Chief Justice (whose
name is Seyton), and after the Insignia of the Garter, bestowed
by Henry on 'Miss Arcourt', have been hurled through the
window of the Palace of Westminster at his horse's feet just
as he arrives for his coronation, all ends happily. Two of the
scenes are closely modelled on Shakespeare, one from each part
of *Henry IV*. That in which Falstaff and the Prince in turn
assume the role of the King takes place in a 'thick wood near
London' with a tree-trunk serving as the throne. The final
rejection of Falstaff at the coronation brings the fat knight
back to the centre of the stage, but he is scarcely a shadow of
himself. Of Shakespeare's other characters, the Duke of Lan-
caster, the Sheriff and Mistress Quickly (under the name of
'Mistress Martinn') make brief appearances. Apart from
two numbers, said to be of poor quality, which survive in a
single copy, Mercadante's music was never published.

Holst's one-act opera 'At the Boar's Head' has a clever
libretto based on the tavern scenes in both parts of Henry IV,
chiefly the fourth scene of Act II in each play. The language
is original, with the bawdier passages omitted and a few old
ballads and two of the sonnets inserted. The music, 'founded
on old English melodies', is ingenious and something more.
Of 38 melodies listed by Holst in his preface, only three are his
own ; the rest are of varying antiquity, some having a modal,
others an eighteenth-century flavour. Yet the opera is all of a
piece — and a Shakespearean piece at that. Few composers
have come closer than Holst to matching the authentic bite
of Shakespeare's language. The moments of sentiment in
particular — the Sonnets on the passage of time, sung by the
Prince in his disguise as a drawer, and Falstaff's parting from

Doll Tearsheet — are admirably judged.  Holst's use of folk-song is far more successful than that of Vaughan Williams in 'Sir John in Love', chiefly because he keeps the texture spare. Although the score is full of contrapuntal ingenuities, including a combination of two keys as well as two tunes in the Pistol scene, its impact is fresh and exhilarating.  This little opera deserves to be revived.

Of the two almost contemporary operas on *Richard III*, that of Canepa (1879) was revived in Italy as recently as 1962. Salvayre's (1883) is a French grand opera, translated into Italian for the benefit of a Russian audience in St. Petersburg. It is a spectacular work of the type created by Scribe and Meyerbeer, full of massive ensembles and eccentric pageantry, in which choruses of gipsies, huntsmen, clergymen, Welshmen and ghosts are variously employed.  The music too has a Meyerbeerian panache and rhythmic bounce, combined with a weak melodic idiom centred on Gounod and a tendency to harmonic 'boldness' that is merely inconsequent.  There is some English local colour which (apart from one startling ingredient) sounds like a French parody of Sir Hubert Parry. The opera is a monument of flatulence and would not be worth attention but for the hilarious gloss it places upon English history and upon Shakespeare, whose *ipsissima verba* crop up in the most unexpected contexts.

It begins with a funeral march immediately followed by an 'orgie'.  Richard, having buried his Queen, orders drinks and a song from his court jester, Puck.  Puck begins one about Queen Mab, but grief for the Queen's death prevents him finishing it, and he is sacked on the spot.  The voice of a minstrel is heard in the street describing Richard's warlike exploits (there may be some confusion with Cœur de Lion here).  The King summons him and gives him Puck's vacant post.  He says his name is Nick, but we soon learn that he is Henry of Richmond, the future Henry VII, who has just set in train a rebellion in another part of the kingdom.  Two Elizabeths enter, the widow of Edward IV and her daughter, conveniently known as Betty.  Richard pays instant court to the latter (his own niece, though the librettist does not seem to have spotted this), only to be met with 'imprécations'.  Henry, who is himself secretly engaged to her, offers the King his aid and experience with women, and under cover of a Ballade pleads his own love but tells her to accept Richard.  The latter proclaims her Queen, puts on his armour and starts a tremendous war song against the Lancastrians, in which Henry is able to join by substituting 'red' for 'white' whenever a rose is mentioned.

Act II takes place in 'a forest of druidic aspect' near Leicester. It is inhabited by gipsies led by a professional soothsayer known as 'Madgy', who turns out to be Queen Margaret of Anjou, widow of Henry VI. She is consulted first by the two Elizabeths (a trio based on the early part of Shakespeare's IV. 4) and then by Richard, who — like Henry, but for opposite reasons — laughs at her prophecy of a Lancastrian triumph. Margaret concocts a philtre of the type used in *Romeo and Juliet* that will send Richard to sleep for a few days, during which time Henry can become King and marry Betty. The latter's wedding to Richard now begins, celebrated by Cardinal Bourchier and a quartet of bass bishops and introduced by a grand nuptial march based on the tune of 'Rule, Britannia'. The Elizabeths have put the philtre in the sacred goblet in which the couple must pledge themselves. Richard craftily makes Betty drink first; she collapses; Richard accuses her mother of murder; she appeals to the judgment of God, with the inevitable consequence in a romantic opera : a knight in black armour rides in on a black horse and takes up the challenge. It is of course Henry; Richard remarks that this is going a bit far, even for a court jester. No sooner has Henry identified himself than a troop of revolting Welshmen rush in led by Margaret brandishing a naked sword, and the entire company, with a nice anticipation of history, cries 'à Bosworth !'

Henry wins the battle and goes off to celebrate, but omits to kill Richard, who wanders alone among the piles of slain praying to Satan and periodically offering his kingdom for a horse. The ghosts of his victims rise, bidding him despair and die — a scene misplaced from the play — and Margaret, having set the forest on fire, comes to gloat over his body. After a melodramatic duet he kills her and arrives in Leicester just in time to see the Cardinal place the crown on Henry's head outside a conveniently situated cathedral. He whips it off, snatches the sceptre and brandishes it defiantly. Just when the history of England seems to have been successfully reversed, he falls dead on the cathedral steps (with a quotation from Henry's song about his military exploits), and the chorus acclaim the reconciliation of the roses — though the librettist, whose treatment of politics is nothing if not casual, has never mentioned this aspect or even explained that Betty represents the house of York.

## 5. THE TRAGEDIES

That *Romeo and Juliet* should have been the most popular of the tragedies was to be expected. An ill-starred love-story against a background of family feud is one of the archetypes of opera. Its wide appeal is attested by premières in places as improbable as Minorca, Middlesbrough and Mexico City. At least seven *Romeo and Juliet* operas were very successful in their day, though none has quite stood the test of time.

The diverse treatment of the story, especially in the earlier operas, is fascinating. The lovers are the only constant factors; all the other characters disappear in one version or another, and Schwanenberger dispenses with the family feud. Of the composers who retain the tragic end, only Barkworth and Blacher include the final reconciliation. All the Italian and French romantics from Vaccai to Zandonai keep Romeo alive long enough to sing a duet with Juliet. (For generations this was traditional in the straight theatre, since Otway's version of 1679 exiled the lovers to ancient Rome.) Friar Laurence undergoes some curious metamorphoses, especially in the anti-clerical period of the French Revolution. In Steibelt's opera he becomes Cébas, the Greek guardian of the Capulet family vault; in Zingarelli's he is Gilberto, a friend of both houses who acts as druggist, priest and general stand-in, and makes a thorough mess of it; in Romani's two librettos he is the family doctor. Tybalt, who in the three earliest operas has been killed by Romeo before the action begins, enjoys various relationships with Juliet — brother, cousin, fiancé, rejected lover. In the last two instances he is fused with Paris. Marchetti conflates the latter with Mercutio and Benvolio, giving the plot a very odd twist. Capulet generally remains the heavy father, but Juliet's Nurse dwindles into the conventional confidante under such names as Laura, Cécile, Matilda, Bianca, Gertrude, Marta and Isabella.

The earliest libretto, set by Schwanenberger and perhaps by another composer before him, has only three characters: the third is Benvolio, a doctor who also fulfils the function of

Friar Laurence. This is an Italian opera with recitatives, arias and occasional duets. The libretto is full of sweet reason, as befits its date (1773). Capulet, having promised Juliet to Romeo, has revoked his consent on hearing of Tybalt's death, procured Romeo's banishment and ordered Juliet to marry Paris. Benvolio thinks up the device of the potion, and has the sense to wait at the tomb when his message to Romeo goes astray. Having prevented his suicide, he puts the screw on Capulet, promising to redeem Juliet from the doors of death if he will allow Romeo to return and marry her. Which done, the opera ends with a happy trio, the only piece for more than two voices. Though remote from Shakespeare, this libretto is clear, natural and consistent in its characterization.

Gotter's libretto, set by Benda, belongs to the *Sturm und Drang* school, half realistic and half sentimental. Juliet is an intensely passionate girl who takes the lead throughout. Already married in secret to the exiled Romeo, she threatens to stab herself in the first act and to create a disturbance in church if her father insists on marrying her to Count Lodrona in the second. Friar Laurence, who is Capulet's private chaplain, again brings off a skilful piece of blackmail by forcing him into a declaration that if he could only revive Juliet he would give her any husband she wanted. Gotter, in a defensive preface, justified his changes on the ground that a tragic end suited neither the musical economy nor the capacity of the singers. But his last act goes to pieces for another reason, the deplorably false sentiment of Romeo's scene in the tomb: he sheds tears over the childless old age of Capulet and Montague and looks forward to hovering with Juliet in the moonlight above the wanderer who with heavy heart brings roses to their grave. The libretto, like many another early *Singspiel*, has far too much spoken dialogue, some of it concerned with superfluities like Juliet's Aunt Camilla. Friar Laurence does not sing at all. Benda has one fine scene, the funeral ceremony at the beginning of Act III, which employs the chorus for the first and only time (offstage) and recalls similar episodes in Gluck and Traetta. Otherwise his music is fluent and superficial, rich in period clichés and sparing of surprises. The vocal parts are encrusted with shallow ornament and long cadenzas. He has almost no feeling for character; the air in which Capulet loses his temper with Juliet's obstinacy is jovial, if not positively jocose.

Steibelt's is the best Shakespeare opera of the eighteenth century. The composer was a German pianist whose morals gave such offence in Paris, even during the Revolution, that he was forced to leave for London. The libretto, originally written for the Paris Opéra (with recitative instead of spoken dialogue), tells the story clumsily, supplying the audience with information in the manner of Sheridan's parody in *The Critic*. Capulet has sworn to give Juliet to whoever will avenge Tybalt's death by killing Romeo. A Spaniard, Don Fernand, has undertaken this task; but when the Capulets discover Romeo unarmed in Juliet's tomb and propose to kill him he reacts with the quixotry expected of operatic Spaniards and leaps to his defence. The fight that follows wakes Juliet — not surprisingly, since it involves three choruses as well as the principals. This is a typical French Revolution *opéra-comique*, starting with realistic comedy (supplied by the husband of Juliet's Nurse, an old family retainer reluctant to take part in any dirty work), working up to a great dramatic climax in the last act and ending happily. The music owes something to Cherubini and more to Mozart. The romantic scoring foreshadows Weber. Act I contains a long love-duet that ends as a trio when the Nurse, playing the part of Brangäne, warns the lovers of the approach of dawn, and a vengeance air for Capulet, rather like the Count's air in Act III of 'The Marriage of Figaro'. Romeo's air in the tomb is a beautiful piece with obbligato horn, cello and clarinet. Best of all are the ensembles, especially the finale of Act II, which ends quietly after Juliet has defied her father and Don Fernand and collapsed under the influence of the potion, and the mourning sequence at the beginning of Act III, where a four-part female chorus is accompanied by muted drums and tamtam — the first operatic appearance of this instrument. Steibelt had learned from Mozart the art of prolonging suspense by harmonic control, and some of his modulations, notably that which marks Juliet's awakening, are both imaginative and prophetic.

By comparison the operas of Zingarelli and Guglielmi seem retrograde. The former's libretto is weak in design and motivation. The marriage is made by declaration before Gilberto and never consummated, for Gilberto at once separates the parties (in one version he plays a double game, consoling Romeo in one scene and Tybalt in the next). All

the characters strike conventional attitudes, especially Capulet,
who rejoices in the Christian name of Everardo; all plunge
into a *preghiera* or prayer aria on the slightest provocation.
Zingarelli, like Vaccai and Bellini, wrote the part of Romeo
for female mezzo-soprano; this was quite common at a time
when heroic parts had not finally passed from the castrato to
the tenor. The music, which resembles weak Cimarosa and
lacks substance or distinction, was a particular favourite of
Napoleon. It is difficult to grasp Guglielmi's plot in the absence
of a complete libretto; it ends happily with a trio for the lovers
and Friar Laurence. Paris was sung by a woman contralto,
Romeo by a tenor. The music, again replete with prayers, is
imperturbably platitudinous.

Two things are remembered of Vaccai's opera: that it
has the same libretto as Bellini's and that Malibran ended
her performances of Bellini with Vaccai's finale. Both are
untrue. The librettos, though both by Romani, are very
different; even the list of characters is not identical. Vaccai's
*penultimate* scene replaced Bellini's finale, and this innovation
(according to her biographer Pougin) was not the work of
Malibran. A comparison of the librettos is interesting.
Vaccai's is much the better. Capulet and Lorenzo (Friar
Laurence) are drawn with considerable subtlety, and so is
Juliet's mother Adèle, who is sympathetic but not in her confidence. Tybalt, though he is killed before Act II, is genuinely
in love with Juliet, and has more consideration for her feelings
than Capulet; this is the one opera in which he is not odious.
There are several admirable episodes that Bellini suppressed,
in particular a long duet for Lorenzo and Juliet before she
drinks the potion (which is her own idea) and a scene in which
the report of her death rouses contradictory emotions of
vengeance and remorse in Capulet. Less happy perhaps is
the melodramatic finale: after Romeo's death Juliet re-
proaches first Lorenzo and then Capulet and throws herself
on the body, from which she is dragged on Capulet's orders
when on the point of death.

Bellini's libretto concentrates on the conventional triangle
of Romeo, Juliet and Tybalt. Capulet and Lorenzo are
reduced to ciphers; Adèle disappears; Tybalt survives till
halfway through Act II (each libretto has two acts), but becomes almost a caricature of an operatic villain. Nor are the
lovers so sensitively drawn. Romeo is a headstrong man of

action, Juliet a timorous creature who cannot make up her mind to defy her father (it is now Lorenzo who suggests the potion). There is one neat new touch: Capulet sets a guard on Lorenzo and so prevents him getting his message about the potion to Romeo. The end is changed; the lovers die together, and when Capulet breaks in and asks who killed them, Lorenzo and the chorus reply: 'You with your inhumanity'. In both librettos Romani identifies the Capulets and Montagues with the Guelphs and Ghibellines and makes Capulet's ball (as in Zingarelli's opera) a celebration of Juliet's engagement to Tybalt. A few pieces — the opening chorus, much of the first finale, and the duet for the lovers in the tomb — are common to both.

When it comes to the music, there is no doubt of Bellini's superiority. Vaccai's score is not negligible, but no strong personality emerges. A tendency to elegiac sentiment, derived from his master Paisiello and akin to Bellini, who drank at the same source, seems to reflect his natural voice. Some of the slow melodies, for instance in Capulet's Act II aria and Romeo's scena in the tomb, are beautiful. But the flimsy cabalettas with their automatic thirds and empty pyrotechnics and the repetitive ensembles echo Rossini's mannerisms without his glitter. The recitative is less expressive than that of Bellini, who was not above taking a few hints from Vaccai, especially in Romeo's death scene; in both operas the hero dies in the middle of uttering Juliet's name.

Bellini composed his opera in a great hurry, and borrowed two items from his early 'Adelson e Salvini' and ten from the suppressed 'Zaira'; but these were completely reworked, and they include some of the freshest music in the opera. (One piece in 'Zaira' supplied a cavatina for Romeo in Act I and a cabaletta for Juliet in Act II.) The characterization is not subtle, but Bellini does convey the ardour and innocence of the lovers, especially in their Act I duet, and Romeo's proposal in the first scene to heal the feud by marrying Juliet comes across with touching sincerity. As in all his operas Bellini scores principally with long slow melodies, of which there are many exquisite examples. The choruses and the tinkling quick tunes — with one noble exception in the first finale — are scarcely better than Vaccai's. But Bellini's dramatic gifts were potentially much greater. His orchestral introductions, sometimes with a beautiful obbligato for horn or clarinet, are adept at establishing atmosphere, and there are moments in the first finale and the tomb scene where an unexpected detail in declamation or harmony anticipates Verdi. The end of the opera, without a showy cabaletta for either singer, reveals a good taste absent from Vaccai's setting and from Bellini's own 'Beatrice di Tenda'.

The next five operas are much closer to Shakespeare — in intention. Marchetti made this clear in his preface, while compromising with the conventional operatic finale. Most of his scenes end with a big tableau of threats, prayers or perturbation. The second scene of Act I and the first of Act II both build up to an interrupted duel between Romeo and Tybalt, which after two replays is decided offstage. This is not a bad libretto of its type, though the conflation of Paris, Benvolio and Mercutio is awkward; apparently Romeo never learns that the friend who took him to the Capulets' ball to help him forget Rosaline not only loves Juliet himself but is her father's choice for her husband. The music imitates the manner of 'Rigoletto' and 'Il Trovatore' without its supreme virtue of melodic energy. It constantly drops into an amble or a jaunty trot just where it should take wing; the duet at the lovers' first meeting is almost a polka. Marchetti falls below the big emotional climaxes, except perhaps in the finale of Act II, where Paris and the Capulets hear of Tybalt's death, and the very Verdian scena in which Juliet, after a prayer to the Virgin, drinks the potion.

Gounod and Ivry set the story almost simultaneously, though the latter, a titled amateur, had to wait more than ten years for a performance. There are marked similarities between the librettos; both insert a languorous duet of postnuptial bliss before the lark-nightingale scene (III. 5) and then bring Friar Laurence hot on Capulet's heels; in both Romeo forgets that he has taken poison in the tomb duet, which ends with a reference to the lark-nightingale music. Ivry's treatment of this scene owes several details to Romani. His generally skilful libretto is marred by the third finale, where he tried to improve on Shakespeare by making Juliet reproach Romeo to his face for killing Tybalt (but he added a more orthodox alternative in an appendix). Gounod could not resist a substantial wedding service complete with responses, and introduced a new character in Romeo's page, Stephano, who provokes the riot in which Mercutio and Tybalt are killed. In 1888, when adapting the work for the Paris Opéra, he added a superfluous second scene to Act IV in order to drag in a ballet.

Gounod's opera is considerably the better, but as remote in spirit from Shakespeare as his 'Faust' is from Goethe. He attires both stories in the same voluptuous and sugary envelope. The two garden scenes are musically almost interchangeable. In either opera Gounod is at his best when lyrical, at his worst when sanctimonious (as in the Friar Laurence scenes or the chorale-like ensemble after the brawl in Act III), and the attempts at strong drama ring hollow. The story loses its epic quality and declines into a salon intrigue of the Second Empire. Juliet's well-known waltz-ariette is typical; this and her earlier outburst of coloratura evoke a more sophisticated character than Shakespeare's young girl. Gounod's charming orchestration, especially in the garden scene, deserves mention. His is the first 'Romeo and Juliet' opera to include Mercutio's Queen Mab speech, and the only one to begin with Shakespeare's Prologue, sung by the characters in chorus. Ivry dedicated his score to the future King Edward VII, presumably for social rather than artistic reasons. It is an insipid affair, impoverished in melody and still more in rhythm, founded on Gounod and Mendelssohn with periodical lapses into the scented opulence of an organ voluntary.

The English-speaking countries now take a hand. Harry R. Shelley, composer of innumerable sentimental and religious ballads, was an American organist and a pupil of Dvořák. All this could be deduced from his 'Romeo and Juliet', which suggests a mixture of Gounod, Barnby and Johann Strauss, with occasional whiffs of Wagner. The texture is stodgy, the harmony stuffy, the word-setting insensitive. The libretto contracts the story but does not falsify it. A dumb-show marriage and the despatch of the potion by post eliminate Friar Laurence except as a mute. Barkworth's opera fails for different reasons. He includes nearly all the play's characters and more of the text than any other composer (not to mention two extra choruses based on Elizabethan poems), and handles it with a real feeling for language. Even the shadowy Rosaline appears. As a result the opera is enormously long, and copious use of leitmotives fails to bind it together, partly because their organization is insufficiently close (except perhaps in the last scene, where no fewer than fourteen are used), and partly

L

because many of them lack savour. There are exceptions:
the principal love motive is attractive, and the phrase intended
to suggest night birds in the tomb scene strangely haunting.
Otherwise the competent but derivative style, based on
romantic models in France, Germany and England, and
relying too much on rich harmony at the expense of rhythm,
is not strong enough to bear the weight.

Zandonai gives us a *verismo* 'Romeo and Juliet'. The
influence of Puccini is omnipresent, both in the libretto and
the music, and that of Mascagni (Zandonai's teacher) and
'Carmen' conspicuous. Only the bare bones of the play
remain, and not all of them. Sampson and Gregory loom
large, but Capulet, Paris, Mercutio, Benvolio and Friar
Laurence are cut; the lovers are already married, and the
Nurse produces the potion. The three main characters come
from stock; Tybalt is a vicious baritone who denounces
Juliet as a prostitute, Juliet a Puccinian heroine who refers
to herself as 'piccioletta come l' ombra d' un fiore' and is com-
forted by Romeo 'come una bimba'. The libretto is full of
more or less picturesque irrelevances — semichoruses of all
kinds (and a backstage semi-orchestra in Act I), distant voices
and bells from a convent, a torch-dance for Juliet's attendants,
a travelling ballad-singer with his lute, a town-crier, and
various flunkeys galloping about on horses in the Mantua
scene. This is linked to the finale in the tomb by a typical
intermezzo representing Romeo's ride to Verona through the
stormy night. The design of Act I is modelled on that of
'Madam Butterfly', an elaborate build-up with much circumstantial detail leading to a long love-duet. The whole opera
is a professional but uninspired job. The synthetic lyrical style
has neither Mascagni's coarseness nor Puccini's concentration.
As in other *verismo* operas the fringe characters, such as the
town-crier and ballad-singer, enjoy better music than the
principals. The sinister little phrase representing the feud is
managed with some skill and makes its point in many contexts.

Sutermeister's is another eclectic opera that sacrifices the
substance for the frills. Tybalt is omitted, and Romeo not
banished; the scenes between the chief characters are so short
that there is scarcely time for them to be established as individuals. Yet the score is cluttered up with extraneous devices —
Voices of Night and the Deep, and four brace of supernumerary

lovers who intrude upon the action at most unsuitable moments, including the garden scene. Although intended to supply a quality of fantasy and a link with the universal cosmos, they merely obstruct the plot, so that the opera has no central core. The device of the offstage chorus is grossly abused; like other operatic gambits (including *Sprechgesang* and the spoken word) it is apt to succeed in inverse ratio to its frequency, besides rendering the words inaudible. The composer's aim to simplify his style in reaction against the complexity of much modern music was no doubt praiseworthy, but it produces a stale *verismo* idiom based on Orff, Strauss and Mascagni, complete with a juicy intermezzo between scenes in the last act. The freshness of lyrical invention essential for this subject is wanting. The orchestration is strident, and a backstage band of piccolo, five trumpets, piano, organ and percussion is used too much. The most effective scene is the initial riot, which gives an impetus to the action that all too soon evaporates.

The two latest settings, both dating from 1950, turn their backs on the romantic treatment current for a century and a half, but have nothing else in common. Malipiero's is part of a larger work, 'Mondi celesti e infernali', described as 'tre atti con sette donne'. The seven heroines range over a period of three thousand years, from the Assyrian Sammuramai (Semiramis) to a twentieth-century She, and include Medea, Poppea and the Virgin Mary. This is one of several such dramatic experiments by Malipiero which seem to fight against theatrical coherence. The *Romeo and Juliet* episode is a very condensed account taken verbatim from three scenes in the play; the lovers are the only characters, and an audience could scarcely grasp the situation without previous knowledge. The music employs a restless, partly modal, harmonic style without much rhythmic drive or vitality in the voice parts. It cannot, however, be judged outside the conspectus of femininity of which it forms part.

Blacher's 'Romeo und Julia' is a one-hour chamber opera originally written for radio. This explains the prominence of the chorus, which describes the action by appropriating the speeches of various characters without regard for dramatic verisimilitude. The libretto consists of eighteen short scenes, a third of them entirely choral, taken direct from Schlegel's translation. The only important soloists are the two lovers.

The music, which owes something to Stravinsky and Hinde-
mith, relies on ostinato, rhythmic complexity (asymmetric
patterns variously superimposed) and an oblique attitude to
tonality in which concords, bitonal collisions and inconsequent
progressions and cadences are handled with equal detachment.
It eschews traditional lyricism and pictorial effects, and shows
no feeling for character or drama as commonly understood.
This cool antiseptic approach, which depends of course on
the pull against the associations of the text, provides (up to a
point) a refreshing antidote to *verismo*; but it cannot hope to
recreate Shakespeare's drama. It remains at best a wry gloss
in the margin. The musical invention varies in quality. The
exhilarating scherzo movements are the most successful. The
one comic scene, mostly spoken, misfires, and there are touches
of selfconsciousness, as when a Verdian vocal line is yoked to
a bitonal chordal accompaniment at Juliet's 'Is there no pity
sitting in the clouds?' (III. 5).

The four Roman tragedies have attracted few composers,
and the only opera on *Timon of Athens* is the work of a Holy
Roman Emperor in the late seventeenth century.[1]  Malipiero's
operas on *Julius Caesar* and *Antony and Cleopatra* are worthy
failures. Both librettos are shortened versions of the plays,
sensitively compiled by the composer with few insertions (none
at all in 'Antony and Cleopatra'); but the task defeated him,
partly because Shakespeare's dramatic design all but repels
operatic treatment, and partly because he adopts too low a
tone in the music.

*Julius Caesar* is a difficult play, since the focus of attention
shifts half way through from Caesar to Brutus and Cassius. If
the conspirators are to hold our interest, they and their motives
for murdering Caesar must be firmly established at the outset.
This is just what Malipiero fails to do. By severely cutting the
conversation between Brutus and Cassius in the second scene
of the play and omitting the third scene altogether, he reduces
Cassius to a cipher and Brutus to little more. Their quarrel
also goes overboard, Shakespeare's last two acts being compressed into a single scene on the battlefield. This is inevitably
an anticlimax, since the only fully realized character, Caesar
himself (whose part is not cut at all), has disappeared in Act II.
To English ears the score suggests a cross between Vaughan

[1] Leopold I. The subject would seem to have been suitable, since according
to the Maréchal de Grammont 'his sole delight is to compose doleful melodies'.

Williams and the later Puccini, with a little Debussy and Stravinsky. There are affinities with Pizzetti's 'Murder in the Cathedral' in Malipiero's scrupulous care for the text,[1] avoidance of set arias and strong modal harmony, and the same danger of monotony in the constant use of *parlando* recitative. This impression is reinforced by the predominance of low voices (all the chief characters except Antony are baritones, and the women have only a few lines each) and the family likeness in many of the instrumental motives. Caesar's however is an exception. Heard first at the beginning of the prelude, it has a powerful character of its own, and seldom fails to make its mark. The phrase to which the Soothsayer utters his warning about the Ides of March also enriches a texture that is often genuinely symphonic. At two points, Caesar's refusal of the crown in Act I and the closing bars of the opera, Malipiero introduces poems by Horace, sung by the chorus in Latin. The idea was happy, and it affords the only opportunity for sustained vocal writing. The former scene, in which the crowd sing part of an Ode offstage against percussion accompaniment and a fanfare version of Caesar's motive, while Brutus and Cassius plot in the foreground, is the best in the opera. The 'Carmen Saeculare' at the end suffers from an undistinguished tune. Offstage choruses play an effective part in the battle scenes.

Klebe's version of *Julius Caesar*, another short radio opera, makes no attempt to grapple with Shakespeare's tragedy or his characters, even in the single act (III) which it takes as text. It is a projection of the moral disintegration of the Roman people, suggested perhaps by the collapse of the Nazi régime in Germany. Everything is concentrated on creating an impression of growing chaos: the fragmented vocal idiom, with much spoken dialogue and *Sprechgesang* and no effort to match Antony's eloquence in the forum scene; the strangely balanced orchestra with single woodwind, no violins or violas, five saxophones, heavy brass (including three tubas) and a huge battery of percussion; and the use of pre-recorded electric tapes. These are sometimes deployed stereophonically, two or three at a time, and for the most part carry shouts, murmurs, footsteps and other more or less concrete noises, chiefly to suggest the uproar of the crowd in the forum. The

---

[1] He even apologizes for changing the Nervii into the Lusitanians in Antony's forum speech to avoid a *double entendre* in Italian ('the day he overcame his nerves').

method is dodecaphonic, and the design based on classical procedures perceptible only on paper, as in 'Wozzeck' (though Klebe's kinship, except in the huge crescendo from *ppp* to *fff* on the last note of the score, is with Webern rather than Berg). The result, insofar as it can be judged from the score, appears wasteful. It suggests the point-blank discharge of a field-gun at a brick wall; the target is demolished, but the operation scarcely seems worth the expense.

In *Antony and Cleopatra* Malipiero was confronted with a subject of the most formidable dimensions. He reduces its scale by omitting all the scenes outside Egypt except that on Pompey's galley (with Enobarbus's description of Cleopatra inserted) and a brief battle-piece for Actium. Octavius Caesar has only a few words, Octavia does not appear, and the political elements are thrust into the background. Even so, what remains demands a lyrical sweep, a grandeur of characterization and a power to fascinate that only the greatest opera composers have possessed. Malipiero's melodic self-denial is fatal here. However sensitive the word-setting, recitative is not enough; it only hampers the greatest poetry, as in Enobarbus's speech about Cleopatra in her barge. The composer's style is more lyrical (and less modal) than in 'Giulio Cesare', but this brings him more under the influence of Puccini, whom he often recalls in his drooping arioso phrases, mosaic method of constructing sequences, and a similar type of dissonance. He uses leitmotives in a symbolic as well as a direct sense and in combination (effectively in the last scene), but sometimes with a curiously imprecise reference. It is difficult to see why the prelude to the opera should begin with two phrases associated with Antony's marriage to Octavia, or why the dance in Pompey's galley and 'Come, thou monarch of the vine' should develop one of Cleopatra's themes, first sung by Antony to the words 'Where's my serpent of old Nile?' The fact that the same phrase is later connected in a literal sense both with the Nile and with serpents is scarcely to the point. Another Cleopatra motive is a chromatic arabesque very like the orientalisms of Rimsky-Korsakov. The chorus is little used except to speak a few sentences of narrative between the scenes.

Of the great tragedies *Macbeth* is the most amenable to opera, since the story has no subplot and is easily grasped on a straightforward human level. The first big work on the subject, by the French composer Hippolyte Chélard, has a very strange libretto by Rouget de Lisle, author of the 'Marseillaise'. The list of characters is enough to raise a smile. Banquo, Macduff and Malcolm are not among them; Duncan's only child is a daughter, Moïna, who is engaged to Douglas, Prince of Cumberland (Macbeth has a son, but the obvious complication does not ensue, though one passage suggests that Rouget de Lisle considered it); the Witches rejoice in the good Scots names of Elsie, Nona and Groeme. The libretto covers only the first two acts of the play, with one or two later events worked in. The murder occurs during the finale of Act II and is not discovered till the very end of the opera, when Lady Macbeth gives it away by talking in her sleep.[1] She wakes up red-handed; the Ghost of Duncan appears, followed by the Witches, who claim Macbeth as the spoil and sport of hell;[2] Lady Macbeth commits suicide, and Macbeth is led off to execution.

Some surprising things have happened earlier. The opera begins with a chorus of depressed soldiers who propose to discard their arms and bury their flags because they cannot find Macbeth. He has been waylaid by the Witches, who have killed his horse under him; their prophecy causes him to recite part of the dagger speech on the blasted heath. In Act II he recoils repeatedly from the crime and is about to swear loyalty to Duncan when the Witches enter with poison, dagger and crown (visible — and audible — only to Macbeth, like Banquo's ghost in the banquet scene of the play) and, supported by Lady Macbeth in a massive ensemble, urge him to be worthy of his destiny. This act contains a ballet, whose highlight is the appearance of 'Auld Lang Syne' in a somewhat corrupt text, and a chorus of bards invoking the shades of dead heroes to protect Duncan's rest, an idea borrowed from the Ossianic operas popular in Napoleonic France. The time between the murder and its discovery is occupied by a brilliant aria for Moïna on the beauties of Highland scenery and a love-duet with Douglas. The music shows a lively sense of the theatre but an incongruously mixed style derived from Rossini, Spontini, Weber and Spohr. It veers abruptly between

---

[1] In a 'Ballo mimico' by C. Pugni (Milan, 1830) Lady Macbeth while sleep-walking kills her own son, whom she mistakes for Duncan.

[2] This seems to have been contributed by Chélard; it does not occur in the printed libretto.

skittish coloratura and the utmost chromatic succulence. The
Witches have a disturbing tendency to drop into anthems.
But the second finale (with the murder) has considerable
harmonic power, and Lady Macbeth's first aria (the equivalent of 'Come, you spirits/That tend on mortal thoughts', I. 5)
and the sleep-walking scene, which recalls the music of the
murder, are lively and effective.

Taubert's 'Macbeth' has a remarkably good libretto —
until the last scene. All the principal episodes are included —
even the Porter, though his obscenities are replaced by an
*echt-deutsches Volkslied* — and the only insertions are a ballad for
Macduff in the banquet scene, accompanied by bards on their
harps, and another harper who just before the battle of Dunsinane moves Macbeth with a song about an old king dying
hallowed by his country's love. Then the fun starts. Lady
Macbeth appears on the castle wall wearing the crown and a
night-dress, and apostrophizes the god of battles. After first
mistaking the advancing enemy for the ghosts of those whom
Macbeth has murdered, she keeps up a running commentary
during his fight with Macduff. After his death (on stage) she
throws first the crown and then herself over the battlements;
whereupon the Witches rise from the spot where she disappeared, cry 'You have the crown, we have the King; Scone
summons you, our kingdom is here', and vanish into the earth.
Taubert was not the composer for this drama. Apart from a
good motive for the Witches' prophecy, which returns at
suitable moments, and a not unimaginative setting of the sleep-
walking scene, his music is very tame, especially in melodic
invention. He devised a German-Scottish dialect involving
the addition of Scotch snaps to square Teutonic tunes and
even polaccas. Lady Macbeth's first air appears to be
modelled on Weber's Eglantine in 'Euryanthe'. She is a
mezzo-soprano, Malcolm a soprano, Hecate a tenor.

Verdi's 'Macbeth', though far from an unflawed masterpiece, is one of the most interesting of all Shakespeare operas,
since it shows the impact of the dramatist on a great composer
at two different stages of his career. The first version dates
from 1847, the second from 1865; the latter — the form in
which the opera is always performed — incorporates a good
deal of the original score. The libretto, first drafted by Verdi
himself, contains much literal translation; Lady Macbeth's
part in the sleep-walking scene follows the play word for word.

The action is compressed, but there are surprisingly few concessions to convention. The form of Lady Macbeth's first aria, as already noted, and of her *brindisi* (drinking song), interlocked with the two appearances of Banquo's ghost, is actually imposed by the play (the music of both these scenes has been unjustly assailed; the jerky lilt of the *brindisi* fits the context perfectly). Macduff and Malcolm are reduced in stature, the former's role at the end of the banquet scene being weakly drawn, and the Porter (who would surely have inspired the later Verdi) is cut; the murder of Banquo is no longer planned by Macbeth alone. The one serious weakness lies in the first act, where everything before the murder happens far too quickly. Macbeth barely hesitates. Above all, Duncan is reduced to a mute, who cannot engage our sympathy. It is a great pity that Verdi omitted Shakespeare's I. 6, with Duncan's comments on the 'pleasant seat' of Macbeth's castle and Banquo's on 'the temple-haunting martlet', surely a wonderful opening for his trenchant gift of dramatic irony.

While the revision was directed largely to the music, three scenes were given new words and actions; the introduction of Lady Macbeth at the end of the cauldron scene is an unconvincing deviation from the play. The new pieces of the 1865 score are Lady Macbeth's aria in the first scene of Act II, the cauldron ballet, the vengeance duet at the end of Act III, the chorus of Scottish exiles (replacing a not negligible chorus on the same words), and the whole of the final scene from the cry of women announcing Lady Macbeth's death. In the first and last of these contexts shoddy stuff was replaced by great music, though Verdi scarcely rose to the 'Tomorrow and tomorrow and tomorrow' speech. Elsewhere he made detailed improvements to the vocal line and harmony, strengthened accompaniment figures and eliminated flashy ornament, chiefly in the murder-duet (rewritten and much improved at the end), the appearances of Banquo's ghost, the scene of the Apparitions and the coda of the Birnam Wood duet and chorus. But a comparison of the two scores provides two surprises: so much of the best music, including the gem of the whole opera, the sleep-walking scene, belongs to 1847; and so many of the poorer features were allowed to survive the revision. These include the *buffo* march — more municipal than regal and almost worthy of Sousa — for the entry of Duncan, the chorus of Banquo's murderers, absurd alike in its verbal, musical and

dramatic aspects, and most of the Witches' music. Verdi not
only treated the Witches as a comedy chorus but increased
their prominence to the detriment of the drama, giving them a
superfluous number at the end of the first scene.[1]

Nevertheless, the good far outweighs the bad, and it
springs directly from Verdi's contact with Shakespeare. This
would be clear without the evidence of his letters. Despite its
weak spots the opera does seriously challenge the play in the
stature of the two principals, especially Lady Macbeth, the
realization of the patriotic background (which came naturally
to Verdi), and the screwing-up of suspense at moments of
climax — the dagger speech, the murder-duet, the entry of
Banquo's murderer during the banquet and later of his ghost,
and many others. Verdi achieves this partly by dramatic
declamation, still more by intensification of the harmony and
darkening of the orchestral colour. The scoring of the show
of eight kings, built on Shakespeare's own specification of wind
instruments (Hautboys), and of the sleep-walking scene is
extraordinarily imaginative. Other well-judged strokes are
the strident trumpets of the fugue during the battle, the spoken
word when Lady Macbeth reads the letter (repeated in a
similar scene in 'La Traviata') and the marvellous depiction
of Macbeth's relief after the second disappearance of Banquo's
ghost. These details, even more than the great swinging tunes
of the first two finales, show the impact of Shakespeare raising
Verdi above his current level of inspiration.

We know that he attached enormous importance to 'Macbeth' — he told Barezzi he loved it above all his other works —
and its manner of presentation. He saw the play in London
with Macready as Macbeth and wrote there for costume
designs, besides doing a little research into Scottish history.
At a time when *bel canto* singing was regarded as the chief
justification of opera he not only chose a subject without love
interest, but rejected certain singers because their voices were
too good. He wrote Macbeth's part for a baritone who sang
notoriously out of tune, and wanted Lady Macbeth to have
'a voice rough, hoarse and gloomy' with 'something diabolical
about it' and 'not to sing at all'. He continually urged both

[1] In a Rome libretto dated 1852 the Witches' parts are entirely rewritten for
gipsies, who in the first scene tell Macbeth's fortune with the aid of a pack of
cards. In Act III Macbeth drinks the contents of the cauldron to make himself
clairvoyant, and the words of the Apparitions appear written on the wall, as at
Belshazzar's feast. Was this the result of the Roman censorship?

artists to study the words and let the music come of itself. No wonder he was furious when a Paris critic in 1865 charged him with ignorance of Shakespeare.

One lost 'Macbeth' opera deserves mention for its incredible libretto. This is Lauro Rossi's 'Biorn' (London 1877), in which the action for some reason was transferred to Norway. The critic Joseph Bennett, who described the first night in his memoirs, could not decide whether to take it seriously or as a joke. The Witches became Norns, and Lady Macbeth (re-named Editha) had a scene in bed. The librettist, one Frank Marshall, gave the chorus some choice comments on the action, of which the following are samples. Lady Macbeth's attendants, when she enters reading the letter:

> If we only had a letter
> We might ponder o'er it too.

Macbeth's servants, roused by the murder:

> What means this noise? O say, O say,
> Why wake us at this time of day?

The women, weary of watching their sleepless mistress:

> When shall we know the sweet delight
> Of sleeping well for one whole night?

Of all little-known Shakespeare operas Bloch's 'Macbeth' most deserves professional revival. It is an early work and not a masterpiece, since the composer's style was not fully formed; it exhibits certain mannerisms and the undigested influence of Debussy and Puccini, especially in the orchestral interludes. But it has atmosphere, strength and a grandeur not unworthy of the play, due chiefly to its convincing treatment of leitmotive as a dramatic and structural principle. It is the one opera in which the Wagnerian method is applied successfully to Shakespeare. This more than makes up for any lack of melodic distinction. The solo voice parts are mostly rhetorical; but the ensembles and choruses, especially the substantial finales to all three acts, supply plenty of contrast and energy.

The libretto leaves out nothing essential and preserves much of the original language. Its obvious defect is that the cauldron scene containing the First Apparition's warning against Macduff comes *after* the murder of the latter's wife and children and so produces a partial anticlimax. The Second

Apparition is omitted, and so are the watchers in the sleep-walking scene. Banquo's ghost makes a third appearance when Macbeth turns to embrace his wife after the guests have left the banquet, and it is this that seals his resolve to shed more blood.

Like Verdi, Bloch is particularly successful at generating tension. His principal means are a very flexible rhythmic style, with constant changes of time, and a resourceful handling of ostinato. He uses irregular or halting metres with great effect — 11/8 when Lady Macbeth taunts Macbeth with fear before the murder, 7/8 during the murder, 5/4 in much of the cauldron scene. Many of the most dramatic scenes are founded on ostinatos : Macduff's discovery of the murder of his family, the sleep-walking (very spare in texture) and the magnificent ensemble after the murder, based on a two-note bass figure that constantly changes the direction of the harmony. The set pieces are all successful except the Porter's song, where a simpler, less consciously grotesque type of irony was required.

The leitmotives have a strong individual character, marked by distinctive rhythms and melodic intervals ; many of them, like those of 'The Ring', can be identified by rhythm alone. Here Bloch, unlike so many composers, has absorbed the true lesson of Wagner. They are often linked and combined and assume a Protean power of changing into each other, thus lending themselves to constant development by distortion or variation and the expression of a wide range of emotions and ideas, direct, oblique or symbolical. Macduff's theme with its syncopated rising fifth serves with equal aptness for the idyllic calm of his family life (a passage of great lyrical beauty) and his fiery revolt against tyranny. The figure first heard in the orchestra at the Witches' words 'Thou shalt be King here-after' illumines countless references to 'the imperial theme' in connection with Macbeth or Banquo's issue, blazes forth in the major when Macbeth enters as King in Act II, and forms a superbly ironical background to the show of eight kings. Still more eloquent is the phrase associated with peace and innocence, first heard when Duncan comments on the sweet air of Macbeth's castle and haunting Macbeth's later references to his lost peace of mind ('After life's fitful fever he sleeps well', 'I have lived long enough', 'Life's but a walking shadow'). At least five leitmotives are interlaced in this last speech, and so expressively that the composer's footnote 'As though here were embodied the philosophical essence of the drama' is not strictly necessary : it is all in the music. Sometimes the Wagnerian allusion is explicit, for example in the final fragmentation of the heroic motive of Macbeth the soldier (like that of Wotan's spear), and structurally in the Prologue (equivalent to I. 3 of the play), a powerful symphonic tissue based on three or four motives. One stroke of acute dramatic perception lights up a central feature of the play. When at the end of the banquet scene Macbeth assumes the leading role ('It will have blood ; they say blood will have blood') he appropriates his wife's motive (cruelty) ; in the sleep-walking scene ('What's done cannot be undone') she borrows one of his, associated hitherto with his guilty conscience.

'Macbeth', Bloch's only opera, reveals dramatic gifts of a very high order. Its original failure, said to be due to jealousies in the Paris cast, prevented the realization of a projected 'King Lear' with the same librettist. Something of rare price may have been lost here. Both *Hamlet* and *King Lear* have tempted the angels, but only lesser beings have rushed in, mostly in Italy and France, with results that could have been predicted. Some of the librettos nevertheless have considerable interest. Two of the best librettists of the nineteenth century tried conclusions with *Hamlet*.

Romani's work, written for Mercadante, is a wild melodrama whose links with Shakespeare are tenuous. His preface points out that the story is the *Oresteia* of the north, and he modelled the three chief characters on Orestes, Clytemnestra and Aegisthus. Amelia (Ophelia) is the daughter of Claudius, who, though she loves Hamlet, promises her to Aldano Prince of Norway to cement a political alliance. Hamlet has gone abroad on his father's murder and is thought to be dead. But he returns secretly, tormented by the Ghost's order to avenge crime with crime and uncertain if the whole thing is not a product of his own fevered imagination ; in his first scene he compares himself with Orestes in the grip of the Furies. He proclaims himself the rightful king, thereby splitting the court into two factions, and his mother surrenders the crown. This provokes a violent quarrel with Claudius, who conspires with Aldano to kill Hamlet. In the first finale, which anticipates a famous scene in 'Simon Boccanegra', Hamlet orders Claudius to swear publicly that he is guiltless of the murder ; the sky darkens, the Ghost appears, and Gertrude offers herself as a sacrifice to the Eumenides. Later Hamlet presses her to take a similar oath on the ashes of his father, but when she cannot do so he pities and tries to comfort her. Claudius's partisans are on the point of murdering Hamlet when a subterranean voice stops them, and they abruptly change sides. At the end Hamlet kills Claudius; Gertrude forgives him as the avenger of his father, begs him to forgive her, and falls dead. The second (and last) act is considerably weaker than the first, which brings the action to a climax in which nothing is resolved — a common situation at this period. Mercadante's music appears not to have survived. The part of Hamlet was sung by a woman.

If a 'Hamlet' opera in the style of 'Ernani' could be taken seriously, that of Antonio Buzzolla, composed in the same year as Verdi's 'Macbeth',[1] might have some claims. The librettist, Peruzzini, copies Romani in fathering Ophelia on Claudius, bestowing the name Norcesto on Horatio, and in several other details, but he keeps closer to the play, at any rate to start with. Polonius, a kind of Iago to Claudius, and Gertrude are both privy to the murder. Gertrude, torn between her son and her paramour, tries to break free from Claudius, but he blackmails her by pointing out that poison was her choice. Act I ends with the Ghost's midnight appearance on the battlements and Hamlet's oath, enforced by its commands from the cellarage. In Act II Gertrude concedes that public affairs must take precedence over private anxiety and, in a big concerted finale, is on the point of accepting marriage and coronation with Claudius when Hamlet asks if there is nothing on her conscience and drops hints about poison. Claudius declares him obviously mad and puts him in Polonius's charge. When Hamlet suddenly begs Ophelia to marry him, she too doubts his sanity. Gertrude, terrified that Hamlet may know too much, dismisses the council without giving her hand to Claudius, who begins to plot further crimes with Polonius, while Hamlet, ignoring Norcesto's advice to mask his feelings, rejoices that vengeance is nigh.

These two acts, with the chief characters powerfully developed, are superior to anything Piave was offering Verdi at this time. But the last two are a jumble of stock situations. Act III introduces an absurd compound of a *brindisi* and a

---

[1] Varesi, Verdi's first Macbeth, was Buzzolla's Claudius.

conspiracy: Claudius, Polonius and their party plan the death of Hamlet, and, with a dagger in one hand and a wineglass in the other, contrive to draw lots as to who shall do the deed. As in the similar scene in 'Un ballo in maschera', we can be sure that the lot will fall on the baritone (Claudius). They invite the Ghost to join the party, whereupon a mysterious subterranean noise alarms them; Claudius begins to have sinister presentiments, while the chorus repeat the *brindisi* in a different rhythm. Meanwhile Gertrude in the mausoleum asks pardon of her husband's shade. Hamlet forces a confession from her and is about to stab her when he fancies he hears his father's voice bidding him be merciful. He accepts her as a victim rather than a criminal and turns his attention to Claudius, whose conspiracy has been penetrated by Norcesto. Claudius, cornered, determines to drag down Gertrude for betraying him; warning her that it will be her turn soon, he stabs himself.

Buzzolla's music is by no means ineffective, especially in the slower movements and the first two finales. It owes a great deal to early Verdi and the Donizetti of 'La Favorite', and tends to break down at the same points; the cabalettas vary between the comically jaunty and the frankly awful (Hamlet's address to his dagger early in Act IV). But the opera has a rude vigour, and the scene on the battlements, with the Ghost confined to two notes, is, within the limits of the idiom, distinctly impressive.

Faccio's 'Amleto' also has a good battlements scene, with five solo cellos and periodical interruptions from a distant brass band as Claudius's coronation festivities continue inside the castle. All the music, as one would expect from a distinguished opera conductor, has a strong sense of the theatre, but the melodies are a pale reflection of Verdi and too weak to support the weight placed upon them, especially in the ensembles. By far the most interesting feature is the superb libretto, the first ever written by Boito, admirable alike in language, construction and handling of the play. Every step is clearly motivated, every character developed in action. As in 'Otello', Boito reconciles Shakespeare with operatic conventions without debasing him, and it is astonishing how little he needs to omit or alter. All the big scenes — the mousetrap play, the closet, Ophelia's funeral — fall easily into place, and so do the soliloquies 'O that this too too solid flesh would

melt' (at the beginning of Act I) and 'To be or not to be'.
There is no model for the unorthodox *brindisi* in the coronation
scene, led by Claudius, with Gertrude, Hamlet and Ophelia
each contributing a stanza (the last two aside) and the King
at intervals repeating his first words: 'Requie ai defunti',
dutifully answered by the courtiers with 'E gloria al re!';
but it expresses the situation and the characters with singular
economy and irony. The chief differences from the play are
that the Ghost does not mention Gertrude on either of his
appearances, and Boito actually shows Ophelia's death (as
described by Shakespeare), preceding and accompanying it
with distant rumbles of revolt against Claudius. There is a
telling detail during Claudius's monologue in the closet scene:
he tries to repeat the Lord's Prayer, but repeatedly breaks down
and flies in terror. At the first production the last act followed
the play almost exactly; when the opera was revived for a
single disastrous performance in 1871, a much shorter and
weaker end with only one death, that of Claudius, was
substituted. We can only regret that Verdi did not set this
libretto.

Aristide Hignard's 'Hamlet' takes in even more of the
play than Faccio's — too much, in fact (though the composer
did not set the full libretto as printed); virtually the entire
cast appears, including Rosencrantz, Guildenstern, Osric and
Fortinbras. Much of the text is a literal translation. Hamlet
has an air with the refrain: 'Fragilité! ton nom est femme'.
The changes are trivial and sometimes amusing: in Hamlet's
description of Claudius's feast (I. 4) 'the kettledrum and
trumpet' are replaced by 'des femmes sans pudeur', a necessary component of all French operatic orgies. This opera was
composed before that of Ambroise Thomas, on whose account
it could not be produced for twenty years: hence the bitter
tone of the librettist's preface. His work, though pedestrian
by comparison with Boito's, shows a reverence for Shakespeare
astonishing in the France of the Second Empire. According
to Pougin's edition of Clément's *Dictionnaire lyrique*, the music
was on a new plan, recitative being replaced by a broad
declamation as used later by Massenet. Hignard was known
as a fertile composer of drawing-room romances and waltzes.

Thomas's opera, still performed in France, is a compound
of the impressive and the deplorable. The libretto contracts
the plot and alters it in important particulars, notably Hamlet's

relations with Polonius and his family, and the conclusion. Polonius's only scene is new, a short dialogue with Claudius in which he reveals his complicity in the murder. Hamlet overhears this; hence his spurning of Ophelia. There is no combat with foils and no poison in the last act; the Ghost simply turns up at Ophelia's funeral, orders Hamlet to kill Claudius and mount the throne, despatches Gertrude into a nunnery, and having done his duty as *deux ex machina* vanishes. Much of the text is the characteristic pabulum of French grand opera, but a few episodes — the first entry of the Ghost on the battlements, the play and closet scenes and the 'To be or not to be' soliloquy — preserve something of the flavour and even the language of Shakespeare. They also contain by far the best music. The first, introduced by the E flat minor prelude to the opera, with fanfares from inside the castle and the chimes of midnight cutting across the harmony, is highly dramatic. The play scene has many points of interest, the ironic recitative for solo saxophone (its first appearance in opera), the strong foretaste of 'L'Arlésienne' in the pantomime music (Bizet arranged the vocal score of 'Hamlet') and the big Verdian ensemble at the end, in which Hamlet's recall of the drinking-song from the previous scene is a brilliant touch. There is some striking harmonic detail at the end of 'To be or not to be', and the closet scene has an admirable prayer for Claudius and another powerful scene for the Ghost.

Elsewhere Thomas's courage, or his artistic integrity, seems to have failed. He wrote the opera for the Swedish soprano Christine Nilsson. Hence the curious distribution of the voices (Hamlet is a baritone, there is no important tenor, and only Ophelia has a high tessitura), the inclusion of Scandinavian motives, among them an almost Griegian ballade in the mad scene, and the expansion of Ophelia's part beyond the demands of the drama. Her music is wholly conventional — and quite indistinguishable from Gertrude's; their consecutive and equally Gounodesque solos at the beginning of Act II could almost be interchanged. Having devised one or two good motives, especially that for Hamlet's first entry, Thomas omitted to use them consistently, perhaps through fear of being branded a Wagnerian heretic. His style veers unpredictably between Gounod (especially in the love music) and Rossini (the players, the drinking-song, the Danish March and most of the ballet). The first scene is an odd mixture of

M

the grandiose, the succulent and the flippant, represented respectively by Meyerbeer, Gounod and Offenbach. In its early years the opera was damned for its virtues and exalted as a great tragic masterpiece for its lapses. Sutherland Edwards (1881) regarded the piffling fourth act, which contains nothing but the ballet and the mad scene, as the sole justification for the work, dismissing the fifth as superfluous and the first three as 'in a great measure irrelevant'. Clément's essay (*c.* 1869), using Thomas as a cudgel to belabour Wagner, is a historical curiosity : he regretted that the librettists had seen fit to preserve 'To be or not to be' and the 'odious' grave-diggers' scene ('which will always be intolerable in the eyes of people of taste') and considered the mad scene an improvement on Shakespeare.

*King Lear* presents an even stiffer challenge than *Hamlet*, as a glance at one opera, that of Vito Frazzi, sufficiently indicates. The effort to include as much as possible of a singularly rich and intricate plot forced the librettist into desperate measures. He left out the vital first scene, in which Lear divides his kingdom, and the entire character of Cordelia except as a posthumous voice at the very end of the opera, where she sings a few lines from Shakespeare's Act IV. Edmund's deception of Gloucester (I. 2) is likewise only mentioned, and we never learn the ultimate fate of Goneril and Regan. Even thus truncated, the opera is very long and devoid of lyrical expansion. The music, in a post-*verismo* idiom, has a certain power of creating atmosphere, but does not begin to match the richness and subtlety of the play's characterization. It is heavily orchestrated, with six additional horns and four trumpets behind the scenes. The motives, though sometimes ingeniously transformed, lack pungency, and the score is too turgid to take wing.

There remains *Othello*, which has inspired three operas, two of them by composers of genius. Until the appearance of Verdi's masterpiece Rossini's enjoyed a high reputation, by no means wholly undeserved. Its uneven quality reflects that of the libretto ; like Berlioz and Thomas, Rossini responded by some instinct to the scenes based closely on Shakespeare, and much of his last act survives comparison with Verdi's. This cannot be said of the first two, which the librettist turned into a conventional *opera seria* plot spun from Shakespeare's Act I. Othello never leaves Venice, and Cassio is omitted. Iago, a rejected suitor of Desdemona, is not married to Emilia, who becomes a colourless confidante. Roderigo is the typical scorned lover, who fights a duel with Othello, Elmiro (Braban-tio) a still more orthodox heavy father with a powerful curse, on which the first two finales reach their climax. He tries to trick Desdemona into marriage with Roderigo, and she does not leave his house till halfway through Act II. Othello him-self, rather sketchily presented as a soldier in the first scene, is little more than a touchy tenor with an ungovernable temper. He has no love music with Desdemona, and no scene with her before the murder — a strange omission in an opera of this period (was it the outcome of a perverted respect for Shake-speare?). The handkerchief is replaced by an insufficiently addressed love-letter from Desdemona to Othello, which is intercepted by Elmiro; Iago gets hold of it and has no diffi-culty in convincing Othello that it was meant for Roderigo. The last act, though weakened by the absence of an earlier love scene to which the unhappy pair can look back, suddenly adheres to the play, with two additions: a storm at the climax (transferred from Shakespeare's second act), which is accept-able, and a snatch of tune from a gondolier in the distance just before the 'Willow' song, which is a stroke of genius. The words are a quotation from Dante's *Inferno*, Canto V, about the pain of recalling past happiness in time of grief ('Nessun maggior dolore/Che recordarsi del tempo felice/Nella miseria'); Rossini inserted them against the wish of his librettist.

The music strikes us today as an incongruous mixture of the serious and the comic. The lapses into Neapolitan *buffo* style are most disconcerting at Othello's first and last appear-ances, in the second finale, and in the murder duet, which employs the same instrumental crescendo motive as Basilio's 'La calunnia' in 'The Barber of Seville', composed earlier the same year. But this piece of laziness is not typical of the whole opera, which in some respects was a work of innovation. It is the first Rossini opera, and one of the earliest in Italy, to accompany the recitatives with full orchestra in place of the keyboard; the scoring, especially for woodwind, is exception-ally rich; the tragic end was unorthodox in 1816 (so much so that it had to be modified in a number of revivals); and Rossini is beginning to transcend the *buffo* idiom and create a style capable of genuine tragic emotion. The powerfully-concentrated first finale, based on organic use of ostinato figures and abrupt modulations, contains many suggestions of Verdi's 'Macbeth' (in the beautiful slow quintet), and of 'Rigoletto'. The duet for Iago and Otello in Act II is also echoed in 'Rigoletto',[1] and Verdi's 'Willow' song may owe something to Rossini's.

Desdemona is by far the most convincing character. Rossini could respond to the pathos of her situation more easily than to the villainy of Iago or the jealousy of Othello. Almost all her music is not only beautiful but profoundly expressive : the chromaticism and hesitant rhythm of her duet with Emilia in Act I, her E minor aria with its agitated syncopation in Act II, and most of all the exquisite 'Willow' song and prayer, which may have suggested the similarly placed 'Ave Maria' in Verdi's opera. In this context the Gondolier's few haunting bars suddenly burst through the barrier between the ephemeral and the universal — and belie the legend that there was nothing romantic in Rossini. The three chief male parts are all tenors, though Rossini later adapted Iago's music for a baritone. Roderigo has a beautiful aria, but none of them comes within measurable distance of Shakespeare.

Boito's 'Otello' is less perfect than his 'Falstaff', but *Othello* was a far harder play to tackle. It is so rich in character, incident and overtone that much is inevitably lost, and it is absurd to claim that what remains has the full range of Shakespeare. Boito concentrated on the three central characters. Very little is left of Emilia and Roderigo, not much of Cassio, and nothing at all of Bianca. They play their parts, but as little more than shadows of their original selves. Iago, while retaining his smooth human cunning, is nearer an incarnation of the devil, thanks to his famous 'Credo', but he remains a theatrical figure of immense potency. Boito, perhaps wisely, omitted his suspicions about Othello's misconduct with Emilia, which in the play sound like a pretext ; it is difficult to see why he also suppressed the deadly suggestion in Iago's line 'She did deceive her father, marrying you' (III. 3), even if Desdemona's father had to be excluded. Othello and Desdemona are essentially unchanged, but the intense compression to which the plot is subjected modifies the emphasis. The key points are the speed with which Othello's jealousy grows from nothing to an unshakeable conviction of Desdemona's guilt,

---

[1] The tune of the cabaletta, where the resemblance is closest, had been used in an earlier Rossini opera, 'Torvaldo e Dorliska'.

and her tactless reiteration of her plea for Cassio. Shakespeare by very careful timing makes both seem credible. Boito encompasses the former in one short act, and facilitates it by two clever modifications, the introduction of the choral serenade to Desdemona, which supplies contrast and a sense of passing time, and the transposition of Desdemona's first plea for Cassio, so that it takes place after, not before, Othello's suspicions have been fully roused by Iago. But her pleas are much harder to swallow in the opera than in the play, because so much of the intervening matter has been cut and Boito makes the last of them, after the entry of Lodovico and the ambassadors, more explicit. When Othello in Act III of the opera denounces his wife as 'that cunning whore of Venice' (a conflation of two scenes in the play), it is hard to believe that she could possibly take his demands for the handkerchief as 'a trick to put me from my suit'.

Nevertheless the libretto is a staggering piece of craftsman-ship. Boito's decision to skip the first act of the play and begin the opera in Cyprus gave him the advantage of the storm to project the psychological as well as the physical background, to show the elements as it were in league with human passions; but it put him to the need of unfolding the past along with the present. In a few lines he and Verdi established Othello as a great soldier so effectively that we never question it — and the entire opera depends on this, for the tragedy lies in the extent of his fall. The love-duet, so far from being a con-ventional insertion, is supremely functional: it not only explains the origin of this strange marriage but supplies a key to all that follows by revealing the quality of the relationship that is so soon to be undermined, a deep spiritual love and no mere sensual passion. Here, and in three other places, Boito made the most skilful use of material from Shakespeare's first act.

In this complex manipulation of set pieces — for revelation of character, development of plot, lyrical expansion and structural design — the opera is unique. *Othello* is less prodigal of such opportunities than almost any other Shakespeare play. Yet Boito and Verdi not only introduced a great many, but have fooled later commentators into supposing that they did nothing of the sort. While 'Otello' conveys an impression of effortless flow, it makes copious use of forms native to the tradition that Verdi inherited from Rossini and Donizetti: in Act I the storm and bonfire choruses, Iago's *brindisi* and the love-duet; in Act II Iago's 'Credo', the serenade, the quartet and the duet of vengeance; in Act III Othello's monologue 'Dio mi potevi scagliar'' (not a soliloquy in the play), the trio for the three men and the extended finale; in Act IV Desdemona's 'Willow' song and prayer and Othello's final solo. All these have earlier operatic parallels, and even the several dialogues (they can hardly be called duets) between Othello and Desdemona and Othello and Iago can be linked with the tradition. Yet with the partial exception of the Act III finale none of them holds a *tableau* in the old romantic manner. All the time the action is moving forward and the music is reflecting it. The *brindisi*, a linear descendant of Lady Macbeth's, exposes Iago's character, his objectives and the details of his plot against Othello. The quartet develops all four characters in different directions and, with the dropping, picking up and theft of the handkerchief, presents several events simultaneously with their underlying motives. The early stages of the serenade and the Act III finale are dovetailed into the whispered machinations of Iago and Othello for trapping Desdemona, thus serving the interests of economy, dramatic irony and continuity all at once. In the trio we watch Iago convincing the hidden Othello of Desdemona's guilt by engaging Cassio in a bantering conversation about Bianca, while every bar of the music carries a double dose of dramatic irony as well as its direct meaning for Cassio. The solos are so intimately linked to the dramatic action and so concentrated in expression and design (most of them based on a free use of ostinato figures in the orchestra) that we scarcely think of them as arias.

The finale of Act III deserves special mention out of justice to Boito, who rewrote the words three or four times, on one occasion to gratify a suggestion of Verdi's which he knew to be misconceived. Verdi wanted the act to end with an attack by the Turks, an offstage battle, and a curtain with Desdemona alone on the stage praying for Othello's victory. Boito supplied all this, and only when Verdi asked his opinion pointed out that it would destroy the psychology of the last act.[1] The present finale is less static than it appears, since Iago is urging Othello and Roderigo to explicit and violent action, and it contains more subtlety of detail than can possibly be conveyed in performance: all seven soloists and the male and female

---

[1] Walker, pp. 478-9. The facts have been suppressed in the Italian biographies.

chorus are simultaneously singing different sets of words. After this it is fitting that the act should end with one of the most superb *coups de théâtre* in all opera : the maddened Othello falls down in a fit (Boito transferred this from an earlier scene), and while the chorus and people offstage sing the praises of the Lion of Venice Iago spurns his body with his foot and cries : 'Ecco il Leone !'

Verdi originally wished to exclude the chorus altogether, but when Boito sent him the words of the serenade he replied : 'What a splash of light amid so much gloom !' He welcomed the 'Credo' as 'most powerful and wholly Shakespearean'. This judgment is open to dispute. Verdi was fascinated by Iago, whose name was to be the opera's original title, and whose physical appearance he discussed in detail in some interesting letters. His musical characterization is masterly. The opera has no leitmotives — though the two returns of the love-duet in Act IV, when Othello kisses Desdemona before strangling her and when he kills himself, are perhaps the most moving of all examples of the simple reminiscence motive — but certain characteristic details, low trills on the voice and in the orchestra, triplet accompaniment figures and sinister chromatic shading at the cadences (for instance in the *brindisi*) bind Iago's music into an overwhelming personification of evil. Yet it can be extraordinarily beautiful at the same time, as in his enquiry of Othello whether Cassio knew Desdemona in the early days of their love, his description of Cassio's dream, and the opening of the trio in which he questions Cassio about Bianca. The music of this scene, especially the scherzo 'Questa è una ragna', is astonishingly like 'Falstaff'.

The wonderful lyrical beauty of Desdemona's music quite conquers our impatience with her stupidity. One tiny detail, her spontaneous echo of the theme of the serenade, gives a key to her character, which lacks all guile. She first pleads for Cassio ('Tu gli perdona') with an unconscious but revealing quotation from the 'Agnus Dei' of Verdi's 'Requiem'. The quartet, the scene with Othello early in Act III and the finale of that act each begin with a phrase of ravishing tenderness from her. Her music in the last act is beyond criticism. Its utter simplicity conceals much artifice; both in the 'Willow' song and the 'Ave Maria' it depends on a very subtle manipulation of rhythm and phrase-length.

Othello by contrast might have been merely repulsive ;

but Verdi never forgets his heroic quality, which blazes forth at intervals from his opening 'Esultate!' to the sudden cry 'Oh Gloria!' in his final monologue, and reveals his agony in the distortion of phrases associated with other characters, which carry their old overtones and somehow retain our sympathy for him. The triplet accompaniment figure of 'Dio mi potevi scagliar' recalls Iago's 'Credo'. His denunciation of Desdemona as a whore twists the gentle phrase with which she greeted him a few minutes earlier. His last speech is introduced in the orchestra by a throbbing chordal repetition associated with Desdemona's 'Buona notte' at the beginning of the act. Most of the solo passages, including Othello's two big monologues, the 'Credo' and the 'Ave Maria', begin with the reiteration of a single note by the voice while the orchestra reveals the emotional leaven working within.

'Otello' is one of the very few operas in which everything is in perfect balance — music and drama, voice and orchestra, arioso and set number. Although this may suggest a cool approach, the outstanding feature of the music is its emotional intensity. Wherever one looks there is something exceptional : the scoring, in which every instrument from the guitar to the bass drum, the organ to the cor anglais, leaves a print on the memory, the rhythmic energy of the instrumental bass, the occasional very bold harmony (Iago's warning against jealousy, his description of Cassio's dream), and the variety and power of the cadences, whether in those titanic gestures that conclude the first three acts or as a means of punctuating the arioso sections. Here, as in 'Falstaff', Verdi's resource is wonderful and multifarious. The lilting cadence figure that runs through the scene for Iago and Cassio at the beginning of Act II is not only exquisite in itself; its effect is redoubled by the fact that we never quite know when it is coming. The process is still more eloquent in Act IV, where again and again the mere placing of a cadence (perfect or interrupted) produces an overpowering emotional impact, for example at Desdemona's 'Son mesta tanto, tanto!', 'Povera Barbara!', and most of all when she calls Emilia back for that last heart-breaking 'Addio!' — surely the perfect musical equivalent for those phrases of almost unbearable simplicity with which Shakespeare adorns his scenes of tragic climax.

This is unquestionably the greatest opera based on any of Shakespeare's tragedies, and if Boito was compelled to subtract something from the original, Verdi has so made up the deficiency that we are not conscious of any falling from the loftiest standards. We can only echo Boito, most sensitive of librettists, when he wrote to Verdi in the early stages of the composition : 'One can't escape one's destiny, and by a law of intellectual affinity that tragedy of Shakespeare's is predestined for you'.

# Shakespeare in the Concert Hall

BY

ROGER FISKE

IT will be my concern to deal here with concert music inspired by Shakespeare's plays — overtures, for instance; incidental music that has outlived the production for which it was written; and ballets based on the plots of the plays. The quantity of this music is astonishingly large, and only a fraction of it can be mentioned. I hope, however, to include everything that has been both published and recorded, together with a handful of other works that seem to me of unusual interest.

Early in the Romantic period Mendlessohn and Berlioz wrote the first and arguably the best of all concert music based on Shakespeare's plays, and I have given them a section to themselves. In the lists that follow, timings, in minutes, are added to indicate the scale of the works; an asterisk indicates that incidental music was added later for a theatre production:

1826, Mendelssohn: Overture, 'A Midsummer Night's Dream' * (11½)
1830, Berlioz: Fantasia, 'The Tempest' (part of 'Lélio') (14½)
1831, Berlioz: Overture, 'King Lear' (14)
1839, Berlioz: Symphony, 'Romeo and Juliet' (91)
1848, Berlioz: Two short 'Hamlet' pieces (part of 'Tristia') (7 + 7)

In the second half of the Romantic period, and of the century, Shakespeare music was written in very much greater quantities, but usually with less success. It was stereotyped into the descriptive overture:

1851, Schumann: Overture, 'Julius Caesar' (8)
1858, Liszt: Symphonic Poem, 'Hamlet' (14)
1858, Smetana: Symphonic Poem, 'Richard III' (13)
1859, Balakirev: Overture, 'King Lear' * (11)
1869, Tchaikovsky: Fantasy Overture, 'Romeo and Juliet' (20)
1873, Tchaikovsky: Fantasy, 'The Tempest' (23)
1875, Svendsen: Fantasy, 'Romeo and Juliet' (12)
1888, Tchaikovsky: Fantasy Overture, 'Hamlet' * (18)

177

1888, Strauss : Tone Poem, 'Macbeth' (19)
1891, Dvořák : Overture, 'Othello' (17)

In our own century the spate has dried to a trickle, and there is but one work worth adding; it ranks with the very best :

1913, Elgar : Symphonic Study, 'Falstaff' (33)

I can detect no difference in method or scope between the overtures in the above lists and the symphonic poems or fantasies. One might expect the latter to tell their story in more detail, but that is not the case. Apart from Berlioz's 'Romeo and Juliet' and Elgar's 'Falstaff', which have obvious symphonic aspirations, the other works listed above are roughly similar in plan and in degree of descriptiveness. All can be regarded as symphonic poems.

### 1. MENDELSSOHN AND BERLIOZ

The one-movement theatre overture was established on the Continent by about 1780, but overtures to operas and plays were seldom or never descriptive until after 1800. Any Handel overture would do equally well before any Handel opera. Mozart tied some of his later opera overtures to what followed by anticipating a theme later to be sung, but none of his overtures could be called descriptive. The earliest descriptive overtures in the modern repertoire are by Beethoven, and two of them, 'Coriolan' (1807) and 'Egmont' (1810), were written for plays and not operas. In these, anticipatory quotation was impossible, and the only way Beethoven could tie his music to what followed was by making it reflect the actual plot. 'Coriolan' was written not for Shakespeare's *Coriolanus*, but for a play on the same theme by the Viennese court poet H. J. Collin; in fact, it would be equally suited to Shakespeare's tragedy. Like all classical overtures it is in sonata form and scarcely distinguishable in plan from the opening movement of a symphony. The first subject is angry and intractable, and clearly represents Coriolanus himself. The second offers a picture of Volumnia pleading, her mounting anxiety expressed by repetitions of the pleading phrase ever a tone higher. At the end of the overture we hear Coriolanus relent; his theme gradually loses its strength and subsides into quiet acquiescence. Thus the music makes a suitable overture to this particular story, and would lose its effect if played before any other. A new concept is creeping into music. A theatre overture is no longer a mere accompaniment to the shuffling of late-comers. It is functional, being intended to prepare the audience for what follows. From now on, the tunes of a theatre overture and their development must reflect the dramatic action; if they do not, the overture is an irrelevance, and there is no point in playing it.

With one possible and unimportant exception, all Beethoven's overtures were composed for theatrical performances, though they were being repeated at concerts soon after they were written. So far as I can discover, the first descriptive overture specifically intended for a concert rather than a dramatic entertainment was Mendelssohn's 'A Midsummer Night's Dream'.

This landmark both in descriptive overtures and in Shakespeare music was the work of a seventeen-year-old prodigy, and it began almost as a family prank. Mendelssohn and his adored sister Fanny had seen the play in Berlin and read it together with enthusiasm in the Schlegel-Tieck translation. About this time Mendelssohn was finishing his astonishing Octet for strings, of which the Scherzo has a fairy flavour that possibly resulted from his new enthusiasm for Shakespeare. The experience gained in the writing of it must have been a help when he set himself the agreeable task of translating *A Midsummer Night's Dream* into music. The first version was a piano duet for himself and Fanny to play. He cast the piece in classical sonata form, and yet managed to relate every bar to some character or incident. Indeed, the unprecedently close relationship between music and drama must have provided a lot of fun at the original family performance. Soon he was orchestrating the piano duet with an easy mastery unequalled by any other composer of his generation, and this orchestral version was first played at Stettin in 1827, just a month before Beethoven died. Two years later it had a couple of performances in London, with the twenty-year-old composer conducting.

After four slow magical chords for wind, we hear four themes, one for each group of characters. First, the fairies, who dominate the action; then some grand music for Theseus and Hippolyta, who open it; next an amorous tune for the

lovers; lastly a silly one (with a suggestion of a donkey's bray)
for the rude mechanicals. In the development the fairy music
grows nocturnal and menacing, and it is easy to imagine the
lovers beset by fears in the wood at night. Five minutes from
the start, at bar 335, there is a curious passage consisting of
four slow descending scales; the first three are pizzicato beneath a held *tremolando* note high on the violins. This music
in no way derives from the main themes, and can only be
explained as a description of the four lovers coming one after
the other to the same clearing in the wood, lying down, and
going to sleep. The last of them, Hermia, is allowed a special
touch of dejection. When all are asleep we hear again the
magic chords of the opening, and can imagine Puck applying
the purple juice to the appropriate eyes and making all well.
Immediately Mendelssohn plunges into his classical recap,
but two touches show he has not forgotten the play. The fairy
music is accompanied by uncouth low notes on horn or
ophicleide to suggest Bottom snoring in the arms of Titania,
and the Theseus tune comes last instead of second, for Theseus
is the last mortal to speak. Because Shakespeare has a coda of
fairies, Mendelssohn has one too, and marvellously catches
the candle-lit charm of the closing lines. Just before the magic
chords end the overture, we hear the Theseus theme delight-
fully transformed, no longer noble but drowsy with sleep.

It is likely that some readers will be disturbed by the
paragraph above, for the belief that there is something dis-
tasteful, and even improper, about descriptive music is still
widely held, and I was myself brought up to think absolute
music a much higher form of art. Those who hold this theory
tend to feel that if they like a piece of music it cannot be
descriptive, and they will try to defend their favourites from
what they regard as an accusation. Berlioz enthusiasts, as we
shall see, are especially prone to claim that he can distil the
essence of a story into music without going into details: in
other words, without 'sinking' to descriptive music.

The alleged superiority of absolute music springs from the
idea that it allows more freedom to the composer's inspiration.
But most composers seem to work better under some form
of limitation, and there is no real evidence that self-chosen
limitations inhibit them. Symphonic form is in itself a limitation, and so is the twelve-note system. The words of a song
or an opera allow even less freedom than a descriptive pro-

gramme, and one might add that it is almost impossible to succeed as a song-writer or opera composer without a flair for descriptive music. Schubert and Wagner would not have understood the theory that absolute music is best.

The theory seems to have originated at the turn of the century when Brahms was being raised onto his pedestal by people who felt little enthusiasm for Wagner and Richard Strauss. Almost alone in his generation, Brahms made no attempt to write descriptive music, which therefore seemed to his admirers a low form of art. But very few composers have shown bias against it. It was being written and admired at least as early as the sixteenth century, and both Bach and Handel wrote quantities of it. Its fortunes declined in the Classical period, and boomed again in the Romantic, when there was a reaction against the classical composers' emphasis on the absolute. Mendelssohn managed to integrate, as did perhaps no other composer, a marvellous sense of classical form with a typical romantic's craving for programme music, and, for me at least, the overture to *A Midsummer Night's Dream* is evidence that a literary programme need not preclude the writing of great music.

It is not easy to succeed on two levels, as Mendelssohn did. Plenty of composers have been defeated by the limitation of a programme, just as Chopin was sometimes defeated by the limitations of classical form. The problem can be illustrated by the two orchestral interpretations of *Hamlet* that Liszt and Tchaikovsky composed. Liszt showed great insight into Hamlet's character; the trouble is that what he wrote is not very interesting as music. Tchaikovsky, on the other hand, produced a finer piece of music, but most of it shows little or no comprehension of the play. Thus both are partial failures, though both, in quite different ways, can be enjoyed. Only when a composer fails at both levels, as Schumann did in his overture to *Julius Caesar*, is descriptive music best left on the shelf.

I doubt if Mendelssohn had any vision of a new musical genre when he wrote his Shakespeare overture, but it looks as though he quickly realized the implications, for his 1830 tour of Scotland resulted in a concert overture with no theatrical associations whatever — the 'Hebrides'. The symphonic poem had been established. But for two decades it had only one other notable advocate, the French composer Hector

Berlioz.   Berlioz wrote scarcely any absolute music, and
almost always needed some literary stimulus to start him off.
The story of his excitement when Charles Kemble, youngest
brother of Mrs. Siddons, took a Shakespeare company to Paris
in 1827 has been told many times.   Berlioz developed an almost
frantic enthusiasm both for Shakespeare and for Harriet
Smithson, the Irish actress who played Ophelia and Juliet
and whom he later married.   But his love of Shakespeare was
to prove more lasting.

Berlioz chose *The Tempest* for his first Shakespearean
experiment.   When he wrote it, the English season at the
Odéon was over, the company had returned to London and
Berlioz had temporarily put Harriet out of his mind; in any
case he had so far worshipped her only from afar.   In 1830 his
affections were directed towards a more approachable girl,
Camille Moke, whom he called his Ariel.   Surprisingly, Ariel
was to play no direct part in his *Tempest* music.

It would be difficult to exaggerate the originality of this
piece.   Berlioz at first called it an overture because he did not
know what else to call it, but finally settled for 'Fantaisie'.
Before the first performance, which took place at the same
concert as the first performance of the 'Symphonie fantastique',
he described it in the press as 'an overture divided into four
parts, yet so connected as to form but one piece : the Prologue,
the Storm, the Action, the Dénouement'.   This gives little
idea of the unique design of the work.   Two of its most original
touches are largely responsible for keeping it out of concerts
today.   First, it needs a chorus, which bars it from orchestral
programmes, and secondly, it does not need any bass singers,
which prejudices choral societies against it.   Furthermore, the
score includes two players on one piano, and so far as I know
this is the first use of the piano as an orchestral instrument.
The words are by Berlioz himself, and he chose to write them
in Italian, perhaps because he did not want his French
audience to bother their heads about them.   It was choral
effects that he was after.   The words are sung by a 'Chœur
d'Esprits de l'air' as a sort of farewell epilogue to the play.
The spirits repeat Miranda's name a great many times, and
refer to her 'sposo' and to Caliban ('orrido mostro'), but not
to Prospero.   There is no attempt to tell the story, and no use
is made of Shakespeare's words.   As the composer himself put
it, 'Choruses of airy spirits, fantastically mingled with the

orchestral sound, speak to lovely Miranda in sweet harmonious strains, then to the gross Caliban in menacing tones. And I want the voices of the sylphs to be carried on light clouds of harmony, aglow with the glitter of their wings.' [1] The resulting texture anticipates that of 'Sirènes', the finale of Debussy's 'Nocturnes'.

The Fantasy opens with a spirit chorus accompanied by the upper instruments of the orchestra and the delicious tinklings of the piano duet. Scarcely a note of the music falls below middle C, and the effect is of a floating etherial delicacy. Then comes a purely orchestral storm, with the spirits returning in the dying moments to call Miranda's name in hushed agitation. The third section — the 'Action' — is much the longest. After some preliminary bustling, the orchestra settles down to a very long Italianate tune in six-four, more conventionally melodious than is usual with Berlioz. There is an uncouth 'second subject' that sounds as though it is in five time, and the chorus briefly intervenes to ensure that we recognize Caliban in these strange sounds. The Italianate tune returns, this time in canon, and eventually the chorus, which has had nothing but brief interjections since the Prologue, sings a new common-time version of the Italianate theme. This is ravishingly lovely, and much more characteristic of Berlioz. The tinkle of the piano duet again colours the texture, and the final *pianissimo* farewells to Miranda are exquisite. A loud energetic coda for orchestra alone ends the work.

With all its practical disadvantages, the *Tempest* Fantasia might have had occasional performances if only Berlioz had left it alone. Two years later, after many months in Italy, he returned to Paris and found Harriet Smithson there too. He quickly got up in her honour a concert consisting of the 'Symphonie fantastique' and its sequel, 'Lélio, ou le Retour à la vie', which he too-rapidly concocted especially for the occasion. This consisted of songs and choruses from previous compositions linked by a narrator called Lélio, representing the composer himself. Harriet was lured into the theatre where the concert was given and to her astonishment discovered that both items were inspired by the composer's almost hysterical love for herself.

The 'Symphonie fantastique' is a blazing masterpiece.

[1] From Lélio's narrative.

N

'Lélio' is not. The *Tempest* Fantasia is both the longest item and, with the tenor solo 'Chant de bonheur', the best, and it is tragic that it should be so little known merely because 'Lélio' as a whole is so seldom done.[1]

We must now go back a year or more and follow Berlioz to Italy with his Prix de Rome. In March 1831 he met Mendelssohn in Rome, and for a week or more spent part of each day listening to his talk and piano-playing. Though Mendelssohn was the younger by six years, he was the better-known of the two, Berlioz being still a student. We do not know what Mendelssohn played (we can be sure that Berlioz played nothing, for he was no pianist), nor what he talked about, but we know that Shakespeare was mentioned and, with two such enthusiasts, he was surely mentioned with great frequency. Berlioz later recorded a chance remark of his own to the effect that an exquisite orchestral scherzo could be based on the Queen Mab speech in *Romeo and Juliet*:

> I instantly regretted having put the idea into his head. For several years afterwards I lived in dread that he would carry it out. Luckily he never thought of it.

Now what can have led up to this very remarkable conversation? Composers at that time did not write scherzos on speeches in Shakespeare. Mendelssohn and Berlioz must surely have been talking of the possibilities of Shakespeare in the concert hall. Mendelssohn must have played all or part of his overture to *A Midsummer Night's Dream*, and the fairy music at the beginning would lead quite naturally to the subject of Queen Mab. I believe these conversations played a vital part in Berlioz's development, turning his mind from a generalized approach to Shakespeare towards a more direct kind of descriptive music. I think too that his ambition to translate *Romeo and Juliet* into music originated during these conversations.

His immediate reaction was to read *King Lear* for the first time, which he did early in April, lying in the grass by the Arno at Florence and, as he himself put it, 'writing in ecstasy'.[2]

---

[1] The Edinburgh Festival performance in 1963, the first to be given in public in Britain, revealed that with a good narrator and imaginative production, 'Lélio' is surprisingly effective.

[2] In his *Berlioz and the Romantic Century*, 2 vols. (1950), Barzun gives a confused account of these events, implying that Berlioz met Mendelssohn *after* writing 'King Lear'. But Mendelssohn was not in Rome when Berlioz returned there, and his

By the end of the month he was in Nice, perhaps the least suitable place in Europe in which to write an overture to *King Lear*, but that is where he wrote it. He described the occasion characteristically and at length in his autobiography :

> I spent a whole month in Nice wandering about in the orange groves, bathing in the sea, sleeping in the heather on the hills above Villefranche, and looking down from those wonderful heights on the ships silently coming and going far below. I live entirely alone. I write the overture to *King Lear*. I sing. I believe in a God.

'King Lear' is a splendid overture, though not, I think, wholly successful as a translation of Shakespeare into music. One must remember that Berlioz had never seen the play on the stage, and had only just met it in print. The few writers who have considered the overture have not found a clear delineation of the plot in the music, and the best of all Berlioz writers, Jacques Barzun, would not wish to find such a thing, for he is ever anxious to defend his hero from the 'accusation' of writing descriptively. Nevertheless I think Berlioz tried to depict the play in some detail. The overture begins with a powerful recitative-like tune for the strings, which represents Lear himself, pronouncing the terms of his will in the opening scene. The six phrases are punctuated by short chattering asides on the wind instruments, which suggest the reactions of the courtiers who are listening. Then comes a much more lyrical theme which we hear three times ; first quite simply on the oboe, then on full woodwind, and finally, after a change of key, on the brass, with a richer and warmer accompaniment. This passage surely represents the replies of the three daughters. Berlioz has failed in the almost impossible task of giving this affectionate tune a touch of insincerity on its first two appearances. The Lear theme is then repeated with angry outbursts on the timpani, which admirably express the old king's reaction to Cordelia's silence.

All this constitutes the slow introduction, which at six minutes is longer than in most overtures. The subsequent Allegro is marked both *disperato* and *agitato*. The desperation never quite comes across; titanic energy seems more in evidence. Quite soon we seem to hear a suggestion of storm winds howling. Then comes a beautifully compassionate theme on

letter describing his meeting with Berlioz is dated March ; see, for instance, the article on Mendelssohn in the first edition of Grove's *Dictionary of Music* (1879–89).

the oboe for Cordelia (see example p. 198) ; it would not, in my opinion, suit any other Shakespeare heroine so well. A third theme which follows immediately and in somewhat similar mood is pleasant but a little ordinary, and I am not clear as to its dramatic purpose. Perhaps at this point Berlioz had only musical considerations in mind. In a brief development bits of the Allegro themes are intertwined. The recap is much lengthened ; this points to dramatic rather than musical considerations holding sway. Just after its start, the Lear theme from the introduction is brought back in a *fortissimo* passage of great power, and this is surely the old king battling against the storm. The storm music subsides into a few broken phrases that suggest his mind is breaking up. The return of Cordelia's theme is preceded by a striking suggestion of sobbing high on the violins. The long coda includes another appearance of the Lear theme *fortissimo* on lower strings (it needs the addition of trombones, and usually gets them), and the overture ends in a blaze of somewhat inappropriate glory.

The only contemporary evidence known to me for the pictorial nature of this music comes from Berlioz himself, who quotes in his autobiography some remarks made to him by the young King of Hanover :

> Magnificent, M. Berlioz, magnificent! Your orchestra speaks; you have no need of words. I could follow each scene — the entrance of the King into the Council Chamber, the storm on the heath, the terrible prison scene, and the lament of Cordelia. And what a Cordelia ! How wonderfully you have painted her ! So tender and so timid ! It is heart-rendingly beautiful.

Though it is possible Berlioz wrote this with his tongue in his cheek, I think it much more likely that he hoped intelligent listeners would react in this way.

Berlioz found inspiration in six Shakespeare plays (once for an opera [1]), and in each case his musical response was utterly different. He called 'Romeo and Juliet' a symphony, and it was by far the longest that had till then been written. Indeed, its ninety minutes are a lot even by Bruckner-Mahler standards. The work is not consistently good. The Prologue includes one rather undistinguished song, while the finale has *longueurs* in the middle. Nevertheless, this is one of music's masterpieces, a colossal conception carried through with irresistible bravura and sincerity.

[1] See above, pp. 133-5.

Berlioz used to complain that he could never afford the time to write a long work, and it was only by a miracle that he ever had time to write 'Romeo and Juliet'. In 1839, to his astonishment, he received a present of 20,000 francs from the violinist Paganini, expressly to enable him to drop all other work and compose something on a large scale. Paganini was usually thought a mean man, and writers are divided as to whether his name was used as a cover for some rich friend of Berlioz, or whether he was prompted by a sudden and unique wish to prove that he was not mean at all. It could also be that he genuinely wanted to enable Berlioz to write a masterpiece.

Berlioz decided to treat 'Romeo and Juliet' as a choral symphony with soloists. He began by roughing out the text in prose, and then got his friend Émile Deschamps to put it into verse. Only a small part of it derives directly from Shakespeare. Berlioz had no wish to tell the entire story (he was not, after all, writing an opera), but there had to be some indication of the action here and there for the sake of those in the audience who did not know the play, and in the tragic finale there had to be a good deal of rather aimless versifying to carry the sort of music he wanted at this point. But little more than a third of the symphony is vocal, and once more Berlioz sacrificed the possibilities of countless performances by his indifference to practical details. It is almost an hour before the full chorus is given a chance to sing, so the work has little appeal for choral societies. It has even less for the three soloists. Contralto (Prologue) and tenor (Mercutio) have nothing to sing after the Introduction, and not much there, while the baritone (Friar Laurence) has nothing until the finale. There are no vocal parts for Romeo or Juliet, while Tybalt and the Nurse are nowhere mentioned. One can hardly accuse Berlioz of a conventional approach to his subject.

'Romeo and Juliet' took nearly a year to write, and the composer conducted three performances of it in Paris at the end of 1839, by which time poor Paganini was dying. Wagner was at the first performance, and remembered to his own advantage some of the more striking passages when he came to write 'Tristan und Isolde'. Later on Liszt heard Berlioz conduct the work in Prague, an experience that influenced his own 'Dante' and 'Faust' Symphonies. The music was blazingly original, and its influence was immense.

'Romeo and Juliet' is in five parts, which show only faint affinities with a normal symphony. These are:

1. Introduction. Soloists, small chorus and orchestra. Four short sections.
2. Romeo's Rêverie and Fête. Orchestra alone. The equivalent of a symphonic first movement with long slow introduction.
3. Love Scene. The slow movement. Orchestral, except for voices 'off' at the start.
4. Queen Mab, or the Dream Fairy. Scherzo. Purely orchestral.
5. The Finale, though not so called. Mainly vocal and in three main sections. Deals with the deaths, supposed and real, of the lovers, and the final reconciliation between the two families. Takes over half an hour.

The Introduction begins with a short quick fugue for full orchestra on this theme:

This represents the squabbling and fighting of the opening scene. The tumult is quelled by a quarter-speed major version of the same tune (the first eight notes) very loud on the trombones; this, of course, represents the Prince of Verona. The end suggests that the crowd's pent-up resentment has not been stamped out, but has gone underground. The Prologue which follows establishes the plot, the voices, and three of the main tunes. Much of it leaves the voices (contralto solo and small chorus) unaccompanied, and the composer makes doubly sure that we shall concentrate on the words and take in the basic situation by giving the voices endless repeated notes without any musical interest. (His intentions are undone whenever an English audience is given a performance in French.) The opening words are from the first four lines of Shakespeare's Prologue, and then comes a précis of the action up to the balcony scene. This allows for brief orchestral interjections of, respectively, the Fête theme (including the six-eight version heard at the start of the Love Scene), a sighing tune on the cellos from Romeo's Rêverie and part of the Love-Scene melody. This last is sung, for the only time in the work, and as it is the first occasion on which the singers have had a tune the effect is unexpected and overwhelming. The third of the four short movements comprising the Introduction is

'Strophes', a rather dull song for the contralto with a very light accompaniment, mainly from the harp. The words are a tribute to Shakespeare by the composer. The song comes to life in the second verse when Berlioz adds a vibrant counter-theme on the cellos. Lastly, after a brief recitative establishing Mercutio, the tenor sings what is described as a Scherzetto, of which the words are a much-cut version of the Queen Mab speech from I. 4 of the play. As there is later to be a long Queen Mab scherzo for orchestra, the composer's preoccupation with her amounts to an obsession. She is not, after all, fundamental to the plot, and there are those who find the speech somewhat out of keeping with Mercutio's character. Nevertheless, both Queen Mab movements are superb music, and one would not be without them.

If Berlioz' directions are observed, there is now a moment of chaos while the chorus goes out. It stays out for forty minutes, missing some of the loveliest and most exciting music in the world. The next three movements, being almost entirely orchestral, are sometimes played at concerts on their own. The result is not very satisfying, largely because the first is for full orchestra, and the others for small orchestra, the third being a quiet, delicate piece. However, it is better to hear some of this music than none.

'Roméo seul — Tristesse — Concert et bal — Grande Fête chez Capulet' is usually known in England as 'Romeo's Rêverie and Fête'. Berlioz' title is curious. In the play we never see Romeo alone before the Capulets' party, and the nearest he comes to sadness is in his discussion with Benvolio about his first love, Rosaline, who 'hath sworn that she will still live chaste' (I. 1). Can it really be that the first half of this movement shows Romeo in sad contemplation of the quite unimportant Rosaline? For the moment let us leave this problem, and contemplate the music, which is extremely 'modern' and 'Tristan'-like at the start. No definite tune; just a thin melancholy thread of sound on the violins. Soon we hear the sighing theme of which there was a hint in the Prologue:

The music dies to nothing, hinting at tune A below (the Fête
theme), and leads into a larghetto aria for the oboe (tune B
below).   This seems to cry out for a voice, and it had one
originally, for Berlioz lifted it from one of his Conservatoire
cantatas, 'La Mort de Sardanapale'.   It is a lovely tune, and
does excellently for Romeo's 'tristesse'.   The tempo quickens,
and after a climactic pause we are plunged into the tumultuous
and very exciting Fête theme.   This is one of those angular,
awkward Berlioz tunes that somehow triumph by sheer energy
and enthusiasm.   We soon discover why it is awkward.   It
has been specially devised as a counter-theme to the
'Sardanapale' aria :

There is a rather similar effect in the 'Carnaval romain'
overture.   Here the combination of the two tunes denotes
Romeo's arrival at the party.   There is a splendidly exuberant
coda, which starts by building up from nothing over a ground
bass of descending minims, itself a derivative of the Fête theme.
The whole piece is carried through with astonishing brilliance.

The 'Scène d'amour ; Nuit sereine — Le jardin de Capulet
silencieux et désert' begins with some slow, soft, mysterious
chords, after which 'voices off' represent drunken revellers in
the distance, going home from the party.   They sing a simplified six-eight version of the Fête theme, and there is a good
deal of tra-la-la-ing.   This is the most nearly operatic effect
in the whole work.   The sublime Adagio that follows is scored
for strings, woodwind and horns, with no heavy brass, percussion or harp.   It can only be paralleled by the rather
similar love scene in 'The Trojans'.[1]   Both seem to me the
equal of the more famous love-duet in Wagner's 'Tristan und
Isolde' ; unlike Wagner, Berlioz manages to suggest a youthful
fervour with the bloom still on it.   For some time he fobs us
off with impressionistic music for the lower strings which

[1] See above, p. 134.

suggests the moonlit garden below Juliet's balcony. Soon a miraculous tune emerges :

This tune never seems to start; suddenly it is there, and your heart turns over. After its second and more impassioned appearance, there is an unmistakable and realistic imitation of the lovers talking. Juliet's utterances on the oboe (with flute doubling) are breathless and agitated ; Romeo on the violas is reassuring. The love theme returns and again we are enraptured. While the orchestra sings the theme very softly, there are some curious loud interruptions for violins and violas. These can only be the Nurse's offstage warnings. After a final passionate outburst, Romeo vanishes, leaving the garden hushed and still.

The very fast and very soft Queen Mab scherzo is scored for the same smallish orchestra as the love scene, with the addition of harps and percussion. Berlioz found he got better ensemble by cutting down the strings. He himself wrote of the 'immense difficulty' of the piece, and it is still a severe test for any orchestra. The last part is a nightmare for the horns, who are asked to play very fast, very high and very soft for a long time, a desperate combination. The actual coda was an afterthought, written because someone in Vienna told Berlioz he thought the end too abrupt. The composer's aim was to depict :

> Queen Mab in her microscopic car, attended by the buzzing insects of a summer's night, and launched at full gallop by her tiny horses.

The theme of the slower trio section is a close relative of the main one, but I must not suggest that this inventive movement is in conventional form. Instead of an exact recap, we are given a miracle of continuous development, one idea giving birth to the next.

We have had almost an hour's music of the highest quality, but with scarcely a hint of tragedy. Berlioz realized he must give due weight to the tragic conclusion, for which he has been keeping his main chorus in reserve. But it must be confessed that parts of this enormous finale do seem to drag, especially at a first hearing. Beginners can be reassured that the last five minutes are magnificent, and at least there is no hint of decline in our next piece, Juliet's Funeral Cortège. This is scored for woodwind and strings alone (the orchestration is surprisingly light and restrained in the greater part of this symphony), and is a march of a very curious kind. The orchestra embarks on a measured fugue whose subject in its first phrase suggests the Fête theme from earlier on. Against this a chorus of Capulets intones a dirge on one note, the words based on Friar Laurence's

> Stick your rosemary
> On this fair corse.                     (IV. 5)

Towards the end chorus and orchestra exchange roles, the voices taking over the fugue while the violins and violas have the repeated-note phrases of the dirge.

Now follows an orchestral movement elaborately but not lucidly headed :

ROMÉO AU TOMBEAU DES CAPULETS
*Invocation    —    Reveil de Juliette*
*Joie délirante, désespoir, dernières angoisses et mort des deux amants*

Whatever else this music is, it is quite certainly descriptive from start to finish (and as it ill accords with Barzun's theories, he ignores it). Writers on Berlioz do not seem to have noticed the problems here. There is no call for 'joie délirante'; Romeo should arrive in the depths of gloom rather than delirious joy, for he thinks Juliet already dead. And what can be the point of the quiet recitative-like dialogue between clarinet and bass strings, and the extraordinary outburst that follows it ?

The impossibility of relating this music to Shakespeare's last scene eventually led me to examine contemporary acting versions of the play. Garrick's appeared in 1750, and in 1812 the *Biographia Dramatica* felt able to say that 'it is now universally and repeatedly performed in all the British theatres'. It was republished as late as 1819, and John Philip Kemble's version of five years earlier admits to being based on Garrick's, from which it scarcely differs. There can be no doubt that this was the version Charles Kemble took to Paris, and that Berlioz had it in mind when writing his symphony. All three of Garrick's major alterations are reflected in the music.

As Shakespeare wrote the play, we hear of Romeo's

melancholy and 'solitary walks' before we see him. Eventually Benvolio worms out of him that the cause is his love for Rosaline. The scene is inevitably played down so that Romeo can later make as much as possible of his far more important love for Juliet. To provide himself with a stronger entrance, Garrick cut all reference to Rosaline and had Romeo in love with Juliet from the start. The melancholy and the 'solitary walks' are now relevant to the main plot and so need emphasis rather than under-statement. We first see Romeo in Garrick's I. 3, 'A Wood near Verona':

> *Romeo passes through the wood from left to right*
> *Mercutio.*
>> See where he steals — told I not you, Benvolio,
>> That we should find this melancholy Cupid
>> Lock'd in some gloomy covert, under key
>> Of cautionary silence, with his arms
>> Threaded, like these cross boughs, in sorrow's knot?

Then comes most of Shakespeare's dialogue about Rosaline, but here applied to Juliet.

It is easy to understand how struck Berlioz was with such an entrance when played in the somewhat exaggerated style of the day, and he naturally tried to express it in his symphony. 'Roméo seul — Tristesse' makes sense when we know that Romeo is in love with Juliet before going to the Capulets' Ball.

Garrick's Act V begins with a purely operatic scene for which William Boyce provided the music. It consists of a dirge for soloists, chorus and orchestra accompanying 'the Procession to the Funeral of Juliet'.[1] But for this interpolation, I doubt if Berlioz would have devoted a movement to the 'Convoie funèbre de Juliette'. Garrick follows Shakespeare over Friar Laurence's ill-fated scheme, so his Romeo showed no 'delirious joy' on arriving at the tomb. The opening music expresses more a wild desperation (it is marked *Allegro agitato e disperato*), and the subsequent quiet chords separated by long silences suggest Romeo's arrival in the tomb and discovery of the 'corpse'. His Invocation to Juliet represents the long and wonderful speech after the death of Paris:

> O my love! My wife!
> Death, that hath suckt the honey of thy breath,
> Hath had no power yet upon thy beauty.

(V. 3)

[1] See above, p. 62.

The sad melody sounds the sadder for being played in hollow
unison by cor anglais, horn and four bassoons, an extraordinary
combination. The sound fades to nothing as Romeo drinks
the poison. So far the music accords with modern performances. But at this point Garrick parts company with Shakespeare; he does not allow Romeo to die immediately. Juliet
wakes slowly as he drains the phial, and there follow some
sixty lines of dialogue between the lovers, who in the original
do not speak to each other at all. Juliet is at first unaware of
where she is. 'Bless me, how cold it is!' she remarks. As soon
as she has grasped the situation, Romeo begins to weaken from
the effects of the poison, but before dying he gives frenzied
expression to his love, and *this* is the 'joie délirante'. The whole
scene is unmistakably parallelled in the music. The clarinet
represents the waking Juliet, the lower strings Romeo, who is
at first questioning and then horrified:

Suddenly the whole orchestra blazes into a ghastly parody of
the love theme from the 'Scène d'amour'. Broken phrases
on the strings show us Romeo's collapse, a hollow-sounding
passage for woodwind perhaps suggests the arrival of Friar
Laurence outside, and, most extraordinary of all, the strings
repeatedly ejaculate a wild desperate phrase that might have
come out of Nielsen's Fifth Symphony; I take this to represent
Romeo's death agonies. At the final two-note *fortissimo* Juliet
stabs herself.

The movement as a whole is too disjointed to qualify as
great music, and perhaps depends overmuch on its programme.
But it is an astonishing invention, and the originality of the
orchestral effects would be hard to parallel even in Berlioz.
The last two or three minutes sound much more like the work
of a twentieth-century composer than an early Romantic.

My interpretation of the piece is strengthened by a passage in the composer's autobiography. Berlioz is engaged on a violent diatribe against those who 'correct' the masterpieces of Mozart, Beethoven, Molière and Shakespeare. He allows but one exception :

> I know that Garrick improved *Romeo and Juliet* by putting his exquisite, pathetic ending in the place of Shakespeare's; but who are the miscreants who doctored *King Lear, Hamlet, The Tempest, Richard III*?

Berlioz is obviously giving us Harriet's views. The Garrick scene in the last act of *Romeo and Juliet* may well have been a favourite of hers.

Berlioz did not use only Garrick's version of the play. He drew on a good text both for the Prologue, which Garrick omitted, and for several lines in the choral finale now to be described.[1] This starts with a chorus of Capulets and Montagues running to the tomb. Friar Laurence addresses them in recitative, the words keeping fairly close to his final speech in the play :

> Romeo, there dead, was husband to that Juliet;
> And she, there dead, that Romeo's faithful wife.
>
> (V. 3)

This leads into a not-very interesting arioso, based on the same speech. But the Friar's first proper aria, 'Pauvres enfants que je pleure' (the words are by Berlioz) is lovely. The quicker section reverts to Shakespeare, rather freely deriving from the Prince's speech, 'Where be these enemies?' It seems that Berlioz was aware he was going on too long, and made some cuts; but in fact one would have welcomed a return to the lovely first part of this aria, a return that never comes. His crowd is less easily swayed by the tragedy than Shakespeare's, and there is now an animated double chorus of Montagues and Capulets quarrelling to the fugal theme that opened the symphony (see example 1, p. 188). The Friar checks them with a second aria, converting them to a saner and more humane attitude; the chorus joins in the repeat of his aria theme. By now we have had more than enough of the Friar, but Berlioz achieves the miracle of making his third and last aria, the 'Sermon', so beautiful that we forgive him all.

[1] Garrick cut the final speeches of the play to shreds, allowed no reconciliation between the families, and gave only five lines to Friar Laurence.

Soloist and chorus build this up into a tremendous gesture of reconciliation, ecstatic and noble. The key, B major, brings us full circle, for the symphony began in B minor, though in fact most of the work hovers round the remote key of F.

True to form, Berlioz invested his two short *Hamlet* pieces with attributes which to all intents and purposes prevent their ever being performed, and true to form he produced a couple of minor masterpieces. They constitute two of the three items in 'Tristia' (Op. 18), the first being a setting for chorus and small orchestra of a poem by Thomas Moore. He originally wrote 'La Mort d'Ophélie' for voice and piano. The words were adapted by Ernest Legouvé from the Queen's speech 'There is a willow grows aslant a brook'. It is a lovely little piece, soft all through except for a sudden *forte* on the word 'tombe'.

The 'Funeral March for the Last Scene of Hamlet' is headed by Fortinbras's speech which ends the play:

> Let four captains
> Bear Hamlet, like a soldier, to the stage.

The stage directions after this speech read: *A dead March. Exeunt, bearing off the dead bodies; after which a peal of ordnance is shot off.* Besides a large orchestra, the music requires drums 'off' for the ordnance, and a chorus to sing a single despairing unison 'ah' at the start, another at the end, and one or two more in the middle. This briefest of choruses may be effective, but it is not indispensable, and the only recording of the march omits it. Nevertheless, many concert promoters must have shied at the sight of the first bar, and performances are very rare indeed. The music is impressive, and would make a superb though appallingly expensive end to the play. The closing bars suggest utter nullity; this is one of Berlioz's most staggering pages.

Both the *Hamlet* pieces date from 1848, and the first was written in London, where there was a plan (which came to nothing) to get Berlioz to conduct an entire concert of his own Shakespeare music. A study of 'Lélio' might suggest that he wrote yet a third *Hamlet* piece. After the opening song the narrator talks about Shakespeare at some length, and in particular about *Hamlet*:

> What a marvellous and penetrating scene is the one in which the Ghost speaks to the youthful Hamlet of the crime which has

robbed him of his father.  I have always thought that this passage would make an admirable subject for music of a grand and sombre kind.[1]

The implication is that the Chorus of Ghosts which follows was inspired by this scene, but in fact Berlioz lifted it from a cantata about Cleopatra which failed to win him the Prix de Rome in 1829.


## 2. SYMPHONIC POEMS (1850–1900)

As we have seen, in the late nineteenth century Shakespeare music was written in vast quantities, mostly in the form of descriptive overtures.  These came increasingly to be called symphonic poems.  Such music was usually planned, like the first movements of symphonies, in sonata form; this involves at least two contrasted themes which together constitute the first and last sections.  In the middle section these themes are developed.  By chance this is a suitable plan for giving a musical impression of Shakespeare's tragedies.  The chief protagonists will be a man and a woman who can be represented by the first and second subjects; even in symphonies these are usually masculine and feminine in quality.  The confusion expected in the middle of any tragedy can be convincingly depicted by the development of the themes.  In the recap the heroine's theme can be emotionally heightened to suggest a declension in her fortunes.  It thus seems that one overture may suit several tragedies equally well.  How far can a composer particularize?  Intelligent people might guess the subject of Tchaikovsky's 'Romeo and Juliet' from the sound alone (but only if the first five minutes were left out, for the *religioso* opening would baffle them.  What play begins with monks? or in a church?)  They might just possibly guess Liszt's 'Hamlet' and Elgar's 'Falstaff', but they would be lucky if they identified any of the others described below.  Yet a symphonic poem is not a failure just because the sound does not reveal the intention.  It must be accepted that an audience

---

[1] Mozart was less impressed by the scene.  In his only known comment on Shakespeare, he wrote to his father that he wanted to keep the music sung off-stage by Neptune in 'Idomeneo' as brief as possible on the grounds that an audience soon tires of a disembodied voice.  In Mozart's view, the Ghost's speech in *Hamlet* was much too long.  He had seen the play in Salzburg, given by a company of which Schikaneder was a member.

needs non-musical clues before it can appreciate descriptive
music.   In opera and ballet there is the action, in songs the
words.   In descriptive overtures the clues are in the title, and
if a knowledge of the subject cannot be assumed the composer
may have to provide a synopsis in words.   Thus an audience
needs to be properly briefed.

But music is limited in what it can describe.   It could not
distinguish between Macduff and Banquo, or translate into
sound so complex a character as Malvolio.   I doubt if any
comedy is susceptible to orchestral treatment, other than *A
Midsummer Night's Dream* and *The Tempest*, and these are
possible mainly because of those musical stand-bys, the fairies
and the storm.   The other comedies have inspired little concert music of value; the plots are more involved than those of
the tragedies, the atmosphere less individual.   Composers
generally have found the tragedies easier to deal with just
because their substance can be expressed more simply.

Let us now probe the limitations of individual composers and
see how far the best of them can rise above the generalized overture described at the beginning of this section.   For the purpose
we shall consider the heroines of the four great tragedies :

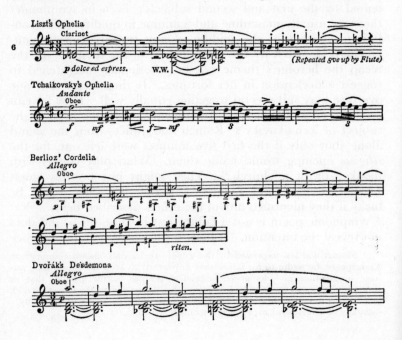

Strauss' Lady Macbeth
*Appassionato, molto rubato*
Flutes, Clarinets
Violins

*pp* [over a held A]        *pp*

The Liszt is shown with all its accompaniment, the Berlioz,
Dvořák and Strauss examples with at least some indication of
what is going on below. The Tchaikovsky has a complex and
unmemorable accompaniment which I have omitted. Unlike
the other tragic heroines, Lady Macbeth is middle-aged and
her intentions are evil. Strauss has given her a succession of
chords rather than a melody, but her baleful nature seems to
call for darker instruments than flutes; perhaps a bass clarinet
or the bottom octave of a cor anglais. Strauss had already
used bass instruments for Macbeth, and perhaps chose high
ones for musical reasons, but the result is a portrait that shows
no likeness to its subject.

It was normal Romantic usage to depict young heroines
by a woodwind melody, usually on the oboe. Thus for touches
of characterization we must look at the shape rather than the
colour of the melodies given above. But first we must try to
differentiate ourselves between Ophelia, Cordelia and Desdemona, and in simple terms within music's range it is no
easy task. All three girls are virtuous and kindly. Ophelia is
the most reserved, and we know least about her until madness
uncovers her tortured mind. Cordelia has the most matured
mentality; she is the most assured, and perhaps the most
compassionate. Desdemona is a bit of a ninny, but her sweet
innocence is irresistible. Is there anything here for music?
Of the two Ophelia tunes Tchaikovsky's is an almost total
failure. The melody suggests a Russian girl suffering from
Russian melancholy by the lakeside at night; when day dawns
she will turn into a swan. That may be how Russians see
Ophelia, but to our ears Liszt's tune is incomparably better.
The false relation effect on the third chord suggests the girl's
uncertainty, the rising phrase that follows her inner yearning,
and its lack of direction her incomprehension. Berlioz'
Cordelia tune is almost as good. The falling phrases suggest
compassion, the touches of *rubato* positive acts of sympathy.
She is eager to give, whereas Liszt's Ophelia can only wait
passively for whatever the fates may bring. Both tunes pass

o

the crucial test : they suit the intended heroine better than any other, and it would be catastrophic to switch them. Dvořák's Desdemona is descriptive at an altogether lower level. This is a nice tune which would do passably for any nice girl, and convincingly for none. One can detect no act of imagination behind it other than a musical one, and we shall see that Dvořák's overture, though a fine piece of music, lacks a strong sense of the dramatic.

Liszt is usually regarded as the father of the symphonic poem, though he was in fact forestalled by both Mendelssohn and Berlioz. But he was more of a father-figure, and as his symphonic poems piled up in the 1850s composers all over Europe began to explore the intriguing possibilities of matching dramatic events with music. Liszt's 'Hamlet' began life in 1858 as an overture, given before a performance of the play at the Weimar Court Theatre. Later it was rewritten, but as a symphonic poem it was not performed until 1876. Before writing the music Liszt is said to have been impressed by a performance of the title-role in *Hamlet* by a Hungarian actor, Bogumil Dawison, who saw the character not as an indecisive dreamer, but as a clever man of action awaiting the right moment. I take this information from the sleeve of a current recording, but it does not seem to me very convincing, for the music suggests precisely the opposite. Liszt's Hamlet is indecisive to a degree, and very far from being a man of action. At the start the timps, playing a dotted rhythm which I take to represent Hamlet himself, are marked *schwankend*, which means irresolute. The trouble is that the whole piece is irresolute, and as music it keeps sagging. It suffers from the minor fault of some very corny ghost music in the slow introduction, and the major one of too much repetition. Two-bar phrases, four-bar phrases, and complete pages are instantly repeated with little or no modification, and this is not intended to suggest Hamlet's mind going round in circles, for it is a characteristic of other Liszt symphonic poems, for instance, 'Mazeppa'.

Nevertheless, as a character study Liszt's 'Hamlet' is fascinating. It is full of original touches, some of them (for instance, Ophelia's tune) strangely like Wagner's 'Tristan' Prelude, which was being written at about the same time. Usually similarities between these two composers are caused

by Wagner's borrowing propensities, but in this case we must
assume coincidence.

Smetana had visited Liszt at Weimar as early as 1849, and
apparently they discussed together the problems of writing
symphonic poems.   In 1856 Smetana, still virtually unknown,
settled at Gothenburg in Sweden, where he worked as a
teacher, pianist and conductor.   He also wrote three symphonic poems, confessed imitations of the Lisztian method,
and quite lacking the nationalist touches to be found in his
later and better-known music.   Nevertheless, they are well
worth occasional performances.

Of his 'Richard III' Smetana wrote to Liszt:

> The emphasis follows more or less the action of the tragedy, the
> attainment of the goal after all obstacles have been surmounted,
> the triumph and finally the downfall of the hero.   In the bass
> theme I have imagined the hero himself, who is active throughout,
> and in the second *motiv* the opposing party.

One would not expect Smetana to have a clear grasp of
the Wars of the Roses, but his last two words do suggest that
he could not remember whom Richard was up against, and
this is confirmed by the 'opposing party's' tune, which
suggests Imogen rather than a bunch of Lancastrian rebels:

However, Smetana had a clear picture of Richard himself,
and manages the alleged deformity extremely well.   The
quiet start has a halting syncopation that admirably suggests
the uneven walk.   Soon a slowly rising melody in the bass
gives us an idea of Richard's aspirations and evil nature.   The
'opposing party' sound quite incapable of resisting his machinations.   In the middle of the overture Richard's coronation is
splendidly managed.   A derivative of his tune blazes magnifi-
cently, its rhythm knocked a little askew here and there to
suggest the cripple's moment of triumph.   After some underground intrigue, the march theme blazes anew, but with an
undercurrent of evil, and the plaintive melody of the 'opposing

party' suggests good people trampled underfoot. Then, after a long drum roll to arouse suspense, we are given music for the Battle of Bosworth Field based on fragments of both the main tunes, and this section ends with the 'opposing party' tune (now representing the future Henry VII) rising symbolically to the top and being delivered by woodwind and trombones *fortissimo e vittorioso*. It is all too common in Liszt-type music for delicate and beautiful tunes to be ruined by being blown up larger than life, and that is what happens here. Richard's theme falls into the bass to signify that he has been vanquished, and he dies to the sound of loud, irregularly-placed descending chords. Strauss was later to kill Macbeth in the same way. In spite of the one error of taste, 'Richard III' is an enjoyable work, and deserves more attention.

It is seldom possible to date with accuracy the start of a new trend, and 1860 is only the roughest of guides to the start of the nationalist movement in music. This was a break-away from the Italian and German styles that had served most of Europe for nearly two centuries, and, more positively, an attempt to found new styles on the melodies and rhythms of folk music. In Prague Smetana turned from the international, but really German, style of 'Richard III' to the parochial style of 'The Bartered Bride', with its fresh Czech rhythms. In St. Petersburg Balakirev was self-appointed leader of a group of young nationalist composers known as 'the Five' (the other important members being Borodin, Moussorgsky and Rimsky-Korsakov). All were amateurs, and none had had what would now be considered adequate training, but Balakirev, their instructor, triumphed over ignorance by sheer genius and enthusiasm. They were not the first to evolve a Russian style, for Glinka and others had been grappling with the problem for several decades, but 'the Five' greatly accelerated the Russianization of music in St. Petersburg and Moscow. Their contemporary, Tchaikovsky, flirted now and then with nationalist tenets, but his Russian colouring is usually much paler, and often invisible.

Balakirev taught the other members of his group to study late Beethoven, Schumann and Liszt, as well as such Russian models as were available, and the Liszt influence resulted, as elsewhere, in a number of symphonic poems, some of which were based on Shakespeare. Balakirev himself produced the first, an overture to *King Lear*, which he wrote in 1859 when his nationalistic ideas were still forming. Almost at once he began to plan incidental music for the same play, but this was neither performed nor published until 1904 (see p. 228).

It might seem unnecessary to devote more than a short paragraph to an early work by a neglected composer which, as I write, has never been recorded. But, in support of my own admiration for this overture I can quote our leading authority on Russian music, Gerald Abraham, who has described it as 'the most satisfactory interpretation of the tragic side of Shakespeare yet made in music'. Balakirev himself described the plan behind his 'King Lear' in a letter to Tchaikovsky of 1869. The translation is Professor Abraham's :

> Having first read the play . . . I fired my imagination with a general outline. I planned an introduction, *Maestoso*, and then something mystical (Kent's prediction). The introduction dies away, and a stormy passionate *allegro* begins. This is Lear himself, the discrowned but still mighty lion. The characteristic themes of Regan and Goneril serve as episodes, and finally the second subject of the calm and tender Cordelia. Then the middle section (storm, Lear and the Fool on the heath), with the repetition of the *allegro* ; Regan and Goneril finally crush their father, and the overture dies away softly (Lear over Cordelia's corse) ; Kent's prediction, now fulfilled, is heard again, and then comes the grave and quiet death.

This is much more classical in mould than either Liszt's 'Hamlet' or Smetana's 'Richard III', both of which abandoned sonata form in the interests of the story. Balakirev is as classical as Berlioz on the same subject, and achieves a closer parallel. Balakirev's analysis of his 'King Lear' needs a little amplifying. The slow introduction begins with a noble tune on the brass for Lear himself, as he is in Act I :

'Kent's prediction' consists of a very soft and slowly falling tune for the horn over persistent drum taps. The main *allegro* section starts by setting before us three important themes almost simultaneously :

Tune A is a worried version of the noble tune in the introduction — a good example of Lisztian transformation of themes. Tune B suggests Lear's great age and infirmity, while the stuttering semiquavers of C represent Goneril and Regan. All three tunes occur frequently in the incidental music, where they are developed on their own. Cordelia's theme, the official second subject, is (inevitably) for woodwind, and as in Berlioz the falling phrases suggest compassion. The rest of the piece has been adequately described by the composer.

Balakirev was an eager pug-nosed little man with something of the dictator in his make-up. He was prodigal of advice, ever wanting to write other people's music for them, and he saw their mistakes with a clarity that did little to make him loved. He could, in fact, be extremely irritating, and perhaps the most irritating thing about him was that he was nearly always right. With his own compositions he was a prey to constant doubts, and in middle life became so neurotic that he ran away from the world of music and became a railway clerk. In old age he emerged from anonymity and finished a handful of masterpieces that had been mouldering on a shelf for nearly half a century.

Just before he fell into the chasm that divides his career Balakirev turned his attention to Tchaikovsky, possibly because Borodin and Moussorgsky would no longer suffer his advice. He never made Tchaikovsky a whole-hearted nationalist, but his influence did lead to some of Tchaikovsky's finest and most Russian works, among them 'Romeo and Juliet'. Balakirev virtually planned this overture. The description of his own 'King Lear' from which I have quoted already was written in a letter to Tchaikovsky as a model for him to follow. Balakirev advised him to go for long walks and think things over ('take goloshes and a walking-stick'), and even offered him a theme for the duelling. Tchaikovsky was not so servile as to accept it, but may have been influenced by it, for instance in bars 140-50.

A month or so later Balakirev was asking to see the themes on which Tchaikovsky proposed to base his overture. He was rightly critical of the original opening :

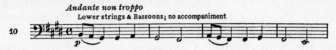

*Andante non troppo*
Lower strings & Bassoons; no accompaniment

Balakirev thought that this did not sufficiently suggest the character of Friar Laurence (who would ever suspect that it was meant to?), and he wanted something 'less like a Haydn Quartet and more like a Liszt Chorale in "Hunnenschlacht" or "St. Elizabeth"'. But he was fascinated by the famous Love Theme. 'I often play it, and I'd like to hug you for it.' He added that he thought the loud ending of the work a mistake. In spite of these criticisms, this version of 'Romeo and Juliet' was performed in March 1870. It was not a success.

The score of this first version has recently been published in the Soviet Complete Works Series, Vol. 23. The slow introduction is based almost entirely on the theme quoted above, which occurs five times, eventually on full orchestra. Then, after a brief anticipation of the Love Theme, come the first 160 bars of the quick music exactly as we know them today. In the remainder there are many differences. The original Friar Laurence theme was not suitable for development, and instead of it, at the equivalent of bar 334, the trumpets played the Love Theme against the same striking accompaniment. The Friar Laurence theme does return a little later, and again in the coda, which is completely different, but there can be no doubt Balakirev was right in thinking it spoilt the work. Soon after the first performance Tchaikovsky took his advice and wrote a new introduction, the one we know today :

*Andante non tanto quasi moderato*
Clarinets & Bassoons

He much improved the development, incorporating the rising minims of the new Friar Laurence theme with tremendous

effect, and he completely rewrote the last five minutes. This
second version of 'Romeo and Juliet' was the first to be
published, and it was played in a number of European countries, though still without much acclaim. Balakirev was
furious when he found it still ended loudly. In 1880, by
which time Balakirev was no longer interested in music,
Tchaikovsky rewrote it yet again, confining his alterations to
the end. He cut a rather pointless episode at the equivalent
of bar 483, and added the marvellous melody for strings just
before the final chords. Composers do not always improve
when they revise, but Tchaikovsky's revisions resulted in a
masterpiece. Even so, success came slowly. In Britain the
work did not become really popular until the 1930s, and it took
a 'pop' version of the Love Theme to make it big box-office.

I do not know why Balakirev thought the overture should
begin with Friar Laurence. Other composers who have
tackled this play, and it is the easiest of the tragedies in which
to succeed, have begun with the street fighting or the lovers
themselves. For us, the solemn chords with their Russian-
Church flavour may conjure up a vision of a black-bearded
priest in one of those tall chimney-pot hats, but they are both
memorable and effective, and no doubt it was a help to
Tchaikovsky to establish them quietly at the start before
tension had been created.

This slow introduction is a little long, and, Friar Laurence
apart, I do not understand what it is meant to represent. But
once the main Allegro is reached, Tchaikovsky is at the very
top of his form. The music is extremely original and evocative,
and it triumphantly equates musical form with dramatic
purpose. The Allegro starts with the street duelling, and
everything possible is done to present two groups in conflict :

This suggests the cut and thrust of rapiers with great vividness.
Often the strings seem to represent the Montagues and the
woodwind the Capulets, or vice versa. At all the great
climaxes cymbals clash like sword on sword. When the street

fighting dies down, cor anglais and muted violas in unison
give us a taste of the Love Theme, a tune too famous to need
quotation here.  Before it has had time to flower, muted strings
on their own are swaying gently and very quietly like the
leaves in the Capulet garden at night.  From these sweet
nocturnal sounds rises the great Love Theme in full on flutes
and oboes; a horn accompanies with a rocking figure that
adds to the effect of yearning.

The central development section lays the rising minims
of Friar Laurence's tune on the horn against the confused
bustling of the street fighting, and we feel the opposition of
Good and Evil.  The music rises to one of the great climaxes
of the concert hall, with the Friar's theme ringing out on two
trumpets against blood-hungry rhythms from the rest of the
orchestra.  Evil seems to win the day, for in the subsequent
recap the duelling music sounds more brilliant than ever.
When the quiet garden music returns, this time on the woodwind, there is an undercurrent of unrest on the strings, and we
sense that tragedy is imminent.  Even though the glorious
Love Theme finds ecstatic expression on unison strings, it
cannot stand up to the family feud.  But at last pride and
anger and stupidity tumble in the dust.  After a momentary
silence, a funeral drum-rhythm beneath snatches of the Love
Theme suggests a cortège.  Friar Laurence delivers his appeal
to the two families to end their vendetta (slow woodwind
chords, as at the start), the strings bid a final valediction to the
dead lovers, and with a few loud chords this splendid overture
comes to an end.  It is without doubt one of Tchaikovsky's
very greatest achievements.

Shortly before his death in 1893 Tchaikovsky was persuaded that the Love Theme would sound well as a Love Duet.
He sketched, but never orchestrated, a scena with words
deriving from the beginning of Shakespeare's III. 5 for soprano
and tenor, with a few optional bars in the middle to be sung 'off'
by the Nurse.  Much of the earlier material is new and rather
attractive, though the words that go with it defy translation.
The author of the following deserves pity rather than blame:

*Juliet*  Love, 'tis not the day; the nightingale is singing.  Then
be not fearful.
*Romeo*  No, not the nightingale.  'Tis the lark.
*Juliet*  Nightly she sings on yonder pomegranate.  Believe me,
love, it is the nightingale.

*Romeo* No, not the nightingale, no ; alas, 'tis the lark, 'tis the lark,
    the herald of the morning.   The night is over.
*Juliet* (*dogged*) No, 'tis the nightingale.
*Romeo* (*sticking to it*) No, 'tis the lark.

Later they return to the subject for the sake of a musical recap,
but in the meantime they have undergone a mutual con-
version, Juliet repeatedly stating her view that it is the lark
after all, and Romeo being equally earnest on the side of the
nightingale.   After Tchaikovsky's death Taneiev orchestrated
the sketch, adding a long and unnecessary introduction taken
from the overture and also an orchestral postlude.   He even
threw in a few stage-directions in case anyone felt an urge to
sing the thing in costume.   Had Tchaikovsky finished the duet
himself, it might possibly have been worth taking into the
repertoire.   In its present state it has little but curiosity value.

    Associated with 'the Five' was a Russian music critic
called Stassov, whom we shall meet again in connection with
the incidental music Balakirev wrote for *King Lear*.   Though
'Romeo and Juliet' seemed a failure, Stassov was eager to
persuade Tchaikovsky to try his hand at another symphonic
poem.   Tchaikovsky asked for suggestions, and Stassov offered
him *The Tempest, Ivanhoe* or *Taras Bulba*.   (As will be gathered,
Stassov was a life-long Anglophile.)   Tchaikovsky chose *The
Tempest*, and by return post received a synopsis which he more
or less followed.   In the published full score it is given in
Russian with a French translation :

The Sea
Ariel, spirit of the air, obeying Prospero's will, raises a tempest
The wreck of the ship bringing Ferdinand
{The enchanted island
{First timid signs of love between Miranda and Ferdinand
{Ariel
{Caliban
The loving couple 'se livre au prestige triomphant de la passion'
    (which I do not feel capable of translating)
Prospero divests himself of his magic powers and leaves the island
The Sea

This is much too complex a plan for a single piece of music.
It demands too many contrasted tunes while allowing too
little opportunity for their interplay on one another, and in
the middle Tchaikovsky loses his grip entirely.   The sea-music

at the start is splendid.  The composer told Rimsky-Korsakov that he wrote it with the Prelude to 'Das Rheingold' in mind, but one would never suspect this.  It would be easier to believe that Rimsky-Korsakov had Tchaikovsky's 'Tempest' in mind when he wrote the sea-music in 'Scheherazade'.  The work is easy to follow, for each section is in a markedly different tempo and mood from its predecessor, except those bracketed together, which flow more or less continuously.  Thus the effect is almost that of a suite in eight shortish movements.

In all three of Tchaikovsky's Shakespeare pieces there is one character who sounds Russian, and in this case it is Prospero :

This would do for a Boyar in a Moussorgsky opera.  Ariel is prettily managed, but Caliban was beyond Tchaikovsky's comprehension and sounds like a relative of Mendelssohn's 'rude mechanicals' with his ass's-bray sevenths.  The storm-music is exciting, and there are some lovely quiet chords moving chromatically to suggest Prospero's magic.  One has the curious feeling that the composer was as innocent of the failure of this piece as of the success of 'Romeo and Juliet'.  In the one case he took bad advice, in the other good.

For this third Shakespearean venture Tchaikovsky relied on his own instincts, and they did not serve him any too well.  He had seen *Hamlet* in Venice in 1876, and no doubt in Russia too, but he clearly did not feel the situations from the dramatic point of view.  The usual slow introduction takes nearly five minutes, and starts well with a melancholy theme that presumably represents Hamlet himself.  The trouble is that it never appears in the main Allegro section, and we do not hear it again until the coda.  It should have been integrated into the quick music in some way.  After this the introduction concerns itself with some hectic music, whose purpose is not clear, and a representation of a clock striking midnight.  The main Allegro theme is also hectic and would not be out of place in the Inferno music of 'Francesca da Rimini'.  The second subject portrays Ophelia (see example 6, p. 198), and then comes a lovely tune, heard first on the woodwind and then very lushly on the strings, which in any other work would

signify Love.   The plot of *Hamlet*, one would think, hardly
calls for a Love Theme.   Rhythmically it is very like Hamlet's
tune at the start; this may or may not be intentional.   After
a quick climax comes a surprisingly trenchant dramatic stroke.
The music drops suddenly and unexpectedly to a *pianissimo*,
and we hear a distant march for brass and drums which clearly
represents Fortinbras in search of the sledded Polacks.

There is little or no development.   The recap is notable
for the way Ophelia's tune is rewritten.   The accompanying
triplets are probably meant to suggest the weeping brook into
which she falls, and the music fades effectively into a silence
which indicates her death.   But the ardour of the subsequent
Love Theme, if it be one, shows no diminishment.   The coda
involves the Hamlet theme from the introduction in exciting
music which must represent the final duel with Laertes, and
once again there is a sudden and very effective drop from
*fortissimo* to *pianissimo* when the Fortinbras march returns.   It
should really have returned later, at the very end of the overture, but musically we cannot complain.   There is then a
tremendous climax on the Hamlet theme with a return to the
hectic music from the Introduction (why?), and the work ends
quietly with a brief funeral march over persistent drum taps.
Though the music suggests a performance of Hamlet without
the Prince, it is, as music, very enjoyable.

We now leave Russia and work our way west and south.
Svendsen's music was less piquantly Norwegian in style than
that of his fellow-countryman Grieg, but he was far more
competent both at orchestrating and at constructing music in
the larger forms.   His 'Romeo and Juliet' deals only with the
aspect of Love, and for once the generalized approach succeeds
because, in this alone of Shakespeare's plays, the one aspect
expresses the whole.   The work is nearly monothematic in that
all the tunes start like the first one, and I can detect no sign
of sonata form.   The start is slow, the end tragic and slower
still; the central *Allegro con fuoco* shows the touch of Wagner
in the frequent chromaticisms.   This highly romantic piece
conveys the mood of the play with considerable success.

No composer showed such ingenuity at descriptive music
as Richard Strauss, whose symphonic poems were leading
events of the 1890s.   Sad to say, 'Macbeth' was the least

successful of them.  Strauss began it in extreme youth, but laid it aside to write 'Don Juan', which he would not have done had it been going well.  With most of his symphonic poems he was happy to expound their meaning, but about 'Macbeth' he was somewhat cagey, even though its construction is clearly dictated by programme rather than musical considerations.

The brief opening fanfare must represent the coveted crown of Scotland, and after it we hear simultaneous themes labelled 'Macbeth' in the score; the upper one surges ambitiously, the lower strides up in the bass in a mildly evil way. The second subject aims to show us Lady Macbeth (see example 6, p. 199), and at this point the score carries six lines from Shakespeare's I. 5 beginning :

> Hie thee hither,
> That I may pour my spirits in thine ear.

Four minutes from the start the dark mood is interrupted by an agreeable tune for the violins which seems to me a fatal break in style.  The intention may have been to show the innocent Duncan and the contrast between Good and Evil. The new tune is soon combined with Lady Macbeth's and at the first big climax some seven minutes from the start we can assume that Duncan is being murdered.  The fanfare theme blossoms regally as Macbeth is crowned in triumph.  Then the music sinks to nothing.  The two Macbeth tunes are developed quietly and ominously to suggest doubts and conscience-pricks.  After what I take to be a glimpse of Banquo's ghost, we reach the final battle; Macbeth's lower theme with its rising bass is inverted to symbolize that his star is in the descendent, and he dies to irregularly-spaced chords falling into limbo.  A quiet coda broods effectively over most of the themes.  Originally the work ended loudly and triumphantly, but after the first performance Hans von Bülow told Strauss that he had made Macduff the hero instead of Macbeth, and Strauss rewrote the final pages.  The new coda is one of several fine passages, but as a whole 'Macbeth' suffers from a programme which even the informed listener cannot follow, while at the same time it depends too much on its programme to stand up as absolute music.

Dvořák's 'Othello' originated in some muddled thinking that involved two other overtures as well.  According to the excellent Czech miniature score, Dvořák 'decided to express in music his ideas, in a sense pantheistic, about nature as the giver of life's beauties and shadows'. He planned three independent overtures under the common title 'Nature, Life and Love', and he meant them to be played consecutively. However, he published them separately, giving them individual titles: 'Nature, or In Solitude', 'Carnival' and 'Othello'. The three works are linked by a common theme:

This, we are told, represents Nature in all three works. Already one feels confusion setting in. What kind of 'nature' does Dvořák mean? In his first overture he must mean the countryside with its living creatures and plants. In the second he appears to mean human nature at its most high-spirited. Having shown 'nature as the giver of life's beauties', he presumably gives us the 'shadows' in 'Othello'. But he also equated the Othello theme with Love, not, one would have thought, the subject of this play. Did he think of the eventual title only after writing the music?

This convenient solution is upset by the Czech miniature score, which reveals that in his autograph the composer pencilled references to Shakespeare's plot in no less than eleven places. Though we may never be clear as to what 'nature' has to do with this music, the connection with Shakespeare is not open to question. We shall see later that some of the pencilled references, as indeed much of the music itself, suggest a rather sketchy knowledge of the play. No copy of it was found among Dvořák's possessions when he died,[1] though he had plenty of chances of getting to know it. For instance, in 1865 *Othello* was given twelve times in the theatre where he was employed as a viola player, and nearer the year when he wrote his overture there were performances in the new National Theatre. Furthermore, he must have known Fibich's symphonic poem on the same play, which appeared in 1873, and Rossini's 'Otello', which was given in Prague on several occasions in his younger days. But I have come to suspect

---

[1] I would like to thank the Czech musicologist and Dvořák expert Jarmil Burghauser for some of this information.

that Verdi's 'Otello',[1] first given in Prague in January 1888, made a stronger impression on Dvořák than the play had ever done, and influenced the composition of his overture three and a half years later to a very considerable extent.

Like Tchaikovsky's 'Romeo and Juliet', Dvořák's 'Otello' has a slow *religioso* introduction, the purpose of which is far from clear. These rather beautiful modal chords return after Desdemona's death when, according to Dvořák but not to Shakespeare, 'he prays'. (Nobody prays on stage in the play; Desdemona does so in a memorable passage in Verdi's opera.) Othello is represented by a descending four-note scale, which I give as it occurs in the introduction and at the start of the main Allegro :

The introduction is based on the Prayer, Othello and Nature themes. The Allegro starts with an alternation between the Othello theme in the treble and the Nature theme in the bass. The second subject represents Desdemona (see example 6, p. 198), and it is accompanied by Othello's descending triplets on the second violins. After some indecisive moments, the oboes insinuate their way slowly up a scale till, at the top, they produce a sentimental major seventh, and it is at this point that Dvořák pencilled his first reference, 'they embrace in silent ecstasy'. Their love finds further expression in some beautiful slow chromatic chords pilfered from the Sleep theme in Wagner's 'Die Walküre'. Then come some rather dull pages in which, for all too long, slow woodwind chords (Iago?) alternate with Othello's chattering triplets. After a climax, 'jealousy and rage begin to grow in the mind of Othello' to the music of the Nature theme beneath a sort of Forest Murmurs effect on the flutes. Some of the music flows too amiably for tragedy, and one keeps wondering if a doom-laden atmosphere is possible in a quick three time. We are some way into the recap when (at bar 480 according to the Artia score, but surely 492 is much more likely) 'Othello murders her at the height of his anger'. Pencilled identifications come thick and fast hereabouts. After some indecisive bars, Desdemona's

---

[1] For a detailed account of Verdi's opera, see above, pp. 170-5.

theme returns, as it should at this point in a sonata-form movement, and 'she tells him for the last time of her innocence'. She dies. Just after the next *ff* climax 'Othello begins to regret his deed'; the pain in his soul lessens, 'he prays', and 'he kisses her for the last time' (that major seventh again). After the unintentional Fire Music chords, the timps start a long *pianissimo* roll as 'he broods on his terrible deed' while the cellos play the Nature theme. He decides to kill himself, and does so as the music reaches its last *fortissimo* climax.

No one should count on being able to follow the events described above from the sound alone. Dvořák at heart was an 'absolute' composer, like his idol Brahms, and he never showed very much sense of musical characterization or dramatic effect. From the programme point of view the overture has two grave faults. First, Othello is shown as a static character, whereas in fact no Shakespeare hero alters more as the play proceeds. Dvořák's hero begins and ends as a strong man in love. The murder seems a purely temporary aberration for which there is scarcely any musical preparation. Secondly, and this failing is closely allied to the first, there is no recognizable sign of Iago or of the jealousy motive. Dvořák does not seem to have realized that Shakespeare's theme is the green-eyed monster. Instead there seems an almost excessive emphasis on love (in a sense, the original title of the work), and one wonders if this emphasis arose from memories, conscious or otherwise, of the marvellous Love Duet at the end of Verdi's Act I. There are further hints of Dvořák's admiration for this opera. In Shakespeare Othello and Desdemona talk *before* he smothers her; afterwards she revives to murmur no more than three half-lines. In Verdi, as in Dvořák, there is no 'dialogue' before the smothering, but a great deal after it. In Shakespeare there is no evidence that the pain in Othello's soul lessens, nor does he pray, and 'to die upon a kiss' are his last words *after* stabbing himself. Verdi makes much more of the kiss than Shakespeare, and a masterstroke is his repetition of the kiss theme from the Act I duet at the very end of the opera. Dvořák attempts the same masterstroke.

It is only fair to add that Dvořák himself had doubts about the title of his overture. When he sent the score to his publisher, he wrote 'Overture in F sharp minor, "Othello" or "Tragic" or even "Eroica"? Or should I just call it Overture? But it is to some extent programme music.' In writing of attempts to express Shakespeare's plays in orchestral music one cannot do otherwise than censure this work as a failure. As music, on the other hand, it can sound magnificent, and Dvořák seldom showed such powers of organization in a long movement. It is taut and strong and beautifully constructed. It may not convince as a musical profile of Othello, but you cannot help liking it.

### 3. THE ENGLISH CONTRIBUTION

Mendelssohn's style was a good deal more imitated in England than his descriptive innovations. The first direct result of the early London performances of his overture to *A Midsummer Night's Dream* were two concert overtures by a composer still in his 'teens, William Sterndale Bennett. These were 'The Tempest' (1832) and 'The Merry Wives of Windsor' (1834); neither has ever been published. 'The Tempest' begins with Mendelssohnian fairy music for Ariel, but the connection between music and drama is less subtle and detailed than in its model. It is sad that Sterndale-Bennett did not return to Shakespeare music when he was older.

A work of great originality is the overture to *Macbeth* by R. L. Pearsall. Pearsall did not start serious composition until he was 30, and he spent most of his subsequent life in Germany, living first in Karlsruhe and later in a castle on Lake Constance. Almost alone among English musicians of the day he was deeply interested in the English Madrigal School, and he himself wrote madrigals and intricate part-songs of real quality. In 1839 Schotts of Mainz published in parts his Grand Characteristic Overture to Shakespeare's *Macbeth*, described as an 'Introduction to the famous Witches' Choruses in the Tragedy'. Pearsall provided a Foreword in German in which he states (incorrectly, as it happens) that for a hundred and fifty years Matthew Locke's splendid choruses have always been sung whenever the play was acted.[1] 'Locke wrote no overture, so I decided to do so.' Pearsall explains that he has been consciously archaic in places in order to fit in with the style of the old music; hence the fugal passages. He goes into his programme at some length. Of the four sections, the first three deal with the general mood of the play, the demoniac

---

[1] See above, p. 53.

P

element, and Macbeth's mental strife occasioned by the witches' prophecies and his wife's promptings. A clarinet solo briefly and appositely quotes from the witches' chorus then sung in Act II, 'He must, he will, he shall have blood' (words by Davenant). Eventually Macbeth, 'overcome by witchcraft . . . manages the bloody deed. The dark powers triumph and loud is the jubilation in Hell.' After which the overture ends quietly. There is a touch of the amateur in the way the music flows, but the macabre mood of the play is surprisingly well caught, and the whole overture is imaginative. It deserves occasional performance today.[1]

Early in Victoria's reign a number of Shakespeare overtures were written by the Macfarren brothers and others. None was published in score, but an overture to *Romeo and Juliet* by G. A. Macfarren appeared in a piano duet arrangement in 1840, and the autograph full score is in the Fitzwilliam Museum, Cambridge. Like Mendelssohn, Macfarren manages with a single Allegro movement, with sonata form only modified at the end. The main themes suggest the Vendetta and Love respectively. In the development they are effectively worked together in double counterpoint. Macfarren delays the recap of the Love Theme until the coda to achieve a Death Scene, and he precedes this with some slow *religioso* bars for Friar Laurence. This Love Theme is engaging in spite of some harmonium-type harmonies, and the whole overture has more power than might be expected.

Henry Hugh Pearson, later known as Hugo Pierson, was a product of Harrow and Cambridge, and studied music at Leipzig, where he was praised by Schumann. After a brief period as Reid Professor of Music at Edinburgh, he spent the last twenty-five years of his life in Germany, living much of the time as a recluse. Many of his works were performed and published in Germany; his music for the second part of Goethe's *Faust* was repeatedly given in Hamburg, Frankfurt and elsewhere. Two of his Shakespeare overtures, both for concert use, were published in full score in Leipzig. Pearson's models are Liszt and Schumann, and the music is imaginative but disorganized. In 'Romeo and Juliet' the all-too-numerous themes are seldom repeated or developed, and the music is shapeless. 'Macbeth' is much better, but here too the com-

---

[1] I would like to thank Dr. Nicholas Temperley for drawing my attention to this overture, and for other information.

poser is over-concerned with finding musical equivalents for passages in the play.   More than twenty quotations are printed over the score (in German), though the unprepared listener could in no case divine the intention from the sound.   The work starts with a splendid slow unison theme headed 'Hours dreadful and things strange' (said by the Old Man in II. 4), and then introduces the witches, who are poorly managed. Macbeth and his soldiers arrive on the blasted heath to a Scots-style march with snap rhythms.   The witches' 'All hail!' predictions are translated as follows, with Macbeth reacting after the second one :

Lady Macbeth is given a too-beautiful clarinet melody.   All the best-known quotations turn up : 'If it were done when 'tis done . . .', 'Is this a dagger . . .' and 'It is a knell/That summons thee to heaven or to hell'.   The long Witches' Dance in the middle of the piece has no quotations from the play over the music, which becomes descriptive again in the third and last section.   This includes a March for the English army, Lady Macbeth's death (rather well done) and a brief battle. The work ends quietly with the opening theme and the First Witch's 'All hail!'

There is no need to linger over such late Victorian symphonic poems as Edward German's 'Hamlet' (1895).   The musical renaissance in our own century ensures a higher standard of Shakespeare music, though it affords fewer examples.   Frank Bridge's 'There is a Willow grows aslant a Brook' is an evocative little piece for small orchestra which is strangely overlooked. A miniature score is available. Vaughan Williams's 'Serenade to Music' was written for Sir Henry Wood's Jubilee in 1938, and is a setting for voices and orchestra of selected lines from *The Merchant of Venice* (V. 1), beginning 'How sweet the moonlight sleeps upon this bank!' All names and references to people are cut, so that the words lose their dramatic significance and becomes an Ode to Music. At the first performance the work was sung by sixteen famous soloists, but it is now usually given by four soloists and chorus, or even by chorus alone. The music is static but sensuously lovely, and it has all the moonlit beauty of the words.[1]

I have left until the last the one giant among English concert works based on Shakespeare, Elgar's 'Falstaff'. Though as fine as anything he ever wrote, it has not been a favourite with the general public, partly, perhaps, because it is based on the two parts of *Henry IV*, which are not well known to most concert-goers, and partly because, as with Wagner's 'The Ring', the listener needs to do some homework in advance. But such homework is amply rewarded.

We know Elgar's intentions with unusual exactness. In the *Musical Times* for September 1913 he wrote an Analytical Essay on the music which is still available from Novello's as a pamphlet. In this he is at pains to point out that the caricature of Falstaff in *The Merry Wives of Windsor* (and in Verdi's opera?) must be forgotten. His subject is the far more subtle Falstaff of *Henry IV*. He had prepared for this composition by reading Maurice Morgann's famous *Essay on the Dramatic Character of Sir John Falstaff* (1777) as well as the writings of other Shakespeare commentators, from some of whom he quotes.

The Symphonic Study, as Elgar calls it, falls into four main sections played without a break, and in addition there are short interludes for small orchestra after the second section and towards the end of the third. The timings below will give a rough idea of when the various events can be expected, but it must be remembered that performances can vary considerably in tempo :

1. *Falstaff and Prince Henry* (0 to $3\frac{1}{4}$). A character-study without action. Elgar presents us with several Falstaff themes and the one associated with Prince Hal. The jovial rotund tune at the start captures the rolling walk of his hero. Prince Hal's theme is suitably handsome and dashing, but the im-

[1] See also above, p. 85.

mediate repeat of the opening phrase in the minor hints at underlying seriousness:

A 'cajoling' tune on the cellos shows Falstaff amusing the Prince on their pub-crawls. 'Sweet wag, shall there be gallows standing in England when thou art king? . . . Do not thou, when thou art king, hang a thief'. (*1 Henry IV*, I. 2).

There is a moment of silence between this and the next section.

   2. *Eastcheap — Gadshill — The Boar's Head, Revelry and Sleep* (based on *1 Henry IV*, I. 2, II. 2, II. 4) (3¼ to 15¾). Short spikey tunes suggest the chatter of the city riff-raff, and the one with a trill a few seconds from the start is for Mistress Quickly, Doll Tearsheet and the other 'honest gentlewomen'. The first long tune (3.40) is a vast affair for Falstaff, singing and boasting in his cups. Another with absurdly exaggerated leaps exactly catches his monstrous tongue-in-the-cheek exaggerations:

After a rumbustious climax things quieten down as Falstaff and his friends set off (without the Prince) to rob a coach by night on Gadshill. Here is their 'cheerful out-of-door ambling theme' (6.5):

A mood of quiet nocturnal suspense is built up, and we hear the Prince and Poins in disguise waiting to leap out on Falstaff's party and rob them of their stolen booty; this is neatly conveyed by a disguised version of the Prince's tune (example 16):

The Prince's object, it will be remembered, is to see what account Falstaff will give of the occasion next day. Falstaff is duly routed (example 18 above treated as a quick *fugato* and then combined with the broad boasting theme), and when the climax subsides, Falstaff is back in London at the Boar's Head, 'battered but once more in tolerable case'. There is a lot of chattering ('Shall we be merry?') and rather too much of the women's tune with the trill. Eventually (12) Falstaff gives his ridiculous account of what happened at Gadshill, a bassoon playing example 18 above with even wider leaps. 'I am a rogue, if I were not at half-sword with a dozen of them two hours together'. They all laugh uproariously at him. When next the bassoon plays example 18, Falstaff is no longer coherent in his speech (14) and soon we hear him heaving three vast snores behind the arras—'How hard he fetches breath!' A held note on the violins links this section on to the first interlude.

In *The Dream Interlude* (15.45 to 18) the sleeping Falstaff recalls his youth as page to Thomas Mowbray, Duke of Norfolk. Verdi in his opera lets Falstaff sing this hint of his past, but Shakespeare gave it not to Falstaff at all, but to Justice Shallow in *2 Henry IV*, III. 2.

3. *Falstaff's March — Return through Gloucestershire — The New King — The Ride to London* (18 to 25). In this scherzo section we move on to *2 Henry IV*. After a moment's silence and a few bars of bustling the brass twice flings out a call to arms. The inevitable rebellion has broken out in the Midlands, and Falstaff's services are required in support of the King. There are two fragments of tune for his recruiting march; the second is especially scruffy and gives us the scarecrow army of Wart, Feeble and the rest (*2 Henry IV*, III. 2):

In the ensuing battle-music we hear the rotund Falstaff theme of the opening bars. A brief repeat of example 21 tells us 'the

army is dischargèd all, and gone' (*2 Henry IV*, IV. 3).  Falstaff
decides to return 'through Gloucestershire; and there will I
visit Master Robert Shallow, esquire'.  The music that depicts
this anticipates the second interlude and we hear once more
the 'ambling' theme (example 19).  This *Second Interlude:
Shallow's Orchard* (22¼ to 23¾) has what Elgar calls 'sadly merry
music for pipe and tabor' (the pipe, rather oddly, is an oboe) and
in between times muted strings show Falstaff snoozing under
the apple-trees, shaded from the warm sun (V. 3).  Suddenly
Pistol discharges himself into this rural scene. 'Sir John, thy
tender lambkin now is king;/Harry the Fifth's the man'.  We
hear examples 16, 18 and 21 in rapid succession as Falstaff sets
off with all speed for London, boasting of his hopes — 'I know
the young king is sick for me'.  There is an expectant silence.

4. *King Henry V's Progress to his Coronation — The Repudiation
of Falstaff and his Death* (25 to 33½).  A solemn march-rhythm
builds up, and we hear music of stern purpose for the new king.
Falstaff, in the crowd near Westminster Abbey, awaits his
approach with high confidence.  But after a sudden drop to
*pianissimo* example 20 tells us that Falstaff, who did not recognize his friend at Gadshill, is in a sense not going to do so now
either.  There is a tremendous climax as the new king comes
near in his robes of state, and example 16 rings out gloriously.
The king sees Falstaff (the opening rotund tune in the bass) and
there is a sudden silence as he stops the procession (28¼).  He
speaks to his old friend like a stranger.  Falstaff is not yet
disillusioned (the 'cajoling' theme, example 17), and example
18 suggests a misguided attempt at humour.  But the king is
determined to put his old life behind him, and he rejects Falstaff utterly and cruelly. 'How ill white hairs become a fool
and jester! . . . I banish thee, on pain of death'.  The
procession passes on, leaving Falstaff broken.

The Death Scene (31), described by Mistress Quickly in
*Henry V* (II. 3), begins with a reminiscence of Shallow's
Orchard ('a' babbled of green fields') and there is a nightmare
memory of Doll Tearsheet's tune.  But Falstaff recalls Prince
Hall without rancour (example 16).  To a short clarinet phrase
his soul abandons his mountainous body.  Elgar gives the last
word to the young king.  All this closing music is extremely
moving.  But then the whole work is masterly, and the way in
which Elgar welds the fascinatingly diversified material into a
whole is beyond praise.

## 4. SHAKESPEARE ON THE PIANO

Shakespeare's plays have inspired little or no chamber music, and only a handful of piano pieces, of which much the most considerable is Beethoven's stormy Sonata in D minor, Op. 31, no. 2. Schindler records that he once asked Beethoven what the first movement meant. The question is not nearly so silly as it sounds; I do not think Schindler would have asked it of any other Beethoven first movement. This one begins very oddly with a brief imitation of recitative, and there are several recitative-like interruptions in the middle. Such writing was unknown in classical keyboard music, and one might well wonder what it 'meant'. Beethoven's reply to Schindler was 'Read Shakespeare's *The Tempest*'. Presumably the recitatives represent Prospero bidding Ariel raise a storm, and the quick music is the storm itself.

The wonderful slow movement of Beethoven's first String Quartet, Op. 18, No. 1, is said to have been inspired by the final scene in *Romeo and Juliet*, but this is certainly not descriptive music in any detailed sense.

At a much less inspired level are three piano pieces deriving from *Macbeth*. Schumann's 'Novelette' Op. 21, no. 3 (1838) has a central Intermezzo section which was originally headed 'When shall we three meet again?' In later editions this was deleted. The music is quick, romantic, and not in the least macabre, and it will not suggest Shakespeare's witches to British ears. In view of the lack of perception in both this piece and in his overture to *Julius Caesar* (1851), it is surprising that Schumann, angling just before his marriage for a doctor's degree at Jena University, seriously considered writing a thesis on *Shakespeare and his Relation to Music*.

In 1859, while he was in Gothenburg, Smetana wrote a long piano piece called 'Macbeth and the Witches'. Unfortunately it has been out of print for many years, and I have not been able to find a copy.

The third of Grieg's Lyric Pieces (Set I, 1867) is called 'Watchman's Song'; it used to be a great favourite with teachers of the piano. Incredibly Grieg had in mind the Porter in *Macbeth*. Thus a bawdy old Scotsman putting on his clothes in the middle of the night to answer the door has become an honest son of the soil singing a stirring presbyterian hymn.

Much more Shakespearean is Debussy's 'La Danse de Puck', No. 11 in his first book of Preludes. The music is suitably nimble and pert, but one must bear in mind Debussy's habit of finding names for his Preludes *after* he had written them.

## 5. INCIDENTAL MUSIC

In the eighteenth and for much of the nineteenth centuries incidental music for English productions of Shakespeare was surprisingly long-lived. The *Macbeth* music attributed to Locke was in constant use throughout this period, and though new productions sometimes offered a new song setting, this would be in addition to music taken over from previous productions. Thus Arne set 'Where the bee sucks' for Garrick's production of *The Tempest*, but much of Purcell's music [1] was still played then and indeed in all productions until well into the next century. In 1818, as an overture to *The Comedy of Errors*, Sir Henry Bishop wrote a pot-pourri of the best-known Shakespeare music, instrumental and vocal, from Purcell's time to his own. It would be impossible to write such an overture today, for there is no comparable corpus of familiar music associated with the plays.

The Continent of Europe lacked a similar tradition on which to draw, and when in the late 1700s Shakespeare productions became the rage complete sets of incidental music had to be commissioned for them, and eventually well-known composers were called on. Thus, in 1825 Spohr wrote music for a Leipzig production of *Macbeth*; only the overture was published, a singularly feeble piece. The music Mendelssohn wrote in 1843 for a production of *A Midsummer Night's Dream* in the King of Prussia's theatre at Potsdam set new standards, and was largely responsible for a musical revolution in London theatre productions. Mendelssohn's popularity in England was such that there was an immediate demand for anything he wrote, and a London production of *A Midsummer Night's Dream* with his music made the traditional type of Shakespeare music sound thin and old-fashioned. Well before the end of the nineteenth century the old songs had almost entirely disappeared, to be replaced by newly commissioned and more

[1] See above, p. 55 and p. 105.

elaborate music. Sullivan wrote goodish music for *The Merchant of Venice* and rather less good for *The Merry Wives of Windsor*, *Henry VIII* and *Macbeth*. Edward German's music for *Romeo and Juliet*, *Much Ado About Nothing*, *Richard III* and *Henry VIII* followed in the 1890s. Apart from the 'Three Dances' from the last named, none of this music outlived the production for which it was intended, nor have the comparable scores which Humperdinck wrote in Germany for many of the comedies. Producers were becoming scornful of anything written for other producers, and this made such music ephemeral. Only Mendelssohn's for *A Midsummer Night's Dream* enjoyed something of the longevity of Purcell's for *The Tempest*, to be killed eventually by the disappearance of the full-scale theatre orchestra.

The late nineteenth century was the golden age of the entr'acte. The realistic sets of the Victorians were heavier than Georgian sets had been, and took longer to change, and the resultant intervals were agreeably filled with orchestral music. In Garrick's day interval-music had consisted of *concerti grossi* with no relevance to the play being performed, but by Irving's time entr'actes were expected to anticipate the mood or the events of the scene to come. Composers could take plenty of time, and entr'actes were sometimes as long as overtures. Many such pieces, mostly by Continental composers, survive in the concert repertoire today.

In the modern theatre conditions for inspiring incidental music of lasting quality no longer exist. Except in Russia, theatres no longer employ symphony orchestras. Shakespeare's plays are so peppered with songs and sennets that some form of music is essential, and the modern solution in England is to have a few wind and percussion players either under or behind the stage, positions in which string players would not be heard. Wind and percussion players produce more decibels per man, and so give shoe-string theatres better value for money, but they cannot hope to sound as effective out of sight as a balanced orchestra in the pit. Apron stages and theatres-in-the-round have many attractions, but they are not kind to musicians.

Today's cinema-fed audiences are intolerant of intervals, which are conveniently avoided by the use of permanent sets. The need for entr'actes has gone, and composers are called on for little more than song settings and brief bursts of background

music.  As these will be unacceptable to other producers and
too curiously scored for the concert-hall, they cannot hope to
be published and they die as the last-night curtain falls.

In 1600 the music that decorated a play was enjoyed by all.
But today's song-settings are often too difficult both for the
actors who sing them and for the musically-untutored audience.
Background music, perhaps accompanying a stylized battle,
can be serial, electronic or what you will and still be effective,
for it does not demand undivided attention.  But a song does,
and it will waste everyone's time unless it is simple and immediately enjoyable, for it will have no chance of impressing
through repetition like concert music.  Difficulties and perhaps
embarrassments are caused by the lack of visual contact in
the modern theatre between singer and band, nor are wind
and percussion instruments well suited to accompanying songs.

It is strange that producers should be so chary of trying
the Elizabethan method, which worked splendidly then and
still would today.  Singers should accompany themselves, or
be accompanied by someone close by on the stage.  The lute
was not too hard for Elizabethans, and should be within the
capabilities of at least one or two modern actors, while the
guitar, an excellent substitute, is the easiest of all instruments.
If drama schools would start lute and guitar classes for the
musically-inclined, we would be able to enjoy both modern
guitar settings in what is loosely known as the folk style, and
also Elizabethan settings, including those actually written for
the plays.  Producers worry constantly about the authenticity
of the texts they use.  Why not about that of the music?

Only incidental music that survives in the concert hall, or
deserves to do so, will be discussed here in detail.  My seven
examples are : Mendelssohn's 'A Midsummer Night's Dream'
(1843) ; Sullivan's 'The Tempest' (1862) ; Balakirev's 'King
Lear' (composed c. 1860–1, though not published until 1904) ;
Fauré's 'Shylock' (1889) ; Tchaikovsky's 'Hamlet' (1891) ;
Sibelius's 'The Tempest' (1926) ; Kabalevsky's 'Romeo and
Juliet' (1956).  These have all been published complete, or
virtually so, and also recorded, except for Sullivan's 'Tempest'
and Balakirev's 'King Lear'.  These are also odd-men-out
in that they were composed without a production in view.

It is easy for us to lose sight of the astonishing originality
of Mendelssohn's music for *A Midsummer Night's Dream*.  There

had been nothing like it before, and indeed few composers
since have shown an equal understanding of Shakespeare.
Quick music of a fairy-like delicacy came naturally to Mendelssohn, and the Scherzo that precedes Act II makes a perfect
introduction to Puck's 'How now, spirit! whither wander
you?' and the 'Over hill, over dale' reply. Fragments of it
spill over into the spoken dialogue, accompanying it in the
style musicians call 'melodrama'. A miniature march heralds
the arrival of Oberon and Titania with their trains, and
snatches of this too are injected under the subsequent dialogue.
The speeches that begin II. 3 ('Come now, a roundel and a
fairy song') are also accompanied, the music leading into 'You
spotted snakes', which is sung by two soloists and a four-part
female chorus. Without a break we hear a new unaccompanied
theme of four minims rising menacingly as Oberon squeezes
the juice on Titania's eyelids, and we hear it again later on
when Puck does the same for Lysander.

The Intermezzo between Acts II and III looks both back-
wards at Hermia's terror alone in the wood, and forwards, in
its final bars, to the Pyramus and Thisbe rehearsal, which is
precisely suggested by an amiably inane bassoon tune. Act
III has more 'melodrama' in the fairy scenes. The snatches
that accompany Puck's routing of the rehearsing mechanicals
would not be very effective in the theatre, but when Titania
is roused from sleep by the 'magic' of Bottom's tuneless song,
the magic chords from the beginning of the overture are
irresistibly parodied :

As the curtain falls on the sleeping lovers, we hear the famous
Nocturne, with its wonderfully tranquil horn solo and subtly
disturbed middle section, suggestive of unquiet dreams. Towards the end the sleep-drenched mood lightens as the curtain
rises on Act IV. Titania and Bottom enter over the closing
bars, and Mendelssohn manages to reflect this in the music
without upsetting the piece as a whole. When Oberon restores
Titania's eyes to their former state, Mendelssohn inverts his
four-minim theme to suggest a return to normality, a surprisingly modern touch. Titania's 'Music, ho! music, such
as charmeth sleep' (IV. 1) produces a repeat of the Nocturne

horn melody, but Theseus's arrival to *Wind horns* needs more virile music, which Mendelssohn takes from bars 70-77 of the Overture. Perhaps he had had Theseus's hunting horns in mind when he wrote this passage sixteen years earlier.

The Wedding March which stands before Act V contains Mendelssohn's best-known tune; it is perhaps the best-known tune by any great composer. In the play within the play Pyramus and Thisbe die to a fatuous little funeral march full of those one-time horrors, consecutive fifths; it is scored only for clarinet, bassoon and drum. The mechanicals' theme from the Overture proves ideal for the Bergomask. The mortals retire to bed to a snatch of the Wedding March which quickly merges into the fairy music. Puck's 'Now the hungry lion roars' is spoken cold, but the following speeches of Oberon and Titania are accompanied by the four magic chords, and the same words are then sung by a fairy chorus to a new tune that ingeniously fits the fairy music from the Overture. The end is almost the same as the end of the Overture, and makes a lovely midnight valediction.

When Sullivan was a 19-year-old student in Leipzig, he wrote elaborate incidental music for *The Tempest*, which he rescored the following year — 1862 — for concert perform-ances at the Crystal Palace. It was these that first made him famous. Later on, in Paris, he several times played the piano-duet arrangement with Rossini, who is said to have much admired the music. Later still it was published in full score as Sullivan's Op. 1. By 1890, when Grove was writing about Sullivan in his famous *Dictionary of Music and Musicians*, the music had still not been used for a stage production. Yet it seems both apt and inventive, and a modern producer would be lucky indeed if he was able to commission anything so good.

Mendelssohn's influence is both obvious and beneficial. Instead of an Overture there is a three-minute Introduction which starts quietly with a picture of the magic island and ends with the storm; in between Prospero calls up the ele-ments in a recitative-like passage for the violins. There is no point in describing the twelve numbers individually. All are scored with facility and grace, and Ariel's songs are specially good. I must admit to a banal 'Banquet Dance', and it is disappointing to find no Caliban, but I agree with Grove that this was one of Sullivan's best works. How to let people hear it is a problem. Most of the music would sound delightful in the theatre and pointless in the concert hall.

Balakirev's music for *King Lear* was written in the same flush of enthusiasm that produced the overture, laid aside, and then after forty years touched up and published in 1904. I have not traced a theatre performance, and even in 1904 theatres would hardly have accepted it in its complete form. The first piece carries impracticability to stupendous heights. After the opening lines of the play there is a stage direction: *Sennet. Enter one bearing a coronet, King Lear, Cornwall, Albany, Goneril, Regan, Cordelia and Attendants.* At seven minutes this must be the longest Sennet in existence, and it is scored for a large stage military band of some thirty players as well as the very considerable orchestra in the pit. Clarinets, trumpets and trombones would scarcely look at home in Lear's Ancient Britain, no audience would want to listen to so long a piece of music just after a full-length overture, and no producer could devise effective business to cover it. Balakirev provided an alternative version of his Procession without the stage band, but even this demands triple woodwind and four trumpets, as does the Overture. Except for a quiet trio section with a Russian flavour, the Procession is based on tunes from the Overture, but in Polonaise rhythm. Stassov thought this the best of the incidental pieces, and certainly the antiphonal effects between the stage band and the orchestra in the pit would sound tremendous.

The short Prelude to Act II is called 'Lear's evil Daughters; their Father's Curse'. It is based on the semi-quaver theme from the Overture (example 9, page 204, tune C).

Stassov was connected by marriage with an English family, and he possessed a number of English books, including Chappell's 'Popular Music of the Olden Time' (1855). He sent several tunes from this collection to Balakirev for possible inclusion in his *King Lear* music. One was the well-known 'traditional' setting of 'When that I was and a little tiny boy', sung by Feste in *Twelfth Night*:

23 When that I was and a lit-tle ti-ny boy, With a heigh ho! the wind and the rain.

Stassov told Balakirev that this had been in use in Shakespeare's day, but Chappell does not suggest this, and it is almost certainly untrue.  The song was first printed in *c.* 1770, and was probably composed by the singer Joseph Vernon.[1]  Chappell points out the resemblance of the words to the Fool's song in *King Lear*, III. 2 :

> He that has and a little tiny wit,
> With a hey, ho, the wind and the rain, etc.

Stassov does not seem to mention this highly relevant point in his letter about the song, but it would be too much of a coincidence if Balakirev had used the tune in his Storm Entr'acte by mere chance.  The piece is called 'Lear and the Fool on the Heath; the Storm', and it presupposes that the first scene in Act III is cut.  It starts by alternating between Lear's 'infirm' tune (example 9, tune B) and the Fool's Song given above.  Then comes some of the storm music from the overture, at the height of which the curtain rises.  This is a most attractive piece.

The Prelude to Act IV is better still.  It is called 'Lear's awakening in Cordelia's Tent, to the Accompaniment of an English Folk Tune'.  It is Balakirev's whim to have his *thème anglais* played by a cor anglais; the result is entrancing :

There are two oddities here.  The first is that though Balakirev must have got the tune from Stassov, it does not seem to be mentioned in Stassov's correspondence, and it is not in Chappell.  The second is that it is not English.  The tune, which has not, I think, been identified before, was first printed in 1784 by Edward Jones in his 'Musical and Poetical Relicks of the Welsh Bards'.  By the second edition of this it had acquired its modern name, *Difyrrwch Gwyr Dyfi* — The Men of Dovey's Delight.  (There is a version of it in The National Song Book.)  Early Welsh scholars suggested the tune looked more Irish than Welsh.  In Balakirev's entr'acte it alternates

---

[1] Stassov mentions a German theory that Mendelssohn borrowed a version of the song for the end of the Act III Entr'acte in his *Midsummer Night's Dream* music — the bassoon tune that represents the mechanicals. The likeness, if any, is surely coincidental.

with Lear's theme (example 9, tune A), and towards the end Cordelia's is played by muted strings. This is a beautiful and imaginative piece, very well scored.

The 'English' tune is played again in IV. 7, at the point when the Doctor attending Lear in the French camp calls for louder music, apparently for prophylactic reasons. The cor anglais is accompanied only by clarinets, bassoons and harp, and though the music is only a background to dialogue, the beauty and naïveté of the melody seem exactly right for Lear in his madness. In the last act there are four short pieces (some of which employ the stage band), but none of the music in this act is distinguished.

It is tragic that the best of Balakirev's *King Lear* music should be heard so seldom. An effective half-hour suite, satisfying as to key, might consist of

The Overture
The Prelude to Act III (Lear and the Fool on the Heath; the Storm)
The Prelude to Act IV (Lear awakening in Cordelia's Tent)
The Procession in Act I (the single-orchestra version)

This music has never had much hope of performance in the theatre; the concert hall is its place, and a rescue operation is called for.

Fauré's 'Shylock' was written in 1889 for a three-act French version of *The Merchant of Venice* by Edmond Haraucourt, who also produced a version of *Macbeth*. To reduce scene-changing to a minimum, Haraucourt completely altered the order of events. Thus there are only two scenes at Belmont before the trial, as opposed to seven in the original, and any one scene in the French version is likely to be an amalgam of three or four widely-separated scenes in Shakespeare's play. In other respects Haraucourt follows the original fairly closely.

The published suite consists of two songs and four orchestral pieces scored for small orchestra. There is nothing in the French text to show where the orchestral pieces occur. If Fauré wrote an overture, he cannot have thought well of it, for no such piece has been published. Koechlin, Fauré's biographer and himself a composer, found an evocative Venetian charm in the score, which for him conjured up a vision of gondolas and rose-marble palaces, but to me the music sounds

wholly French — so French as to be scarcely conceivable as a
background to Shakespeare's words. But much of it is
ravishingly lovely.

The opening song, 'Oh! les filles! Venez, les filles aux voix
douces', is sung off-stage at the beginning of the second scene
('La nuit, sur le canal'), and immediately after it Jessica comes
out of Shylock's house in disguise. The singer is directed to
sing 'dans la coulisse' even in the concert version. No. 2,
an Entr'acte, is bold, assertive and delightful, and starts with
a trumpet-call; there is a very faint Elizabethan atmosphere.
Clearly the piece stands immediately before Act II, in which
we first meet Portia ('Bien vrai! Mon petit corps est las de ce
grand monde!') and the three suitors. During this scene, the
first suitor, the Prince of Arragon in Haraucourt's version,
sings the remaining song outside Portia's window before he
has been seen on the stage. For some inscrutable reason
Fauré calls it a Madrigal, and very charming it is, though
un-Elizabethan to a fault. Next comes one of Fauré's loveliest
inventions, 'Épithalame'. This was presumably played before
Act III, which corresponds with Shakespeare's Act V. After
a gravely beautiful opening there is a second tune which turns
out to be a softened amorous version of the Entr'acte theme;
perhaps it represents Portia. We also hear again a quiet
trumpet rhythm borrowed from the Entr'acte. This last act
is laid in the garden of Belmont at night, and Haraucourt asks
for music at the same point as does Shakespeare himself; the
Nocturne for muted strings is charmingly right as a background to Jessica's 'I am never merry when I hear sweet
music' and Lorenzo's comforting reply. The Finale begins
with a *pizzicato* imitation of lutes, which was probably played
under the closing dialogue, and no doubt the rest of the piece
was danced by the whole company.

Tchaikovsky cannot have taken much trouble over the
music he wrote in 1891 for a production of *Hamlet* in St.
Petersburg. The theatre employed an orchestra of only 27
players, and though Tchaikovsky managed to have nine more
engaged, the band was still unequal in numbers or skill to the
previously-composed overture, which in any case was too long.
The composer reduced it by half, simplified the syncopated
rhythms, cut the more difficult semi-quaver passages and
ruined the piece. The loveliest tune (the one that follows

Q

Ophelia's) disappears altogether, and the Fortinbras march episodes lose all their dramatic impact.

It is significant that so few of the overture tunes are repeated in the incidental music.  It looks as though Tchaikovsky had an imperfect notion as to what they represented, whereas Mendelssohn, in his *Midsummer Night's Dream* music, worked in tunes from his overture with triumphant ease.  So casual is Tchaikovsky's attitude that he actually has the Alla Tedesca movement from the Third Symphony as an entr'acte before Act II.  He might as suitably have used 'The Dance of the Sugar Plum Fairy' had he written it in time.  The entr'acte before Act IV is especially unpleasant.  Tchaikovsky roused himself for Ophelia's songs, which have the right touch of pathos, and the English words can be fitted to them without too much difficulty:

The Grave-digger's song manages to be banal without being appropriate, and it may be taken that those of the sixteen numbers I have not mentioned are not worth mentioning.

In 1937 Prokofiev wrote incidental music for a production of *Hamlet* in Leningrad, and a little later Shostakovich did so too, which suggests that Soviet producers are no more anxious to use music written for their rivals than are our own.  Neither score has been published, and this is especially tantalizing in the light of an article Prokofiev wrote about his own music.

Of the ten numbers, four are songs for Ophelia in which the composer 'partly used folk-airs of the Shakespeare period'. He avoided 'mysticism' in the Ghost scene for the curious reason that Shakespeare did not intend any; 'the music should rather convey the emotions of the wronged father'. For the 'mousetrap' scene he wrote in the style of a gavotte, superficially gay at the start, and for the end of the play he composed 'a triumphal march, or rather an Adagio in march rhythm, starting softly . . . and rising to a triumphant C major' on the strange grounds that though almost everyone is dead 'life triumphs, the life that Shakespeare loves and in which he believes'. A suite of this music for small orchestra had its first concert performance in Russia in 1954. I should like to hear it.

In 1904 André Antoine commissioned Debussy to write incidental music for a production of *King Lear* at the Odéon in Paris. Debussy pecked away at the problem, but accomplished little. In 1926, long after his death, two short pieces were published, amounting in all to about five minutes of music. 'Fanfare' for brass, drums and harp was reconstituted from barely legible sketches by Roger-Ducasse. 'Sommeil de Lear', scored for flute, four horns, harp, timps and strings, is gravely beautiful. Sketches for six more pieces exist.

As I write, Sibelius is languishing in a trough of official disfavour of which I happen not to approve. But though I have less wish than usual to beat the bones of the dead, I cannot champion his music for *The Tempest*. He wrote it in 1926, at the end of his active career, at about the same time as the incomparable Seventh Symphony and 'Tapiola', but most of the eighteen short pieces seem to me dramatically inappropriate, and some of them are trivial. Other reasons besides its quality prevent this music from being used for English productions of the play. First, the song-tunes were written for Danish translations that did not preserve Shakespeare's rhythms; thus they will not fit the original words. Secondly, Sibelius has provided more numbers than the play seems to call for but without covering all Shakespeare's demands; for instance, in the masque. Thirdly, the music calls for an enormous orchestra, and one wonders how the Danish National Theatre ever found the money for it.

As a prelude Sibelius wrote the most onomatopoeic storm-music in existence (Op. 109, no. 1). Chromatic scales howl up and down the pages of the score, and the effect is so exciting that we do not notice the virtual absence of musical content. The rest of the music is published in two suites with the vocal items arranged as instrumental pieces. Op. 109, no. 2, described inaccurately as for small orchestra, consists of nine pieces entitled (in German) The Oak, Humoresque, Caliban's Song, The Harvesters, Canon, Scene, Intrada: Lullaby, Entr'acte: Ariel's Song and The Storm. The last is a shortened version of the prelude, and must have been played after the first scene. The second suite (Op. 109, no. 3) really is for small orchestra (double woodwind, four horns, timps, harp and strings), and consists of: Chorus of Winds, Intermezzo, Nymph's Dance, Prospero, Song I, Song II, Miranda, Naiads and Dance Episode. Miranda's music has a sweet melancholy that is engaging, but little else deserves attention. This music may have been adequate in the theatre, but divorced from the action it barely holds our interest.

The Soviet composer Kabalevsky (born in 1904, and a pupil of Mayakovsky) set ten of Shakespeare's Sonnets in 1953, and three years later he wrote the music for a production in Moscow of *Romeo and Juliet*. A concert score of the latter has recently been published with useful information in English and other languages, and entitled 'Musical Sketches to the Tragedy of W. Shakespeare for Big Symphony Orchestra'. Triple woodwind are required; also harp, xylophone, piano and a great deal of percussion. No theatre could accommodate so large an orchestra, and the scoring must have been blown up for concert use.

The ten pieces reveal a leitmotive system simple enough for theatre-goers to appreciate. The first, which probably formed the overture, is called 'Enmity and Love', and there is a theme for each. For Enmity the trombones stride down from tonic to dominant to tonic, while in the middle of the piece muted violins have a suitably languishing melody for Love. 'Morning in Verona' is fresh and slight; here, as elsewhere, Prokofiev's ballet-music on the same play has been influential. 'Preparations for the Ball' is rather feebly pretty, 'Procession of the Guests' more interesting, with a main theme deriving from the Enmity motive. After a 'Merry Dance' (for the

Capulets' Ball?), there is a rather beautiful piece called
'Lyrical Dance : Romeo and Juliet meet'; this has a derivative of the Love theme in the middle. 'In Friar Laurence's
Cell' starts with an Adagio deriving from the Enmity theme
and becomes desperate and impassioned at the end. 'Scene
in the Square' shows more Prokofiev influence, is very long,
and presumably covers the duelling with Tybalt. Most of
these pieces seem too long for a stage production, and one
suspects that for concert use they have been blown up in
length as well as in instrumentation. 'Romeo and Juliet' is
followed by 'Finale : Death and Reconciliation', based on
both leitmotives. All this music is fresh and competent, and
though perhaps rather characterless, it holds the interest
pleasantly.

## 6. SHAKESPEARE IN THE CINEMA

Hollywood's pre-war *Romeo and Juliet* with Leslie Howard
and Norma Shearer made intelligent use of Tchaikovsky's
Fantasy Overture for background music. Almost all other
Shakespeare films have had new music specially composed
for them, and in this country all such music has been written
by William Walton. Of his first venture, *As You Like It* (1936),
only one song has been published, an indifferent setting of
'Under the Greenwood Tree'. The picture itself will be
remembered, if at all, as a dismal failure. Since then Walton
has written the music for Laurence Olivier's three Shakespeare
films, contributing very considerably to their great success.
Two short pieces for strings from *Henry V* (1944) have been
published : the lovely Purcellian Passacaglia that accompanies the Hostess's account of Falstaff's death (II. 3), and
'Touch her soft lips, and part', which is said at the end of the
same scene by Pistol when encouraging Bardolph to bid farewell to the Hostess. (What he actually says is 'Touch her soft
mouth, and march'; Walton appears to have been improving
on the text.) These two pieces and other music constitute a
suite for full orchestra and optional chorus, which can be
hired; the suite includes a stirring arrangement of the old
'Agincourt Song', and much of it is very exciting.

After *Henry V* Walton decided against the publication of
his film music, feeling that it can only make its full effect in

its proper context, but in 1963 he relented so far as to allow the splendid Funeral March from *Hamlet* to appear. There is a long-playing record with music from *Henry V* on one side and *Hamlet* (1947) on the other, all of it taken from the respective sound-tracks. The entire sound-track of *Richard III* (1954) is available on three long-playing records. The fact that most of this music remains unpublished puts it outside my self-imposed limits; everyone seems agreed on its brilliant effectiveness in the cinema.

Equally effective was the music Walton wrote for Gielgud's wartime production of *Macbeth* (1942); this too is unpublished. There can be little doubt that he has found closer and more dramatic musical parallels for Shakespeare's characters and events than most of the composers I have mentioned. But then he is English, and it should be easier for him.

## 7. SHAKESPEARE AT THE BALLET

Shakespeare ballets have a long history. Noverre created one in London on *Macbeth* in the 1780s, but it is not known what music he used; it was almost certainly undistinguished. Good ballet-music was not written on Shakespeare themes until recent times.

A marginal candidate for inclusion in this book is a ballet called *Romeo and Juliet* with music by Constant Lambert. This was written in 1926 for the Diaghilev company while Lambert was still a student, and it was the first time Diaghilev had commissioned a ballet from an English composer. The décor was by Mirò and Ernst, the chief dancers were Karsavina and Lifar, and the ballet was not very successful. The story is about an actor and actress rehearsing Shakespeare's tragedy who are themselves thwarted lovers. We see them rehearsing, and later eloping in an aeroplane. The music looks smart and lacking in feeling, but I have not heard it.

Nijinska, sister of the great Nijinsky, did most of the choreography for Lambert's ballet, and in 1934 she devised a ballet on the story of Hamlet, to the music of Liszt's symphonic poem. She herself danced the part of Hamlet in Paris and elsewhere. Eight years later Robert Helpmann did the same. His idea was to show the thoughts that flit through Hamlet's mind as he lies dying, so the ballet began with Hamlet's death and funeral cortège, and then became a flash-back. This was practicable because Liszt's music happens to begin funereally. When the choreography had been devised, it was found that the music lasted under a quarter of an hour. So short a ballet was felt to be an uneconomic proposition, and at the last moment Tchaikovsky's symphonic poem of the same name was substituted for the Liszt. Apparently the dancers took the change in their stride, if that is the right expression, and the ballet was much admired. There must be a moral to be drawn from this story, but I shall leave it alone.

Much the finest Shakespeare ballet is *Romeo and Juliet* with music by Prokofiev; it is also the only full-length one known to me. Prokofiev wrote the music in 1935–6 to his own plan, without advice from any choreographer. I do not know of any other great ballet created in this way. He had not long returned to Russia after many years abroad, and this may partly account for the reluctance of the authorities to stage the work; there must still have been suspicions about his 'correctness'. Furthermore, of the four ballets he had written previously, none had had much success even abroad, so that there was no reason to have high hopes of the new one. At the time Russian ballet was still living in the past, and nothing was known of the Diaghilev developments abroad. Ulanova, the first Russian Juliet, has recalled [1] how when at last rehearsals did begin none of the company could make head or tail of the music. 'To tell the truth, we were not accustomed to such music, and we were a little afraid of it.' They found the beat hard to hear because of 'the unusual orchestration and the chamber-music quality', and they were unused to ballets whose music 'expressed genuine human emotions'.

The first performance was not given in Russia, but in Brno, in December 1938. By this time Prokofiev, despairing of ever getting the music heard in his own country, had published two orchestral suites (a third followed in 1947), both of them confusing jigsaw puzzles of bits and pieces from all over the ballet. However, in 1938, a Russian choreographer, Lavrovsky, did become fired by the music, and he at last got the ballet staged in Leningrad on 11 January 1940. He found

---

[1] The Ulanova and Lavrovsky reminiscences can be found in S. Prokofiev, *Autobiography, Articles, Reminiscence*, published in English in Moscow in the late 1950s. It is of some relevance that in 1929 the Bolshoi started work on Prokofiev's second ballet, *Le Pas d'acier*, but abandoned it because of 'sharp criticism' by the Association of Proletarian Musicians.

Prokofiev more than reluctant to make changes. For instance, Lavrovsky thought the opening scene in the square needed a set dance as well as the mimed numbers. Prokofiev refused to write one. Later he came to a piano rehearsal and found Lavrovsky concocting what he called a 'Morning Dance' for the first scene out of the Scherzo in Prokofiev's Second Piano Sonata. The composer left the theatre in a rage. But neither then nor later could he afford to dig his toes in too far, and eventually he did write a 'Morning Dance' for this scene. (One wonders if Lavrovsky was right. No choreographer in Western Europe in 1938 would have insisted on a set dance in a mime scene.) Under pressure Prokofiev also added Juliet's Variation at the Capulets' Ball, and when, at the start of Act III, they made him sit up-stage on the couch with the two main dancers and hear for himself that the beat was inaudible, he did agree to strengthen the scoring. There were doubts to the last. A fortnight before the first night the orchestra wanted the production cancelled 'to avoid a scandal'. However, it took place, and the ballet has been a huge success in Russia ever since.

Ulanova, who began by disliking Prokofiev because he seemed bad-tempered and aloof, ended by liking him very much and thinking *Romeo and Juliet* her favourite ballet. 'His vividly drawn characterization literally dictated the pattern of the dance, making our task incomparably easier'. At a party after the first night she gave him a toast:

> Never was told a tale of greater woe
> Than Prokofiev's music for Romeo!

Later that night she discovered, when attempting to fox-trot with him, that his sense of rhythm was deplorable.

The Russians have long made amends for their initial lack of understanding. Today it is we who should be ashamed. Though Ashton did the choreography in 1955 for a Royal Danish Ballet production of *Romeo and Juliet*, it has taken Shakespeare's Quatercentenary to bring about a production in England. I would have thought this ballet ranked as high as Tchaikovsky's; it should surely be in every company's repertoire.

The music is based on a leitmotive system. The tunes given below recur throughout at appropriate moments. Romeo's sometimes recurs to show Juliet is thinking of him. In the short Introduction before the curtain goes up, there is a yearning tune for Romeo and a light youthful one for Juliet :

During the street fighting in the first scene we meet Tybalt, whose relentless tune is usually to be heard on the lower brass. Sometimes it comes in canon :

The Nurse has an amiably fussy theme which fits her exactly :

Early in the second scene we meet Juliet, whose second melody is of great beauty :

The well-known 'Dance of the Knights' is really a dance for the more brash and assertive Capulets at the Ball, but the dotted-rhythm arpeggios recur later as well :

When Romeo first glimpses Juliet at the Ball, a Love Theme flowers :

Ulanova says that at first the company could not hear any suggestion of love in either this or the other tunes heard in the balcony scene; they improve on acquaintance. For the departure of the guests from the Ball, Prokofiev wrote an expanded version of the delightful little Gavotte in his Classical Symphony.[1] Act I ends with the first Balcony Scene, but in Juliet's bedroom. Romeo has a Variation based on a waltz-time version of the Love Theme (example 31).

Act II starts in the square with a great deal of merry-making by the crowd. Scene 2 moves to Friar Laurence's cell; the Friar is the only important character whom Prokofiev fails to portray successfully. Back in the square, there is more merry-making, in fact rather too much. The ballet suddenly springs to life when Tybalt appears. His duels with Mercutio and Romeo are accompanied by thrilling music, and the alternation between his brassy effrontery when challenging Romeo and Romeo's reluctance to accept his challenge is brilliantly done. Tybalt's death produces a tragic gesture of the highest musical order.

Act III begins with Romeo taking leave of Juliet in her bedroom. After she has refused to marry Paris, the music wells up into a passionate surge of sound as she hurries off once more to Friar Laurence. As she drains the phial, alone and apprehensive in her bedroom, a rising, menacing theme is heard, perhaps representing Destiny :

This becomes high tragedy in the tomb scene, which Prokofiev calls an Epilogue, and Juliet dies to sublime music based on

[1] This has caused trouble. The rights in the Classical Symphony belong to an American firm. In Russia, which is outside the copyright area, the Gavotte can be printed, but no version can be sold elsewhere, for instance in England, unless published by the American firm. Incredibly, this is given as the main reason why the piano score of *Romeo and Juliet* has not for many years been obtainable in England.

her second theme (example 29).   The last ten minutes of this ballet contains some of Prokofiev's most profound and spiritual invention.

It is arguable that the three finest examples of Shakespearean orchestral music all derive from *Romeo and Juliet*; one is by a Frenchman, and two are by Russians, and it is a chastening thought that England has never had a composer worthy of the subject.   For some deep reason we have had no talent for love-music, at least, not since Purcell's day.

# Catalogue of Musical Works Based on the Plays and Poetry of Shakespeare

COMPILED BY

## WINTON DEAN, DOROTHY MOORE
## AND PHYLLIS HARTNOLL

THIS catalogue, which makes no claims to completeness, was compiled with the idea of showing the wide range of composers, famous and otherwise, who have found inspiration in Shakespeare. It contains mainly published works, and no attempt has been made to list the vast quantity of unpublished, and often ephemeral, incidental music written for the theatre, cinema, radio and television, often by hard-working resident musicians. The archives of the Royal Shakespeare Theatre at Stratford-upon-Avon alone would provide material for a list as long again as the present one, and the same is probably true of innumerable theatres all over Europe.

Our researches have been confined to Western music, though here again investigation into the music of the Far Eastern countries would no doubt reveal unsuspected quantities of incidental music written for productions of Shakespeare in translation. We have also, for reasons of time and space, omitted the many settings of non-Shakespearean words which embellished the productions of ages less preoccupied with the importance of the original text. The field of spurious Shakespeareana is a vast and fascinating one, and deserves study. Some of its products were laid aside without regret, but it was sad to have to exclude such gems as 'Arise, ye subterranean winds', 'To fair Fidele's grassy tomb', 'My gentle Jessy', and the interpolated dirges in *Romeo and Juliet*. A complete catalogue of Shakespearean music would have to take these into account, since some composers no doubt thought they were setting Shakespeare when they made use of them, and they can even be said to have been 'inspired' by Shakespeare, since they were mainly written for specific productions.

Considerations of space have also dictated the omission of all but the briefest notes on each work, even where information is available, and in general we have limited ourselves, for orchestral works and songs, to date (usually of publication) and opus number. Nor have the 'arrangements' of earlier works, or of traditional melodies, been deliberately included, though some may have slipped in by mistake. The only exception is where composers have themselves later arranged incidental music for performance in the concert hall, and there a cross-reference has been made. Lack of space also accounts for the omission of a note on those songs which were set for, and used in, a production of a play other than that from which they come. All songs, in other words, have been assigned to their original source, irrespective of the use made of them.

The plays are listed alphabetically, followed by the poems, and by a general section into which have been put works that cannot be assigned to any particular play or poem, and works in honour of the dramatist himself; among these are the commemorative odes called for by successive centenary celebrations. It is hoped that additions to this list will be necessary after 1964.

Under each heading the works are divided into three sections. Part 1 deals exclusively with operas based on Shakespeare's plays, and appears to be the first attempt to map this field. It was compiled by Mr. Winton Dean as a supplement to his article, *Shakespeare and Opera* (p. 89), and should be used in conjunction with it. The composers are listed alphabetically, and where possible the following information is given: title, librettist (in brackets), place and year of first stage performance. An * indicates that a full or vocal score (or both) has been published (in a few cases incomplete), a † that no score has been found, but that a libretto has been published. Square brackets indicate a first publication date. Among the 180 operas listed — a total which took even the compiler by surprise — one or two may not be based on Shakespeare, since it has proved impossible so far to establish the connection with certainty. For the numerous operas which might be thought to be by Shakespeare, but are not, see p. 96 *n*.

Parts 2 and 3 of the catalogue are the responsibility of the editor, but rest mainly upon the devoted and meticulous research undertaken by Miss Dorothy Moore, Hon. Librarian of The Society for Theatre Research. Part 2 (*a*) lists published incidental music used in the theatre, with a few additions from film and radio, 2 (*b*) works composed for the concert hall. This includes overtures which stand alone without other incidental music, and concert works adapted from incidental music. Large-scale choral works have also been included here, and not in Part 3, which consists of settings of single lyrics, or isolated passages from the plays, as solos, part-songs or choruses. These are arranged alphabetically by first words (omitting 'a', 'and' and 'the'), and are numbered consecutively, with act and scene reference (based on the Globe edition). Where composers have supplied titles for their songs, or quoted a line from the body of the work, or begun part-way through it, this has been noted in brackets, and a cross-reference made from the new title to the main entry, together with the composer's name. This may seem unnecessary in some of the shorter lists, but is a help in dealing with the 100-odd settings of such lyrics as 'It was a lover and his lass' and 'O mistress mine'. Where possible, each setting is given a date (usually of publication), and its number within the opus number if it forms part of a collection of songs by one composer. Where no date is given, an approximate date can sometimes be deduced by reference to the birth and death dates in the checklist of composers (see p. 291).

Much research remains to be done on Shakespearean music, but it would be ungrateful in the compilers of Parts 2 and 3 not to acknowledge their debt to their predecessors, particularly to Alfred T. Roffe's *Handbook of Shakespeare Music* (1878), to the New Shakspere Society's volume, *A List of all the songs and passages in Shakespeare which have been set to music*, compiled by J. Greenhill, W. A. Harrison and F. J. Furnival (1884), and to H. Kelsey White's *Index to songs, snatches and passages in Shakespeare which have been set to music* (1900). Jaggard's *Shakespeare Bibliography* (1911) and the Supplement to it by Ebisch (1937) have also been consulted; but the greater part of the material for the catalogue came from the British Museum, where use was made not only of the catalogues of the Music Section, but of the collections of catalogues of music publishers in Great Britain and abroad. The editor would also like to record her gratitude to the Music Librarians of the Birmingham and Liverpool Public Libraries for their help in checking or expanding entries, to Mr. Karl Kroeger of the Music Division of the New York Public Library, and to many friends and fellow-workers for supplying missing information, dates or opus numbers, and for eliminating a number of mis-attributions. Reference should also be made to Mr. Alan Boustead's useful handbook, *Music to Shakespeare* (O.U.P., May, 1964), which was published too late to be used here.

Since it is hoped that this first tentative list will form the basis of a more extensive catalogue of Shakespearean music, the compilers would be grateful for any corrections or additions which those who use it may care to send them.


LONDON, 1964

### All's Well That Ends Well

I

AUDRAN, E.  'Gillette de Narbonne' (H. C. Chivot and A. Duru), Paris, 1882*

CASTELNUOVO-TEDESCO, M.  'Tutto è bene quello che finisce bene' (composer), [comp. 1958]

2

(a) HOÉRÉE, A. C. E. ;  RANKY, Gy. (Budapest)

3

(a) 'Was this fair face the cause' (I. 3): LINLEY, W. ;  THOMSON, V. (N.Y., 1961)

### Antony and Cleopatra

I

KAFFKA, J. C.  'Antonius und Kleopatra' (duodrama), Berlin, 1779
MALIPIERO, G. F.  'Antonio e Cleopatra' (composer), Florence, 1938*
SAYN-WITTGENSTEIN-BERLEBURG, E. F. von.  'Antonius und Kleopatra' (J. Mosenthal), Graz, 1883
YUFEROV, S. V.  'Antony i Kleopatra' (composer) *[1900]

2

(a) BISHOP, H. R. (1913) ;  HOPKINS, A. ;  IBERT, J. ; JACOBSON, M. ;  KLE-NOVSKY, N. S. ;  LEVEY, W. C. ;  MADETOJA, L. A. (Op. 80, 1944) ;  NORMAN, F. V. L. ;  PORTER, Q. ;  RABAUD, H. B. ;  RÔZE, R. ;  RUD-NICKI, M. T. ;  SCHMITT, F. (Paris, Opéra, 14 June 1920) ;  THOMSON, V. (1937)
(b) GURLITT, M. (Symphony) ;  HAYDEN, W. (Five dances, pf., No. 2 : 'Cleopatra') ;  HERBERIGS, R. (Symphonic poem, 1949) ;  INDY, P. V. d' (Overture, Op. 6, 1876, unpub.) ;  KREUTZER, R. (Ballet) ;  PROKOFIEV, S. S. (Suite : 'Egyptian Nights', Op. 61, 1934) ;  RUBIN-STEIN, A. G. (Overture, Op. 116) ;  SCHMITT, F. (Two suites of six episodes, Op. 69, 1921) ;  SMYTH, E. M. (Overture, 1890) ;  WISSMER, P. (Symphonic Suite, 1943)

3

(a) 'Come, thou monarch of the vine' (II. 7): BISHOP, H. R. (Glee, 1864) ;  BRIDGEWATER, L. (1964) ;  CHILCOT, T. (1744) ;  JACOBSON, M. (1953) ;  LINLEY, W. ;  SCHUBERT, F. (Op. 105, No. 3, 1826, D.888) ;  WEISS, W. H. (1863)

## As You Like It

### 1

VERACINI, F. M. 'Rosalinda' (P. A. Rolli), London, 1744 *
WICKHAM, FLORENCE 'Rosalind' (operetta), Dresden, 1938

### 2

(a) ARNE, T. A. (D.L., 20 Dec., 1740); BARBER, S. (N.Y.); BARBOUR, J. M. (1948); BENSON, J. A. (Scenes for recitation with music, 1900); BISHOP, H. R. (1824); BLISS, A. (Lyric, Hammersmith, 1920); DUGGAN, J. F. (1834); ELLIOTT, M.; FARKAS, F. (1937); GERMAN, E. (St. James's, 1896); KAZASOGLU, G.; PELLEG, F.; PIZZETTI, I. (Florence, Boboli Gardens, May, 1938); PONC, M. (1941, 1948); RIETZ, J.; ROGOWSKI, L. M.; TAUSCH, J.; TAYLOR, Mrs. Tom (1879); TOCH, E. (1931); WALTON, W. (Film, 1936); WETZLER, H. H.; ZILCHER, H. (1917)

(b) BATH, H. (Two pieces for pf., No. I: 'Rosalind', Ballade, 1916); BOYCE, E. M. ('Under the greenwood tree', six pieces for pf., 1921); CARPENTER, J. A. (Orchestral suite: 'Seven Ages', 1945); CLIFFORD, H. J. (Four sketches for strings); GADSBY, H. (Intermezzo and Tantarra: 'The Forest of Arden', 1886); HAYDEN, W. (Five dances, pf., No. 3: 'Touchstone'); LUCAS, C. (Overture); MILFORD, R. H. (Idyll for vl. and pf.: 'Under the greenwood tree', 1949); PAINE, J. K. (Overture); PIERSON, H. H. (Overture, unpub.); QUILTER, R. (Suite, Op. 21, 1921); THOMAS, R. H. (Overture, 1864); WAGNER, J. K. (Overture)

### 3

(a) 'All the world's a stage' (II. 7): LEVEY, S. (Recitation with music, 1908); PINSUTI, C. E. (1861)
'Amiens sings', see 'Blow, blow, thou winter wind': WISTER, O.

(b) 'Blow, blow, thou winter wind' (II. 7): ALFERAKI, A. N. (Op. 13, No. 2, 1892); ALVENSLEBEN, A. (Op. 4, No. 1); ANTCLIFFE, H. (1931); ARNE, T. A. (1740); BARTON, G. (Boston, 1903); BENSON, J. A. (Recitation with music, 1900); BRIDGE, Frank (1916); BRIDGE, Fred.; BRIDGEWATER, L. (1964); CASTELNUOVO-TEDESCO, M. ('Winter Wind'); CLEMENS, T. (1883); CLOKEY, J. (Boston, 1927); CROW, E. J. (1906); DADGE, R. (1907); DUNCAN, W. E. (1894); DYCE-SOMBRE, Hon. Mrs.; ELLISTON, M.; FAULKES, W. (Op. 204, No. 3, 1920, unpub.); FISHER, W. A. (Op. 5, No. 4); GALE, J. R. C. ('Ingratitude', 1895); GATTY, N. C. (1915); GIBBS, C. A. (1951); HOBY, J. (1900); HOPKINS, F. (N.Y., 1913); HORN, C. E.; HORROCKS, A. E. (1891); HOTHAM, C. (1904); HUDSON, H. (1909); JENKINS, D. C. (1914); KETÈLBY, A. W. (1952); KIESERLING, R. (Phil., 1924); KILBURN, N. (1911); LINLEY, W.; LOVATT, S. E. (1932); MACFARREN, G. A. (1864); MANSFIELD, P. J. (Op. 92, No. 1, 1926); MARZIALS, T. J. H. ('Unto the holly', 1890); MERWIN, R. A. (N.Y., 1927); MOORAT, J. S. (1904); MOUNSEY, Mrs. Ann; NOBLE, T. T. (Boston, 1924); OSBORNE, M. C. (N.Y., 1915); PARKER, H. T. (1895); PARRY, C. H. H.; PASCAL, F. ('Ingratitude' — 'Sing heigh-ho, the

R

holly'); QUILTER, R. (1905, 1919); SARJEANT, J. (1890); SCHACHNER, R.; SELBY, B. L. (Boston, 1903); SHAW, M. F.; SIMMONDS, T. F. (1915); SLINN, E. B. (Op. 13, 1906); SOMERVELL, A. (1925); STEVENS, R. J. S. (Glee, ? 1830); STONE, N. M. (1938); TREHARNE, B.; VOWLES, W.; WASSALL, G. (Sh. Song Cycle, No. 3, Cincinnati, c. 1904); WEBBE, S. *the younger* (1830); WILLIAMS, A. (1937); WISTER, O. ('Amiens sings', N.Y., 1936); WOOD, C.; YOUNG, A. (4 Sh. songs in swing, 1940); ZIMMERMANN, A. *See also* GENERAL: BOCHSA, R. N. C.

'Fairy life', *see* 'It was a lover': LUCKE, K. E.

(c) 'From the East to Western Ind' (III. 2): SULLIVAN, A. S. ('Rosalind')

'Horn, The', *see* 'What shall he have?': CASTELNUOVO-TEDESCO, M.; EDGAR, E.

'Huntsman's Song, The', *see* 'What shall he have?': CAREY, H.

'If it do come to pass', *see* 'Under the greenwood tree': BENSON, J. A.

'In [the] springtime', *see* 'It was a lover': LAHMEYER, C.; LINTON, A. H.; NEWTON, E.

'Ingratitude', *see* 'Blow, blow, thou winter wind': GALE, J.; PASCAL, F.

(d) 'It was a lover and his lass' (V. 3): ADAMS, D. S. (N.Y., 1937); ALDERSON, A. P. (1897); ALLEN, W. R. ('Sweet lovers'); AMBROSE, P. (Op. 13, No. 1, Boston, 1898); ANDREWS, G. F. (1904); ARKWRIGHT, G. E. P. (? 1902); ATTWATTER, J. P. (1898); AUSTIN, F. (1909); BARKWORTH, J. E. (1928); BARNBY, J. (Madrigal, 1885); BARRATT, W. A. (N.Y., 1915); BARTON, G. (Boston, 1903); BENDALL, W. E. (1886); BESLY, E. M.; BEVIS, T. A. (1896); BISHOP, H. R.; BLAKELEY, W.; BOOTH, J.; BREWER, A. H.; BRIAN, H.; BRIDGE, Fred.; BRIDGEWATER, L. (1964); BROWN, A. G. Y.; BUCK, D. ('Spring Song', N.Y., 1904); BURY, W. (1927); BUSH, G. (1945; 'The Sweet Season', No. 4, 1961); CARDEW, H. W. (1895); CARMICHAEL, M. G.; CASTELNUOVO-TEDESCO, M. ('Springtime'); CHADWICK, G. W.; CHAMBERS, C.; CHAPMAN, E. T.; CHAPPELL, W.; COATES, E. (1908); COWDELL, E.; DANNREUTHER, E. G.; DAVENPORT, D.; DAVIES, D.; DELIUS, F. (1916); DICKS, E. A.; DUNHILL, T. F. (Op. 62, No. 3, 1923); EDESON, D. J. S. (1937); ELLISTON, M.; FINZI, G. (1942); FOSTER, M. B.; FULTON, R. N.; GERMAN, E.; GIBBS, C. A. (1932); GIBSON, S. A.; GREENHILL, J.; HARKER, F. F.; HARTLEY, B. W.; HEISE, P. A.; HILES, H.; HIND, J. (1956); HOSMER, E. S.; HUDSON, H. (1910); HUSS, H. H. (Op. 22, No. 2); HUTCHINSON, J. T. (1895); JENNER, H. ('Sweet lovers'); JOHNSON, Reginald; KNIGHT, H.; KOVEN, R. de (Op. 159, No. 1, Cinn., 1900); LAHMEYER, C. ('In the springtime'); LANG, E. (Boston, 1915); LAW, H. (1909); LEHMANN, L. (1907); LEIGHTER, H. Clough- (Boston, 1906); LEVEY, S.; LINLEY, W.; LINTON, A. H. ('In the springtime'); LODER, E.; LUCKE, K. E. ('Fairy Life', N.Y., 1906); MACFARREN, G. A. (1869); MARZIALS, T. J. H. (1892); MEISSLER, J. (1877); MILFORD, R. H. (1940); MINETTI, C. (N.Y., 1908); MOERAN, E. J. ('The lover and his lass', 1934); MORLEY, T. (First Book of Airs, 1600); NEEDHAM, A. A. (1907); NEVIN, G. B. (Phil., 1910); NEWTON, E. ('In springtime'); OGILVY, A. W. (1905); O'NEILL, N. (N.Y., 1922); OSBORNE, M. C. (N.Y., 1915); PARKER, H. T.; PARRY, C. H. H. (Op. 21, No. 2, 1874); PASCAL, F. (1889); PEINIGER, O.; PHILLIPS, M. F. (Op. 66, No. 5, 1941); QUILTER, R. (Op. 23, 1921); REAY, S. (1897); REYNOLDS, C. T. (1890);

Ricci, C. R. (N.Y., 1916) ; Rodgers, J. A. (1909) ; Rowley, A. (1951) ;
Rubbra, E. (Op. 13, 1935) ; Sampson, Godfrey ('Spring Song', 1931) ;
Scull, G. C. (1938) ; Selby, B. L. (1878) ; Slinn, E. B. (Op. 13, No. 1,
1906) ; Smale, P. (1910) ; Stanislaus, F. (1868) ; Stevens, R. J. S.
(Chearful glee, prize medal, 1786) ; Stoessel, A. F. (Boston, 1933) ;
Sullivan, A. S. (part of 'Kenilworth', 1865) ; Taubert, W. (Op. 33,
No. 4) ; Thiman, E. (Spring Garland, No. 2) ; Troup, E. J. ; Van Etten,
J. ; Walker, E. (Op. 1) ; Wallbank, N. S. (Op. 8, No. 1) ; Walthew,
R. H. ; Warlock, P. ('Pretty ring-time', 1925) ; Warrell, A. S. (1938) ;
Wassall, G. (Sh. Song Cycle, No. 5, Cincinnati, c. 1904) ; Watson,
W. N. (1883) ; Williams, D. C. (1913) ; Williams, R. Vaughan
(1922) ; Wood, C. ; Wood, R. W. (1922) ; Young, A. (4 Sh. songs in
swing, 1940)

'Lover and his lass, The', see 'It was a lover' : Moeran, E. J.

'Pastoral', see 'Under the greenwood tree' : Demuth, N. F.

'Pretty ring-time', see 'It was a lover' : Warlock, P.

'Shakespeare's Carol', see 'Blow, blow, thou winter wind' : passim

'Sing heigh-ho, the holly', see 'Blow, blow, thou winter wind' : Pascal, F.

'Spring Song', see 'It was a lover' : Buck, D. ; Sampson, G.

'Springtime', see 'It was a lover' : Castelnuovo-Tedesco, M.

'Sweet lovers', see 'It was a lover' : Allen, W. R. ; Jenner, H.

(e) 'Then is there mirth in heaven' (V. 4) : Arne, T. A. ; Bishop, H. R.

(f) 'Under the greenwood tree' (III. 5) : Anstruther, P. N. (1907) ;
Arkwright, G. E. P. (1902) ; Arne, T. A. (1740) ; Benson, J. A.
(Recitation with music, 1900) ; Biggs, E. S. (1800) ; Bishop, H. R. ;
Brian, H. ; Bridgewater, L. (1964) ; Brydson, J. C. ; Busch, C.
(1906) ; Buzzi-Peccia, A. ; Carmichael, M. G. ; Castelnuovo-
Tedesco, M. ; Challinor, F. A. ; Chapman, E. T. ; Chappell, W. ;
Coates, E. (1909) ; Davidson, M. ; Davie, C. Thorpe ; Demuth, N.
('Pastoral', 1925) ; Dunhill, T. (1934) ; Dunn, J. P. ; Elliston, M. ;
Faulkes, W. (Op. 204, No. 8, 1920, unpub.) ; Ffoulkes, S. ; Forsyth,
C. ; Foster, M. B. ; Fulton, R. N. ; Gardner, J. (Op. 36, No. 5,
1958) ; Gurney, I. ; Harris, C. ; Harrison, J. A. G. (N.Y., 1913) ;
Hoby, J. (1903) ; Hook, J. ; Hopkins, F. (N.Y., 1913) ; Hotham, C.
(1904) ; Howells, H. ; Jacob, G. (A Goodly Heritage, No. 1, 1954) ;
Kelly, T. J. ; Lee, E. M. (1923) ; Lehmann, L. (1912) ; Linley, W.
('Who doth ambition shun') ; Linton, A. H. ; Lovelock, W. ; Mac-
farren, G. A. (1869) ; Marzials, T. J. H. (1890) ; Moeran, E. J.
(Songs of Springtime, No. 1, 1933) ; Montgomery, R. B. (1948) ;
Ogilvy, A. W. (1904) ; Osborne, M. C. (N.Y., 1915) ; Parke, J. ;
Parke, M. H. ; Parnell, C. W. ; Parry, C. H. H. (1903) ; Penny,
E. M. (1909) ; Peterkin, G. N. (Boston, 1919) ; Phillips, M. F. (Op.
67, No. 2, 1940) ; Quilter, R. (Op. 23, 1921) ; Richards, A. (1909) ;
Ritchie, J. (1951) ; Rowley, A. ; Sampson, Godfrey (1938) ;
Shaw, J. (1895) ; Shaw, M. F. (1917) ; Smith, J. S. (c. 1812) ;
Somervell, A. (1925) ; Sykes, H. H. ; Tremain, R. ; Walker, E. ;
Walton, W. ; Wareing, H. W. ; Wassall, G. (Sh. Song Cycle, No.
11, Cincinnati, c. 1904) ; Williams, F. (1937) ; Wood, C. ; Wurm,
M. J. ; Young, A. (1948).

'Unto the holly', see 'Blow, blow, thou winter wind' : Marzials,
T. J. H.

(g) 'Wedding is great Juno's crown' (V. 4) : CHILCOT, T. ; LINLEY, W. ; TOURS, B. ; WOOD, F. H.

(h) 'What shall he have that killed the deer ?' (IV. 2) : BENSON, J. A. (Recitation with music, 1900) ; BISHOP, H. R. (1824) ; BRIDGEWATER, L. (1964) ; CAREY, H. ('The Huntsman's Song' in C. Johnson's adap. *Love in a Forest*, D.L., 1723) ; CASTELNUOVO-TEDESCO, M. ; DAVIDSON, M. ; EDGAR, E. ; FULTON, R. N. (Songs in Arden, No. 3) ; HAYES, P. (? 1780) ; HILTON, J. ; QUILTER, R. (1924) ; SHAW, G. T. (1912) ; SMITH, J. S. (c. 1792) ; SOMERVELL, A. (1888) ; STEVENS, R. J. S. ; WOOD, F. H. (Op. 33, No. 2)

'Who doth ambition shun', *see* 'Under the greenwood tree' : BENSON, J. H. ; LINLEY, W.

'Winter Wind', *see* 'Blow, blow, thou winter wind' : CASTELNUOVO-TEDESCO, M.

## The Comedy of Errors

### 1

KREJČÍ, I.   'Pozdvižení v Efesu' (J. Bachtík), Prague, 1946
LORENZ, A.   ' Die Komödie der Irrungen' [c. 1890]
STORACE, S.   'Gli equivoci' (Lorenzo da Ponte), Vienna, 1786 †

### 2

(a) BISHOP, H. R. (1819) ; LORENZ, K. A. (Op. 40, 1892) ; PONC, M. (1930) ; RODGERS, R. (*The Boys from Syracuse*, N.Y., 1938) ; SHAPORIN, Y. A. (1940) ; ZILCHER, H. (1934)

(b) FOGG, C. W. E. (Overture, 1922) ; GOLDSCHMIDT, B. (Overture)

### 3

(a) 'Oh, for my beads' (II. 2) : KEMP, J. (1814)

(b) 'Teach me, dear creature' (III. 2) : PASCAL, F. ('Lehr' mich, Geliebte', 1902)

## Coriolanus

### 1

BAEYENS, A.   'Coriolanus', Antwerp, 1940
SULEK, S.   'Koriolan' (composer), Zagreb, 1958

### 2

(a) COOKE, T. S. (1821) ; HOFFER, P. (Radio) ; SÖDERMAN, J. A.

(b) COOKE, T. S. (Triumphal March, pf. duet, 1820) ; LUX, F. (Scene for voices and orch.) ; MACKENZIE, A. C. (Suite dramatique pour orch., 1909) ; WEBER, B. A. (Overture)

## Cymbeline

### 1

EGGEN, A. 'Cymbelin' (composer), Oslo, 1951
KREUTZER, R. 'Imogène, ou la gageure indiscrète' (J. E. B. Dejaure), Paris, 1796
MISSA, E. J. L. 'Dinah' (M. Carré and P. de Choudens), Paris, 1894 *
SOBOLEWSKI, E. 'Imogene', Königsberg, 1833

### 2

(a) ALPAERTS, F.; CLARKE, J. H. S. (1896); DIETRICH, A. H. (1896); GERHARD, R.; TIESSEN, H.
(b) BENNETT, G. J. (Overture, 1895); BIRTCHNELL, A. J. (Valse for pf. with cornet acc.)

### 3

'Arise', see 'Hark, hark! The lark': CASTELNUOVO-TEDESCO, M.
'Come to dust', see 'Fear no more': CASTELNUOVO-TEDESCO, M.
'Dirge', see 'Fear no more': passim
'Elegy', see 'Fear no more': NARES, J.
(a) 'Fear no more the heat of the sun' (II. 2): ANDERTON, H. O. (1920); ARNE, T. A. (C.G., 1759); BOYCE, W. (C.G., 1746); BRIAN, H. (1922); BRIDGEWATER, L. (1964); BUSH, G. (In 'Farewell, Earth's Bliss', 1950); CALLCOTT, J. W.; CARDEW, H. W. (1898); CASTELNUOVO-TEDESCO, M. ('Come to dust'); COOK, J. E. (1954); CRICHTON, M. (1929); DANKWORTH, J. (1964); DAVIES, H. Walford (Op. 18, No. 6, 1905); ELLISTON, M.; FINZI, G. (1942); GARDINER, H. B. ('Fidele'); GARDNER, J. (Op. 36, No. 4, 1958); GIBBS, C. ('Fidele', 1954); GODFERY, M. van S.; GRAY, A.; GREENHILL, J.; HALAS, F.; HALES, H. J. (Op. 15, 1932); HAYES, F. M. ('Dirge of Fidele'); HOPKINS, D. (1937); HOWENSTEIN, J. H. ('Funeral Chant'); JACOB, G. (1939); KEEL, F. (1948); LAMBERT, C. (1942); LAW, A. (1909); LINLEY, W. (2nd verse only); MACFARREN, G. A. (1864); MARZIALS, T. J. H. (1890); MOORE, M. (1937); NARES, J. ('Elegy', c. 1780); PARRY, C. H. H. (1906); PENDER, T. (1943); PIERSON, H. H. (Op. 63, No. 3); QUILTER, R. (Op. 23, No. 1, 1921); ROBERTON, H. (1941); SARSON, H. M. (1933); SMITH, A. B. (Op. 14, No. 2, 1926); STONE, N. M. (1949); WEIGL, V. (N.Y., 1958); WICKENS, D. (1955); WILLIAMS, R. Vaughan (1922)
'Fidele', see 'Fear no more': GARDINER, H. B.; GIBBS, C.
'Funeral Chant', see 'Fear no more': HOWENSTEIN, J. H.
(b) 'Hark, hark! The lark at heaven's gate sings' (II. 3): ARKWRIGHT, G. E. P. (1902); ATTWATER, J. P. (1898); AUSTIN, E. (Op. 6, No. 2, 1907); AYLWARD, T. (1765); BAYLEY, T. H. R. ('The Lark', 1902); BRIDGEWATER, L. (1964); CASTELNUOVO - TEDESCO, M. ('Arise'); CHILCOT, T.; CLARKE, J. H. S.; COOKE, B.; CURSCHMANN, C. F. ('Morgengruss', 1851); EMMERICH, R. (Op. 42); GAMBOGI, F. E.; GARDNER, J. (Op. 36, No. 1, 1958); GLENDINNING, R. R. (1897); JOHNSON, Robert (Bod. MS. Don. C. 57); KERR, Mark, Lord (1888); KLEIN, J.; KÜCKEN, F. W.; MACFARREN, G. A.;

MARZIALS, T. J. H. (1890); MOCHRING, F.; PARKER, H. T. (1895);
PYE, K. J. (1889); QUILTER, R. (1946); SCHUBERT, F. (1828, D. 889);
STEGGALL, R. (Op. 28, No. 1); THORNE, E. H.; TROUP, E. J.;
WALKER, E.

'Lark, The', see 'Hark, hark! The lark': BAYLEY, T.


## Hamlet

### 1

BUZZOLA, A.   'Amleto' (G. Peruzzini), Venice, 1847 *
CARUSO, L.   'Amleto', Florence, 1789
FACCIO, F.   'Amleto' (A. Boito), Genoa, 1865 *
HEWARD, L. H.   'Hamlet' (comp. 1916, unfinished)
HIGNARD, J. L. A.   'Hamlet' (P. de Garal), Nantes, 1888 *[1868]
KAGEN, S.   'Hamlet', Baltimore, 1962
KALNINŠ, J.   'Hamlets' (composer), Riga, 1936
MACHAVARIANI, A.   'Hamlet', Tbilisi, 1964
MARECZEK, M.   'Hamlet', Brno, 1840
MERCADANTE, S.   'Amleto' (F. Romani), Milan, 1822 †
MORONI, L.   'Amleto', Rome, 1860
STADTFELD, A.   'Hamlet' (J. Guilliaume), Darmstadt, 1857
THOMAS, C. L. A.   'Hamlet' (J. Barbier and M. Carré), Paris, 1868 *
ZAFRED, M.   'Amleto' (composer and L. Zafred), Rome, 1961

### 2

(a) ADAMS, R. (1955); ALBERT, K.; ANDRIESSEN, J.; BARDI, B.; BISHOP,
H. R.; CAREY, H. (Goodman's Fields, 9 Feb. 1736); CLARKE,
J. H. S. (1878); DUPUY, J. B. E. (1819); EASDALE, B.; ECCLES, J.
(c. 1698); FERRARI, G. (for Irving, 1905); HAYDN, F. J. (? authen-
ticity doubtful); HENSCHEL, G. (Op. 50); HOLLAND, J. D. (Music for
the dumb-show, Schroeder's prod., Hamburg, 1776); HOLLY, F. A.
(Breslau, 1 May 1778); HONEGGER, A. (1946); JACOBSON, M.;
JONCIÈRES, V. de (Nantes, 21 Sept. 1867); LAMBERT, C.; LEVY, H.
(1953); MILHAUD, D. (Paris, Th. de l'Atelier, April 1939); MONIUSZ-
KO, S.; MOYZES, A. (Op. 29, 1938); O'NEILL, N. (Op. 13, 1904);
PIERNE, H. C. G.; PROKOFIEV, S. (Leningrad, 1937); REY, J. B.;
RIETZ, J. (Düsseldorf, 28 Dec. 1834); SHOSTAKOVICH, D. (Op. 32,
1931, unpub. ms. at Vakhtangov Th.); STENHAMMAR, W. E.;
TCHAIKOVSKY, P. (Op. 67b, St. Petersburg, Mikhailovsky, 21 Feb.
1891); THOMSON, V. (1938); TIESSEN, H.; VOGLER, G. J. (Mannheim, 1779); WALTON, W. (Film, 1947)
(b) ADLAM, F. ('Alas, poor Ghost', pf., 1886); BERLIOZ, H. ('Tristia',
1848: No. 2: 'La Mort d'Ophélie'; No. 3: 'Marche funèbre');
BLACHER, B. (Ballet, Op. 35, 1950); BORGSTRØM H. (Symphonic
poem and ballet); BOURGAULT-DUCOUDRAY, L. A. ('L'Enterrement
d'Ophélie'); BRIDGE, F. ('There is a willow': Impression for sm.
orch., 1928); BUSH, G. (Overture, 'Yorick', 1949—in memory of
Tommy Handley); CLARKE, J. H. S. (Overture, 1875); DURAND, E.
(Scène: Recitative, 1863); GADE, N. V. (Concert Overture, Op. 37,

1861); GALLENBERG, W. R. (Ballet, 1815); GERMAN, E. (Symphonic poem, 1895); HART, F. B. (Fantasy on 'Bonny Sweet Robin' for strings, Op. 145, 1941); JACOBSON, M. (Mime music for Dumb Show, 1930); JOACHIM, J. (Overture, Op. 4); LAZZARI, S. ('Ophélie': Symphonic poem); LEKEU, G. ('Marche d'Ophélie', 1887; Second Symphonic study, 1890); LISZT, F. (Symphonic poem, 1858); MAC-DOWELL, E. ('Hamlet' and 'Ophelia': Symphonic poems, Op. 22, 1 and 2, 1885); MACFARREN, G. A.; NICHOLL, H. W. (Symphonic poem, Op. 14); PIERSON, H. H. ('Funeral March', 1850); PRO-KOFIEV, S. (inc. m., concert version, 1954, unpub.); ROGERS, B. (Prelude, 1926); SHAKESPEARE, W. ('Dramatic Overture', Op. 15); SHOSTAKOVICH, D. (Suite based on inc. m., Op. 32a, 1932, pub. 1960); TANEIEV, A. S. (Overture); TCHAIKOVSKY, P. (Fantasy Overture, Op. 67a, 1888); THOMAS, C. L. A. (Ballet: 'Festival of Spring'); WEIGL, V. (Cantata, 1791); WOYRSCH, F. (Overture, Op. 56, 1913)

### 3

'Clown in the Churchyard, The', *see* 'In youth, when I did love': CASTELNUOVO-TEDESCO, M.

(a) 'Doubt thou the stars are fire' (II. 2): BARRY, J.; DAVY, J. (c. 1820); DIGNUM, C.; FISIN, J.; KELLY, M. (? 1810); KEMP, J. (c. 1810); PARRY, J.; RUSSELL, W. (1808); STEVENS, R. J. S. (Op. 2); STEVEN-SON, J. A.; TINDAL, W. (Op. 5, c. 1786)

(b) 'For Bonny Sweet Robin is all my joy' (IV. 5): HADLEY, H. K. (Op. 81, N.Y., 1918)

'Gracious time, The', *see* 'Some say': MILFORD, R. H.

'Hamlet's Letter to Ophelia', *see* 'Doubt thou the stars': *passim*

'Hamlet's Soliloquy', *see* 'To be or not to be': *passim*

(c) 'How should I your true love know' (IV. 5): BRAHMS, J. (1873); BURROWS, B. (1928); BUSH, G. ('The Sweet Season', No. 3, 1961); CASTELNUOVO-TEDESCO, M. ('Ophelia'); CHAUSSON, E. (Op. 28, No. 4); FAULKES, W. (Op. 204, No. 5, 1920, unpub.); GARDINER, H. B.; MACONCHY, E. (1946); QUILTER, R. (Op. 30, 1933); STEVENSON, J. A.; STRAUSS, R. ('Wie erkenn' ich mein Treulieb?', Op. 6, No. 1); WHITE, M. V. ('Ophelia's Song'); WHITTAKER, W. G. (1928)

(d) 'In youth, when I did love' (V. 1): CASTELNUOVO-TEDESCO, M. ('The Clown in the Churchyard')

'Mort d'Ophélie', *see* 'There is a willow': BERLIOZ, H.

'Pensées', *see*, 'To be or not to be': PERABO, E.

'Ophelia', *see* 'How should I': CASTELNUOVO-TEDESCO, M.

'Ophelia's Song', *see* 'How should I': WHITE, M. V.

'So runs the world away', *see* 'Why, let the stricken deer': KING, M. P.

(e) 'Some say that ever 'gainst that season comes' (I. 1): MILFORD, R. H. ('The gracious time', 1926)

(f) 'There is a willow grows aslant a brook' (IV. 7): BERLIOZ, H. ('La Mort d'Ophélie', 1848). *See also* 2 (b), BRIDGE, F.

(g) 'They bore him barefac'd on the bier' (IV. 5): BRAHMS, J. (1873); LINLEY, W.; STRAUSS, R. ('Sie trugen ihn auf der Bahre bloss', Op. 67, No. 3)

(h) 'To be or not to be' (III. 1): BUCK, D. (N.Y., 1904); ? MORELLI, C.; PERABO, E. ('Pensées', Op. 11)

(*i*) 'To-morrow is St. Valentine's Day' (IV. 5): BRAHMS, J. (1873);
STRAUSS, R. ('Guten Morgen, 's ist Sankt Valentinstag', Op. 67, No.
2)
(*j*) 'White his shroud as the mountain snow' (IV. 5): BRAHMS, J. (1873)
(*k*) 'Why, let the stricken deer go weep' (III. 2): KING, M. P. ('So runs
the world away', Glee, 1803)
(*l*) '[And] will 'a not come again' (IV. 5): BRAHMS, J. (1873); BRIAN,
H.; BRIDGEWATER, L. (1964); ELLISTON, M.; MELLERS, W. H.;
STEVENSON, J. A. (Glee, ? 1821)

## Henry IV, Parts 1 and 2

### 1

HOLST, G.   'At the Boar's Head' (1 act) (composer), Manchester, 1925 *
MERCADANTE, S.   'La gioventù di Enrico V' (F. Romani), Milan, 1834 †
VERDI, G.   'Falstaff', *see Merry Wives of Windsor*

### 2

(*a*) BISHOP, H. R. (Pt. 2 only, 1821); CORBETT, W. (*c.* 1699); PAISIBLE,
J. (*The Humours of Sir John Falstaff*, adap. by Betterton, 1700); *see also*
GENERAL: COPLAND, A.
(*b*) ELGAR, E. ('Falstaff', Symphonic study, Op. 68, 1913); GURLITT, M.
(Symphony); JOACHIM, J. (Overture, Op. 7); SMITH, D. S. ('Prince
Hal', Overture, Op. 31); WILLIAMS, G. ('Owen Glendower',
Symphonic impression)

### 3

(*a*) 'Do nothing but eat' (2HIV, V. 3): BISHOP, H. R. ; LINLEY, W.
(*b*) 'Give me a cup of sack, boy' (1HIV, II. 4): HATTON, J. L.
(*c*) 'Health to my sovereign' (2HIV, IV. 4): SHIELD, W. ('The King',
a glee)
(*d*) 'How many thousands of my poorest subjects' (2HIV, III. 1):
SARJEANT, J. ('King Henry's Soliloquy', 1932)
   'King, The', *see* 'Health to my sovereign': SHIELD, W.
   'King Henry's Soliloquy', *see* 'How many thousands': SARJEANT, J.
(*e*) 'O gentle sleep' (2HIV, III. 1): LESLIE, H. D. (Op. 13)
(*f*) 'She bids you on the wanton rushes lay you down' (1HIV, III. 1):
ROGERS, L. J.

## Henry V

### 2

(*a*) BARDI, B.; ISAACSON, B. (Princess's, 1859); O'NEILL, N. (Alhambra,
1933); WALTON, W. (Film, 1944); *see also* GENERAL: COPLAND, A.
(*b*) BOUGHTON, R. ('Agincourt', dramatic scene, 1924); DYSON, G.
('Agincourt'); MACFARREN, W. C. (Overture, 1881); RÔZE, R.
('Wedding March', Boston, 1910); WILLIAMS, R. Vaughan ('Thanks-
giving for Victory' words partly IV. 8, 1945)

3

'England's pleasant land', *see* 'O England!': DAVIES, H. Walford
(a) 'O England! Model to thy inward greatness' (Prologue, Act V):
DAVIES, H. Walford ('England's pleasant land', No. 3, Op. 22, 1907)

## Henry VI, Parts 1, 2 and 3

2

*See*; GENERAL: COPLAND, A.

3

(a) 'God's goodness hath been great to thee' (2HVI, II. 1): BRIDGE, F.
(Tercentenary Celebrations, 1916)

## Henry VIII

2

(a) DAVIE, C. Thorpe (1949); ENGEL, L.; FOULDS, J. H. (Empress, 1926);
GERMAN, E. (Lyceum, 1892); HATTON, J. K. (1855); SCHUMAN,
W. H.; SULLIVAN, A. S. (1877)
(b) LINLEY, W. ('Sad and solemn music' for IV. 2)

3

'In sweet music', *see* 'Orpheus with his lute': MAINZER, J.
(a) 'Orpheus with his lute' (III. 1): ALCOCK, G. A. (1938); ALWYN,
W. C. (1875); ARKWRIGHT, G. E. P. (1902); ARNE, T. A.; ASPA,
E.; AUSTIN, F. (1949); BAIRSTOW, E. C. (1919); BARRATT, W. A.
(N.Y., 1915); BAYLEY, T. H. R. (1908); BISHOP, H. R. (1820);
BREWER, A. H. (In Springtime, No. 3: 'The power of music');
BRIDGEWATER, L. (1964); BUSCH, C. (1906); BUSH, G. (Portraits, No.
1, 1942); BUTT, J. H. B.; CASTELNUOVO-TEDESCO, M.; CHILCOT, T.;
COATES, E. (1909); DAVIE, C. Thorpe; DAVIES, H. Walford (1931);
DUNHILL, T. F. (1935); FAULKES, W. (Op. 204, No. 11, 1920, unpub.);
FOX, A. M. (1901); GABRIEL, M.; GATTY, N. C. (1915); GERMAN,
E.; GIBBS, C. A. (1959); GILBERT, E. T. B.; GREATOREX, T. (1833);
GREENE, M. (c. 1745); GURNEY, I. (Five Songs, No. 2); HARKER, C.;
HART, F.; HATTON, J. L. (1905); HEATHCOTE, E. D.; HOPKINS, F.
(N.Y., 1913); HULBERT, H. R.; JACQUES, R.; KEEL, F. (1950);
KNIGHT, H.; LASSEN, E.; LEFEBVRE, C. (N.Y., 1958); LINLEY, W.;
LOCKE, M. (1673); MACFARREN, G. A. (1864); MAINZER, J. ('In
sweet music'); MANNEY, C. F. (Op. 3, No. 5, Boston, 1897); MILNER,
A.; MORNINGTON, Lord; NEWTON, E. R. (1926); PARKE, J.; PAR-
KER, H. T. (1895); PASCAL, F. (1899); PAYNE, R. (1883); QUILTER,
R. (Op. 32, No. 1, 1939); RATHBONE, G. (1921); RHODES, H. W.
(1925); RICCI, C. (Boston, 1902); SCHUMAN, W. H. (N.Y., 1944);
SHARMAN, C. (1931); SLINN, E. B. (Op. 13, No. 4); SMITH, J. C.
(1755); SOMERVELL, A. (1927); STEGGALL, R. (Op. 28, No. 4);

STEVENS, R. J. S.; SULLIVAN, A. S.; THOMAS, D. V.; WALKER, E. (Op. 3, No. 1); WESTRUP, J. A.; WILLIAMS, L. P. (1933); WILLIAMS, R. Vaughan (1903; 1926); WILSON, H. R.; WOOD, C.
'Power of music, The', see 'Orpheus with his lute': BREWER, A. H.


## Julius Caesar

### 1

GARCÍA ROBLEZ, J. 'Julio César'
KLEBE, G. 'Die Ermordung Cäsars' (1 act) (composer), Essen, 1959 *
MALIPIERO, G. F. 'Giulio Cesare' (composer), Genoa, 1936 *

### 2

(a) AKSES, N. K. (1942); BLITZSTEIN, M. (N.Y., Mercury, 1937); BÜLOW, H. von (Op. 10); CARPI, F. (Verona, 1949); DORET, G.; FOULDS, J. H. (Op. 39); FRÄNZL, I. (Mannheim, 1785); FRANKEL, B. (Film); GALLIARD, J. E. (Hickford's Rooms, 1740); IRELAND, J. (Radio, 1942); JACOBSON, M.; MILHAUD, D. (Paris, Th. de l'Atelier, 1937); O'NEILL, N. (St. James's, 1920); RÔZE, R. (Op. 16, 1899); SEYFRIED, I. von
(b) CASTELNUOVO-TEDESCO, M. (Concert overture, 1935); DRAESEKE, F. A. B. (Overture and Symphonic poem, 1854); FALCHI, S. (Overture); FOERSTER, J. B. (Overture, Op. 116); GURLITT, M. (Symphony); LUNSSENS, M. (Symphonic poem); PIERSON, H. H. (Overture); RUBENSON, A. (Overture, 1859); SCHUMANN, R. (Overture, Op. 128, comp. 1851, perf. 1857)


## King John

### 2

(a) DEMUTH, N. F. (Radio); WIRÉN, D.
(b) CASTELNUOVO-TEDESCO, M. (Concert overture, 1942); RADECKE, R. (Overture, Op. 25)

### 3

(a) 'That pale, that white-faced shore' (II. 1): GOVER, G. ('This sceptred isle', 1943)
'This sceptred isle', see 'That pale, that white-faced shore': GOVER, G. (see also Richard II, 3a)


## King Lear

### 1

CAGNONI, A. 'Re Lear'
COTTRAU, G. 'Cordelia' (composer), Padua, 1913 *
FRAZZI, V. 'Re Lear' (G. Papini), Florence, 1939 *
GHISLANZONI, Alberto. 'Re Lear' (composer), Rome, 1937 *.

GOBATTI, S.   'Cordelia', Bologna, 1881
REYNAUD, A.   'Le Roi Lear . . .', Toulouse, 1888
SÉMÉLADIS, M.   'Cordélia' (E. Pacini and E. Deschamps), Versailles, 1854

2

(a) ANDRÉ, J. (Berlin, 1778); BALAKIREV, M. A. (c. 1860; see also 2 (b));
    BARRAINE, E. (1945); CLARKE, J. H. S. (1892); HATTON, J. L. (1858);
    MISSA, E. J. L.; O'NEILL, N. (Op. 36, Haymarket, 1909); PAUM-
    GARTNER, B.; PEDRELL, F.; RAWSTHORNE, A.; REY, J. B.; SALM-
    HOFER, F.; SHAPORIN, Y. A. (1920); SHOSTAKOVICH, D. (Op. 58a,
    1940, unpub., ms. at Gorky Th., Leningrad); STEGMANN, C. D.
    (Hamburg, 1778)
(b) BALAKIREV, M. A. (Overture, 1859); BANTOCK, G. (Overture for
    brass band, 1936); BERLIOZ, H. (Overture, Op. 4, 1831); BLITZSTEIN,
    M. ('Lear, a study'); DEBUSSY, A. C. (1. Fanfare; 2. 'Sommeil de
    Lear', comp. 1904, pub. 1926; also 6 unpub. sketches); DUKAS, P.
    (Overture, unpub.); KLAMI, U. K. (Op. 33, 1944); LUENING, O.
    (Suite for tape recorder); PERSICHETTI, V. (Ballet); SCHULZ-BEUTHEN,
    H. (Symphony, No. 6); WEINGARTNER, F. von (Symphonic poem,
    Op. 20)

3

(a) 'Fathers that wear rags' (II. 4): CASTELNUOVO-TEDESCO, M.
(b) 'Fools had ne'er less grace' (I. 4): CASTELNUOVO-TEDESCO, M.;
    LINLEY, W. (as 'Ne'er less wit')
(c) 'Have more than thou owest' (I. 4): CASTELNUOVO-TEDESCO, M.
(d) 'He that has but a little tiny wit' (III. 2): CASTELNUOVO-TEDESCO, M.
(e) 'Saint Withold footed thrice the wold' (III. 4): BISHOP, H. R.
(f) 'That lord that counselled thee' (I. 4): CASTELNUOVO-TEDESCO, M.
(g) 'That sir that serves and seeks for gain' (II. 4): CASTELNUOVO-
    TEDESCO, M.
(h) 'Then they for sudden joy did weep' (I. 4): LINLEY, W.


## Love's Labour's Lost

1

BEECHAM, A.   'Love's Labour's Lost' *[1936]
FOLPRECHT, Z.   'Lásky hra osudná' (Čapek brothers), Bratislava, 1926

2

(a) BISHOP, H. R. (1839); FINZI, G. (Op. 28, 1948); FOERSTER, J. B.
    (Op. 116); MENGES, H. (1949)
(b) CUSINS, W. H. (Overture, 1875)

3

'Cuckoo, The', see 'When daisies pied': ARNE, T. A.; LEVERIDGE, R.
'Cuckoo and the Owl, The', see 'When daisies pied' and 'When icicles
    hang by the wall': CASTELNUOVO-TEDESCO, M.
'Cuckoo Song, The', see 'When daisies pied': ELLIOT, M.; FFOULKES, S.

'Do not call it sin in me', *see* 'On a day': KING, M. P.; SMITH, J. C.

(*a*) 'If love make me forsworn' (IV. 2): HUGHES, R.; MAJOR, J.

(*b*) 'If she be made of white and red' (I. 2): LESTER, W. (N.Y., 1914)

'King's Song, The', *see* 'So sweet a kiss': BEECHAM, A.

(*c*) 'Lover's eyes will gaze an eagle blind, A' (IV. 3): KEMP, J. (*c*. 1810); PARRY, J.

'Merry Note, A', *see* 'When icicles hang by the wall': SARSON, H. M.

'Mockery', *see* 'When daisies pied': WARLOCK, P.

(*d*) 'On a day, alack the day!' (IV. 3): ARNE, T. A.; BISHOP, H. R. (1864); BLUM, E. (Op. 10, No. 2, Boston, 1912); CHILCOT, T. (1744); CUMMINGS, W. H.; ELLA, J.; HOPKINS, F. ('That I am forsworn for thee', N.Y., 1913); JACKSON, W. (Op. 3, 1762); KING, M. P. ('Do not call it sin in me'); LYON, T.; PARRY, C. H. H. (1874); PYE, K. J.; SMITH, J. C. ('Do not call it sin in me', 1755); STEVENS, W. P. (1864); SULLIVAN, T. D.; WASSALL, G. (Sh. Song Cycle, No. 7, Cincinnati, *c*. 1904)

'Owl, The', *see* 'When icicles hang by the wall': ARNE, T. A.

(*e*) 'So sweet a kiss the golden sun gives not' (IV. 3): BEECHAM, A. ('The King's Song', 1934); SAMPSON, George, 1893)

'Spring', *see* 'When daisies pied': FISKE, R.; MÜLLER, J.

'That I am forsworn for thee', *see* 'On a day': HOPKINS, F.

'Tu-whit! Tu-whoo!', *see* 'When icicles hang by the wall': JACOB, G.; TREHARNE, B.

(*f*) 'When daisies pied and violets blue' (V. 2): ARKWRIGHT, G. E. P. (1902); ARNE, T. A. ('The Cuckoo', 1740); BRIDGEWATER, L. (1964); CASTELNUOVO-TEDESCO, M. ('The cuckoo and the owl'); CRICHTON, M. (1928); DANNREUTHER, E. G.; DRAKEFORD, R. (1961); ELLIOT, M. ('Cuckoo Song'); FFOULKES, S. ('The Cuckoo Song'); FINZI, G. (1948); FISKE, R. ('Spring', 1948); JUDD, P.; KEEL, F. (1940); LEVERIDGE, R. ('The Cuckoo', ? 1725); MACFARREN, G. A. (1864); MOERAN, E. J.; MÜLLER, J. ('Spring', 1905); PARKE, J.; RICKARDS, E. H. (1918); SHARMAN, C. (1930); SHAW, M. F. (1921); SIMPSON, R.; SMITH, J. S. (*c*. 1812); STRAVINSKY, I. (1953); TAUBERT, K. G. W. ('Wenn Veilchen blau und bunter Klee', Op. 33); WARLOCK, P. ('Mockery'); WOOD, F. H. (Op. 16)

(*g*) 'When icicles hang by the wall' (V. 2): ANDERSON, R. G. ('Winter', 1910); ARKWRIGHT, G. E. P. (1902); ARNE, T. A. ('The Owl', words altered to '. . . on the wall', 1720); BAINES, H.; BRIAN, H.; BRIDGEWATER, L. (1964); BROOKS, W. W.; CASTELNUOVO-TEDESCO, M. ('The cuckoo and the owl'); CHANDLER, M.; DANKWORTH, J. ('Winter', 1964); DANNREUTHER, E. G.; DUNCAN, W. E. ('Winter', 1892); DYSON, G.; EVANS, D. M.; FINZI, G. (1948); GIBBS, C. A. (1951) GILBERT, N. ('Winter', 1938); HAND, C.; HARDY, T. M.; JACOB, G. ('Tu-whit! Tu-whoo!', 1938); KEEL, F. (1927); KEIGHLEY, T.; LEHMANN, L. (1911); LONGMIRE, J.; MACFARREN, G. A. (1851); MARZIALS, T. J. H. ('Winter's Song', 1890); MOERAN, E. J.; MOORAT, J. S. ('Winter', 1904); MONTGOMERY, R. B. (1947); PARRY, C. H. H. (1886); PERCY, J.; QUILTER, R. (Op. 32, No. 2, 1939); SARSON, H. M. ('A Merry Note', 1933); SELBY, B. L. (Boston, 1903); SHARMAN, C. (1931); SHAW, G. T. (1912); SIMPSON, F. J. (Op. 1, No. 7, 1888); STONE, N. M. (1945); THIMAN, E. ('A Winter's

Song'); TREHARNE, B. ('Tu-whit! Tu-whoo!'); TREMAIN, R.; WALKER, E. (Op. 1); WAREING, H. W. ('Winter'); WILLIAMS, L. P. (1933); WILLIAMS, R. Vaughan (1926); WILSON, H. R. ('Winter'); WISTER, O. ('Winter's Song', N.Y., 1936); WOOD, F. H. (Op. 16); WOOD, R. W.

'Winter', 'Winter's Song', see 'When icicles hang by the wall': *passim*

## Macbeth

### 1

ASPLMAYR, F. 'Leben und Tod des Königs Macbeth' (pantomime) (Moll), Vienna, 1777
BLOCH, E. 'Macbeth' (E. Fleg), Paris, 1910 *
CHÉLARD, H. 'Macbeth' (C. J. Rouget de Lisle), Paris, 1827 *
COLLINGWOOD, L. 'Macbeth' (composer), London, 1934
GATTY, N. C. 'Macbeth'
ROSSI, Lauro. 'Biorn' (F. Marshall), London, 1877
TAUBERT, W. 'Macbeth' (F. Eggers), Berlin, 1857 *
VERDI, G. 'Macbeth' (F. M. Piave and A. Maffei), Florence, 1847 *; (C. Nuitter and A. Beaumont), Paris, 1865 *

### 2

(a) ARNOLD, S. (1778); ASSAFIEV, B. V.; BALMER, L.; BANTOCK, G. (1926); BRAUNFELS, W. (Op. 14); BUSH, A. (1947); CARR, B. (N.Y., 1795); DEMUTH, N. (Radio); ECCLES, J. (c. 1695); FISHER, J. A.; FRÄNZL, I. (Mannheim, 1788); FRANKEL, B. (Film); HATTON, J. L. (1853); HOLLY, F. A. (Breslau, 1780); IBERT, J. (Film); IRVING, K. E.; JACOBSON, M.; KELLEY, E. S. (Op. 7); KHACHATURIAN, A. I.; KLUG, E.; KOHS, E. (1947); LEVERIDGE, R. (1702); LINLEY, T. *the elder* (1794); LOCKE, M. (c. 1662–8; 1674, lost) [1]; MEDERITSCH, J.; MILHAUD, D. (New, for Old Vic company, 1937); NECHAYEV, V. V.; NEEFE, C. G. (Mannheim, 1779); O'NEILL, N. (Aldwych, 1920); PONC, M. (1939); PURCELL, D.; REY, J. B.; RIETZ, J. (Düsseldorf, 1834); RUBBRA, E.; SPOHR, L. (Op. 75, 1825); STEGMANN, C. D.; SUTOR, W.; TRANCHELL, P. A. (1949); WALTON, W. (1941); WEYSE, C. E. F. (Copenhagen, c. 1820); WHITAKER, J. (*The Weird Sisters: or, the Thane and the Throne*, pantomime, Sadler's Wells, 1819); ZUMSTEEG, J. R.

(b) BANTOCK, G. ('Dance of Witches', 1927); BLOCH, E. ('Deux Interludes symph.', Milan, 1946); BRÜLL, I. (Overture, Op. 43); DANKWORTH, J. ('Dunsinane blues', voices and orch., 1964); DUPUIS, S. (Symphonic poem, overture and 2 suites for orch.); EBERWEIN, T. M. (Overture, 1828); FRY, W. H. (Overture and Witches' Incantation); GRIEG, E. H. (Lyric Pieces, Set I, No. 3 : 'Watchman's (*i.e.* Porter's) Song', Op. 12, 1867); LE FLEM, P. ('Mimodrame dansé', 1936); LUCAS, C. (Overture); OBERTHÜR, C. (Overture); PEARSALL, R. L. (Overture, Op. 35, 1839); PIERSON, H. H. (Symphony, Op. 54, 1874;

---

[1] On the question of Locke's music for *Macbeth*, see p. 53.

Overture, unpub.) ; REICHARDT, J. F. ('Hexenscenen', pf., 1787) ;
SCHUMANN, R. ('When shall we three meet again?', Op. 21, No. 3,
1838) ; SMETANA, B. ('Macbeth and the Witches', pf., 1859) ; SPOHR,
L. (Overture, Op. 75, 1825) ; STRAUSS, R. (Tone Poem, Op. 23,
1890) ; SULLIVAN, A. S. (Overture, 1888) ; TCHEREPNIN, N. N.
('Witches' scene' for orch.) ; TIPPETT, M. (Suite)

### 3

'Ashmansworth', *see* 'This castle hath a pleasant seat' : MILNER, A.
(*a*) 'Round about the cauldron go' (IV. 1) : KING, M. P.
(*b*) 'This castle hath a pleasant seat' (I. 6) : MILNER, A. ('Ashmansworth',
1963)
(*c*) 'When shall we three meet again?' (I. 1) : HERSCHEL, W. ; HORSLEY,
W. ; KING, M. P. ('The Witches', Glee, *c.* 1810); WEBBE, S. *the
elder.*
(*d*) 'Where the place?' (I. 1) : KING, M. P. (Glee, *c.* 1805)
'Witches, The', *see* 'When shall we three?' : KING, M. P.

## Measure for Measure

### 1

WAGNER, R. 'Das Liebesverbot, oder die Novize von Palermo' (composer), Magdeburg, 1836 *

### 2

(*a*) KABALEVSKY, D. B. ; O'NEILL, N. (Haymarket, 1929) ; PONC, M.
(1935)
(*b*) ADLAM, F. ('Take, o take', pf. 1886)

### 3

'Mariana's Song', *see* 'Take, o take' : MELLERS, W. H.
'Seals of Love', *see* 'Take, o take' : CASTELNUOVO-TEDESCO, M.
(*a*) 'Take, o take those lips away' (IV. 1) : ALCOCK, J. (? 1775) ; ANDER-
TON, H. O. (1910) ; ATTERBURY, L. ; AYRES, F. (Op. 3, No. 1, 1906) ;
BARRATT, W. A. (N.Y., 1916) ; BARRY, Hon. A. (1810) ; BEACH, J. P.
(1906) ; BENNETT, T. C. Sterndale- (1909) ; BISHOP, H. R. (1819) ;
BORCH, G. (Op. 11, No. 3, 1907) ; BRIDGEWATER, L. (1964) ; CALL-
COTT, J. W. ; CARMICHAEL, M. ; CASTELNUOVO-TEDESCO, M. ('Seals
of love') ; CHAUSSON, E. (Op. 28, No. 2) ; CHILCOT, T. (1744) ;
CLARK, H. (Madrigal) ; COVER, C. E. (1895) ; COWARD, J. (1872) ;
COWEN, F. H. ; DIEREN, B. van ; DIXON, C. (*c.* 1760) ; FAULKES, W.
(Op. 204, No. 7, 1920, unpub.) FOX, A. M. (1900) ; GALLIARD, J. E.
(*c.* 1730) ; GAMBOGI, F. E. ; GARDINER, W. (? 1795) ; GIORDANI, T.
(1781) ; GRAZIA, E. N. (1872) ; GREENHILL, J. ; HUEFFER, F. (1873) ;
ILES, E. (1891) ; JACKSON, W. (Op. 9, No. 7, *c.* 1770) ; JOHNSON, G. F.
(1907) ; LA FORGE, F. (N.Y., 1909) ; LANCELOTT, F. (1858) ;
LEHMANN, A. (1899) ; LETTS, E. (1915) ; LINLEY, W. ; MACFARREN,
G. A. (1869) ; MACIRONE, C. A. ; MELLERS, W. H. ('Mariana's

Song', 1944); MELLON, A. (1864); MONTGOMERY, R. B. (1948); MOORE,
E. C. (Chicago, 1914); PARRY, C. H. H. (Op. 11, No. 3, 1875);
PEARSALL, R. L. (Op. 6, 1819); PIERSON, H. H. (Op. 26, No. 3);
PLUMSTEAD, M. (1956); PRENDERGAST, A. H. D.; QUILTER, R. (Op.
23, 1921); REAY, S.; RUBBRA, E. (1928); SAUGUET, H.; SELBY,
B. L. (Boston, 1903); SMITH, J. S. (c. 1812); SOMERVELL, A. (1898);
STEGGALL, R. (Op. 28, No. 3); STEVENSON, J. A.; STRELEZKI, A.;
TAYLOR, J. A.; THOMSON, V. (1961); TINDAL, W. (Op. 1, c. 1786);
TREHARNE, B.; TREMAIN, R. (1958); TREMAIN, T. (1786); WARLOCK,
P. ('Saudades', No. 2, 1916; also 1918); WELDON, J. (c. 1710);
WESTRUP, J. A.; WILLIAMS, R. Vaughan (1926); WILSON, C.;
WILSON, J. (pub. 1652); WOOD, R. W.; YOUNG, A. (Six Songs, No.
4, 1947)

## The Merchant of Venice

### 1

ALPAERTS, F. 'Shylock' (H. Melis), Antwerp, 1913
BEECHAM, A. 'The Merchant of Venice', London, 1922 *
BRUMAGNE, F. 'Le Marchand de Venise', Brussels
CASTELNUOVO-TEDESCO, M. 'Il mercante di Venezia' (composer),
Florence, 1961 *
DEFFÈS, L. P. 'Jessica' (J. Adenis and H. Boisseaux), Toulouse, 1898
FOERSTER, J. B. 'Jessika' (J. Vrchlický), Prague, 1905
HAHN, R. 'Le Marchand de Venise' (M. Zamaçoïs), Paris, 1935 *
LAUFER, B. 'Shylock' [1929]
PINSUTI, C. 'Il mercante di Venezia' (G. T. Cimino), Bologna, 1873 *
RADÓ, A. 'Shylock' (composed 1913-14, unfinished)
TAUBMANN, O. 'Porzia', Frankfurt/Main, 1916

### 2

(a) ARNE, T. A. (D.L., 1741); ASSAFIEV, B. V.; BUSH, G.; CARTER, E.
(1939); CLARKE, J. H. S. (1879); EASDALE, B.; FAURÉ, G. (Odéon,
1889); GREENWOOD, J.; HATTON, J. L. (1858); HUMPERDINCK, E.
(Berlin, 1905); MONIUSZKO, S.; MÜHLDORFER, W. C. (Op. 29,
1873); NYSTROEM, G.; O'NEILL, N. (N.Y., Lyceum, 1922); RABAUD,
H. B. (Th. Antoine, 1917); RATHAUS, K.; RÓŻYCKI, L.; SABATA, V.
de; SIMON, A.; SULLIVAN, A. S. (Prince's, Manchester, 1871);
TRANCHELL, P. A. (1950); WIRÉN, D. (1943)
(b) BUSH, G. ('Prince of Morocco's fanfare and march', wind ensemble
from inc. m., see 2(a), 1964); CASTELNUOVO-TEDESCO, M. (Concert
overture, 1935); FAURÉ, G. (Four orch. pieces from inc. m., see 2 (a);
'Nocturne of Shylock', vl.); FOERSTER, J. B. (Orch. suite, 1908);
HALES, H. J. (Concert overture, Op. 1); MACFARREN, G. A. (Overture); O'NEILL, N. (Sh. sketches for orch., No. 2, 1928); RILEY, A.
('Shakespeare's lovers in a garden'); ROSSE, F. (Intermezzo 'Portia'
and 'Doge's March', 1905); SAUSSINE, H. de ('Le Marchand
de Venise', voice and pf.); WHITE, F. H. (Overture: 'Shylock',
1907)

3

(a) 'All that glisters is not gold' (II. 7) : HORN, C. E.
  'Cheerfulness', *see* 'Let me play the fool' : PINSUTI, C.
  'Fancy', *see* 'Tell me, where is fancy bred?' : BOLLINGER, S.; CASTEL-
  NUOVO-TEDESCO, M.
(b) 'For do but note a wild and wanton herd' (V. 1) : COOKE, T. S.
  ('I do but note . . .')
(c) 'How sweet the moonlight sleeps upon this bank' (V. 1) : BEDFORD,
  H. ('Lorenzo to Jessica', 1922); BENDALL, W. E. (1889); BERLIOZ, H.
  (*see* 'Les Troyens', Act IV); BLANCHARD, T.; BRYAN, R. (1922);
  CALLCOTT, J. G. (1886); DIGNUM, C.; EVANS, D. E. (1895); FANING,
  J. E. (1905); GARDNER, C.; HATHAWAY, J. (Rhapsody for ch. and
  orch., Op. 17, 1905); HILL, M. (1926); HUTCHINSON, J. T. (1897);
  HUTCHINSON, T.; KING, M. P. (Glee, 1820); LEHMANN, L. (1912);
  LESLIE, H. D. (Op. 23, No. 4); LEVEY, S. (Recitation with music,
  'Sweet Music', 1918); LOVATT, S. E. ('Nocturne', 1923); NAYLOR,
  E. ('Moonlight', 1845); PERCY, J. (? 1790); RATHBONE, G. (1926);
  REED, W. (Boston, 1901); RUSSELL, O. N. (1960); SMITH, W. E.
  (1930); SULLIVAN, A. S. (part of 'Kenilworth', 1865); TAYLOR,
  E. D.; THOMAS, D. V.; WEBBE, S. *the younger*; WILLIAMS, R. Vaughan
  ('Serenade to music', 1938); WILSON, H. R.; WOOD, C.
  'Kenilworth', *see* 'How sweet the moonlight' : SULLIVAN, A. S.
  'I do but note', *see* 'For do but note' : COOKE, T. S.
(d) 'In such a night' (V. 1) : GARDNER, C.; SULLIVAN, A. S.
(e) 'Let me play the fool' (I. 1) : LESLIE, H. D. (1885); PINSUTI, C.
  ('Cheerfulness', Glee, 1879)
  'Lorenzo to Jessica', *see* 'How sweet the moonlight' : BEDFORD, H.
  'Love', *see* 'Tell me, where is fancy bred?' : HADLEY, H. K.
  'Moonlight', *see* 'How sweet the moonlight' : NAYLOR, E.
  'Nocturne', *see* 'How sweet the moonlight' : LOVATT, S. E.
(f) 'Quality of mercy is not strained, The' (IV. 1) : BANTOCK, G. (1938);
  THORNE, E. H.
  'Serenade to music', *see* 'How sweet the moonlight' : WILLIAMS, R.
  Vaughan
  'Sweet music', *see* 'How sweet the moonlight' : LEVEY, S.
(g) 'Tell me, where is fancy bred?' (III. 2) : ARNE, T. A. (1741); BART-
  LETT, H. N. (Op. 241, No. 2, N.Y., 1912); BESLY, E. M. (1919);
  BLYTON, C. ('What then is love?', 1960); BOLLINGER, S. ('Fancy',
  Op. 16, No. 1, N.Y., 1910); BRIDGEWATER, L. (1964); BRITTEN, B.
  (1964); BUSH, G. (1964); CALLCOTT, J. G. (1881); CARMICHAEL,
  M.; CASTELNUOVO-TEDESCO, M. ('Fancy'); COATES, E. (1912);
  COOK, J. E. (1958); CUISSET, F. F. (? 1840); DUNHILL, T. (1931);
  EDESON, D. J. S. (1928); FAULKES, W. (Op. 204, No. 1, 1920, unpub.);
  GÁL, H. (Op. 75, No. 3, 1959); GORDON, P. (N.Y., 1958); HADLEY,
  H. K. ('Love', Op. 81, No. 1, N.Y., 1918); HALES, H. (Op. 31, No. 1,
  1942); HARCOURT, J. A.; HATTON, J. L. (1859); HIND, J. (1953);
  HODGE, M. T. (1926); JEFFERSON, P. (N.Y., 1957); KNIGHT, R.
  (1901); KODÁLY, Z. (1964); KOVEN, R. de (Op. 159, No. 5, Cin-
  cinnati, 1900); LEHMANN, L. (1911); LINLEY, W.; LUETGEN, B.
  (1877); MACFARREN, G. A. (1869); MACKENZIE, A. C. (1924);
  MONTGOMERY, R. B. (1948); MOUNSEY, A. S.; OBERHOFFER, R. W.

(1902); O'NEILL, N. (N.Y., 1922); PIERSON, H. H. (Op. 63); PIN-
SUTI, C. (1884); POINTER, J. (1917); POULENC, F. (1964); QUILTER,
R. (1951); RICHMOND, L. (1790); ROSSE, F. (1905); SHARMAN, C.
(1929); SHAW, G. T. (1937); SLINN, E. B. (Op. 13, No. 3); STEVENS,
R. J. S. (Glee); STEVENSON, J. A. (? 1795); TAUBERT, W. ('Sagt
woher stammt Liebeslust?', Op. 33, No. 3); THOMSON, V. (1961);
TOYE, J. F.; WASSALL, G. (Sh. song Cycle, No. 7, Cincinnati, c. 1904);
WEBER, B. A.; WEBER, C. M. F. von (1821); WILLIAMS, F. (1936);
WOOD, F. H. (Op. 35, No. 1)
'What then is love?', see 'Tell me where is fancy bred?': BLYTON, C.

## The Merry Wives of Windsor

### I

ADAM, A. 'Falstaff' (1 act) (J. H. Vernoy de Saint-Georges and A. de
Leuven), Paris, 1856
BALFE, M. W. 'Falstaff' (S. M. Maggioni), London, 1838 *
DITTERSDORF, K. Ditters von. 'Die lustigen Weiber von Windsor und der
dicke Hans' (G. C. Roemer, altered), Öls, 1796
NICOLAI, O. 'Die lustigen Weiber von Windsor' (S. H. Mosenthal),
Berlin, 1849 *
PAPAVOINE 'Le Vieux Coquet, ou les deux amies', Paris, 1761
PHILIDOR, F. A. D. 'Herne le chasseur' (Douin), (composed 1773)
RITTER, P. 'Die lustigen Weiber' (G. C. Roemer), Mannheim, 1794
SALIERI, A. 'Falstaff osia le tre burle' (C. P. Defranceschi), Vienna,
1799 *
VERDI, G. 'Falstaff' (A. Boito), Milan, 1893 *
WILLIAMS, R. Vaughan. 'Sir John in Love' (composer), London, 1929 *

### 2

(a) ANDRIESSEN, J.; BARDI, B.; BINET, J. (1940); BISHOP, H. R. (1824);
HORN, C. E. (part only, 1823); MONIUSZKO, S.; PONC, M. (1937);
SALMHOFER, F.; SULLIVAN, A. S. (1874)
(b) ADAM, A. (Quadrille et valse, 1856); BENNETT, W. Sterndale- (Overture) 1834, unpub.); HERBERIGS, R. (Symphonic poem, 1950);
KAUN, H. ('Sir John Falstaff': Humoresque for orch., Op. 60);
NICOLAI, O. (Overture, see I above); TRANCHELL, P. A. ('Falstaff',
ballet, 1950); WILLIAMS, R. Vaughan ('In Windsor Forest', cantata
from 'Sir John in Love' see I above, 1929)

### 3

(a) 'By shallow rivers' (III. 1): ARNOLD, S. (see also The Passionate
Pilgrim, 8)
(b) 'Fie on sinful phantasy' (V. 5): ADDISON, J.; BRIDGEWATER, L.
(1964); CASTELNUOVO-TEDESCO, M. ('Roundel')
'Roundel', see 'Fie on sinful phantasy': CASTELNUOVO-TEDESCO, M.
(c) 'Thine own true knight' (II. 1): ELLISTON, M.

S

## A Midsummer Night's Dream

### 1

ARUNDELL, D. 'A Midsummer Night's Dream'

BRITTEN, B. 'A Midsummer Night's Dream' (composer and Peter Pears), Aldeburgh, 1960 *

DELANNOY, M. 'Puck' (A. Boll), Strasbourg, 1949 *

DOUBRAVA, J. 'A Midsummer-Night's Dream' (composed 1945)

LAMPE, J. F. 'Pyramus and Thisbe' (1 act) (mock-opera, libretto partly based on Leveridge, *see below*), London, 1745 *

LEVERIDGE, R. 'The Comick masque of Pyramus and Thisbe' (1 act) (composer), London, 1716 †

MANCINELLI, L. 'Sogno di una notte d' estate' (F. Salvatori), (composed 1917) *

MANUSARDI, G. 'Un sogno di primavera', Milan, 1842

ORFF, C. 'Ein Sommernachtstraum' (composer), 1952 *

PURCELL, H. 'The Fairy Queen' (? E. Settle), London, 1692 *

SMITH, J. C. 'The Fairies' (composer), London, 1755 *

SUPPÉ, F. von. 'Der Sommernachtstraum', Vienna, 1844

VREULS, V. 'Un Songe d'une nuit d'été' (P. Spaak), Brussels, 1925

WOLF, E. W. 'Die Zauberirrungen' (F. H. von Einsiedel), Weimar, 1785

For SERPETTE and THOMAS, *see* GENERAL

### 2

(a) ARNE, M. (for Colman's *The Fairy Tale*, 1763); ARNOLD, S. (Haymarket, 1777); AYLWARD, T.; BISHOP, H. R. (1816); COOKE, T. S. (1816); GREENWOOD, J.; HALL, P. (Oslo, 1948); HAWKINS, H. A. (1924); IBERT, J.; KŘENEK, E. (Op. 46, 1926); LEIGH, W. (1937); MALAWSKI, A. (1954); MENDELSSOHN, F. (Op. 61, 1842); PAUMGARTNER, B.; PERCY, J. (c. 1795) REYNOLDS, F. (1816); SATIE, E. (1914); SHARP, C. J. (1914); WEISMANN, J. (1934); WIRÉN, D.

(b) ANSON, H. ('Puck in the Belfry', pf. 1924); BAYNHAM, T. ('The Titania Polka', pf., 1855); BIDGOOD, T. ('Titania: Mazurka russe'); CASTELNUOVO-TEDESCO, M. (Concert overture, 1940); DEBUSSY, C. (Preludes, Book I, No. 11: 'La Danse de Puck', 1910); EWING, M. ('Titania', pf., 1922); HAYDEN, W. (Five dances for pf., No. 4: 'Titania'); HOWELLS, H. (Two pieces for small orch., No. 1: 'Puck's Minuet', 1918); IBERT, J. ('Suite élisabéthaine,' 1942); JACOBI, G. (Ballet); MACFARREN, A. G. (Overture); MACONCHY, E. (Suite for orch., 'Puck'); MENDELSSOHN, F. (Overture, Op. 21, 1826); NEWTON, E. ('Titania's dance', pf., 1924); NIXON, H. ('Titania's Overture', 1880); O'NEILL, N. (Sh. sketches for orch., No. 1, 'Nocturne', 1928); SHAW, M. G. ('The Fools and the Fairies', arr. P. A. Scholes, 1955); SPEAIGHT, J. ('Fairy characters' and 'Fantasy', string quartet); TAUBERT, K. G. W. ('Titania', solo pf., 1865); THIMAN, E. H. ('Fairy Scenes', pf., 1934); TRNKA, J. (Puppet-film); VAČKÁŘ, D. C. (Ballet)

### 3

(a) 'Be as thou wast wont to be' (IV. 1): BATTISHILL, J. (1763); BISHOP, H. R.; CRICHTON, M. ('Oberon's song', 1928) (*b*) 'Before the time I did Lysander see' (I. 1) : SMITH, J. C. (1755)

'Blind Cupid', *see* 'Love looks not' : LEHMANN, L.

(*c*) 'By the simplicity of Venus' doves' (I. 1) : BISHOP, H. R. (1864)

'Fairies', *see* 'Ye spotted snakes' : CASTELNUOVO-TEDESCO, M.

'Fairies' Lullaby', *see* 'Ye spotted snakes' : BUZZI-PECCIA, A.

'Fairies' Song, The', *see* 'Ye spotted snakes' : BUTT, J.

'Fairy Blessing, A', *see* 'Now the hungry lion roars' : JOSEPH, J.

'Fairy [Goblin] lead them up and down', *see* 'Up and down' : COOKE, T. S.

'Fairy lullaby', *see* 'Ye spotted snakes' : BEACH, A.

'Fairy song and lullaby', *see* 'Ye spotted snakes' : LUETGEN, B.

(*d*) 'Flower of this purple dye' (III. 2) : BISHOP, H. R. ; SMITH, J. C.

'For night's swift dragons', *see* 'Lo, night's swift dragons' : COOKE, T. S.

(*e*) 'Hand in hand, with fairy grace' (V. 1) : COOKE, B.

(*f*) 'I know a bank where the wild thyme blows' (II. 1) : BARNETT, J. (1830) ; BURY, W. (1934) ; COLLINGWOOD, A. (1933) ; DEMUTH, N. F. (1925) ; GILL, G. (1935) ; HARRISON, J. A. G. (1928) ; HORN, C. E. (1823) ; HUDSON, H. ('Oxlips and violet') ; LEHMANN, L. ('Titania's cradle', 1892); MENDELSSOHN, F. (1842); NEWTON, E. R. ('Where the wild thyme blows', 1924); PARKER, H. T. (1895); PERCY, J. (*c*. 1795); SHARMAN, C.; SHAW, M. F. (1922); WOOD, F. H. (Op. 31, No. 1)

'In Theseus' house', *see* 'Through the house' : BISHOP, H. R.

(*g*) 'Lo [For] night's swift dragons cut the clouds full fast' (III. 2) : COOKE, T. S.

'Loadstars', *see* 'O happy fair !' : SHIELD, W. (1797)

'Love in idleness', *see* 'That very time I saw' : COOKE, T. S.

(*h*) 'Love looks not with the eyes' (I. 1) : LEHMANN, L. (1895) ; SMITH, J. C. (1755)

'Lullaby', *see* 'Ye spotted snakes' : BLITZSTEIN, M. ; DAVIES, H. Walford; HALES, H.

'Lullaby for Titania', *see* 'Ye spotted snakes' : AGER, L.

(*i*) 'Now [When] it is the time of night' (V. 1) : HORN, C. E.

(*j*) 'Now the hungry lion roars' (V. 1) : BISHOP, H. R. ; ELLERTON, J. L. ; GIBBS, C. A. ; HORN, C. E. ; JOSEPH, J. M. ('A Fairy Blessing'); LEVERIDGE, R. (1716) ; LINLEY, W. ; LODGE, J. (1850) ; MENDELSSOHN, F. (1842) ; STEVENS, R. J. S.

(*k*) 'Now until the break of day' (V. 1) : BISHOP, H. R. ('To the best bride-bed will we') ; SMITH, J. C. (1755)

(*l*) 'O happy fair !' (I. 1) : BISHOP, H. R. (1816) ; HIME, E. L. ; LODER, E. J. (1873) ; SALOMON, J. P. ('When hawthorn buds') ; SMITH, J. C. ('O Hermia fair !', 1755) ; SHIELD, W. ('Shakespeare's Duel (see *The Passionate Pilgrim*, 7) and Loadstars', Glee, 1797)

'O Hermia fair !', *see* 'O happy fair !' : SMITH, J. C.

'Oberon's Song', *see* 'Be as thou wast wont to be' : CRICHTON, M.

(*m*) 'On the ground, Sleep sound' (III. 2) : WILSON, C.

'Ousel cock, The', *see* 'Woozel cock' : *passim*

(*n*) 'Over hill, over dale' (II. 1) : ATTWATER, J. P. ('Song of the fairies', 1909) ; BUNNETT, E. ; COOKE, T. S. ; DICKS, E. A. ; DUGGAN, J. F. ; DUNHILL, T. ('Puck's Song', 1932) : FITZWILLIAM, E. ; GODFREY,

H. G. (1929); HATTON, J. L.; HEWARD, L. H.; JACKSON, W. (Op. 11, 1780); LLOYD, C. H. (1907); LODER, E. J. (1857); MACFARREN, G. A. (1856); NEWELL, J. E. ('Song of the fairies', 1886); RÔZE, R. (1900); SHAW, G. T. (1912); SHAW, M. F. (1923); WILKINSON, P. G. (1955); WILLIAMS, R. Vaughan (1951); WILSON, W.

'Oxlips and violet', *see* 'I know a bank': HUDSON, H.

'Philomel', *see* 'Ye spotted snakes': HARRISON, J. A. G.; WATERS, C. F.; YOUNG, A.

'Puck's Song', *see* 'Over hill, over dale': DUNHILL, T. P.

'Shakespeare Lullaby, A', *see* 'Ye spotted snakes': NEWTON, E. R.

'Song of the fairies', *see* 'Over hill, over dale': ATTWATER, J. P.; NEWELL, J. E.

(*o*) 'That very time I saw, though thou couldst not' (III. 1): COOKE, T. S. ('Love in idleness', 1840)

(*p*) 'Through the forest have I gone' (II. 2): GATTIE, Mrs. J. B. (Canzonet)

(*q*) 'Through the house give glimmering light' (V. 1): BISHOP, H. R. ('In Theseus' house . . .'); BOYCE, E. M. (1927); MENDELSSOHN, F. (1842)

'Titania's cradle', *see* 'I know a bank': LEHMANN, L.

'Titania's lullaby', *see* 'Ye spotted snakes': FORSYTH, C.; INGHAM, R.

'To the best bride-bed will we', *see* 'Now until the break of day': BISHOP, H. R.

(*r*) 'Up and down, up and down' (III. 2): BURNEY, C.; COOKE, T. S. ('Fairy lead them', 1835); HATELY, W.; SMITH, J. C. (1755)

'When hawthorn buds', *see* 'O happy fair!': SALOMON, J. P.

'When it is the time of night', *see* 'Now it is': HORN, C. E.

'Where the wild thyme blows', *see* 'I know a bank': NEWTON, E. R.

(*s*) 'Woosel cock, so black of hue, The' (III. 1): BURNEY, C. (*c*. 1763); ELLISTON, M.

(*t*) 'Ye [You] spotted snakes with double tongue' (II. 2): AGER, L. ('Lullaby for Titania', 1958); ANDERTON, H. O. (? 1897); BEACH, A. ('Fairy lullaby', Boston, 1907); BLITZSTEIN, Marc ('Lullaby', 1958); BRIAN, H.; BRIDGEWATER, L. (1964); BUTT, J. H. B. ('The fairies' song'); BUZZI-PECCIA, A. ('The fairies' lullaby'); CASTELNUOVO-TEDESCO, M. ('Fairies'); COLLINGWOOD, A. (1933); DAVIE, C. Thorpe; DAVIES, H. Walford ('Lullaby', 1932); DAVIS, J. D.; EARLE, W. B. (? 1794); ELLISTON, M.; FORSYTH, C. ('Titania's lullaby'); GIBBS, C. A. (1923); GRAFFE, G.; HALES, H. ('Lullaby', Op. 39, No. 1, 1952); HALL, J.; HARRISON, J. A. G. ('Philomel', 1938); HILLS, W.; INGRAM, R. ('Titania's lullaby'); KEEL, F. (1937); LEONARD, S. B.; LEPPARD, R.; LUETGEN, B. ('Fairy song and lullaby', 1887); MAC-FARREN, G. A. (1869); MAXWELL, I. (1951); MEISSLER, J. ('The fairies' song', 1879); MENDELSSOHN, F. (1842); MUNDELLA, E. (1886); MYERS, J. (1952); NEWTON, E. R. ('A Shakespeare Lullaby', Boston, 1928); ORCHARD, W. A. (1891); SHAW, G. T. (1912); SHAW, M. F. (1927); SMITH, J. C. (1755); STEVENS, R. J. S. (Glee, ? 1800); TAUBERT, W. (Op. 33, No. 5); TURNBULL, P.; WATERS, C. F. ('Philomel', 1938); WOOD, F. H. (Op. 24, No. 7); YOUNG, A. ('Philomel', 1948)

## Much Ado About Nothing

### I

BERLIOZ, H.   'Béatrice et Bénédict' (composer), Baden-Baden, 1862 *
DOPPLER, A.   'Viel Lärm um Nichts', Leipzig, 1896
HAHN, R.   'Beaucoup de bruit pour rien' (J. Sarment), Paris, 1936
HEINRICH, H.   'Viel Lärm um Nichts', Frankfort/Oder, 1956
MOJSISOVICS, R. von.   'Viel Lärm um Nichts', Graz, c. 1930
PODESTÀ, C.   'Ero', Cremona, 1900
PUGET, P.   'Beaucoup de bruit pour rien', Paris, 1899
STANFORD, C. V.   'Much Ado About Nothing' (J. R. Sturgis), London, 1901 *

### 2

(a) ARNE, T. A. (D.L., 1748) ; GERMAN, E. (St. James's, 1898) ; GODARD, B. L. P. (Odéon, 1887) ; HATTON, J. L. (1858) ; KHRENNIKOV, T. N. (Op. 7, 1935) ; KORNGOLD, E. W. (Op. 11)

### 3

(a) 'Done to death by slanderous tongues' (V. 3) : AYLWARD, T. (c. 1790) 'Heavily', see 'Pardon, Goddess of the night' : CASTELNUOVO-TEDESCO, M.
(b) 'Pardon, Goddess of the night' (V. 3) : ARNE, T. A. ; BRIDGEWATER, L. (1964) ; CASTELNUOVO-TEDESCO, M. ('Heavily') ; CHAUSSON, E. (Op. 28, No. 3) ; CHILCOT, T. ; LINLEY, W. ; THOMSON, V. (1961)
(c) 'Sigh no more, ladies' (II. 3) : ADRIAN, W. (1950) ; AIKIN, W. A. (1911) ; ALFERAKI, A. N. (Op. 13, No. 1, 1892) ; ALLISON, H. C. (1871) ; ARNE, T. A. ; AUSTIN, E. (Op. 10, No. 2, 1908) ; AUSTIN, F. (1910) ; BAINES, H. ; BALFE, M. ; BONAVIA, F. (1935) ; BRIDGEWATER, L. (1964) ; BURTON, H. S. ; BUSH, G. (Eliz. songs, No. 3, 1947) ; CAIROS-REGO, R. de ; CASTELNUOVO-TEDESCO, M. ; COATES, E. (1916) ; COLE, F. G. ; CRICHTON, M. (1932) ; DEARLE ; DEXTER, H. ; DUNHILL, T. ; FARRANT, G. ; FAULKES, W. (Op. 204, No. 5, 1920, unpub.) ; FISHER, W. A. (Op. 5, No. 5) ; FOOTE, A. W. ; FORD, T. (c. 1610, pub. 1925) ; FOX, G. E. ; GILBERT, N. (1961) ; HARRADEN, E. ; HILLER, H. C. ('Vocal Gavotte') ; HUDSON, H. (1910) ; KEEL, F. (1922) ; LAWSON, M. L. (1880) ; LEHMANN, L. (1895) ; LINLEY, W. ; LOUIS, E. (1883) ; LOVATT, S. E. (1909) ; MACFARREN, G. A. (1869) ; MANSFIELD, P. J. (Op. 119, 1938) ; MOERAN, E J. (1933) ; MOORE, D. S. (N.Y., 1944) ; NEVIN, G. B. (Phil., 1915) ; PARKE, J. ; PARKER, H. T. (1880) ; PASCAL, F. (1884) ; PHILLIPS, M. (Op. 67, No. 3, 1949) ; PLUMSTEAD, M. (1955) ; PORTEOUS, N. (1914) ; QUILTER, R. (Op. 30) ; ROGERS, J. H. (Boston, 1900) ; ROOTHAM, C. B. ; ROWLEY, A. (1951) ; SHAW, G. T. (1937) ; SHAW, M. F. (1917) ; SLINN, E. B. (Op. 13, No. 6) ; SMITH, J. C. (1755) ; SOWERBUTTS, J. A. (1920) ; STANISLAUS, F. (1868) ; STEVENS, R. J. S. (? 1790) ; SULLIVAN, A. S. ; THIMAN, E. ; THOMSON, V. (1961) ; TOMPKINS, G. ; TOYE, F. ; TREHARNE, B. ; TREMAIN, R. ; TREVOR, C. ; TWIGG, D. J. ; WARLOCK, P. (1927) ; WILLAN, H. (1930) ; WILLIAMS, R. Vaughan (1931) ; WISTER, O. (N.Y., 1936) ; YOUNG, A. (4 Sh. songs in swing, 1940)

## Othello

### 1

MACHAVARIANI, A. 'Othello', Tbilisi, ? 1963
ROSSINI, G. 'Otello osia il Moro di Venezia' (F. Berio di Salsa), Naples, 1816 *
VERDI, G. 'Otello' (A. Boito), Milan, 1887 *

### 2

(a) ASSAFIEV, B. V.; BARDI, B.; BERNARD, A. (Savoy, 1930); LENTON, J. (1703); PARKER, C.; PONC, M.; SALMHOFER, F.; SHOSTAKOVICH, D.; TITL, E. (Burgth.); ZUMSTEEG, J. R.
(b) AMBROS, A. W. (Overture); BLACHER, B. (Ballet, Op. 50, Berlin, 1955); BORTKIEVICH, S. E. (Symphonic poem, Op. 19); ESPOSITO, M. (Overture); FIBICH, Z. (Symphonic poem, Op. 6, 1873); HADLEY, H. K. (Overture, Op. 96, N.Y., 1921); JANUŠ, J. (Ballet, Prague, Nat. Th.); KREIN, A. A. (Choral ballet); KRUG, A. (Prelude); LUCAS, C. (Overture); MACFARREN, W. C. (Overture, 1896); MUELLER, C. C. (Overture); TAUBERT, K. G. W. (Overture); TAYLOR, S. Coleridge- (Symphonic poem, 1911; orch. suite, 1912)

### 3

'Barbara', *see* 'The poor soul sat sighing': *passim*
'Canakin [Canniken] Song', *see* 'Let me the canakin clink': GAUL, H. B.
'Desdemona's Song', *see* 'The poor soul sat sighing': PITFIELD, T. B.
'Iago's [Drinking] Song', *see* 'Let me the canakin clink': LOOMIS, H. W.; MANNEY, C. F.
(a) 'Let me the canakin clink' (II. 3); BAINES, H. (1898); CASTELNUOVO-TEDESCO, M. ('The soldier drinks'); FOX, G. E.; GAUL, H. B. ('The Canakin Song'); HUMFREY, P.; LINLEY, W. (1816); LOOMIS, H. W. ('Iago's Song'); MACEWEN, J. B.; MANNEY, C. F. ('Iago's Drinking Song', N.Y., 1907)
'My mother had a maid called Barbara', *see* General: BOCHSA, R. N. C.
'Poor Barbara', *see* 'The poor soul sat sighing': SHIELD, W.
(b) 'Poor soul sat sighing by a sycamore tree, The' (IV. 3): BARRATT, W. A. (N.Y., 1915); BIGGS, E. S. (1794); BISHOP, H. R.; BRIAN, H. ('A Song of Willow'); BRIDGEWATER, L. (1964); BRUCE, M. C.; CARMICHAEL, M. G.; CASTELNUOVO-TEDESCO, M.; DUNHILL, T.; DUSSEK, J. L. (in his *Captive of Spilsburg*, D.L., 1798); FAULKES, W. (Op. 204, No. 10, 1920, unpub.); FULTON, R. N.; GIORDANI, T. (1783); HEISE, P. A.; HOBDAY, R.; HOOK, J. (1798); HUMFREY, P.; KEMP, J. (c. 1810); LINLEY, W.; MACKENZIE, A. C. (1899); MOREHEAD, J.: NICHOL, H. E. (1919); NORDOFF, P. (N.Y., 1938); PARKER, H. T. (1895); PARRY, C. H. H. (1885); PITFIELD, T. B. ('Desdemona's Song', 1957); SALTER, L.; SHIELD, W. ('Poor Barbara', Glee, ? 1794); SULLIVAN, A. S.; TAYLOR, S. Coleridge-; VINCENT, C. J.; WATSON, G.; WATSON, W. M.; WILLIAMS, R. Vaughan (comp. 1890; pub. 1913); WILSON, H. J. L.

'Soldier drinks, The', *see* 'Let me the canakin clink': CASTELNUOVO-
TEDESCO, M.
'Song of Willow, A', *see* 'The poor soul sat sighing': BRIAN, H.
'Willow', 'Willow Song', 'Willow, Willow', *see* 'The poor soul sat sigh-
ing'; *passim*

## Pericles Prince of Tyre

1

COTTRAU, G. 'Pericle re di Tiro' (composed for London, *c.* 1915, not
performed) *

2

(*a*) PERFALL, K. von

## Richard II

2

(*a*) AMES, J. C.; CARPI, F. (Milan, 1948); HATTON, J. L. (1857); PITT,
P.; *see also* GENERAL: COPLAND, A.
(*b*) BLOCH, J. ('March', Op. 26, 1904)

3

'England', *see* 'This royal throne of kings': PARRY, C. H. H.
'This England', *see* 'This royal throne of kings': EWING, M. P.; SHAW,
M. F.
(*a*) 'This royal throne of kings' (II. 1): EWING, M. P. ('This England',
1950); GOVER, G. ('This sceptred isle', 1943); PARRY, C. H. H.
('England', pub. 1919); SHAW, M. F. ('This England', 1935);
WILSON, S.
'This sceptred isle' *see* 'This royal throne of kings': GOVER, G. (*see also*
King John 3*a*)

## Richard III

1

CANEPÁ, L. 'Riccardo III' (Fulgonio), Milan, 1879
SALVAYRE, G. 'Riccardo III' (E. R. Blavet), St. Petersburg, 1883 *

2

(*a*) BARDI, B.; CARPI, F. (Milan, 1950); GERMAN, E. (Globe, 1889);
HOÉRÉE, A. C. E.; MÜHLDORFER, W. C. (Op. 50, 1880); MURRILL,
H. J.; SÖDERMAN, J. A.; VOLKMANN, F. R. (Op. 73); WALTON, W.
(Film); *see also* GENERAL: COPLAND, A.
(*b*) ROSENFELD, I. (Overture); SMETANA, B. (Symphonic poem, 1856);
VOLKMAN, F. R. (Overture, Op. 68)

3

(a) 'God, if Thy will be so, Enrich the time to come (V. 5) : BRIDGE, Sir F. (Motet, 'Peace lives again')

'Peace lives again', see 'God, if Thy will be so' : BRIDGE, Sir F.

## Romeo and Juliet

1

BARKWORTH, J. E. 'Romeo and Juliet' (composer), Middlesbrough, 1916 *

BELLINI, V. 'I Capuleti e i Montecchi' (F. Romani), Venice, 1830 *

BENDA, G. 'Romeo und Julie' (F. W. Gotter), Gotha, 1776 *

BLACHER, B. 'Romeo und Julia' (scenic oratorio) (composer), Salzburg, 1950 *

CAMPO, C. del. 'Los amantes de Verona', 1909

DALAYRAC, N. 'Tout pour l'amour, ou Roméo et Juliette' (J. M. Boutet de Monvel), Paris, 1792

GAUJAC, E. 'Les Amants de Vérone', Toulouse, 1955

GOUNOD, C. 'Roméo et Juliette' (J. Barbier and M. Carré), Paris, 1867 *

GUGLIELMI, P. C. 'Romeo e Giulietta' (S. Buonaiuti), London, 1810 *

IVRY, P. X. D., Marquis d'. 'Les Amants de Vérone' (composer), Paris, 1878 *

MALIPIERO, G. F. 'Romeo e Giulietta' (one section of the composite drama 'Monde celesti e infernali'), Italian radio (a broadcast performance), 1950 *

MARCHETTI, F. 'Romeo e Giulietta' (M. M. Marcello), Trieste, 1865 *

MARESCALCHI, L. 'Romeo e Giulietta', Rome, 1789

MERCADAL, A. 'Romeo e Giulietta', Mahon (Minorca), 1873

MORALES, M. 'Romeo y Julieta', Mexico City, 1863

PORTA, B.    ?    Paris, 1806

RUMLING, S. von 'Roméo et Juliette', Munich, 1790

SCHWANENBERGER, J. G. 'Romeo e Giulia'[1] (C. Sanseverino), Leipzig, 1776 †

SHELLEY, H. R. 'Romeo and Juliet' (composer?) * [1901]

STEIBELT, D. 'Roméo et Juliette' (J. A. P. de Ségur), Paris, 1793 *

SUTERMEISTER, H. 'Romeo und Julia' (composer), Dresden, 1940 *

VACCAI, N. 'Giulietta e Romeo' (F. Romani), Milan, 1825 *

ZANDONAI, R. 'Giulietta e Romeo' (A. Rossato), Rome, 1922 *

ZINGARELLI, N. A. 'Giulietta e Romeo' (G. M. Foppa), Milan, 1796 *

2

(a) ALEXANDROV, A. N.; AMANI, N. (Op. 12, 1904); ARNE, T. A. (C.G., 1750); BARBOUR, J. M. (1949); BARDI, B.; BERNSTEIN, L. (West Side Story, N.Y., 1957); BISHOP, H. R. (1814); BOYCE, W. (D.L., 1750); DIAMOND, D. L. (1947); FARKAS, F. (1940); GERHARD, R.; GERMAN, E. (Lyceum, 1895); HUMPERDINCK, E. (Berlin, Deutsches Th., 1907); KABALEVSKY, D. B. (Moscow, Vakhtangov, 1956); MARTIN, F. (1927);

[1] A printed libretto by Sanseverino for a performance given in ? Berlin, 1773, which names no composer, may refer to this opera.

MILHAUD, D. (Paris, Th. des Mathurins, 1937); MUELLER, A. E.;
SALMHOFER, F.; STENHAMMAR, W. E.; THOMÉ, F. (Odéon, 1890);
VLAD, R. (Film)

(b) ARMSTRONG, W. D. ('Souvenir de Verona: The ball of the Capulets',
pf., Chicago, 1903); BARTHOLIN, B. (Ballet, 1938); BEDFORD, H.
('Queen Mab' suite, 1900; Love Scene, 1902); BEETHOVEN, L. van
(String Quartet in F ma., Op. 18, No. 1, 1801 — the slow movement is
said to have been inspired by the last scene of the play); BENDL, K.
('Queen Mab's Waltzes', pf., 1852); BENEDICT, J. (Sarabande and
Minuet, 1882); BERLIOZ, H. (Dramatic symphony, Op. 17, 1839);
CURSCHMANN, C. F. ('Romeo all tomba di Giulietta', 1848); HOL-
BROOKE, J. (Symphonic poem 'Queen Mab', 1904); HOLMES, A.
(Symphony); ILYINSKY, A. A. (Overture); KABALEVSKY, D. B.
(Musical sketches, 1959); LAMBERT, C. (Ballet, 1926); LUNSSENS, M.
(Symphonic poem); MACFARREN, G. A. (Overture, p. duet, 1840 —
full score in ms. in Fitzwilliam, Cambridge); MILHALOVICH, O. (Over-
ture and Funeral March, ? 1872); PARKER, H. T. (Romance, Phil.,
1914); PARROTT, H. I. (Solemn Overture); PERCY, J. ('The garden
scene', Op. 2, 1785); PIERSON, H. H. (Overture, Op. 86, 1874, unpub.);
PROKOFIEV, S. (Ballet, composed, c. 1935, first perf. 1938, Op. 64;
three orch. suites based on this, Op. 64, 1-2, 1938-9, 3, 1947); SCHLOTT-
MANN, L. (Overture, Op. 18); SVENDSEN, J. S. (Fantasy, Op. 18,
1875); TCHAIKOVSKY, P. I. (Fantasy Overture, first version 1869, pub.
Vol. 23 of Complete Works; rev. 1870; final version, 1880; Operatic
duet for orch., ed. Taneiev, 1893); THIENEN, M. van (Prelude, 1951);
WATSON, W. M. ('Queen Mab', fairy dance, pf., 1886)

3

(a) 'Come, black-browed night!' (III. 2): GAUL, H. B.
(b) 'Good night, good night! Parting is such sweet sorrow' (II. 2):
BARRI, O. (1888); GLOVER, H. ('Juliet's song, Sweet, good night!');
KING, M. P. ('Parting is such sweet sorrow')
(c) 'How silver sweet sound lovers' tongues by night' (II. 2): CORELLI,
M. ('Romeo's Good Night')
(d) 'If I profane with my unworthiest hand this holy shrine' (I. 5):
HUTCHINSON, F. (1807)
   'Juliet's Song', see 'Good night, good night!': GLOVER, H.
(e) 'Lady, by yonder blessed moon I swear' (II. 2): KEMP, J. (c. 1810);
STEVENS, W. S.
   'Parting is such sweet sorrow', see 'Good night, good night!': KING, M. P.
   'Sweet, good night', see 'Good night, good night': GLOVER, H.
(f) 'When griping grief the heart doth wound' (IV. 5): EDWARDS, R.
(g) 'Wilt thou be gone?' (III. 5): REEKES, J.


**The Taming of the Shrew**

1

BOSSI, R.    'Volpino il calderaio' (1 act) (L. Orsini), Milan, 1925
CLAPP, P. G.    'The Taming of the Shrew', New York, 1948

COOKE, T. S., and BRAHAM, J. 'The Taming of the Shrew', London, 1828 *
GIANNINI, V. 'The Taming of the Shrew' (composer and Dorothy Fee), Cincinnati, 1953 *
GOETZ, H. 'Der Widerspänstigen Zähmung' (J. V. Widmann), Mannheim, 1874 *
KAREL, R. 'The Taming of the Shrew' (composed 1942–3, unfinished)
MACLEAN, A. 'Petruccio' (1 act), London, 1895 *
PERSICO, M. 'La bisbetica domata' (A. Rossato), Rome, 1931
SAMARA, S. 'La furia domata', Milan, 1895
SHEBALIN, V. Y. 'Ukroshchenie stroptivoi' (A. A. Gozenpud), Kuibyshev, 1957 *
SILVER, C. 'La Mégère apprivoisée' (H. Cain and E. Adenis), Paris, 1922 *

2

(a) ADDINSELL, R.; CARPI, F. (Milan, 1949); IRVING, K. E.; PONC, M. (1939; 1950); PORTER, C. (*Kiss Me, Kate!*, N.Y., 1948); PURCELL, D. (*Sawney the Scot*, ad. by Lacy, 1698); STEVENSON, J. A.; ZILCHER, H. (1926)

(b) BRAHAM, J. (Overture, 1828); CASTELNUOVO-TEDESCO, M. (Concert overture, 1931); MACFARREN, W. C. (1845); PITT, P. (Overture, 1898); RHEINBERGER, J. G. (Overture, Op. 18); WAGENAAR, J. (Overture)

3

(a) 'Say that she rail' (II. 1): BISHOP, H. R. (as 'Should he upbraid', 1823)
'Should he upbraid', *see* 'Say that she rail': BISHOP, H. R.
(b) 'Wilt thou have music?' (Induction, Sc. 2): COOKE, B.


## The Tempest

1

ASPLMAYR, F. 'Der Sturm', Vienna, 1781
ATTERBERG, K. 'Stormen', Stockholm, 1948
CARUSO, L. 'La tempesta', Naples, 1799
EMMERT, A. J. 'Der Sturm', Salzburg, 1806
FABRIZI, V. 'La tempesta', Rome, 1788
FARWELL, A. 'Caliban' (masque), 1916
FIBICH, Z. 'Bouře' (J. Vrchlický), Prague, 1895 *
FLEISCHMANN, F. 'Die Geisterinsel' (F. W. Gotter and F. H. von Einsiedel), Weimar, 1798
FRANK, E. 'Der Sturm', Hanover, 1887
GATTY, N. C. 'The Tempest' (R. Gatty and composer), London, 1920 *
HAACK, F. 'Die Geisterinsel' (F. W. Gotter and F. H. von Einsiedel), Stettin, 1798
HALE, A. M. 'The Tempest' (? composer) * [1917]
HALÉVY, F. 'La tempesta' (E. Scribe, tr. P. Giannone), London, 1850 *
HENSEL, J. D. 'Die Geisterinsel' (composer, based on F. W. Gotter and J. W. Doering), Hirschberg, 1799 †

KUNZEN, F. L. A. 'Stormen'

LATTUADA, F. 'La tempesta' (A. Rossato), Milan, 1922

MARTIN, F. 'Der Sturm' (composer), Vienna, 1956 *

MÜLLER, W. 'Der Sturm' (K. F. Hensler), Vienna, 1798 †

NÁPRAVNÍK, E. 'Der Sturm', Prague, 1860

PURCELL, H. 'The Tempest; or, the Enchanted Island'[1] (J. Dryden, W. Davenant and T. Shadwell), London, 1695 *

RAYMOND, E. 'Der Sturm' (composed c. 1840)

REICHARDT, J. F. 'Die Geisterinsel' (F. W. Gotter and F. H. von Einsiedel), Berlin, 1798 *

RIOTTE, P. J. 'Der Sturm', Brno, 1833

RITTER, P. 'Der Sturm, oder die bezauberte Insel' (J. W. Doering), Aurich, 1799 † [dated 1798]

ROLLE, J. H. 'Der Sturm (Die bezauberte Insel)' (1 act) (Patzke), Berlin, 1784

RUNG, E. 'Der Sturm', Copenhagen, 1847

SMITH, J. C. 'The Tempest' (? D. Garrick), London, 1756 *

SUTERMEISTER, H. 'Die Zauberinsel' (composer), Dresden, 1942 *

URSPRUCH, A. 'Der Sturm' (E. Pirazzi), Frankfurt, 1888 *

WINTER, P. von. 'Der Sturm', Munich, 1793

ZUMSTEEG, J. R. 'Die Geisterinsel' (F. W. Gotter and F. H. von Einsiedel), Stuttgart, 1798 *

2

(a) ARENSKY, A. S.; ARNE, T. A. (D.L., 1746); ARNOLD, M. H. (1954); ARUNDELL, D. (1934); BARDI, B.; BERKELEY, L. (1946); BISHOP, H. R. (1821); BLISS, A. (Gaiety, 1921); BOYCE, W. (masque, C.G., 1746; unpub. ms. in Bodley, Oxford); CHAUSSON, E. (Paris, Th. des Marionnettes, Op. 18, 1888); COOKE, T. S. (1821); DAVY, J. (1821); DEMUTH, N. F. (Radio, 2 versions); DIAMOND, D. L. (1944); DRAGHI, G. B. (1674); FISHER, J. A.; GRIESBACH, J. H.; HESSENBERG, K. (1938); HORN, C. E. (1821); HUMFREY, P. (ms. in Paris Conservatoire); HUMPERDINCK, E. (Berlin, Volksbühne, 1915); LINLEY, T. *the younger* (D.L., 1777) (full score in ms. in B.M.); LOCKE, M. (prod. 1674; pub. in 'English opera, or the vocal music in *Psyche* . . . To which is adjoyned the instrumental musick in *The Tempest*', 1675); MALAWSKI, A. (*Burza*, for radio, 1937; stage versions, 1938, 1940); NYSTROEM, G.; PIJPER, W. (1930); PONC, M. (1937); SALMHOFER, F.; SIBELIUS, J. (Op. 109, 1926, *see also* 2 (*b*) ); STUCKEN, F. van der (Breslau, 1882); SULLIVAN, A. S. (Op. 1, *see* 2 (*b*) ); TAUBERT, K. G. W. (Munich, 1855); TIESSEN, H.; WEINGARTNER, P. F. von (Op. 65, 1918); WESSELY, C. B. (1796, not perf.); WOOD, R. W. (1930)

(b) ADLAM, F. (Ballet of reapers and water-nymphs, pf. 1886); ALWYN, W. ('Magic Island', Sym. prelude, 1953); BATH, H. ('Miranda', Scherzo, pf., 1916); BEETHOVEN, L. van (Sonata in D. Minor, Op. 31, No. 2, based on Ariel and the storm[2], 1803); BENEDICT, J. (Op. 77, 1875); BENNETT, W. Sterndale- (Overture, 1832, unpub.); BERLIOZ, H.

---

[1] But see p. 55 above; also Dr. Margaret Laurie, 'Did Purcell set *The Tempest*', *P.R.M.A.*, 1963-4.    [2] See p. 222.

(Fantasia, part of 'Lélio, ou le retour à la vie', Op. 14*b*, 1832);
BRAUNFELS, W. ('Ariel's Song' for sm. orch., Op. 18); CORDER, F.
('Prospero', Concert overture, 1888); CRUFT, A. F. (Phantasy over-
ture 'Prospero's island', 1963); DALE, B. (1902); DEMUTH, N. F.
(Prelude); DUVERNOY, V. A. (Poème symphonique, 1880); FIBICH,
Z. (Op. 46, 1880); FOSS, L. (Suite, 1941); GILBERT, E. T. B. ('Ariel',
pf., Op. 25); HAGER, J. (Overture); HAYDEN, W. (Five dances for
pf., No. 1: 'Ariel'; No. 5: 'Caliban'); HONEGGER, A. (Prelude,
1923); JOHNSTONE, M. (Symphonic fantasy for brass band); KREUT-
ZER, R. (Orch. introd.); LARSSON, L. E. (Four vignettes); MILFORD,
R. H. ('Ariel', 1940); NEWTON, E. R. (Ballet music, pf., 1924);
NORRIS, T. (Overture); PAINE, J. K. (Symphonic poem); REED, W. H.
(Scherzo fantastique: 'Caliban', 1905); RIETZ, J. (Overture);
SIBELIUS, J. (Suite from inc. m.; Op. 109, 1929); SPEAIGHT, J. ('Ariel',
string quartet); SULLIVAN, A. S. (Inc. m. for concert perf., Op. 1,
1862); TCHAIKOVSKY, P. I. (Symphonic fantasy, Op. 18, 1873);
THOMAS, C. L. A. (Ballet, Paris Opéra, 1889); VIERLING, G. (Over-
ture); WELLESZ, E. (Symphonic suite: 'Prosperos Beschwörungen',
Op. 53, 1936); WHITE, F. H. (Serenade for string orch.: 'To Miranda',
1928); YOUNG, W. J. ('Ariel', polka, pf.)

3

'Amiens [*sic*] sings', *see* 'Come unto these yellow sands' and 'Full
    fathom five': WISTER, O.
'Ariel', *see* 'Come unto these yellow sands': CASTELNUOVO-TEDESCO, M.;
    'Where the bee sucks': STEVENSON, F.
'Ariel's Songs', *see* 'Come unto these yellow sands': BANISTER, J.;
    'Full fathom five': BANISTER, J.; PARKER, H. T.; 'Where the bee
    sucks': HUMFREY, P.; SCHARTAU, H. W.
'Ban! Ban!', *see* 'No more dams': HOBBS, J. W.
(*a*) 'Before you can say come and go' (IV. 1): LINLEY, T. *the elder*
(*b*) 'Be not afeard; the isle is full of noises' (III. 2): DUGGAN, J. F.
'Caliban', *see* 'No more dams': CASTELNUOVO-TEDESCO, M.; HOBBS,
    J. W.
'Ceres' Song', *see* 'Earth's increase': ABEELEN, H. van der; COOKE,
    T. S.
(*c*) 'Cloud-capp'd towers, the gorgeous palaces, The' (IV. 1): GAUL,
    H. B. ('Mirage'); STEVENS, R. J. S. (Glee, 1848); WILLIAMS, R.
    Vaughan (1951)
(*d*) 'Come unto these yellow sands' (I. 2): ARNE, T. A. (*c*. 1746); ARNOLD,
    M. H. (1959); AYRES, F. (Op. 3, No. 3, Newton Center, Mass., 1907);
    BANISTER, J. ('Ariel's Songs', *c*. 1675); BRIDGEWATER, L. (1964);
    CASTELNUOVO-TEDESCO, M. ('Ariel'); CORDER, F. ('Song of the
    spirits', 1899); CRAVEN, J. T. (1856); DANSIE, R. (1911); DUNHILL,
    T. F. (1928); EASSON, J. (1957); ELLISTON, M.; HONEGGER, A. (1923);
    KEEL, F. (1952); LA FORGE, F. (N.Y., 1907); LEE, E. M. (1935);
    LESTER, W. (N.Y., 1914); MANSFIELD, P. J. (Madrigal, Op. 92, No.
    3, 1936); MARTIN, F. (1950); MELLERS, W.; PURCELL, H. ('Hark,
    hark! The watch dogs bark', ? 1695); QUILTER, R. (1951); RIGBY, H.
    (1923); SIMPSON, R.; STEVENSON, J. A. (Dublin, ? 1798); SULLIVAN,
    A. S. ('Hark, hark! The watch dogs bark'); TAUBERT, K. G. W.

('Kommt auf diesen gelben Strand') ; TIPPETT, M. ('Songs for Ariel'
No. 1, 1964) ; WALKER, E. (Op. 2) ; WISTER, O. ('Amiens sings', N.Y.,
1936) ; WOOD, F. H. (Op. 34, No. 1)

'Dirge', *see* 'Full fathom five' : MANSFIELD, P. J.

(*e*) 'Earth's increase, foison plenty' (IV. 1) : ABEELEN, H. van den ('Ceres'
Song') ; COOKE, T. S. ('Ceres' Song)

'Epithalamium', *see* 'Honour, riches' : CASTELNUOVO-TEDESCO, M.

'Fairy Life', *see* 'Where the bee sucks' : LUCKE, K. E.

'Farewell, master !', *see* 'No more dams' : DUGGAN, J. F.

'Friendly wish from Shakespeare, The', *see* 'Honour, riches' : GAM-
BARINI, E. de

(*f*) 'Full fathom [fadom] five thy father lies' (I. 2) : ALDRIDGE, A. N.
(1892) ; ARKWRIGHT, G. E. P. (1902) ; ARNOLD, M. H. (1959) ;
AYRES, F. ('Sea dirge', Op. 4, No. 2, Newton Center, Mass., 1907) ;
BAINES, H. (1891) ; BANISTER, J. ('Ariel's Songs', *c.* 1675) ; BRIDGE-
WATER, L. (1964) ; DUNHILL, T. (Op. 40, No. 3, 1913) ; EASSON, J.
(1941) ; ELLISTON, M. ; FOGG, C. W. E. (Op. 51, No. 2, 1921) ;
HAMAND, L. A. (1912) ; HONEGGER, A. (1923) ; HOWELLS, H. ('A
dirge', Op. 5, No. 5, 1914) ; HUDSON, H. (1909) ; IRELAND, J. (1908) ;
JOHNSON, Robert (*c.* 1610) ; JONES, T. H. (Seven sea-poems, No. 2,
1958) ; KEEL, F. (1935) ; LEE, E. M. 1936) ; MANGELSDORFF, A.
(Madrigal, 1912) ; MANSFIELD, P. J. ('Dirge' Op. 92, No. 2, 1926) ;
MARTIN, F. (1950) ; MELLERS, W. ; MONTGOMERY, R. B. (1948) ;
PARKER, H. T. ('Ariel's Song', 1885) ; PARNELL, C. W. ('Sea Dirge',
1910) ; PARRY, C. H. H. (A Garland, No. 5 ; 'Sea Dirge', 1875) ; PUR-
CELL, H. ('Sea nymphs', ? 1695) ; ROBERTON, H. S. (1957) ; ROOT-
HAM, C. B. ; SHAW, M. F. (1922) ; SMITH, E. (1897) ; STRAVINSKY, I.
F. (1953) ; SULLIVAN, A. S. ; TAUBERT, K. G. W. ('Funf Faden tief
liegt Vater dein') ; TIPPETT, M. ('Songs for Ariel', No. 2, 1964) ;
TREMAIN, R. ; VICARS, G. R. ; WALKER, E. (Op. 1, No. 1, 1892) ;
WARREN, A. M. (1874) ; WILLIAMS, R. Vaughan (1951) ; WISTER, O.
('Amiens sings', N.Y., 1936) ; WOOD, C. ; WOOD, F. H. (Op. 34,
No. 2)

'Hark, hark ! The watch dogs bark', *see* 'Come unto these yellow sands' :
PURCELL, H. ; SULLIVAN, A. S.

(*g*) 'Honour, riches, marriage-blessing' (IV. 1) : ABEELEN, H. van den
('Juno and Ceres', 1859) ; CASTELNUOVO-TEDESCO, M. ('Epithalamium') ; COOKE, T. S. ('Juno's Song', 1840) ; FIELDEN, T. P.
(1959) ; GAMBARINI, E. de ('The friendly wish from Shakespeare', *c.*
1785) ; LINLEY, W. ; MARTIN, F. (1950) ; SHAW, G. T. (1933) ; SULLI-
VAN, A. S. ; TAUBERT, K. G. W. ('Hüll und Füll, gedeihen immer',
1908) ; WOOD, F. H. (Op. 34, No. 4)

(*h*) 'I shall no more to sea' (II. 2) : CASTELNUOVO-TEDESCO, M. ('The
sailor drinks')

'Juno and Ceres', *see* 'Earth's increase' and 'Honour, riches' : ABEELEN,
H. van den

'Juno's Song', *see* 'Honour, riches' : COOKE, T. S.

(*i*) 'Master, the swabber, the boatswain and I, The' (II. 2) : Martin, F.
(1950) ; WHITE, F. H. ('Stephano's Song', 1922)

'Merrily', *see* 'Where the bee sucks' : CASTELNUOVO-TEDESCO, M.

'Mirage', *see* 'Cloud capp'd towers' : GAUL, H. B.

(*j*) 'No more dams I'll make for fish' (II. 2) : CASTELNUOVO-TEDESCO, M.
('Caliban') ; DUGGAN, J. F. ('Farewell, master !') : HOBBS, J. W.
('Caliban : Ban ! Ban !', 1861)

'Sailor drinks, The', *see* 'I shall no more to sea' : CASTELNUOVO-
TEDESCO, M.

'Sea Dirge', *see* 'Full fathom five' : AYRES, F. ; PARNELL, C. W. ;
PARRY, C. H. H. (1875)

'Sea nymphs', *see* 'Full fathom five' : PURCELL, H.

'Song of the Spirits', *see* 'Come unto these yellow sands' : CORDER, F.

'Songs for Ariel', *see* 'Come unto these yellow sands' : TIPPETT, M. ;
'Full fathom five' : TIPPETT, M. ; 'Where the bee sucks' : TIPPETT,
M.

'Stephano's Song', *see* 'The master, the swabber' : WHITE, F. H.

(*k*) 'Where the bee sucks, there suck I' (V. 1) : ALDRIDGE, A. N. (1892) ;
ARNE, T. A. (1746) ; ARNOLD, M. H. (1959) ; AYRES, F. (Op. 3, No.
2, Newton Centre, Mass., 1907) ; BRIDGEWATER, L. (1964) ; CASTEL-
NUOVO-TEDESCO, M. ('Merrily') ; DANSIE, R. (1911) ; DUNHILL, T. F.
(1929) ; FOSS, L. ; HUDSON, H. (1910) ; HUMFREY, P. ('Ariel's Songs',
*c.* 1675) ; JOHNSON, Robert (*c.* 1610) ; KOVEN, R. de (Op. 159, No. 2,
Cincinnati, 1900) ; LUCKE, K. E. ('Fairy Life', N.Y., 1906) ; MARTIN,
P. (1950) ; MOERAN, E. J. (1940) ; PASQUALI, N. (*c.* 1750) ; PITCHER,
R. J. (Phil., 1923) ; PURCELL, H. ; SCHARTAU, H. W. ('Ariel's Song') ;
SLINN, E. B. (Op. 13, No. 7) ; STEVENSON, F. ('Ariel', Op. 59, 1910) ;
SULLIVAN, A. S. ; TAUBERT, K. G. W. ('Wo die Bien' saug' ich mich
ein') ; THATCHER, R. S. ; TIPPETT, M. ('Songs for Ariel', No. 3,
1964) ; WATSON, W. M. ; WHITE, F. H. (1929) ; WILSON, J. *See also*
General : BOCHSA, R. N. C.

(*l*) 'While you here do snoring lie' (II. 1) : ARNE, T. A. (1746) ; LINLEY,
T. *the elder* ; SULLIVAN, A. S. ; WOOD, F. H. (Op. 34, No. 2)

(*m*) 'You sunburnt sicklemen of August weary' (V. 1) : HUTCHINSON, T.
(1807)

## Timon of Athens

### 1

LEOPOLD I, Holy Roman Emperor.    'Timone misantropo', Vienna, 1696

### 2

(*a*) FARKAS, F. (1935) ; FRANCK, J. W. (for the masque, 1692) ; GRABU,
L. (Dorset Garden, *c.* 1678) ; PAISIBLE, J. ; PURCELL, H. (for the
masque, 1694) ; TRAPP, M. (Op. 19)

(*b*) DIAMOND, D. ('A Portrait', 1950) ; LUNSSENS, M. (Symphonic poem) ;
MIHALOVICH, Ö. (Overture, 2nd version, 1867) ; SÖDERMAN, J. A.
(Symphonic poem) ; SULLIVAN, A. S. (Overture, 1857)

### 3

'Apemantus' grace', *see* 'Immortal Gods' : CASTELNUOVO-TEDESCO, M.

(*a*) 'Immortal Gods, I crave no pelf' (I. 2) : CASTELNUOVO-TEDESCO, M.
('Apemantus' grace')

### Titus Andronicus

2

(*a*) CLARKE, J. ; DEMUTH, N. F. (Radio)


### Troilus and Cressida

1

ZILLIG, W.  'Troilus und Cressida' (composer), Düsseldorf, 1951 * [1950]

2

(*b*) GURLITT, M. (Symphony)

3

(*a*) 'Love, love, nothing but love' (III. 1): BRIDGEWATER, L. (1964)
(*b*) 'O heart, o heavy heart' (IV. 4): BISHOP, H. R. (? 1810); KING,
M.P. (Glee, ? 1810)


### Twelfth Night

1

FARINA, G.  'La dodicesima notte', Milan, 1929
FILIPPI, A. de.  'Malvolio', 1937 (? composition)
GIBBS, C. A.  'Twelfth Night' (composed 1947)
HART, F. B.  'Malvolio', 1913 (? composition)
HOLENIA, H.  'Viola' (O. Widowitz), Graz, 1934
KUSTERER, A.  'Was ihr wöllt', Dresden, 1932
RINTEL, W.  'Was ihr wöllt', Berlin, 1872
SMETANA, B.  'Viola' (E. Krásnohorská), Prague, 1924 (composed 1874–
    1884, unfinished) *
STEINKÜHLER, E.  'Cäsario, oder die Verwechslung', Düsseldorf, 1848
TAUBERT, W.  'Cesario' (E. Taubert), Berlin, 1874 *
WEIS, K.  'Viola (Die Zwillinge)' (B. Adler, R. Šubert and V. Novo-
    hradský), Prague, 1892

2

(*a*) ARNE, T. A. (D.L., 1741); BATE, S. ; BISHOP, H. R. (1820); BOWLES,
P. F. (1940); BRAUNFELS, W. (Op. 11); CARPI, F. (Florence, 1948);
CLAY, F. ; DANKWORTH, J. (City of London Festival, 1964); FOERSTER,
J. B. (Op. 116); HUMPERDINCK, E. (Berlin, Deutsches Th., 1907);
PAUMGARTNER, B. ; PONC, M. (1937; 1944); POSTON, E. (Radio,
1947)); SAUGUET, H.; STENHAMMAR, W. E.; STERNEFELD, D.;
TAUSCH, J. (Düsseldorf, 1859); VLAD, R.; WIDOR, C. M. (*Conte
d'avril*, Odéon, 1885)
(*b*) BUSH, G. (Entertainment for tenor solo, chorus and orch., 1950);
CASTELNUOVO-TEDESCO, M. (Concert overture, 1935); DAVENPORT,
F. W. (Overture, 1879); HALES, H. J. (Concert overture, Op. 32);

MACKENZIE, A. C. (Overture, Op. 40, 1888; MULLEN, F. ('Sweet and Twenty', gavotte, pf. 1902); PIERSON, H. H. (Overture); PROUT, E. (Overture); SPEAIGHT, J. (Poem for string quartet: 'She never told her love'); WAGENAAR, J. (Overture)

### 3

'Carpe diem', *see* 'O mistress mine': JOHNSON, B.

(*a*) 'Cesario, by the roses of the spring' (III. 1): WINTER, P. von ('I love thee so', ad. Bishop, 1820)

'Clown's Songs', *see* 'Come away, death', 'O mistress mine', 'When that I was': *passim*

(*b*) 'Come away, come away, death' (II. 4): ALDRIDGE, A. N. (1892); ALLPORT, R. E. H. (1928); ANDERTON, H. O. (1910); ARKWRIGHT, G. E. P. (1902); ARNE, T. A. (two settings, one 1741); BARRATT, W. A. (1901); BRAHMS, J. (Op. 17, No. 2); BRIDGEWATER, L. (1964); BULLOCK, E. (1947); CASTELNUOVO-TEDESCO, M. ('Old Song'): CHAUSSON, E. (Op. 28, No. 1); COCKSHOTT, G. (1959); CORDER, F. (1899); CORNELIUS, P. (duet, four versions); DALE, B. J. (1919); DANKWORTH, J. (1964); DAVIES, H. Walford (Op. 13, No. 2, 1902); DRAYTON, H. U. (1909); DUNCOMBE, W. ('Feste's Song', 1922); DUNHILL, T. (Op. 62, No. 4, 1923); ELTON, A. (1957); FAULKES, W. (Op. 204, No. 6, 1920, unpub.); FINZI, G. (Op. 18, No. 1, 1942); FULTON, R. N.; GODFREY, H. G. ('Dirge', 1914); GREAVES, R. (1928); HARRISON, J. A. G. (1912; 1948); HARRISS, A. (1916); HIND, J. (1958); HOLST, G. T. ('A lover's complaint'); HOPKINS, A.; KAY, U. S. (N.Y., 1954); KAYE, E. (1949); KORNGOLD, E. W. (N.Y., 1943); LINLEY, W.; MACFARREN, G. A. (1864); MOERAN, E. J. (1925); MONTGOMERY, R. B. (1948); MURRILL, H. H. J. (1941); O'NEILL, N. (N.Y., 1922); PALMER, G. M. (Op. 14, No. 1, 1912); PARKE, J.; PARKE, M. H.; PARKER, H. T. (1895); QUILTER, R. (1905); SHAW, M. F. (1929); SIBELIUS, J. ('Komm' herbei, Tod', Op. 60, No. 1, 1911); SMITH, H. P. (1914); STANFORD, C. V. (Op. 65, 1897); STEVENS, R. J. S.; STONE, N. M. (1951); SYMONS, T.; TAUBERT, W. ('Komm' herbei, Tod', Op. 33, No. 2); TOYE, J. F.; TREHARNE, B.; TREMAIN, R.; WEBBE, S. *the younger* (Glee); WESTRUP, J. A. (1948); WILKINSON, P. G. (Madrigal, 1954); WILLIAMS, R. Vaughan (1909); WILSON, C.

'Dirge', *see* 'Come away, death': GODFREY, H. G.

'Epilogue', *see* 'When that I was': BERNARD, A.

'Feste's Song', *see* 'Come away, death': DUNCOMBE, W.

'For the rain . . .', *see* 'When that I was': CASTELNUOVO-TEDESCO, M.

'Hey, ho, the wind and the rain', *see* 'When that I was': QUILTER, R.; WALTHEW, R. H.

(*c*) 'Hey Robin, jolly Robin' (IV. 2): HARRISON, J. A. G. (1948); HORNCASTLE, F. W. (Glee, 1833); KORNGOLD, E. W. (N.Y., 1943); SHAW, G. T. (1912)

(*d*) 'Hold thy peace!' (II. 3): RAVENSCROFT, T. (Catch)

(*e*) 'I am gone, sir!' (IV. 2): KORNGOLD, E. W. (N.Y., 1943); WOOD, F. H. (Op. 32, No. 1)

'I love thee so', *see* 'Cesario, by the roses of the spring': WINTER, P. von

(*f*) 'If music be the food of love, play on!' (I. 1): BEDFORD, H. (1924);

BENSON, G. (1861) ; BLACKALL, A. K. (1928) ; CLIFTON, J. C. (1802) ;
COOKE, T. S. ; DANKWORTH, J. (1964) ; HORSLEY, C. E. ; LEHMANN,
L. (1895); MATTHEY, A. (1847) ; SELLÉ, W. C. (1863) ; STEVENSON,
J. A. ; TRAVERS, A.

'Lover's complaint, A', *see* 'Come away, death' : HOLST, G.

'Little tiny boy', *see* 'When that I was' : LEVEY, A. J.

(*g*) 'Make me a willow cabin at your gate' (I. 5) : BRAHAM, J.

'Old Song', *see* 'Come away, death' : CASTELNUOVO-TEDESCO, M.

(*h*) 'O mistress mine, where are you roaming?' (II. 3) : ADDISON, J. ;
ANDERTON, H. O. ; BAINES, H. ; BARRATT, W. A. (1897) ; BEAUMONT,
H. (1905) ; BREWER, A. H. (*c.* 1900) ; BRIDGEWATER, L. (1964) ;
BULLOCK, E. (1947) ; BURY, W. (1938) ; CAIROS-REGO, R. de (Op. 2,
No. 5) ; CARDEW, H. W. (1895) ; CARMICHAEL, M. ; CARROTT, L. ;
CASTELNUOVO-TEDESCO, M. ; CHALLINOR, F. A. ; CHAPPELL, W. ;
COLLINGWOOD, A. ; COX, W. R. ; CRAVEN, E. (Madrigal, adap.
Major, 1795) ; CRICHTON, M. (1929) ; CRIPPS, A. R. ; CRUICKSHANK,
W. A. C. ; DALE, B. J. (1919) ; DANKWORTH, J. (1964) ; DAVIES, H.
Walford (1902) ; DAYMOND, E. R. ; DILSNER, L. (Madrigal) ; DRAY-
TON, H. U. (1909) ; DRIFFIELD, E. T. (Glee) ; DUNHILL, T. (1935) ;
EDESON, D. J. S. (1937) ; EDMONDS, P. N. ; EDWARDS, W. S. ; EVANS,
D. M. ; FARRAR, E. B. (Op. 13) ; FAULKES, W. (Op. 204, No. 2, 1920
unpub.) ; FINZI, G. (Op. 18) ; FORRESTER, J. C. ; FRYER, G. H. ;
FULTON, R. N. ; GAVALL, J. ; GIBBS, C. A. (1936) ; GLADSTONE, F. E. ;
GRAY, A. ; GREENHILL, H. W. ; GRIFFITH, W. ; HADLEY, H. K. (Op.
81, No. 3, N.Y., 1918) ; HARRISON, J. A. G. (1948) ; HEY, C. E. ;
HILBY, L. ; HOPKINS, F. ('Trip no further', N.Y., 1913) ; HOWE,
M. C. ; JENNER, H. ; JOHNSON, B. ('Carpe diem', 1890) ; JONES, H. F.
(Op. 5, No. 5) ; KORNGOLD, E. W. (N.Y., 1943) ; KOVEN, R. de (Op.
159, No. 3, Cincinnati, 1900) ; LEHMANN, L. (1897) ; LESTER, W.
(N.Y., 1914) ; LEVEY, A. J. ('Little tiny boy') ; LINLEY, W. ; LINTON,
A. H. ('Sweet and twenty') ; MACCUNN, H. ; MACFARREN, G. A.
(1869) ; MEISSLER, J. (1879) ; MONTGOMERY, R. B. (1948) ; MORLEY,
T. (in 'Consort Lessons', 1599) ; MURRILL, H. H. J. (1941) ; NEED-
HAM, A. A. (1894) ; OLIVER, H. (1921) ; PARKER, H. T. (1895) ;
PARRY, C. H. H. (1886) ; PORTER, B. C. (N.Y., 1917) ; POUNDS,
C. C. (1909) ; PRENDERGAST, A. H. D. (Madrigal, 1878) ; QUILTER,
R. (1905) ; REEKES, J. ; SLINN, E. B. (Op. 13, No. 5) ; SOMERVELL, A.
(1927) ; STANFORD, C. V. (Op. 65, 1897) ; STANISLAUS, F. (1870) ;
STEVENS, R. J. S. (Glee, 1790) ; SULLIVAN, A. S. ; TARPEY, W. K. ;
TAUBERT, K. G. W. ('O Schatz, auf welchen Wegen irrt ihr?', Op.
33, No. 1) ; TAYLOR, S. Coleridge- ; THIMAN, E. (1937) ; TOYE,
J. F. ; VICARS, G. R. ; VINCENT, C. J. ; WADDINGTON, S. P. ; WADELY,
F. W. ; WALLIS, A. J. ; WAREING, H. W. ; WARLOCK, P. ('Sweet and
Twenty', 1923) ; WATSON, H. (1891) ; WEST, J. E. ; WILLAN, H.
(1907) ; WILLIAMS, A. (1933) ; WILLIAMS, J. G. (1922) ; WILLIAMS,
R. Vaughan (comp. 1890, pub. 1913) ; WILSON, F. (1934) ; YATES,
E. ; YOUNG, W. J. ('Where are you roaming?')

'Rain it raineth, The', *see* 'When that I was' : STANFORD, C. V.

(*i*) 'She never told her love' (II. 4) : HARINGTON, H. ; HAYDN, F. J.
(Canzonets, Set II, No. 4, 1795) ; HIME, E. L. ; NICKS, G. ; ROWLAND,
A. C. (*See also* SPEAIGHT, J., 2 (*b*)

T

'Sweet and twenty', *see* 'O mistress mine': LINTON, A. H.; WARLOCK, 'Trip no further', *see* 'O mistress mine': HOPKINS, F.

(*j*) 'When that I was and a little tiny boy' (V. 1): BAINES, H. (1891); BARTON, G. (Boston, 1903); BERNARD, A. ('Epilogue', 1943); BISHOP, H. R.; BRIDGEWATER, L. (1964); BULLOCK, E. (1947); CARMICHAEL, M.; CASTELNUOVO-TEDESCO, M. ('For the rain it raineth'); DANKWORTH, J. (1964); DAVIES, H. Walford (Op. 13, No. 3, 1902); DEMUTH, N. F. (1924); DUNHILL, T. F. ('The wind and the rain', Op. 62, No. 1, 1923); FAULKES, W. (Op. 204, No. 12, 1920, unpub.); GIBBS, C. A. (1936); HARRISON, J. A. G. (1948); HATTON, J. L. (1893); HOIBY, L.; KORNGOLD, E. W. (N.Y., 1943); KOVEN, R. de (1891); LEVEY, A. J. ('Little tiny boy'); QUILTER, R. ('Hey, ho, the wind and the rain'); ROBINSON, C. W. (1885); SCHUMANN, R. A. ('Schlusslied des Narren' Op. 127, No. 5, 1850); SHAW, G. T. (1912); SHAW, M. F.; SIBELIUS, J. ('Heisa, hopsa, bei Regen und Wind', Op. 60, No. 2, 1911); SIMPSON, R.; STANFORD, C. V. (Op. 65, 1897); STEVENSON, J. A. (Glee, 1834); VERNON, J. (1763); WALTHEW, R. H. ('Hey, ho, the wind and the rain'); WAREING, H. W.; WILLAN, H. (1931); WILLIAMS, J. G. (1922); WOOD, F. H. ('The wind and the rain', Op. 32); YOUNG, A. (4 Sh. songs in swing, 1940)

'Where are you roaming?', *see* 'O mistress mine': YOUNG, W. J.

'Wind and the rain, The', *see* 'When that I was': DUNHILL, T.; WOOD, F. H.

## The Two Gentlemen of Verona

2

(*a*) BARDI, B.; BISHOP, H. R. (1821)
(*b*) STREET, J. (Overture, Op. 8)

3

(*a*) 'He makes sweet music with the enamel'd stones' (II. 7): ALLNATT, M. M. (Two songs: 'Hinder not my course' and 'He makes sweet music', 1860)
(*b*) 'O, how this spring of love resembleth' (T. 3): BISHOP, H. R. ('The springtime of love', 1820)
'Silvia', *see* 'Who is Silvia?': *passim*
'Springtime of love, The', *see* 'O, how this spring of love': BISHOP, H. R.
'Sylvia', *see* 'Who is Silvia?': *passim*
'Then to Sylvia let us sing', *see* 'Who is Silvia?': HOPKINS, F.
'To Sylvia', *see* 'Who is Silvia?': WEST, J. E.
(*c*) 'Who is Silvia? what is she?' (IV. 2): ALDRIDGE, A. N. (1892); ARKWRIGHT, G. E. P. (1902); BENSON, L. S. (1873); BISHOP, H. R. (Glee, 1864); BRIDGEWATER, L. (1964); CARMICHAEL, M. G.; CASTELNUOVO-TEDESCO, M.; COATES, E. (1909); DICKS, E. A. (Madrigal); DUFF, A. K.; DUGGAN, J. F.; DUNHILL, T. F. (Op. 62, No. 2, 1923); ELLIOTT, J.; FAULKES, W. (Op. 204, No. 9, 1920, unpub.); FINZI, G. (1942); GERMAN, E.; GORDON, W.; GOULD, W. M. (1906); HAM,

A.; HEAP, C. S.; HOPKINS, F. ('Then to Sylvia let us sing', N.Y., 1913); HOWELLS, W. A.; HUDSON, H. (1910); KEARTON, J. H.; LEHMANN, L. (1908); LEVERIDGE, R.; LINLEY, W.; LINTON, A. H.; MACFARREN, G. A. (1864); MACIRONE, C. A.; MARKS, T. O.; MARTINEZ, I.; MARZIALS, T. J. H. (1890); MONTGOMERY, R. B. (1948); OAKLEY, S. H. (1916); PIERSON, H. H. (Op. 63, No. 2); PIGGOTT, H. E. (1955); QUILTER, R. (1927; Op. 30, 1933); RATHBONE, G.; RUBBRA, E. (Op. 8, 1923); SARJEANT, J. (1916); SCHUBERT, F. (Op. 106, No. 4, 1828, D. 891d); SOLLA, I. de (1883); STEGGALL, R. (Op. 281, No. 2); STEVENS, R. J. S. (Glee, 1810); THIMAN, E. H.; THOMAS, D. V.; VERNON, J. (c. 1770); WAITHMAN, R. H.; WEBBE, S. the younger; WEST, J. E. (1896); WILLIAMS, W. A.; WOOD, C.; WOOLLEY, C.; YOUNG, W. J.

## The Winter's Tale

### 1

BARBIERI, C. E. di. 'Perdita oder ein Wintermärchen' (K. Gross), Prague, 1865 †
BERENY, H. 'Das Wintermärchen', 1898
BRUCH, M. 'Hermione' (E. Hopffer), Berlin, 1872 *
GOLDMARK, C. 'Ein Wintermärchen' (A. M. Willner), Vienna, 1908 *
NEŠVERA, J. 'Perdita' (J. Kvapil), Prague, 1897

### 2

(a) BERKELEY, L. (Op. 54, 1960); BOYCE, W. (D.L., ? 1756); FLOTOW, F. von (Weimar, 1859); HUMPERDINCK, E. (Berlin, Deutsches Th., 1906); KŘIČKA, J. (1916); LARSSON, L. E.; LEVEY, A. J.; MILHAUD, D.; MOYZES, A. (Op. 24, 1935); ORR, R.; ROOS, R. de; SOKOLOV, N. A.; ZILCHER, H. (1919)
(b) BARNETT, J. F. (Overture, 1873); CASTELNUOVO-TEDESCO, M. (Concert overture, 1938); EHLERT, L. (Overture); MACFARREN, W. C. (Overture); NEWTON, E. R. (Ballet, pf., 1926); SUK, J. (Op. 9, 1894)

### 3

'Autolycus', see 'When daffodils begin to peer': CASTELNUOVO-TEDESCO, M.
'Autolycus' song', see 'Lawn as white': GREENHILL, J.; 'Will you buy?': MACIRONE, C. A.
(a) 'But shall I go mourn for that, my dear?' (IV. 2): BRIDGEWATER, L. (1964); CASTELNUOVO-TEDESCO, M. ('Merry heart'); LAMPE, J. F. (1745)
'Come buy', see 'Lawn as white': BUZZI-PECCIA, A.
(b) 'Daffodils that come before the swallow dares' (IV. 3): BARRY, K.
(c) 'Get you hence, for I must go' (IV. 3): BIGGS, A. (1926): BOYCE, W.; BRIDGEWATER, L. (1964); CASTELNUOVO-TEDESCO, M. ('Two maids wooing a man'); ELLISTON, M.; HALES, H. (Op. 9, No. 4, 1927)
'Here's lawn', see 'Lawn as white': BIGGS, E. S.
(d) 'Jog on, jog on, the footpath way' (II. 2): BLACKALL, A. K.; BRIDGEWATER, L. (1964); DAVIES, H. Walford ('Merry heart', Op. 33, No.

1); FARRAR, E. B. (Op. 4, No. 3); HALES, H. (Op. 2, 1927); MAC-IRONE, C. A. (1849); ROWLEY, A. ('Song of the pedlar', 1930; Vignettes, No. 5: 'A Merry Heart', 1948); SHAW, M. F. (1932)

(e) 'Lawn as white as driven snow' (IV. 3): BIGGS, E. S. ('Here's lawn', Glee, 1801); BLITZSTEIN, M. ('Vendor's song', 1958); BRIDGEWATER, L. (1964); BUZZI-PECCIA, A. ('Come buy'); CASTELNUOVO-TEDESCO, M. ('The pedlar'); COOKE, B.; DYSON, G. ('The Pedlar's song'); ELLISTON, M.; GREENHILL, J. ('Autolycus' song'); HALES, H. (Op. 9, No. 3, 1927); HUTCHINSON, T. (1807); JOHNSON, Robert; LINLEY, W.; LOVATT, S. E. ('The Pedlar's song', 1914); NESTOR, C.; ROW-LEY, A.; SLATER, G. A. (1925); SOMERVELL, A. (1931); WILKINSON, P. G. ('The pedlar', 1955); WILSON, J.

'Merry Heart', see 'But shall I go mourn?': CASTELNUOVO-TEDESCO, M.; 'Jog on, jog on': DAVIES, H. Walford; ROWLEY, A.

'Pedlar, The', see 'Lawn as white': CASTELNUOVO-TEDESCO, M.; WILKINSON, P. G.; 'Will you buy': BIGGS, E. S.

'Pedlar's song, The', see 'Lawn as white': DYSON, G.; LOVATT, S. E.; 'Will you buy?': LOVATT, S. E.

'Shepherd's song', see 'When daffodils': BLITZSTEIN, M.

'Song of the Pedlar', see 'Jog on, jog on': ROWLEY, A.

'Songs of a wayfarer', see 'When daffodils': IRELAND, J.

'Sweet o' the year', see 'When daffodils': WARLOCK, P.

'Two maids wooing a man', see 'Get you hence': CASTELNUOVO-TEDESCO, M.

'Vendor's song', see 'Lawn as white': BLITZSTEIN, M.

(f) 'When daffodils begin to peer' (IV. 2): AYRES, F. (Op. 5, No. 2, N.Y., 1918); BLITZSTEIN, M. ('Shepherd's song', 1958); BOYCE, W.; BRIDGEWATER, L. (1964); BUSH, G. (1945); CASTELNUOVO-TEDESCO, M. ('Autolycus'); CRICHTON, M. (1931); HALES, H. (Op. 9, No. 1, 1927); IRELAND, J. ('Songs of a wayfarer, No. 2, 1912); JUDD, P.; LOVELOCK, W.; MACIRONE, C. A.; PRATT, A. (1901); QUILTER, R. (Op. 30); REDMAN, D. (1893); WAREING, H. W.; WARLOCK, P. ('The sweet o' the year')

(g) 'Will you buy any tape?' (IV. 3); BIGGS, E. S. ('The Pedlar', Glee); BOYCE, W.; BRIDGEWATER, L. (1964); COOKE, B.; DAVIES, H. Walford (1932); DEMUTH, N. F. (1931); ELLISTON, M.; HALES, H. (Op. 9, No. 5, 1927); HIND, J. (1958); LOVATT, S. E. ('Pedlar's Song', 1914); MACIRONE, C. A. ('Autolycus' song', 1864); NUNN, E. C. (1913); SOMERVELL, A. (1931); WILLIAMS, C. L. (1922); WILLIAMS, R. Vaughan

---

## Lucrece

1. SAEVERUD, H. (Suite, Op. 10)
2. 'Her lily hand her rosy cheek lies under' (Stanza 56): ARNE, T. A. (as 'One of her hands', c. 1746)
   'One of her hands', see 'Her lily hand': ARNE, T. A.
3. ''Tis double death to drown in ken of shore' (Stanza 160): SIMPSON, R.

## The Passionate Pilgrim

(including *Sonnets to Sundry Notes of Music*)

1. 'As it fell upon a day' (SSNM 6): BISHOP, H. R. (two settings, one beginning at l. 29: 'Whilst inconstant [as fickle] fortune smiled'); COOKE, T. S. (Glee); COPLAND, A. (*c.* 1929); COWARD, J. (Glee, 1857); GARDNER, C.; HUDSON, H. (1911); KNYVETT, W.; MORNINGTON, Lord (Glee); PARRY, J.; REAY, S.; RYLEY, G. C. E.; STEVENSON, J. A. (? 1795); WHEELER, A.

2. 'Beauty is but a vain and doubtful good' (PP 13): BISHOP, H. R. ('Beauty's valuation', 1819)

'Beauty's valuation', *see* 'Beauty is but a vain and doubtful good': BISHOP, H. R.

'Come live with me', *see* 'Live with me': *passim*

3. 'Crabbed age and youth cannot live together' (PP 12): BISHOP, H. R.; EDMONDS, P. N.; FANE, J.; GÁL, H. (Op. 75, 1959); GARDNER, J. (Op. 36, No. 2, 1958); GIORDANI, T. ('Youth and age', 1783); GRIFFITH, W.; HORN, C. E.; LOOMIS, H. W.; MOORE, E. C. (Chicago, 1914); MOUNSEY, A. S.; PARRY, C. H. H. (1902); PASCAL, F. (1889); STEVENS, R. J. S. (Glee, ? 1798); WASSALL, G. (Sh. song Cycle, No. 1 and 13, Cincinnati *c.* 1904)

'Duel, Shakespeare's', *see* 'It was a Lording's daughter': SHIELD, W.

4. 'Fair is my love, but not as fair as fickle' (PP 7): BISHOP, H. R. ('Fair was . . .'); MACKENZIE, A. C. (Op. 35, No. 2): SIMPSON, R.

5. 'Good night, good rest, Ah, neither be my share' (PP 14): BISHOP, H. R.; BRIDGEWATER, L. (1964); MACFARREN, W. C.; PYE, K. J. (1879); SIMPSON, R.

6. 'If music and sweet poetry agree' (PP 8): BRAHAM, J.

'In black mourn I', *see* 'My flocks feed not': HORN, C. E.

'Inconsequent ballad, An', *see* 'It was a Lording's daughter': WILLIAMS, J. G.

7. 'It was a Lording's daughter, the fairest one of three' (SSNM 1): BELLERBY, E. J. (Op. 43, 1923); GLOVER, S. (1846); HORN, C. E.; RICHARDSON, T. (Madrigal, 1887); SHIELD, W. ('Shakespeare's Duel' — for 'Loadstars' see *A Midsummer Night's Dream*, 3 (*k*)); WILLIAMS, J. G. ('An inconsequent ballad', 1920)

8. 'Live with me and be my love' (SSNM 5 — by Christopher Marlowe, as 'Come, live . . .'): BISHOP, H. R. (1819); CAIROS-REGO, R. de (Op. 7); CHILCOT, T. (1744); FOX, G. E.; LAWSON, M. L.; TREMAIN, R. (1958); TREMAIN, T. (1786); WEBBE, S. *the elder* (Glee, ? 1855); see also *Love's Labour's Lost*, 3 (*a*).

'Love's Lost, *see* 'Sweet rose, fair flower': SHIELD, W.

9. 'My flocks feed not' (SSNM 3): HORN, C. E. (2nd v., 'In black mourn I'); WEELKES, T.

'On a day, alack the day' (SSNM 2), see *Love's Labour's Lost*, 3 (*d*).

'Shakespeare's Duel and Loadstars', *see* 'It was a Lording's daughter': SHIELD, W.

10. 'Sweet rose, fair flower' (PP 10): BISHOP, H. R. (Cavatina); SHIELD, W. ('Love's Lost', *c.* 1790)

'Youth and age', *see* 'Crabbed age and youth': GIORDANI, T.

### The Phoenix and Turtle

MUSGRAVE, Thea, for chorus and orch.


### Sonnets

(NOTE: Richard Simpson set all the Sonnets, but only those listed below have been published.

The composer's title or first line, if it differs from Shakespeare's, has been quoted in brackets and given a cross-reference.)

5. 'Those hours, that with gentle work did frame': SIMPSON, R. (1878)
6. 'Then let not winter's ragged hand deface': SIMPSON, R. (1878)
7. 'Lo, in the orient': BISHOP, H. R.; SIMPSON, R. (1878)
8. 'Music to hear, why hear'st thou music sadly?': KABELEVSKY, D.; STRAVINSKY, I. F. (1953)
13. 'O that you were yourself': KABALEVSKY, D.
15. 'When I consider everything that grows': FINZI, G.
18. 'Shall I compare thee to a summer's day?': AIKIN, W. A. (1911); BECKETT, W. (N.Y., 1948); BRIAN, H.; CARMICHAEL, M. G.; CHADBOURNE, G.; DANKWORTH, J. (1964); GAUL, H. B.; GOVER, G.; HOAR, R.; HORN, C. E.; KEEL, F. (1935); KELLY, F. S. (1912); LODER, E. (1857); MACKENZIE, A. C. (Op. 50); MOSS, M. H. (N.Y., 1916); PARRY, C. H. H. (1887); PARRY, J. H. (1887); PENDER, T.; RAMSAY, C. F.; RAPHAEL, M.; REEKES, J.; SEIBER, M. (1954); TREHARNE, B.; WASSALL, G. (Sh. Song Cycle, No. 8, Cincinnati, c. 1904)
23. 'As an imperfect actor on the stage': BAIRD, T.; DANKWORTH, J. (1964)
24. 'Mine eye hath played the painter': DANKWORTH, J. (1964)
27. 'Weary with toil, I haste me to my bed': KABALEVSKY, D.; SIMPSON, R. (1878)
29. 'When, in disgrace with fortune and men's eyes': BISHOP, H. R. (1874); BURROWS, B.; CAIROS-REGO, R. de ('Love's Recompense'); CHADBOURNE, G.; MACKENZIE, A. C. (1893); PARRY, C. H. H. (1887); WALTHEW, R. H. (Madrigal); WASSALL, G. (Sh. Song Cycle, No. 12, Cincinnati, c. 1904)
30. 'When to the session of sweet silent thought': CHADBOURNE, G.; CORBETT, H. M. ('Remembrance'); KABALEVSKY, D.; PARNELL, C. W. ('Remembrance'); PARRY, C. H. H. (1887); WASSALL, G. (Sh. Song Cycle No. 10, 'Remembrance', Cincinnati, c. 1904)
32. 'If thou survive my well-contented day': PARRY, C. H. H.
33. 'Full many a glorious morning have I seen': BISHOP, H. R.; REEKES, J.; WORDSWORTH, W. (1941, pub. 1948)
36. 'Let me confess that we two must be twain': O'CONNOR, E. (1896)
40. 'Take all my loves, my love': BISHOP, H. R.; DANKWORTH, J. (on a theme by Duke Ellington) (1964); HORN, C. E. (1825)
43. 'When most I wink, then do mine eyes best see': BRITTEN, B. ('Nocturne', Op. 60); SAUGUET, H. ('Je te vois en rêve')

44. 'If the dull substance of my flesh were thought': SALAMAN, C. K. ('Thought')
53. 'What is your substance, whereof are you made?': RAMATI, R. Haubenstock- ('Mobile')
54. 'O, how much more doth beauty beauteous seem': BARKER, G. A.; BISHOP, H. R.; LYGON, F. (Glee, 1866); RAMATI, R. Haubenstock- ('Mobile')
56. 'Sweet love, renew thy force': BAIRD, T.
57. 'Being your slave, what should I do': HORN, C. E.
58. 'That god forbid that made me first your slave': SIMPSON, R. (1878)
59. 'If there be nothing new': HALE, A. M. (Op. 18, 1926); SIMPSON, R. (1878)
60. 'Like as the waves make towards the pebbled shore': AMES, J. C. (1908); HALE, A. M. (Op. 18, 1926)
61. 'Is it thy will thy image should keep open': HALE, A. M. (Op. 18, 1926); MACKENZIE, A. C. (1887)
63. 'Against my love shall be, as I am now': SIMPSON, R. (1878)
64. 'When I have seen by Time's fell hand defaced': BISHOP, H. R. (as 'When I have seen the hungry ocean', 1821); WOOD, R. W.
65. 'Since brass, nor stone, nor earth, nor boundless sea': CHADBOURNE, G.; WASSALL, G. (Sh. Song Cycle, No. 6, Cincinnati, c. 1904)
66. 'Tired with all these, for restful death I cry': SHOSTAKOVICH, D. (tr. Boris Pasternak) (Op. 62, 1942)
71. 'No longer mourn for me when I am dead': COKE, R. S.; FRYER, G. H. (Op. 2, No. 1); HOLLAND, C. ('The triumph of death'); HUGHES, R. ('Remember not!'); KABALEVSKY, D.; LODER, E. J. (1857); PARRY, C. H. H. (1886); SIMPSON, R. (1878); SOMERVELL, A. (Madrigal, 1892)
73. 'That time of year thou mayst in me behold': BISHOP, H. R. (1821); LOVELOCK, W. ('Twilight of love'); SIMPSON, R. (1878)
75. 'So are you to my thoughts as food to life': JOHNSTONE, M.
78. 'So oft have I invoked thee for my Muse': KABALEVSKY, D.
81. 'Or shall I live, your epitaph to make': KABALEVSKY, D.; SIMPSON, R. (1878)
87. 'Farewell! thou art too dear for my possessing': CARACCIOLO, L.; PARRY, C. H. H. (1887); REEKES, J.
90. 'Then hate me when thou wilt, if ever, now': CHADBOURNE, G.; KABALEVSKY, D.; WASSALL, G. (Sh. Song Cycle, No. 2, Cincinnati, c. 1904)
91. 'Some glory in their birth, some in their skill': BAIRD, T.; CHADBOURNE, G.; WASSALL, G. (Sh. Song Cycle, No. 4, Cincinnati, c. 1904)
92. 'But do thy worst to steal thyself away': BISHOP, H. R. (as 'Say tho' you strive to steal yourself away', 1821)
94. 'They that have power to hurt and will do none': BUTT, J. H. B.
96. 'Some say, thy fault is youth': SIMPSON, R. (1878)
97. 'How like a winter hath my absence been': BAIRD, T.; BISHOP, H. R. (1821); WOOD, R. W. ('. . . hath thine absence . . .')
99. 'The forward violet thus did I chide': MACKENZIE, A. C.
100. 'Where art thou, Muse, that thou forgett'st so long?': GREENHILL, J.; WORSLEY, F. W.

102. 'My love is strengthened though more weak in seeming': KABALEV-
      SKY, D.
104. 'To me, fair friend, you never can be old': BENNETT, G. J. (1883);
      CHAWNER, C. F. F.; HALE, A. M. (Op. 18, 1926); NETTLEFOLD,
      F. J. (1935)
105. 'Let not my love be called idolatry': HALE, A. M. (Op. 18, 1926);
      LEHMANN, L. ('Fair, kind and true', 1898)
106. 'When in the chronicle of wasted time': HALE, A. M. (Op. 18, 1926)
109. 'O, never say that I was false of heart': ARNOLD, C. ('Shakespeare's
      love-song', 1835); BISHOP, H. R. (1821); KABALEVSKY, D.; KING,
      M. P. (Glee, 1812); MALLINSON, A. (1926); PARRY, C. H. H.
      (1907); RANDEGGER, A. ('The Unchangeable')
110. 'Alas, 'tis true, I have gone here and there': HALE, A. M. (Op. 18,
      1926); SIMPSON, R. (1878)
116. 'Let me not to the marriage of true minds': BRAHAM, J. ('Love is an
      ever-fixed mark'); HALE, A. M. (Op. 18, 1926)
123. 'No, Time, thou shalt not boast that I do change': BISHOP, H. R.
138. 'When my love swears that she is made of truth': RIEGGER, W. (Op.
      65)
146. 'Poor soul, the centre of my sinful earth': BEECHAM, A. (1962)
147. 'My love is as a fever': DANKWORTH, J. (on a theme by Duke Elling-
      ton) (1964)
148. 'O me, what eyes hath Love put in my head': BISHOP, H. R.
153. 'Cupid laid by his brand and fell asleep': KABALEVSKY, D.


### Check-List

#### (First Lines and Titles)

'Love's recompense', *see* 29 :  CAIROS-REGO, R. de
'Mine eye hath played the painter', *see* 24
'Mobile', *see* 53 and 54 :  RAMATI, R. Haubenstock-
'Music to hear, why hear'st thou music sadly', *see* 8
'My love is as a fever', *see* 147
'My love is strengthened, though more weak in seeming', *see* 102
'No longer mourn for me when I am dead', *see* 71
'No, Time, thou shalt not boast that I do change', *see* 123
'Nocturne', *see* 43 :  BRITTEN, B.
'O, how much more doth beauty beauteous seem', *see* 54
'O me, what eyes hath Love put in my head', *see* 148
'O, never say that I was false of heart', *see* 109
'Or shall I live, your epitaph to make,' *see* 81
'O, that you were yourself', *see* 13
' Poor soul, the centre of my sinful earth', *see* 146
'Remember not !', *see* 71 :  HUGHES, R.
'Remembrance', *see* 30, *passim*
'Say, tho' you strive to steal yourself away', *see* 92 :  BISHOP, H. R.
'Shakespeare's love-song', *see* 109 :  ARNOLD, C.
'Shall I compare thee to a summer's day', *see* 18
'Since brass, nor stone, nor earth, nor boundless sea', *see* 65
'So are you to my thoughts as food to life', *see* 75
'So oft have I invoked thee for my Muse', *see* 78
'Some glory in their birth, some in their skill', *see* 91
'Some say, thy fault is youth', *see* 96
'Sweet love, renew thy force', *see* 56
'Take all my loves, my love', *see* 40
'That god forbid that made me first your slave', *see* 58
'That time of year thou mayst in me behold', *see* 73
'Then hate me when thou wilt', *see* 90
'Then let not winter's ragged hand deface', *see* 6
'They that have power to hurt and will do none', *see* 94
'Those hours, that with gentle work did frame', *see* 5
'Thought', *see* 44 :  SALAMAN, C. K.
'Tired with all these, for restful death I cry', *see* 66
'To me, fair friend, you never can be old', *see* 104
'Triumph of Death, The', *see* 71 :  HOLLAND, C.
'Twilight of love, The', *see* 73 :  LOVELOCK, W.
'Unchangeable, The', *see* 109 :  RANDEGGER, A.
'Weary with toil, I haste me to my bed', *see* 27
'What is your substance, whereof are you made', *see* 53
'When I consider everything that grows', *see* 15
'When I have seen by Time's fell hand defaced', *see* 64
'When I have seen the hungry ocean', *see* 64 :  BISHOP, H. R.
'When, in disgrace with fortune and men's eyes', *see* 29
'When in the chronicle of wasted time', *see* 106
'When most I wink, then do mine eyes best see', *see* 43
'When my love swears that she is made of truth', *see* 138
'When to the session of sweet silent thought', *see* 30
'Where art thou, Muse, that thou forgett'st so long', *see* 100

### Venus and Adonis

1. 'Alas, poor world, what treasure hast thou lost' (Stanza 180) : GAUL, A. R.
2. 'Art thou obdurate, flinty, hard as steel' (Stanza 34) : BISHOP, H. R. ('O, thou . . .')
3. 'Bid me discourse, I will enchant thine ear' (Stanza 25) : BISHOP, H. R. (1822)
4. 'Even as the sun with purple-coloured face' (Stanza 1) : BISHOP, H. R. ; HORN, C. E.
5. 'If love have lent you twenty thousand tongues' (Stanza 130) : BISHOP, H. R. ; REEKES, J. ('. . . have left you . . .')
6. 'Lo ! here the gentle lark, weary of rest' (Stanza 143) : BISHOP, H. R. ; PASCAL, F. ('Sunrise', 1900) ; WALKER, E. (Op. 2)
   'O, thou obdurate', see 'Art thou obdurate' : BISHOP, H. R.
   'Sunrise', see 'Lo ! here the gentle lark' : PASCAL, F.
7. 'To see his face the lion walkt along' (Stanza 183) : BISHOP, H. R.

## GENERAL AND COMMEMORATIVE PIECES

ARNE, T. A.  *See* 'Shakespeare's Garland'

AYLWARD, T.  Songs in Garrick's *Harlequin's Invasion* (D.L., 1759) ; *see also* 'Shakespeare's Garland'

BALDWIN, F.  Shakespearian Tercentenary March for the pf., 1866

BARNETT, J.  Songs (Titles only from Shakespeare), 1845 ; *also* 'Shakespeare's Birthday Song', words by the composer, 1827

BARTHÉLEMON, F. H.  *See* 'Shakespeare's Garland'

BOCHSA, R. N. C.  'Souvenir de Shakespeare'. A dramatic fantasia for the harp, in which is introduced some of the music in *Macbeth* and *Hamlet*, and the favourite airs, 'My mother had a maid called Barbara', 'Where the bee sucks', 'Blow, blow, thou wintry wind', 1833

BORCHARD, A.  'En marge de Shakespeare', for orch.

BORRIS, S.  'Shakespeare suite', Op. 39, No. 3, for oboe

BOYCE, Dr. W.  'Ode in Commemoration of Shakespeare', words by William Havard ('Titles and ermine fall behind'), 1757, mss. Bodley, Oxford and Barbour Inst., Birmingham ; *also* 'Arise, immortal Shakespeare' (ms. Bodley, extract beginning 'Sweetest Bard' pub. in *Thalia*) ; song in Garrick's *Harlequin's Invasion* (D.L., 1759) ('Thrice happy the nation that Shakespear has charm'd')

COOKE, T. S., and Mr. REEVE.  Incidental music for *Shakespeare v. Harlequin* (based on Garrick's *Harlequin's Invasion*, D.L., 1820)

COPLAND, A.  Inc. m. for Orson Welles's *Five Kings* (Henry IV, V, VI ; Richard II, III), prod. Nat. Th., Washington, 13 March, 1939 ; pub. N.Y., 1941

DIBDIN, C.  *See* 'Shakespeare's Garland'

DIGNUM, C.  'Shakespeare's Epitaph', 1801 ; *see also* HAYES, F. M.

DANKWORTH, J.  'The Complete Works', a setting of the titles of all Shakespeare's plays and poems, 1964 ; 'Witches Fair and Foul'

(Titania, from *Midsummer Night's Dream* and the witches from *Macbeth*), 1964

ELGAR, E.   A pageant of Empire 1924 : 'Shakespeare's Kingdom', words by Alfred Noyes, 1924

ELLINGTON, Duke.   'Such Sweet Thunder', inc. m. for Stratford, Ont., 1960

FOERSTER, J. B.   'From Shakespeare', orch. suite, Op. 76

'Garland, The'.   *See* Shakespeare's Garland'

GILBERT, E. T. S.   'Shakespeare's Dream : a Night in Fairyland', operetta, 1861

'Good friend, for Jesus' sake forbear' — Shakespeare's Epitaph, *see* DIGNUM, C., and HAYES, F. M.

GUERNSEY, W.   'Shakespeare Polka', *c.* 1864

*Harlequin's Invasion*, pantomime, words by David Garrick ; *see* AYLWARD, T., BOYCE, W. and COOKE, T. S.

HAYES, Fanny M.   'Shakespeare's Epitaph' (1911) ; *see also* DIGNUM, C.

HOLMES, A.   'Youth of Shakespeare' : a symphony

HORN, C. E.   'Shakespeare's Seven Ages', illus. by music and poetry, the words by G. Soane, etc., ? 1845

JACOB, G.   Six Shakespeare sketches for strong trio, 1946

JIRÁK, K. B.   'Ouvertüre zu einer Komödie von Shakespeare', Op. 22, 1922

'Jubilee, The Warwickshire', *see* 'Shakespeare's Garland'

KUHLAU, D. F. R.   Incidental music to Boye's *William Shakespeare*, 1826

LEE, G. A.   'Recollections of Shakespeare' ; dramatic overture for pf., 1847

LESLIE, H. D.   'Soul of the age, my Shakespeare, rise', madrigalian chorus, the poetry by Ben Jonson, 1864

LINLEY, T. *the younger*.   'A lyric Ode on the Fairies, Aerial Beings and Witches of Shakespeare', words by Dr. French Lawrence, D.L., 20 March 1776

MACFARREN, G. A.   'England's Minstrel King', for the Tercentenary Celebrations, words by G. L. Banks, 1864

MARTIRANO, S.   'O O O That Shakespeherian Rag', chorus and instr. ensemble (including settings of 'When daisies pied', 'When icicles hang by the wall', 'While you here do snoring lie', 'You spotted snakes'), 1961

NEILSEN, C. A.   'Ariels Sang af Prologen ved Mindefesten for Shakespeare', 1916

PHILLIPPS, M. F.   'Shakespearean Scherzo' for orch.

'Queen Mab, or the Fairies' Jubilee', *see* 'Shakespeare's Garland', SHIELD, W.

REEVE, Mr.   *See* COOKE, T. S.

SALAMAN, C. K.   'Ode for the Shakespeare Commemoration', words by Isaac Cowen, 1830

SERPETTE, H. C. A. G.   'Shakespeare', opéra-bouffe, 1899

'Shakespeare's Epitaph', *see* DIGNUM, C., and HAYES, F. M.

'Shakespeare's Garland' : a collection of odes, songs, glees, catches, etc., performed at the Jubilee Celebrations at Stratford-on-Avon, 1769 ; words by David Garrick, music by ARNE, T. A. ('Thou soft-flowing Avon') ; AYLWARD, T. ; BARTHÉLEMON, F. H. ; DIBDIN, C. ('Queen

Mab, a cantata'); later used as the basis of a dramatic entertainment, *The Jubilee,* or *The Warwickshire Jubilee,* or *The Warwickshire Lad* (D.L., 14 Oct., 1769)

'Shakespeare's Voice to Rome. The Protestant Song of the Nation, God Save our Church and Queen, an original Ballad', 1850 (Prefaced by lines from *King John,* III. 1 : 'Thou canst not, Cardinal')

SKERJANC, L. M.   Incidental music for Shakespeare

SMETANA, B.   'Solemn Festival March' for the Shakespeare Tricentenary Celebrations, 1864

SPEAIGHT, J.   'Shakespeare Fairy Characters' for String Quartet

STEWART, R. P.   'Ode on Shakespeare', Birmingham Festival, 1870

THOMAS, C. L. A.   'Songe d'une nuit d'été' (Opera about Shakespeare)

*Warwickshire Jubilee, Warwickshire Lad, The.*   *See* 'Shakespeare's Garland'

# CHECK-LIST OF COMPOSERS

This list gives the names of all composers (with full Christian names and years of birth and death where possible) whose works are contained in the main catalogue, together with cross-references to each item. A general idea can be gained of the composer's contribution to Shakespearean music if it is remembered that 1 refers to opera, 2a to incidental music, 2b to concert music, and 3, with all its subdivisions, to settings of individual lyrics or isolated passages from each play. The editor will be glad to receive any additions or corrections for this list, particularly dates of birth and death.

ABEELEN, Henri van den. *See* Tempest 3*e, g*

ABRAHAM, John. *See* Braham, J.

ADAM, Adolphe Charles (1803–56). *See* Merry Wives of Windsor 1, 2*b*

ADAMS, D. S. *See* As You Like It 3*d*

ADAMS, Roger. *See* Hamlet 2*a*

ADDINSELL, Richard (1904– ). *See* Taming of the Shrew 2*a*

ADDISON, John (*c.* 1766–1844). *See* Merry Wives of Windsor 3*b*; Twelfth Night 3*h*

ADLAM, Frank. *See* Hamlet 2*b*; Measure for Measure 2*b*; Tempest 2*b*

ADRIAN, Walter (1897– ). *See* Much Ado About Nothing 3*c*

AGER, Laurence Mitchell (1904– ). *See* Midsummer-Night's Dream 3*t*

AIKIN, William Arthur (1857–1939). *See* Much Ado About Nothing 3*c*; Sonnet 18

AKSES, Necil Kâzim (1908– ). *See* Julius Caesar 2*a*

ALBERT, Karel (1901– ). *See* Hamlet 2*a*

ALCOCK, Gilbert A. *See* Henry VIII 3*a*

ALCOCK, John (1715–1806). *See* Measure for Measure 3*a*

ALDERSON, Albion Percy. *See* As You Like It 3*d*

ALDRIDGE, Arthur N. *See* Tempest 3*f, k*; Twelfth Night 3*b*; Two Gentlemen of Verona 3*c*

ALEXANDROV, Anatoly Nicolaievich (1888– ). *See* Romeo and Juliet 2*a*

ALFERAKI, Akhilles Nikolaevich (1846–1920). *See* As You Like It 3*b*; Much Ado About Nothing 3*c*

ALLEN, W. R. *See* As You Like It 3*d*

ALLISON, Horton Claridge. *See* Much Ado About Nothing 3*c*

ALLNATT, M. M. *See* Two Gentlemen of Verona 3*a*

ALLPORT, Ronald Eric Harrison. *See* Twelfth Night 3*b*

ALPAERTS, Flor (1876–1954). *See* Cymbeline 2*a*; Merchant of Venice 1

ALVENSLEBEN, Agibhard (*c.* 1820–?). *See* As You Like It 3*b*

ALWYN, William Crowther (1905– ). *See* Henry VIII 3*a*; Tempest 2*b*

AMANI, Nikolai. *See* Romeo and Juliet 2*a*

AMBROS, August Wilhelm (1816–76). *See* Othello 2*b*

AMBROSE, Paul (1868–1941). *See* As You Like It 3*d*

AMES, John Carlovitz (1860–1924). *See* Richard II 2*a*; Sonnet 60

ANDERSON, R. Graham. *See* Love's Labour's Lost 3*g*

ANDERTON, Howard Orsmond (1861–1934). *See* Cymbeline 3*a*; Measure for Measure 3*a*; Midsummer Night's Dream 3*t*; Twelfth Night 3*b*, *h*

ANDRÉ, Johann (1741–99). *See* King Lear 2*a*

ANDREWS, George F. *See* As You Like It 3*d*

ANDRIESSEN, Jurriaan (1925– ). *See* Hamlet 2*a*; Merry Wives of Windsor 2*a*

ANSON, Hugo Vernon (1894–1958). *See* Midsummer Night's Dream 2*b*

ANSTRUTHER, P. N. *See* As You Like It 3*f*

ANTCLIFFE, Herbert (1875– ). *See* As You Like It 3*b*

ARENSKY, Antony Stepanovich (1861–1906). *See* Tempest 2*a*

ARKWRIGHT, Godfrey Edward Pellew (1864–1944). *See* As You Like It 3*d*, *f*; Cymbeline 3*b*; Henry VIII 3*a*; Love's Labour's Lost 3*f*, *g*; Tempest 3*f*; Twelfth Night 3*b*; Two Gentlemen of Verona 3*c*

ARMSTRONG, William Dawson (1868–1936). *See* Romeo and Juliet 2*b*

ARNE, Michael (? 1740–86). *See* Midsummer Night's Dream 2*a*

ARNE, Thomas Augustine (1710–78). *See* As You Like It 2*a*, 3*b*, *e*, *f*; Cymbeline 3*a*; Henry VIII 3*a*; Love's Labour's Lost 3*d*, *f*, *g*; Merchant of Venice 2*a*, 3*g*; Much Ado About Nothing 2*a*, 3*b*, *c*; Romeo and Juliet 2*a*; Tempest 2*a*, 3*d*, *k*, *l*; Twelfth Night 2*a*, 3*b*; Lucrece 2; General

ARNOLD, Charles. *See* Sonnet 109

ARNOLD, Malcolm Henry (1921– ). *See* Tempest 2*a*, 3*d*, *f*, *k*

ARNOLD, Dr. Samuel (1740–1802). *See* Macbeth 2*a*; Merry Wives of Windsor 3*a*; Midsummer Night's Dream 2*a*

ARUNDELL, Dennis Drew (1898– ). *See* Midsummer Night's Dream 1; Tempest 2*a*

ASPA, Edwin. *See* Henry VIII 3*a*

ASPLMAYR, Franz (1728–86). *See* Macbeth 1; Tempest 1

ASSAFIEV, Boris Vladimirovich (1884–1949). *See* Macbeth 2*a*; Merchant of Venice 2*a*; Othello 2*a*

ATTERBERG, Kurt (1887– ). *See* Tempest 1

ATTERBURY, Luffman (?–1796). *See* Measure for Measure 3*a*

ATTWATER, John Post. *See* As You Like It 3*d*; Cymbeline 3*b*; Midsummer Night's Dream 3*n*

AUDRAN, Edmond (1840–1901). *See* All's Well That Ends Well 1

AUSTIN, Ernest (1874–1947). *See* Cymbeline 3*b*; Much Ado About Nothing 3*c*

AUSTIN, Frederic (1872–1952). *See* As You Like It 3*d*; Henry VIII 3*a*; Much Ado About Nothing 3*c*

AYLWARD, Theodore (1730–1801). *See* Cymbeline 3*b*; Midsummer Night's Dream 2*a*; Much Ado About Nothing 3*a*; General

AYRES, Frederic (1876–1926). *See* Measure for Measure 3*a*; Tempest 3*d*, *f*, *k*; Winter's Tale 3*f*

BAEYENS, August (1895– ). *See* Coriolanus 1

BAINES, HERBERT. *See* Love's Labour's Lost 3*g*; Much Ado About Nothing 3*c*; Othello 3*a*; Tempest 3*f*; Twelfth Night 3*h*, *j*

BAIRD, T. *See* Sonnets 23, 56, 91, 97

BAIRSTOW, Sir Edward Cuthbert (1874–1946). *See* Henry VIII 3*a*

BALAKIREV, Mily Alexeievich (1837–1910). *See* King Lear 2*a*, *b*

BALDWIN, Frederick. *See* General

BALFE, Michael William (1808–70). *See* Merry Wives of Windsor 1; Much Ado About Nothing 3*c*

BALMER, Luc (1898– ). *See* Macbeth 2*a*

BANISTER, John *the elder* (1630–1679). *See* Tempest 3*d*, *f*

BANTOCK, Sir Granville (1868–1946). *See* King Lear 2*b*; Macbeth 2*a*, *b*; Merchant of Venice 3*f*

BARBER, Samuel (1910– ). *See* As You Like It 2*a*

BARBIERI, Carlo Emanuele di (1822–1867). *See* Winter's Tale 1

BARBOUR, J. Murray (1897– ). *See* As You Like It 2*a*; Romeo and Juliet 2*a*

BARDI, Benno (1890– ). *See* Hamlet 2*a*; Henry V 2*a*; Merry Wives of Windsor 2*a*; Othello 2*a*; Richard III 2*a*; Romeo and Juliet 2*a*; Tempest 2*a*; Two Gentlemen of Verona 2*a*

BARKER, George Arthur. *See* Sonnet 54

BARKWORTH, John Edmund (1858–1929). *See* As You Like It 3*d*; Romeo and Juliet 1

BARNBY, Sir Joseph (1838–1896). *See* As You Like It 3*d*

BARNETT, John (1802–90). *See* Midsummer Night's Dream 3*f*; General

BARNETT, John Francis (1837–1916). *See* Winter's Tale 2*b*

BARRAINE, Elsa (1910– ). *See* King Lear 2*a*

BARRATT, William Augustus. *See* As You Like It 3*d*; Henry VIII 3*a*; Measure for Measure 3*a*; Othello 3*b*; Twelfth Night 3*b*, *h*

BARRI, Odoardo. *See* Romeo and Juliet 3*b*

BARRY, Hon. Augustus. *See* Measure for Measure 3*a*

BARRY, John. *See* Hamlet 3*a*

BARRY, Katharine E. *See* Winter's Tale 3*b*

BARTHÉLEMON, François Hippolyte (1741–1808). *See* General

BARTHOLIN, Birger. *See* Romeo and Juliet 2*b*

BARTHOLOMEW, A. S. *See* Mounsey, A. S.

BARTLETT, Homer Newton (1845–1920). *See* Merchant of Venice 3*g*

BARTON, Gerard (1861– ). *See* As You Like It 3*b*, *d*; Twelfth Night 3*j*

BATE, Stanley (1913–59). *See* Twelfth Night 2*a*

BATH, Hubert Charles (1883–1945). *See* As You Like It 2*b*; Tempest 2*b*

BATTISHILL, Jonathan (1738–1801). *See* Midsummer Night's Dream 3*a*

BAYLEY, T. Harold R. *See* Cymbeline 3*b*; Henry VIII 3*a*

BAYNHAM, Thomas. *See* Midsummer Night's Dream 2*b*

BEACH, Amy Marcy Cheney (1867–1944). *See* Midsummer Night's Dream 3*t*

BEACH, John Parsons (1877–1953). *See* Measure for Measure 3*a*

BEAUMONT, Henry. *See* Twelfth Night 3*h*

BECKETT, Wheeler. *See* Sonnet 18

BEDFORD, Herbert (1867–1945). *See* Merchant of Venice 3*c*; Romeo and Juliet 2*b*; Twelfth Night 3*f*

BEECHAM, Sir Adrian Welles (1904– ). *See* Love's Labour's Lost 1, 3*e*; Merchant of Venice 1; Sonnet 146

BEETHOVEN, Ludwig van (1770–1827). *See* Romeo and Juliet 2*b*; Tempest 2*b*

BELLERBY, Edward Johnson. *See* Passionate Pilgrim 7

BELLINI, Vincenzo (1801–1835). *See* Romeo and Juliet 1

BENDA, Jiří Georg Antonín (1722–1795). *See* Romeo and Juliet 1

BENDALL, Wilfred Ellington. *See* As You Like It 3*d*; Merchant of Venice 3*c*

BENDL, Karl (1838–1897). *See* Romeo and Juliet 2*b*

BENEDICT, Sir Julius (1804–1885). *See* Romeo and Juliet 2*b*; Tempest 2*b*

BENNETT, George John (1863–1930). *See* Cymbeline 2*b*; Sonnet 104

BENNETT, Thomas Case Sterndale- (?–1944). *See* Measure for Measure 3*a*

BENNETT, William Sterndale- (1816–1875). *See* Merry Wives of Windsor 2b; Tempest 2b

BENSON, George. *See* Twelfth Night 3f

BENSON, John Allanson (1848–?). *See* As You Like It 2a, 3b, f, h

BENSON, Lionel Solomon. *See* Two Gentlemen of Verona 3c

BERENY, Henry. *See* Winter's Tale 1

BERKELEY, Lennox Randal Francis (1903– ). *See* Tempest 2a; Winter's Tale 2a

BERLIOZ, (Louis) Hector (1803–69). *See* Hamlet 2b, 3f; King Lear 2b; Merchant of Venice 3c; Much Ado About Nothing 1; Romeo and Juliet 2b; Tempest 2b

BERNARD, Anthony (1891–1963). *See* Othello 2a; Twelfth Night 3j

BERNSTEIN, Leonard (1918– ). *See* Romeo and Juliet 2a

BESLY, Edward Maurice (1888–1945). *See* As You Like It 3d; Merchant of Venice 3g

BEVIS, T. A. *See* As You Like It 3d

BIDGOOD, Thomas. *See* Midsummer Night's Dream 2b

BIGGS, Allan. *See* Winter's Tale 3c, e, g

BIGGS, Edward Smith. *See* As You Like It 3f; Othello 3b; Winter's Tale 3c, e, g

BINET, Jean (1893–1960). *See* Merry Wives of Windsor 2a

BIRTCHNELL, Arthur J. *See* Cymbeline 2b

BISHOP, Sir Henry Rowley (1786–1855). *See* Antony and Cleopatra 2a, 3a, h; As You Like It 2a, 3d, e, f; Comedy of Errors 2a; Hamlet 2a; Henry IV 2a, 3a; Henry VIII 3a; King Lear 3e; Love's Labours Lost 2a, 3d; Measure for Measure 3a; Merry Wives of Windsor 2a; Midsummer Night's Dream 2a, 3a, c, d, j, k, l, q; Othello 3b; Romeo and Juliet 2a; Taming of the Shrew 3a; Tempest 2a; Troilus and Cressida 3a; Twelfth Night 2a, 3j; Two Gentlemen of Verona 2a, 3b, c; Passionate Pilgrim 1-5, 8, 10; Sonnets 7, 29, 33, 40, 54, 64, 73, 92, 97, 109, 123, 148

BLACHER, Boris (1903– ). *See* Hamlet 2b; Othello 2b; Romeo and Juliet 1

BLACKALL, Allen Keet (1877–1963). *See* Twelfth Night 3f; Winter's Tale 3d

BLAKELEY, William. *See* As You Like It 3d

BLANCHARD, T. *See* Merchant of Venice 3c

BLISS, Sir Arthur (1891– ). *See* As You Like It 2a; Tempest 2a

BLITZSTEIN, Marc (1905–1964). *See* Julius Caesar 2a; King Lear 2b; Midsummer Night's Dream 3t; Winter's Tale 3e, f

BLOCH, Ernest (1880–1959). *See* Macbeth 1, 2b

BLOCH, Joseph. *See* Richard II 2b

BLUM, Elias (1881– ). *See* Love's Labour's Lost 3d

BLYTON, Carey. *See* Merchant of Venice 3g

BOCHSA, Robert Nicolas Charles (1789–1856). *See* General

BOLLINGER, Samuel (1871–1941). *See* Merchant of Venice 3g

BONAVIA, Ferruccio (1877–1950). *See* Much Ado About Nothing 3c

BOOTH, Josiah (1852–1930). *See* As You Like It 3d

BORCH, Gaston (1871–1926). *See* Measure for Measure 3a

BORCHARD, Adolphe (1882– ). *See* General

BORGSTRØM, Hjalmar (1864–1925). *See* Hamlet 2b

BORRIS, Siegfried (1906– ). *See* General

BORTKIEVICH, Sergei Eduardovich (1877–1952). *See* Othello 2b

BOSSI, Renzo (1883– ). *See* Taming of the Shrew 1

BOUGHTON, Rutland (1878–1960). *See* Henry V 2b

BOURGAULT-DUCOUDRAY, Louis Albert (1840–1910). *See* Hamlet 2b

BOWLES, Paul Frederic (1910– ).
*See* Twelfth Night 2*a*

BOYCE, Ethel Mary. *See* As You
Like It 2*b*; Midsummer Night's
Dream 3*q*

BOYCE, William (*c.* 1710–79). *See*
Cymbeline 3*a*; Romeo and Juliet
2*a*; Tempest 2*a*; Winter's Tale
2*a*, 3*c*, *f*, *g*; General

BRAHAM, John (1777–1856). *See*
Taming of the Shrew 1, 2*b*;
Twelfth Night 3*g*; Passionate
Pilgrim 6; Sonnet 116

BRAHMS, Johannes (1833–97). *See*
Hamlet 3*c*, *g*, *i*, *j*, *l*; Twelfth
Night 3*b*

BRAUNFELS, Walter (1882–1954).
*See* Macbeth 2*a*; Twelfth Night
2*a*; Tempest 2*b*

BREWER, Sir Alfred Herbert (1865–
1928). *See* As You Like It 3*d*;
Henry VIII 3*a*; Twelfth Night
3*h*

BRIAN, (William) Havergal (1876–
). *See* As You Like It 3*d*, *f*;
Cymbeline 3*a*; Hamlet 3*l*; Love's
Labour's Lost 3*g*; Midsummer
Night's Dream 3*t*; Othello 3*b*;
Sonnet 18

BRIDGE, Frank (1879–1941). *See*
As You Like It 3*b*; Hamlet 2*b*;
Henry VI 3*a*

BRIDGE, Sir (John) Frederick (1844–
1924). *See* As You Like It 3*d*;
Richard III 3*a*

BRIDGEWATER, (Ernest) Leslie (1893–
). *See* Antony and Cleopatra
3*a*; As You Like It 3*b*, *d*, *f*, *h*;
Cymbeline 3*a*, *b*; Henry VIII
3*a*; Love's Labour's Lost 3*f*, *g*;
Measure for Measure 3*a*; Mer-
chant of Venice 3*g*; Merry Wives
of Windsor 3*b*; Midsummer
Night's Dream 3*t*; Much Ado
About Nothing 3*b*, *c*; Othello 3*b*;
Tempest 3*d*, *f*, *k*; Troilus and
Cressida 3*a*; Twelfth Night 3*b*,
*h*, *j*; Two Gentlemen of Verona
3*c*; Winter's Tale 3*a*, *c*, *d*, *e*, *f*, *g*;
Passionate Pilgrim 5

BRITTEN, (Edward) Benjamin (1913–
U

). *See* Midsummer Night's
Dream 1; Merchant of Venice
3*g*; Sonnet 43

BROOKS, Walter William. *See* Love's
Labour's Lost 3*g*

BROWN, Allanson Gordon Yeoman.
*See* As You Like It 3*d*

BRUCE, Margaret Campbell. *See*
Othello 3*b*

BRUCH, Max (1838–1920). *See*
Winter's Tale 1

BRÜLL, Ignaz (1846–1907). *See*
Macbeth 2*b*

BRUMAGNE, Fernand (1887–1939).
*See* Merchant of Venice 1

BRYAN, Robert. *See* Merchant of
Venice 3*c*

BRYDSON, John C. *See* As You
Like It 3*f*

BUCK, Dudley (1839–1909). *See*
As You Like It 3*d*; Hamlet 3*h*

BULLOCK, Sir Ernest (1890– ).
*See* Twelfth Night 3*b*, *h*, *j*

BÜLOW, Hans Guido von (1830–
1894). *See* Julius Caesar 2*a*

BUNNETT, Edward (1834–1923). *See*
Midsummer Night's Dream 3*n*

BURNAND, Arthur Bransby. *See*
Strelezki, A.

BURNEY, Charles (1726–1814). *See*
Midsummer Night's Dream 3*r*, *s*

BURROWS, Benjamin. *See* Hamlet 3*c*;
Sonnet 29

BURTON, H. Sanford. *See* Much
Ado About Nothing 3*c*

BURY, Winifred. *See* As You Like
It 3*d*; Midsummer Night's Dream
3*f*; Twelfth Night 3*h*

BUSCH, Carl (1862– ). *See* As
You Like It 3*f*; Henry VIII 3*a*

BUSH, Alan Dudley (1900– ). *See*
Macbeth 2*a*

BUSH, Geoffrey (1920– ). *See*
As You Like It 3*d*; Cymbeline
3*a*; Hamlet 3*c*; Henry VIII 3*a*;
Merchant of Venice 2*a*, *b*; Much
Ado About Nothing 3*c*; Twelfth
Night 2*b*; Winter's Tale 3*f*

BUTT, James Henry Baseden. *See*
Henry VIII 3*a*; Midsummer
Night's Dream 3*t*; Sonnet 94

BUZZI-PECCIA, Arturo (1856– ). *See* As You Like It 3 *f*; Midsummer Night's Dream 3*t*; Winter's Tale 3*e*

BUZZOLA, Antonio (1815–71). *See* Hamlet 1

CAGNONI, Antonio (1828–96). *See* King Lear 1

CAIROS-REGO, Rex de (1886– ). *See* Much Ado About Nothing 3*c*; Twelfth Night 3*h*; Passionate Pilgrim 8; Sonnet 29

CALCOTT, John George. *See* Merchant of Venice 3*c, g*

CALLCOTT, John Wall (1766–1821). *See* Cymbeline 3*a*; Measure for Measure 3*a*

CAMPO Y ZABALETA, Conrado del (1876–1953). *See* Romeo and Juliet 1

CANEPÁ, Luigi (1849–1914). *See* Richard III 1

CARACCIOLO, Luigi. *See* Sonnet 87

CARDEW, Herbert W. *See* As You Like It 3*d*; Cymbeline 3*a*; Twelfth Night 3*h*

CAREY, Henry (c. 1687–1743). *See* As You Like It 3*h*; Hamlet 2*a*

CARMICHAEL, Mary Grant. *See* As You Like It 3*d, f*; Measure for Measure 3*a*; Merchant of Venice 3*g*; Othello 3*b*; Twelfth Night 3*h, i*; Two Gentlemen of Verona 3*c*; Sonnet 18

CARPENTER, John Alden (1876–1951). *See* As You Like It 2*b*

CARPI, Fiorenzo (1918– ). *See* Julius Caesar 2*a*; Richard II 2*a*; Richard III 2*a*; Taming of the Shrew 2*a*

CARR, Benjamin (1768–1831). *See* Macbeth 2*a*

CARROTT, Livesey. *See* Twelfth Night 3*h*

CARTER, Elliot Cook *jun.* (1908– ). *See* Merchant of Venice 2*a*

CARUSO, Luigi (1754–1822). *See* Hamlet 1; Tempest 1

CASTELNUOVO-TEDESCO, Mario (1895– ). *See* All's Well That Ends Well 1; As You Like It 3*b, d, f, h*; Cymbeline 3*a, b*; Hamlet 3*c, d*; Henry VIII 3*a*; Julius Caesar 2*b*; King John 2*b*; King Lear 3*a, b, c, d, f, g*; Love's Labour's Lost 3*f*; Measure for Measure 3*a*; Merchant of Venice 1, 2*b*, 3*g*; Merry Wives of Windsor 3*b*; Midsummer Night's Dream 2*b*, 3*t*; Much Ado About Nothing 3*b, c*; Othello 3*a, b*; Taming of the Shrew 2*b*; Tempest 3*d, g, h, j, k*; Timon of Athens 3*a*; Twelfth Night 2*b*, 3*b, h, j*; Two Gentlemen of Verona 3*c*; Winter's Tale 2*b*, 3*a, c, e, f*

CHADBOURNE, G. *See* Sonnets 18, 29, 30, 65, 90, 91

CHADWICK, George Whitfield [Whitefield] (1854–1931). *See* As You Like It 3*d*

CHALLINOR, Frederick Arthur (1866– ). *See* As You Like It 3*f*; Twelfth Night 3*h*

CHAMBERS, Clifford. *See* As You Like It 3*d*

CHANDLER, Mary. *See* Love's Labour's Lost 3*g*

CHAPMAN, Edward Thomas. *See* As You Like It 3*d, f*

CHAPPELL, William (1809–1888) *See* As You Like It 3*d, f*; Twelfth Night 3*h*

CHAUSSON, Ernest Amédée (1855–1899). *See* Hamlet 3*c*; Measure for Measure 3*a*; Much Ado About Nothing 3*b*; Tempest 2*a*; Twelfth Night 3*b*

CHAWNER, C. F. F. *See* Sonnet 104

CHÉLARD, André Hippolyte Jean Baptiste (1789–1861). *See* Macbeth 1

CHILCOT, Thomas ( ? –1766). *See* Antony and Cleopatra 3*a*; As You Like It 3*g*; Cymbeline 3*b*; Henry VIII 3*a*; Love's Labour's Lost 3*d*; Measure for Measure 3*a*; Much Ado About Nothing 3*b*; Passionate Pilgrim 8

CLAPP, Philip Greeley (1888–1954). *See* Taming of the Shrew 1

CLARK, Harold. *See* Measure for Measure 3*a*

CLARKE, James Hamilton Siree (1840–1912). *See* Cymbeline 2*a*, 3*b*; Hamlet 2*a*, *b*; King Lear 2*a*; Merchant of Venice 2*a*

CLARKE, Jeremiah (*c.* 1673–1707). *See* Titus Andronicus 2*a*

CLAY, Frederic (1838–89). *See* Twelfth Night 2*a*

CLEMENS, Theodor L. *See* As You Like It 3*b*

CLIFFORD, Hubert John (1904–59). *See* As You Like It 2*b*

CLIFTON, John Charles (1781–1841). *See* Twelfth Night 3*f*

CLOKEY, Joseph Waddell (1890– ). *See* As You Like It 3*b*

CLOUGH - LEIGHTER, Henry. *See* Leighter, Henry Clough-

COATES, Eric (1886–1957). *See* As You Like It 3*d*, *f*; Henry VIII 3*a*; Merchant of Venice 3*g*; Much Ado About Nothing 3*c*; Two Gentlemen of Verona 3*c*

COCKSHOTT, Gerald Wilfrid (1915– ). *See* Twelfth Night 3*b*

COKE, R. Sacheverell. *See* Sonnet 71

COLERIDGE - TAYLOR, S. *See* Taylor, S. Coleridge-

COLE, Frederick G. *See* Much Ado About Nothing 3*c*

COLLINGWOOD, Arthur. *See* Midsummer Night's Dream 3*f*, *t*; Twelfth Night 3*h*

COLLINGWOOD, Lawrance Arthur (1887– ). *See* Macbeth 1

COOK, John Ernest. *See* Cymbeline 3*a*; Merchant of Venice 3*g*

COOKE, Benjamin (1734–93). *See* Cymbeline 3*b*; Midsummer Night's Dream 3*e*; Taming of the Shrew 3*b*; Winter's Tale 3*e*, *g*

COOKE, Thomas Simpson (1782–1848). *See* Coriolanus 2*a*, *b*; Merchant of Venice 3*b*; Midsummer Night's Dream 2*a*, 3*g*, *h*, *o*, *r*; Taming of the Shrew 1; Tempest 2*a*, 3*e*, *g*; Twelfth Night 3*f*; Passionate Pilgrim 1; General

COPLAND, Aaron (1900– ). *See* Passionate Pilgrim 1; General

CORBETT, H. M. *See* Sonnet 30

CORBETT, William (?–1748). *See* Henry IV 2*a*

CORDER, Frederick (1852–1932). *See* Tempest 2*b*, 3*d*; Twelfth Night 3*b*

CORELLI, Marie (1855–1924). *See* Romeo and Juliet 3*c*

CORNELIUS, Peter (1824–74). *See* Twelfth Night 3*b*

COTTRAU, Giulio (1831–1916). *See* King Lear 1; Pericles 1

COVER, C. E. *See* Measure for Measure 3*a*

COWARD, James (1824–80). *See* Measure for Measure 3*a*; Passionate Pilgrim 1

COWDELL, Ellen. *See* As You Like It 3*d*

COWEN, Sir Frederic Hymen (1852–1935). *See* Measure for Measure 3*a*

COX, W. Ralph (1884–1941). *See* Twelfth Night 3*h*

CRAVEN, Elizabeth (Baroness Craven, Margravine of Anspach) (1750–1828). *See* Twelfth Night 3*h*

CRAVEN, John Thomas (1796–?). *See* Tempest 3*d*

CRICHTON, Margaret. *See* Cymbeline 3*a*; Love's Labour's Lost 3*f*; Midsummer Night's Dream 3*a*; Much Ado About Nothing 3*c*; Twelfth Night 3*h*; Winter's Tale 3*f*

CRIPPS, A. Redgrave. *See* Twelfth Night 3*h*

CROW, Edwin John. *See* As You Like It 3*b*

CRUFT, Adrian Francis (1921– ). *See* Tempest 2*b*

CRUICKSHANK, William Alexander Campbell. *See* Twelfth Night 3*h*

CUISSET, Frank F. *See* Merchant of Venice 3*g*

CUMMINGS, William Hayman (1831–1915). *See* Love's Labour's Lost 3*d*

CURSCHMANN, Karl Friedrich (1804–1841). *See* Cymbeline 3*b*; Romeo and Juliet 2*b*

CUSINS, Sir William George (1833–1893). *See* Love's Labour's Lost 2*b*

DADGE, Ralph. *See* As You Like It 3*b*

DALAYRAC, Nicolas (1753–1809). *See* Romeo and Juliet 1

DALE, Benjamin James (1885–1943). *See* Tempest 2*b*; Twelfth Night 3*b*, *h*

DANKWORTH, Johnny (John Philip William) (1927– ). *See* Cymbeline 3*a*; Love's Labour's Lost 3*g*; Macbeth 2*b*; Twelfth Night 2*a*, 3*b*, *f*, *h*, *j*; Sonnets 18, 23, 24, 40, 147; General

DANNREUTHER, Edward George (1844–1905). *See* As You Like It 3*d*; Love's Labour's Lost 3*f*, *g*

DANSIE, Redgewell. *See* Tempest 3*d*, *k*

DAVENPORT, Dennis. *See* As You Like It 3*d*

DAVENPORT, Francis William (1847–1925). *See* Twelfth Night 2*b*

DAVIDSON, Malcolm. *See* As You Like It 3*f*, *h*

DAVIE, Cedric Thorpe (1913– ). *See* As You Like It 3*f*; Henry VIII 2*a*, 3*a*; Midsummer Night's Dream 3*t*

DAVIES, D. *See* As You Like It 3*d*

DAVIES, Sir Henry Walford (1869–1941). *See* Cymbeline 3*a*; Henry V 3*a*; Henry VIII 3*a*; Midsummer Night's Dream 3*t*; Twelfth Night 3*b*, *h*, *j*; Winter's Tale 3*d*, *g*

DAVIS, John David (1867–1942). *See* Midsummer Night's Dream 3*t*

DAVY, John (1763–1824). *See* Hamlet 3*a*; Tempest 2*a*

DAYMOND, Emily Rosa. *See* Twelfth Night 3*h*

DEARLE. *See* Much Ado About Nothing 3*c*

DEBUSSY, (Achille) Claude (1862–1918). *See* King Lear 2*b*; Midsummer Night's Dream 2*b*

DEFFÈS, Louis Pierre (1819–1900). *See* Merchant of Venice 1

DE KOVEN, H. L. R. *See* Koven, H. L. R. de

DELANNOY, Marcel François Georges (1898–1962). *See* Midsummer Night's Dream 1

DELIUS, Frederick (1862–1934). *See* As You Like It 3*d*

DEMUTH, Norman Frank (1898– ). *See* As You Like It 3*f*; King John 2*a*; Macbeth 2*a*; Midsummer Night's Dream 3*f*; Tempest 2*a*, *b*; Titus Andronicus 2*a*; Twelfth Night 3*j*; Winter's Tale 3*g*

DEXTER, Harry (1910– ). *See* Much Ado About Nothing 3*c*

DIAMOND, David Leo (1915– ). *See* Romeo and Juliet 2*a*; Tempest 2*a*; Timon of Athens 2*b*

DIBDIN, Charles (1745–1814). *See* General

DICKS, Ernest Alfred (1865– ). *See* As You Like It 3*d*; Midsummer Night's Dream 3*n*; Two Gentlemen of Verona 3*c*

DIEREN, Bernard van (1884–1936). *See* Measure for Measure 3*a*

DIETRICH, Albert Hermann (1829–1908). *See* Cymbeline 2*a*

DIGNUM, Charles (*c.* 1765–1827). *See* Hamlet 3*a*; Merchant of Venice 3*c*; General

DILSNER, Laurence. *See* Twelfth Night 3*h*

DITTERSDORF, Karl Ditters von (1739–99). *See* Merry Wives of Windsor 1

DIXON, Christopher. *See* Measure for Measure 3*a*

DOPPLER, Árpád (1857–1927). *See* Much Ado About Nothing 1

DORET, Gustave (1866–1943). *See* Julius Caesar 2*a*

DOUBRAVA, Jaroslav (1909–61). *See* Midsummer Night's Dream 1

DRAESEKE, Felix August Bernhard (1835–1913). *See* Julius Caesar 2*b*

DRAGHI, Giovanni Battista (*c.* 1640–*c.* 1710). *See* Tempest 2*a*

DRAKEFORD, Richard Jeremy. *See* Love's Labour's Lost 3*f*

DRAYTON, Harry U. *See* Twelfth Night 3*b*, *h*

DRIFFIELD, Edward Townshend. *See* Twelfth Night 3*h*

DUFF, Arthur K. *See* Two Gentlemen of Verona 3*c*

DUGGAN, Joseph Francis (1817–?). *See* As You Like It 2*a*; Midsummer Night's Dream 3*n*; Tempest 3*b*, *j*; Two Gentlemen of Verona 3*c*

DUKAS, Paul (1865–1935). *See* King Lear 2*b*

DUNCAN, William Edmonstoune (1866–1920). *See* As You Like It 3*b*; Love's Labour's Lost 3*g*

DUNCOMBE, William. *See* Twelfth Night 3*b*

DUNHILL, Thomas Frederick (1877–1946). *See* As You Like It 3*d*, *f*; Henry VIII 3*a*; Merchant of Venice 3*g*; Midsummer Night's Dream 3*n*; Much Ado About Nothing 3*c*; Othello 3*b*; Tempest 3*d*, *f*, *k*; Twelfth Night 3*b*, *h*, *j*; Two Gentlemen of Verona 3*c*

DUNN, James Philip. *See* As You Like It 3*f*

DUPUIS, Sylvain (1856–1931). *See* Macbeth 2*b*

DUPUY, Jean Baptiste Édouard (1770/1–1822). *See* Hamlet 2*a*

DURAND, Émile. *See* Hamlet 2*b*

DUSSEK, Jan Ladislav (1760–1812). *See* Othello 3*b*

DUVERNOY, Victor Alphonse (1842–1907). *See* Tempest 2*b*

DYCE-SOMBRE, Hon. Mary Ann Jervis, Mrs. *See* Sombre, Mrs. Dyce-

DYSON, Sir George (1883– ). *See* Henry V 2*b*; Love's Labour's Lost 3*g*; Winter's Tale 3*e*

EARLE, William Benson. *See* Midsummer Night's Dream 3*t*

EASDALE, Brian (1909– ). *See* Hamlet 2*a*; Merchant of Venice 2*a*

EASSON, James. *See* Tempest 3*d*, *f*

EBERWEIN, Traugott Maximilian (1775–1831). *See* Macbeth 2*b*

ECCLES, John (1668–1735). *See* Hamlet 2*a*; Macbeth 2*a*

EDESON, Donald Joseph Scott. *See* As You Like It 3*d*; Merchant of Venice 3*g*; Twelfth Night 3*h*

EDGAR, Edward. *See* As You Like It 3*h*

EDMONDS, Paul N. (1873–1939). *See* Twelfth Night 3*h*; Passionate Pilgrim 3

EDWARDS, R. *See* Romeo and Juliet 3*f*

EDWARDS, Walker Strong. *See* Twelfth Night 3*h*

EGGEN, Arne (1881–1955). *See* Cymbeline 1

EHLERT, Ludwig (1825–84). *See* Winter's Tale 2*b*

ELGAR, Sir Edward William (1857–1934). *See* Henry IV 2*b*; Merry Wives of Windsor 2*b*; General

ELLA, John (1802–88). *See* Love's Labour's Lost 3*d*

ELLERTON, John Lodge (1826–93). *See* Midsummer Night's Dream 3*j*

ELLINGTON, Duke (1899– ). *See* General

ELLIOT, Muriel. *See* As You Like It 2*a*; Love's Labour's Lost 3*f*

ELLIOTT, Joseph. *See* Two Gentlemen of Verona 3*c*

ELLISTON, Marion. *See* As You Like It 3*b*, *d*, *f*; Cymbeline 3*a*; Hamlet 3*l*; Merry Wives of Windsor 3*c*; Midsummer Night's Dream 3*s*, *t*; Tempest 3*d*, *f*; Winter's Tale 3*c*, *e*, *g*

ELTON, Antony. *See* Twelfth Night 3*b*

EMMERICH, Robert. *See* Cymbeline 3*b*

EMMERT, Adam J. *See* Tempest 1

ENGEL, Lehman (1910– ). *See* Henry VIII 2*a*

ESPOSITO, Michele (1855–1929). *See* Othello 2*b*

ETTEN, J. Van. *See* Van Etten, J.

EVANS, David Emlyn (1843–1913). *See* Merchant of Venice 3*c*

Evans, David Moule. *See* Love's Labour's Lost 3*g*; Twelfth Night 3*h*

Ewing, M. Porteous. *See* Richard II 3*a*

Ewing, Montague. *See* Midsummer Night's Dream 2*b*

Fabrizi, Vincenzo (*c.* 1765–?). *See* Tempest 1

Faccio, Franco (1840–91). *See* Hamlet 1

Falchi, Stanislao (1851–1922). *See* Julius Caesar 2*b*

Fane, John, 11th Earl of Westmorland (1784–1859). *See* Passionate Pilgrim 3

Faning, Joseph Eaton (1850–1927). *See* Merchant of Venice 3*c*

Farina, Guido (1903– ). *See* Twelfth Night 1

Farkas, Ferenc (1905– ). *See* As You Like It 2*a*; Romeo and Juliet 2*a*; Timon of Athens 2*a*

Farrant, George. *See* Much Ado About Nothing 3*c*

Farrar, Ernest Bristow (1885–1918). *See* Twelfth Night 3*h*; Winter's Tale 3*d*

Farwell, Arthur (1872–1952). *See* Tempest 1

Faulkes, William (1863–1933). *See* As You Like It 3*b, f*; Hamlet 3*c*; Henry VIII 3*a*; Measure for Measure 3*a*; Merchant of Venice 3*g*; Much Ado About Nothing 3*c*; Othello 3*b*; Twelfth Night 3*b, h, j*; Two Gentlemen of Verona 3*c*

Fauré, Gabriel Urbain (1845–1924). *See* Merchant of Venice 2*a, b*

Ferrari, Gustave (1872–1948). *See* Hamlet 2*a*

Ffoulkes, Sydney. *See* As You Like It 3*f*; Love's Labour's Lost 3*f*

Fibich, Zdeněk (1850–1900). *See* Othello 2*b*; Tempest 1, 2*b*

Fielden, Thomas Perceval (1883– ). *See* Tempest 3*g*

Filippi, Amadeo de (1900– ). *See* Twelfth Night 1

Finzi, Gerald (1901–56). *See* As You Like It 3*d*; Cymbeline 3*a*; Love's Labour's Lost 2*a*, 3*f, g*; Twelfth Night 3*b, h*; Two Gentlemen of Verona 3*c*; Sonnet 15

Fisher, John Abraham (1744–1806). *See* Macbeth 2*a*; Tempest 2*a*

Fisher, William Ames (1861–1948). *See* As You Like It 3*b*; Much Ado About Nothing 3*c*

Fisin, James (1755–1847). *See* Hamlet 3*a*

Fiske, Roger (1910– ). *See* Love's Labour's Lost 3*f*

Fitzwilliam, Edward Francis (1824–57). *See* Midsummer Night's Dream 3*n*

Fleischmann, Friedrich (1766–98). *See* Tempest 1

Flotow, Friedrich von (1812–83). *See* Winter's Tale 2*a*

Foerster, Josef Bohuslav (1859–1951). *See* Julius Caesar 2*b*; Love's Labour's Lost 2*a*; Merchant of Venice 1, 2*b*; Twelfth Night 2*a*; General

Fogg, Charles William Eric (1903–1939). *See* Comedy of Errors 2*b*; Tempest 3*f*

Folprecht, Zdeněk (1900– ). *See* Love's Labour's Lost 1

Foote, Arthur William (1853–1937). *See* Much Ado About Nothing 3*c*

Ford, Thomas (*c.* 1580–1648). *See* Much Ado About Nothing 3*c*

Forrester, James Cliffe (1860–1941). *See* Twelfth Night 3*h*

Forsyth, Cecil (1870–1941). *See* As You Like It 3*f*; Midsummer Night's Dream 3*t*

Foss, Lukas (1922– ). *See* Tempest 2*b*, 3*k*

Foster, Myles Birket (1851–1922). *See* As You Like It 3*d, f*

Foulds, John Herbert (1880–1939). *See* Henry VIII 2*a*; Julius Caesar 2*a*

Fox, Arthur Makinson. *See* Henry VIII 3*a*; Measure for Measure 3*a*

Fox, George E. *See* Othello 3*a*; Much Ado About Nothing 3*c*; Passionate Pilgrim 8

FRÄNZL, Ignaz (1736–1811). *See* Julius Caesar 2*a*; Macbeth 2*a*

FRANCK, Johann Wolfgang (?1641–?). *See* Timon of Athens 2*a*

FRANK, Ernst (1847–89). *See* Tempest 1

FRANKEL, Benjamin (1906– ). *See* Julius Caesar 2*a*; Macbeth 2*a*

FRAZZI, Vito (1888– ). *See* King Lear 1

FRY, William Henry (1813–64). *See* Macbeth 2*b*

FRYER, George Herbert (1877–1957). *See* Twelfth Night 3*h*; Sonnet 71

FULTON, Robert Norman (1909– ). *See* As You Like It 3*d*, *f*, *h*; Othello 3*b*; Twelfth Night 3*b*, *h*

GABRIEL (afterwards March), Mary Ann Virginia (1825–77). *See* Henry VIII 3*a*

GADE, Niels Vilhelm (1817–90). *See* Hamlet 2*b*

GADSBY, Henry (1842–1907). *See* As You Like It 2*b*

GÁL, Hans (1890– ). *See* Merchant of Venice 3*g*; Passionate Pilgrim 3

GALE, James Randolph Courtenay. *See* As You Like It 3*b*

GALLENBERG, Wenzel Robert Graf von (1783–1839). *See* Hamlet 2*b*

GALLIARD, Johann Ernst (*c.* 1680–1749). *See* Julius Caesar 2*a*; Measure for Measure 3*a*

GAMBARINI, Elisabetta de (1731–?). *See* Tempest 3*g*

GAMBOGI, F. Elvira. *See* Cymbeline 3*b*; Measure for Measure 3*a*

GARCÍA ROBLEZ, José (1839–1910). *See* Julius Caesar 1

GARDINER, Henry Balfour (1877–1950). *See* Cymbeline 3*a*; Hamlet 3*c*

GARDINER, William (1770–1853.) *See* Measure for Measure 3*a*

GARDNER, Charles. *See* Merchant of Venice 3*c*, *d*; Passionate Pilgrim 1

GARDNER, John Linton (1917– ). *See* As You Like It 3*f*; Cymbeline 3*a*, *b*; Passionate Pilgrim 3

GATTIE, Mrs. J. B. *See* Midsummer Night's Dream 3*p*

GATTY, Nicholas Comyn (1874–1946). *See* As You Like It 3*b*; Henry VIII 3*a*; Macbeth 1; Tempest 1

GAUJAC, Edmond. *See* Romeo and Juliet 1

GAUL, Alfred Robert (1837–1913). *See* Venus and Adonis 1

GAUL, Harvey Bartlett (1881–1945). *See* Othello 3*a*; Romeo and Juliet 3*a*; Tempest 3*c*; Sonnet 18

GAVALL, John [Hugh Waters]. *See* Twelfth Night 3*h*

GERHARD, Roberto (1896– ). *See* Cymbeline 2*a*; Romeo and Juliet 2*a*

GERMAN, Sir Edward [Edward German Jones] (1862–1936). *See* As You Like It 2*a*, 3*d*; Hamlet 2*b*; Henry VIII 2*a*, 3*a*; Much Ado About Nothing 2*a*; Richard III 2*a*; Romeo and Juliet 2*a*; Two Gentlemen of Verona 3*c*

GHISLANZONI, Alberto (1897– ). *See* King Lear 1

GIANNINI, Vittorio (1903– ). *See* Taming of the Shrew 1

GIBBS, Cecil Armstrong (1889–1960). *See* As You Like It 3*b*, *d*; Cymbeline 3*a*; Henry VIII 3*a*; Love's Labour's Lost 3*g*; Midsummer Night's Dream 3*j*, *t*; Twelfth Night 1 and 3*h*, *j*

GIBSON, S. Archer. *See* As You Like It 3*d*

GILBERT, Ernest Thomas Bennett. *See* Henry VIII 3*a*; Tempest 2*b*; General

GILBERT, Norman. *See* Love's Labour's Lost 3*g*; Much Ado About Nothing 3*c*

GILL, Harry. *See* Midsummer Night's Dream 3*f*

GIORDANI, Tommaso (1730–1806). *See* Measure for Measure 3*a*; Othello 3*b*; Passionate Pilgrim 3

GLADSTONE, Francis Edward (1845–1928). *See* Twelfth Night 3*h*

GLENDINNING, Richard Rashleigh. *See* Cymbeline 3*b*

GLOVER, H. *See* Romeo and Juliet 3*b*; Passionate Pilgrim 7

GOBATTI, Stefano (1852–1913). *See* King Lear 1

GODARD, Benjamin Louis Paul (1849–95). *See* Much Ado About Nothing 2*a*

GODFERY, M. van Someren. *See* Cymbeline 3*a*

GODFREY, H. Graham. *See* Midsummer Night's Dream 3*n*; Twelfth Night 3*b*

GOETZ, Hermann (1840–76). *See* Taming of the Shrew 1

GOLDMARK, Carl (1830–1915). *See* Winter's Tale 1

GOLDSCHMIDT, Berthold (1903– ). *See* Comedy of Errors 2*b*

GORDON, Philip. *See* Merchant of Venice 3*g*

GORDON, William. *See* Two Gentlemen of Verona 3*c*

GÖTZ, Hermann. *See* Goetz, H.

GOULD, William Monk (1858– ). *See* Two Gentlemen of Verona 3*c*

GOUNOD, Charles François (1818–1893). *See* Romeo and Juliet 1

GOVER, Gerald Maxwell (1914– ). *See* King John 3*a*; Richard II 3*a*; Sonnet 18

GRABU [Grabut, Grebus], Louis (*fl.* 1665). *See* Timon of Athens 2*a*

GRAFFE, G. *See* Midsummer Night's Dream 3*t*

GRAY, Alan (1855–1935). *See* Cymbeline 3*a*; Twelfth Night 3*h*

GRAZIA, E. N. [Mrs. Bourne]. *See* Measure for Measure 3*a*

GREATOREX, Thomas (1758–1831). *See* Henry VIII 3*a*

GREAVES, Ralph. *See* Twelfth Night 3*b*

GREENE, Maurice (1695–1755). *See* Henry VIII 3*a*

GREENHILL, Harold Walter. *See* Twelfth Night 3*h*

GREENHILL, James (1840– ). *See* As You Like It 3*d*; Cymbeline 3*a*; Measure for Measure 3*a*; Winter's Tale 3*e*; Sonnet 100

GREENWOOD, John Darnforth Herman (1889– ). *See* Merchant of Venice 2*a*; Midsummer Night's Dream 2*a*

GRIEG, Edvard Hagerup (1843–1907). *See* Macbeth 2*b*

GRIESBACH, John Henry (1798–1875). *See* Tempest 2*a*

GRIFFITH, William (?1876– ). *See* Twelfth Night 3*h*; Passionate Pilgrim 3

GUERNSEY, Wellington. *See* General

GUGLIELMI, Pietro Carlo (*c.* 1763–1817). *See* Romeo and Juliet 1

GURLITT, Manfred (1890– ). *See* Antony and Cleopatra 2*b*; Henry IV 2*b*; Julius Caesar 2*b*; Troilus and Cressida 2*b*

GURNEY, Ivor Bertie (1890–1937). *See* As You Like It 3*f*; Henry VIII 3*a*

HAACK, Friedrich (*c.* 1760– ). *See* Tempest 1

HADLEY, Henry Kimball (1871–1937). *See* Hamlet 3*b*; Merchant of Venice 3*g*; Othello 2*b*; Twelfth Night 3*h*

HAGER, J. *See* Tempest 2*b*

HAHN, Reynaldo (1875–1947). *See* Merchant of Venice 1; Much Ado About Nothing 1

HALAS, František (1901– ). *See* Cymbeline 3*a*

HALE, Alfred Matthew. *See* Tempest 1; Sonnets 59, 60, 61, 104, 105, 106, 110, 116

HALES, Hubert James (1902– ). *See* Cymbeline 3*a*; Merchant of Venice 2*b* and 3*g*; Midsummer Night's Dream 3*t*; Twelfth

Night 2b; Winter's Tale 3c, d, e, f, g

HALÉVY [Lévy], Jacques François Fromental Elias (1799–1862). See Tempest 1

HALL, John. See Midsummer Night's Dream 3t

HALL, Pauline Margaret Markham. See Midsummer Night's Dream 2a

HAM, Albert (1858–1940). See Two Gentlemen of Verona 3c

HAMAND, Louis Arthur. See Tempest 3f

HAND, Colin. See Love's Labour's Lost 3g

HARCOURT, J. Arthur. See Merchant of Venice 3g

HARDY, T. Maskell (1861– ). See Love's Labour's Lost 3g

HARINGTON, Dr. Henry (1727–1816). See Twelfth Night 3i

HARKER, Clifford. See Henry VIII 3a

HARKER, F. Flaxington (1876–1936). See As You Like It 3d

HARRADEN, Ethel. See Much Ado About Nothing 3c

HARRIS, Cuthbert (1870– ). See As You Like It 3f

HARRISON, Julius Allan Greenway (1885–1963). See As You Like It 3f; Midsummer Night's Dream 3f, t; Twelfth Night 3b, c, h, j

HARRISS, Alfred. See Twelfth Night 3b

HART, Fritz Bennicke (1874–1949). See Hamlet 2b; Henry VIII 3a; Twelfth Night 1

HARTLEY, B. W. See As You Like It 3d

HATELY, W. See Midsummer Night's Dream 3r

HATHAWAY, Joseph William George (1870– ). See Merchant of Venice 3c

HATTON, John Liptrot (1809–86). See Henry IV 3b; Henry VIII 2a, 3a; King Lear 2a; Macbeth 2a; Merchant of Venice 2a, 3g; Midsummer Night's Dream 3n; Much Ado About Nothing 2a;

Richard II 2a; Twelfth Night 3j

HAUBENSTOCK-RAMATI, Roman. See Ramati, R. H.

HAWKINS, H. A. See Midsummer Night's Dream 2a

HAYDEN, William. See Antony and Cleopatra 2b; As You Like It 2b; Midsummer Night's Dream 2b; Tempest 2b

HAYDN, Franz Joseph (1732–1809). See Hamlet 2a; Twelfth Night 3i

HAYES, Fanny M. See Cymbeline 3a; General

HAYES, Philip (1738–97). See As You Like It 3h

HEAP, Charles Swinnerton (1847–1900). See Two Gentlemen of Verona 3c

HEATHCOTE, Evelyn Dawsonne. See Henry VIII 3a

HEINRICH, Hermann. See Much Ado About Nothing 1

HEISE, Peter Arnold (1830–79). See As You Like It 3d; Othello 3b

HENSCHEL, Sir Isidor Georg (later George) (1850–1934). See Hamlet 2a

HENSEL, John Daniel (1757–1839). See Tempest 1

HERBERIGS, Robert (1886– ). See Antony and Cleopatra 2b; Merry Wives of Windsor 2b

HERSCHEL, Sir William (1738–1822). See Macbeth 3c

HESELTINE, Philip Arnold. See Warlock, Peter

HESSENBERG, Kurt (1908– ). See Tempest 2a

HEWARD, Leslie Hays (1897–1943). See Hamlet 1; Midsummer Night's Dream 3n

HEY, C. E. See Twelfth Night 3h

HIGNARD, Jean Louis Aristide (1822–1898). See Hamlet 1

HILBY, L. See Twelfth Night 3h

HILES, Henry (1826–1904). See As You Like It 3d

HILL, Mirrie. See Merchant of Venice 3c

2a; Romeo and Juliet 2a; Tempest 2a; Twelfth Night 2a; Winter's Tale 2a

Huss, Henry Holden (1862–1953). *See* As You Like It 3d

Hutchinson, Francis. *See* Romeo and Juliet 3d

Hutchinson, Joseph T. *See* As You Like It 3d; Merchant of Venice 3c

Hutchinson, Thomas. *See* Tempest 3m; Winter's Tale 3e

Hutchison, William Marshall. *See* Meissler, Josef

Ibert, Jacques François Antoine (1890–1962). *See* Antony and Cleopatra 2a; Macbeth 2a; Midsummer Night's Dream 2a, b

Iles, Edward. *See* Measure for Measure 3a

Ilyinsky, Alexander Alexandrovich (1859–1919). *See* Romeo and Juliet 2b

Indy, Paul Marie Théodore Vincent d' (1851–1931). *See* Antony and Cleopatra 2b

Ingram, R. *See* Midsummer Night's Dream 3t

Ireland, John Nicholson (1879–1962). *See* Julius Caesar 2a; Tempest 3f; Winter's Tale 3f

Irving, Kelville Ernest (1878–1953). *See* Macbeth 2a; Taming of the Shrew 2a

Isaacson, B. *See* Henry V 2a

Ivry, Richard d' [Paul Xavier Désiré Marquis d'] (1829–1903) [pseud. Richard d'Yrvid]. *See* Romeo and Juliet 1

Jackson, William (1730–1803). *See* Love's Labour's Lost 3d; Measure for Measure 3a; Midsummer Night's Dream 3n

Jacob, Gordon Percival Septimus (1895– ). *See* As You Like It 3f; Cymbeline 3a; Love's Labour's Lost 3g; General

Jacobi, Georg (1840–1906). *See* Midsummer Night's Dream 2b

Jacobson, Maurice (1896– ). *See* Antony and Cleopatra 2a, 3a; Hamlet 2a, b; Julius Caesar 2a; Macbeth 2a

Jacques, (Thomas) Reginald (1894– ). *See* Henry VIII 3a

Januš, Jan. *See* Othello 2b

Jefferson, Peter. *See* Merchant of Venice 3g

Jenkins, D. Cyril (1889– ). *See* As You Like It 3b

Jenner, Harold. *See* As You Like It 3d; Twelfth Night 3h

Jirák, Karel Boleslav (1891– ). *See* General

Joachim, Joseph (1831–1907). *See* Hamlet 2b; Henry IV 2b

Johnson, Bernard. *See* Twelfth Night 3h

Johnson, George F. *See* Measure for Measure 3a

Johnson, Reginald. *See* As You Like It 3d

Johnson, Robert (c. 1583–1633). *See* Cymbeline 3b; Tempest 3f, k; Winter's Tale 3e

Johnstone, Maurice (1900– ). *See* Tempest 2b; Sonnet 75

Joncières, Victorin de [Félix Ludger Rossignol] (1839–1903). *See* Hamlet 2a

Jones, Henry Festing (1851–1928). *See* Twelfth Night 3h

Jones, Tony Hewitt. *See* Tempest 3f

Joseph, Jane M. *See* Midsummer Night's Dream 3j

Judd, Percy (1892– ). *See* Love's Labour's Lost 3f; Winter's Tale 3f

Kabalevsky, Dmitri Borisovich (1904– ). *See* Measure for Measure 2a; Romeo and Juliet 2a, b; Sonnets 8, 13, 27, 30, 71, 78, 81, 90, 102, 109, 153

Kaffka, J. C. *See* Antony and Cleopatra 1

Kagen, Sergius (1908/9–1964). *See* Hamlet 1

Kalniňš, Janis (1904– ). *See* Hamlet 1

LA FORGE, Frank (1879–1953). *See* Measure for Measure 3*a*; Tempest 3*d*

LAHMEYER, Carl. *See* As You Like It 3*d*

LAMBERT, Constant (1905–51). *See* Cymbeline 3*a*; Hamlet 2*a*; Romeo and Juliet 2*b*

LAMPE, John Frederick (*c.* 1703–51). *See* Midsummer Night's Dream 1

LANCELOTT, F. *See* Measure for Measure 3*a*

LANG, Edith. *See* As You Like It 3*d*

LARSSON, Lars-Erik Vilner (1908– ). *See* Tempest 2*b*; Winter's Tale 2*a*

LASSEN, Eduard (1830–1904). *See* Henry VIII 3*a*

LATTUADA, Felice (1882–1962). *See* Tempest 1

LAUFER, Beatrice. *See* Merchant of Venice 1

LAW, Alice. *See* Cymbeline 3*a*

LAW, Hamilton. *See* As You Like It 3*d*

LAWSON, Malcolm Leonard. *See* Much Ado About Nothing 3*c*; Passionate Pilgrim 8

LAZZARI, Sylvio (1857–1944). *See* Hamlet 2*b*

LEE, Ernest Markham (1874–1956). *See* As You Like It 3*f*; Tempest 3*d, f*

LEE, George Alexander (1802–51). *See* General

LEFEBVRE, Channing (1895– ). *See* Henry VIII 3*a*

LE FLEM, Paul (1881– ). *See* Macbeth 2*b*

LEHMANN, Amelia. *See* Measure for Measure 3*a*

LEHMANN, Liza [Elizabetta Nina Mary Frederika, afterwards Bedford] (1862–1918). *See* As You Like It 3*d, f*; Love's Labour's Lost 3*g*; Merchant of Venice 3*c, g*; Midsummer Night's Dream 3*f, h*; Much Ado About Nothing 3*c*; Twelfth Night 3*f, h*; Two Gentlemen of Verona 3*c*; Sonnet 105

LEIGH, Walter (1905–42). *See* Midsummer Night's Dream 2*a*

LEIGHTER, Henry Clough- (1874–1956). *See* As You Like It 3*d*

LEKEU, Guillaume (1870–94). *See* Hamlet 2*b*

LENTON, John (1656–*c.* 1719). *See* Othello 2*a*

LEONARD, S. B. *See* Midsummer Night's Dream 3*t*

LEOPOLD I, Emperor (1640–1705). *See* Timon of Athens 1

LEPPARD, Raymond (1927– ). *See* Midsummer Night's Dream 3*t*

LESLIE, Henry David (1822–96). *See* Henry IV 3*e*; Merchant of Venice 3*c, e*; General

LESTER, William. *See* Love's Labour's Lost 3*b*; Tempest 3*d*; Twelfth Night 3*h*

LETTS, Egerton. *See* Measure for Measure 3*a*

LEVERIDGE, Richard (*c.* 1670–1758). *See* Love's Labour's Lost 3*f*; Macbeth 2*a*; Midsummer Night's Dream 1, 3*j*; Two Gentlemen of Verona 3*c*

LEVEY, Andrew James. *See* Twelfth Night 3*h, j*; Winter's Tale 2*a*

LEVEY, Sivori. *See* As You Like It 3*a*; Merchant of Venice 3*c*

LEVEY, William Charles (1837–94). *See* Antony and Cleopatra 2*a*

LEVY, Harold (1894– ). *See* Hamlet 2*a*

LINLEY, Thomas *the elder* (1733–1795). *See* Macbeth 2*a*; Tempest 3*a, l*

LINLEY, Thomas *the younger* (1756–1778). *See* General

LINLEY, William (1771–1835). *See* All's Well That Ends Well 3*a*; Antony and Cleopatra 3*a*; As You Like It 3*b, d, f, g*; Cymbeline 3*a*; Hamlet 3*g*; Henry IV 3*a*; Henry VIII 2*b*, 3*a*; Measure for Measure 3*a*; Merchant of Venice 3*g*; Midsummer Night's Dream 3*j*; Much Ado About Nothing 3*b, c*; Othello 3*a, b*; Tempest 3*g*; Twelfth Night 3*b, h*;

MAJOR, Joseph. *See* Love's Labour's Lost 3*a*

MALAWSKI, Artur (1904–57). *See* Midsummer Night's Dream 2*a*; Tempest 2*a*

MALIPIERO, Gian Francesco (1882– ). *See* Antony and Cleopatra 1; Julius Caesar 1; Romeo and Juliet 1

MALLINSON, A. *See* Sonnet 109

MANCINELLI, Luigi (1848–1921). *See* Midsummer Night's Dream 1

MANGELSDORFF, Arthur. *See* Tempest 3*f*

MANNEY, Charles Fonteyn (1872–1951). *See* Henry VIII 3*a*; Othello 3*a*

MANSFIELD, Purcell James. *See* As You Like It 3*b*; Much Ado About Nothing 3*c*; Tempest 3*d*, *f*

MANUSARDI, G. *See* Midsummer Night's Dream 1

MARCHETTI, Filippo (1831–1902). *See* Romeo and Juliet 1

MARECZEK, Massimiliano. *See* Hamlet 1

MARESCALCHI, Luigi. *See* Romeo and Juliet 1

MARKS, Thomas Osborne. *See* Two Gentlemen of Verona 3*c*

MARTIN, Frank (1890– ). *See* Romeo and Juliet 2*a*; Tempest 1, 3*d*, *f*, *g*, *i*, *k*

MARTINEZ, Isidora. *See* Two Gentlemen of Verona 3*c*

MARTIRANO, Salvatore. *See* General

MARZIALS, Théophile Jules Henri. *See* As You Like It 3*b*, *d*, *f*; Cymbeline 3*a*, *b*; Love's Labour's Lost 3*g*; Two Gentlemen of Verona 3*c*

MATTHEY, Alphonso. *See* Twelfth Night 3*f*

MAXWELL, Isobel. *See* Midsummer Night's Dream 3*t*

MEDERITSCH, Johann Georg Anton Gallus (1752–1835). *See* Macbeth 2*a*

MEISSLER, Josef [also Mount, Julian] [real name William Marshall Hutchison]. *See* As You Like It 3*d*; Midsummer Night's Dream 3*t*; Twelfth Night 3*h*

MELLERS, Wilfrid Howard (1914– ). *See* Hamlet 3*l*; Measure for Measure 3*a*; Tempest 3*d*, *f*

MELLON, Alfred (1820–67). *See* Measure for Measure 3*a*

MENDELSSOHN-BARTHOLDY, Jacob Ludwig Felix (1809–47). *See* Midsummer Night's Dream 2*a*, *b*, 3*f*, *j*, *q*, *t*

MENGES, (Siegfried Frederick) Herbert (1902– ). *See* Love's Labour's Lost 2*a*

MERCADAL, Antonio. *See* Romeo and Juliet 1

MERCADANTE, Giuseppe Saverio Raffaele (1795–1870). *See* Hamlet 1; Henry IV 1

MERWIN, Royal Andrews. *See* As You Like It 3*b*

MIHALOVICH, Ödön Péter József de (1842–1929). *See* Romeo and Juliet 2*b*; Timon of Athens 2*b*

MILFORD, Robin Humphrey (1903–1959). *See* As You Like It 2*b*, 3*d*; Hamlet 3*e*; Tempest 2*b*

MILHAUD, Darius (1892– ). *See* Hamlet 2*a*; Julius Caesar 2*a*; Macbeth 2*a*; Romeo and Juliet 2*a*; Winter's Tale 2*a*

MILLER, Anthony. *See* Henry VIII 3*a*; Macbeth 3*b*

MINETTI, Carlo. *See* As You Like It 3*d*

MISSA, Edmond Jean Louis (1861–1910). *See* Cymbeline 1; King Lear 2*a*

MOCHRING, F. *See* Cymbeline 3*b*

MOERAN, Ernest John (1894–1950). *See* As You Like It 3*d*, *f*; Love's Labour's Lost 3*f*, *g*; Much Ado About Nothing 3*c*; Tempest 3*k*; Twelfth Night 3*b*

MOJSISOVICS, Roderich von (1877–1953). *See* Much Ado About Nothing 1

MONIUSZKO, Stanisław (1819–72). *See* Hamlet 2*a*; Merchant of

NIELSEN, Carl August (1865–1931). *See* General

NIXON, Henry Cotter (1842–1907). *See* Midsummer Night's Dream 2*b*

NOBLE, Thomas Tertius (1867–1953). *See* As You Like It 3*b*

NORDOFF, Paul (1909– ). *See* Othello 3*b*

NORMAN, Fredrik Vilhelm Ludvig (1831–85). *See* Antony and Cleopatra 2*a*

NORRIS, Thomas (1741–90). *See* Tempest 2*b*

NUNN, Edward Cuthbert. *See* Winter's Tale 3*g*

NYSTROEM, Gösta (1890– ). *See* Merchant of Venice 2*a*; Tempest 2*a*

OAKLEY, Samuel Harold. *See* Two Gentlemen of Verona 3*c*

OBERHOFFER, Robert Werner. *See* Merchant of Venice 3*g*

OBERTHÜR, Charles (1819–95). *See* Macbeth 2*b*

O'CONNOR, Eustace. *See* Sonnet 36

OGILVY, Alfred Walter. *See* As You Like It 3*d*, *f*

OLIVER, Herbert. *See* Twelfth Night 3*h*

O'NEILL, Norman (1875–1934). *See* As You Like It 3*d*; Hamlet 2*a*; Henry V 2*a*; Julius Caesar 2*a*; King Lear 2*a*; Macbeth 2*a*; Measure for Measure 2*a*; Merchant of Venice 2*a*, 2*b*, 3*g*; Midsummer Night's Dream 2*b*; Twelfth Night 3*b*

ORCHARD, William Arundel (1867–1961). *See* Midsummer Night's Dream 3*t*

ORFF, Carl (1895– ). *See* Midsummer Night's Dream 1

ORR, Robin [Robert Kemsley] (1909– ). *See* Winter's Tale 2*a*

OSBORNE, Mabel C. *See* As You Like It 3*b*, *d*, *f*

PAINE, John Knowles (1839–1906). *See* As You Like It 2*b*; Tempest 2*b*

PAISIBLE, James (*c*. 1650–*c*. 1721). *See* Henry IV 2*a*; Timon of Athens 2*a*

PALMER, Geoffrey Molyneux (1882– ). *See* Twelfth Night 3*b*

PAPAVOINE. *See* Merry Wives of Windsor 1

PARKE, John (1745–1829). *See* As You Like It 3*f*; Henry VIII 3*a*; Love's Labour's Lost 3*f*; Much Ado About Nothing 3*c*; Twelfth Night 3*b*

PARKE, Maria Hester (1775–1822). *See* As You Like It 3*f*; Twelfth Night 3*b*

PARKER, Clifton (1905– ). *See* Othello 2*a*

PARKER, Henry Taylor (1867–1934). *See* As You Like It 3*b*, *d*; Cymbeline 3*b*; Henry VIII 3*a*; Midsummer Night's Dream 3*f*; Much Ado About Nothing 3*c*; Othello 3*b*; Romeo and Juliet 2*b*; Tempest 3*f*; Twelfth Night 3*b*, *h*

PARNELL, Claude W. *See* As You Like It 3*f*; Tempest 3*f*; Sonnet 30

PARROTT, Horace Ian (1916– ). *See* Romeo and Juliet 2*b*

PARRY, Sir Charles Hubert Hastings (1848–1918). *See* As You Like It 3*b*, *d*, *f*; Cymbeline 3*a*; Love's Labour's Lost 3*d*, *g*; Measure for Measure 3*a*; Othello 3*b*; Richard II 3*a*; Tempest 3*f*; Twelfth Night 3*h*; Passionate Pilgrim 3; Sonnets 18, 29, 30, 32, 71, 87, 109

PARRY, John (1776–1851). *See* Hamlet 3*a*; Love's Labour's Lost 3*c*; Passionate Pilgrim 1

PARRY, J. H. *See* Sonnet 18

PASCAL, Florian [Joseph Benjamin Williams] (1850–1923). *See* As You Like It 3*b*, *d*; Comedy of Errors 3*b*; Henry VIII 3*a*; Much Ado About Nothing 3*c*; Passionate Pilgrim 3; Venus and Adonis 6

PASQUALI, Niccolò (?–1757). *See* Tempest 3*k*

X

PRENDERGAST, Arthur Hugh Dalrymple. *See* Measure for Measure 3*a*; Twelfth Night 3*h*

PROKOFIEV, Sergei Sergeievich (1891–1953). *See* Antony and Cleopatra 2*b*; Hamlet 2*a*; Romeo and Juliet 2*b*

PROUT, Ebenezer (1835–1909). *See* Twelfth Night 2*b*

PUGET, P. *See* Much Ado About Nothing 1

PURCELL, Daniel (*c.* 1660–1717). *See* Macbeth 2*a*; Taming of the Shrew 2*a*

PURCELL, Henry (1659–95). *See* Midsummer Night's Dream 1; Tempest 1, 3*d*, *f*, *k*; Timon of Athens 2*a*

PYE, Kellow John (1812–1901). *See* Cymbeline 3*b*; Love's Labour's Lost 3*d*; Passionate Pilgrim 5

QUILTER, Roger (1877–1953). *See* As You Like It 2*b*, 3*b*, *d*, *f*, *h*; Cymbeline 3*a*; Hamlet 3*c*; Henry VIII 3*a*; Love's Labour's Lost 3*g*; Measure for Measure 3*a*; Merchant of Venice 3*g*; Much Ado About Nothing 3*c*; Tempest 3*d*; Twelfth Night 3*b*, *h*, *j*; Two Gentlemen of Verona 3*c*; Winter's Tale 3*f*

RABAUD, Henri Benjamin (1873–1949). *See* Antony and Cleopatra 2*a*; Merchant of Venice 2*a*

RADECKE, Robert. *See* King John 2*b*

RADÓ, Aladár (1882–1914). *See* Merchant of Venice 1

RAMATI, Roman Haubenstock- (1919– ). *See* Sonnets 53, 54

RAMSAY of Banff, Charlotte Fanning, Lady (?–1904). *See* Sonnet 18

RANDEGGER, Alberto (1832–1911). *See* Sonnet 109

RANKY, Gy. *See* All's Well That Ends Well 2*a*

RAPHAEL, Mark. *See* Sonnet 18

RATHAUS, Karol (1895–1954). *See* Merchant of Venice 2*a*

RATHBONE, George. *See* Henry VIII 3*a*; Merchant of Venice 3*c*; Two Gentlemen of Verona 3*c*

RAVENSCROFT, Thomas (*c.* 1590–*c.* 1633). *See* Twelfth Night 3*d*

RAWSTHORNE, Alan (1905– ). *See* King Lear 2*a*

RAYMOND, E. *See* Tempest 1

REAY, Samuel (1822–1905). *See* As You Like It 3*d*; Measure for Measure 3*a*; Passionate Pilgrim 1

REDMAN, Douglas. *See* Winter's Tale 3*f*

REED, William Henry (1876–1942). *See* Merchant of Venice 3*c*; Tempest 2*b*

REEKES, J. *See* Romeo and Juliet 3*g*; Twelfth Night 3*h*; Sonnets 18, 33, 87; Venus and Adonis 5

REICHARDT, Johann Friedrich (1752–1814). *See* Macbeth 2*b*; Tempest 1

REY, Jean-Baptiste (1734–1810). *See* Hamlet 2*a*; King Lear 2*a*; Macbeth 2*a*

REYNAUD, Arnaud. *See* King Lear 1

REYNOLDS, Charles Tom. *See* As You Like It 3*d*

REYNOLDS, Frederic (1764–1841). *See* Midsummer Night's Dream 2*a*

RHEINBERGER, Josef Gabriel (1839–1901). *See* Taming of the Shrew 2*b*

RHODES, Harold William (1889–1956). *See* Henry VIII 3*a*

RICCI, Clara Ross. *See* As You Like It 3*d*; Henry VIII 3*a*

RICHARDS, Arthur. *See* As You Like It 3*f*

RICHARDSON, Thomas. *See* Passionate Pilgrim 7

RICHMOND, Rev. Legh (1772–1827). *See* Merchant of Venice 3*g*

RICKARDS, Ernest H. *See* Love's Labour's Lost 3*f*

RIEGGER, Wallingford (1885–1961). *See* Sonnet 138

RIETZ, Julius (1812–77). *See* As You Like It 2*a*; Hamlet 2*a*; Macbeth 2*a*; Tempest 2*b*

SALTER, Lionel Paul (1914– ). *See* Othello 3*b*

SALVAYRE, Gaston [Gervais Bernard] (1847–1916). *See* Richard III 1

SAMARA, Spiro (1863–1917). *See* Taming of the Shrew 1

SAMPSON, George (1861–1949). *See* Love's Labour's Lost 3*e*

SAMPSON, Godfrey. *See* As You Like It 3*d*, *f*

SARJEANT, James. *See* As You Like It 3*b*; Henry IV 3*d*; Two Gentlemen of Verona 3*c*

SARSON, H. May. *See* Cymbeline 3*a*; Love's Labour's Lost 3*g*

SATIE, Erik Alfred Leslie (1866–1925). *See* Midsummer Night's Dream 2*a*

SAUGUET, Henri [Jean Pierre Poupard] (1901– ). *See* Measure for Measure 3*a*; Twelfth Night 2*a*; Sonnet 43

SAUSSINE, Henri de (1859–1940). *See* Merchant of Venice 2*b*

SAYN-WITTGENSTEIN-BERLEBURG, E. F. von. *See* Antony and Cleopatra 1

SCHACHNER, R. *See* As You Like It 3*b*

SCHARTAU, Herbert William. *See* Tempest 3*k*

SCHLOTTMANN, Louis. *See* Romeo and Juliet 2*b*

SCHMITT, Florent (1870–1958). *See* Antony and Cleopatra 2*a*, *b*

SCHUBERT, Franz Peter (1797–1828). *See* Antony and Cleopatra 3*a*; Cymbeline 3*b*; Two Gentlemen of Verona 3*c*

SCHULZ-BEUTHEN, Heinrich (1838–1915). *See* King Lear 2*b*

SCHUMAN, William Howard (1910– ). *See* Henry VIII 2*a*, 3*a*

SCHUMANN, Robert Alexander (1810–56). *See* Julius Caesar 2*b*; Macbeth 2*b*; Twelfth Night 3*j*

SCHWANENBERGER, Johann Gottfried (1740–1804). *See* Romeo and Juliet 1

SCULL, G. C. *See* As You Like It 3*d*

X 2

SEIBER, Mátyás George (1904–1962). *See* Sonnet 18

SELBY, Bertram Luard (1853–1918). *See* As You Like It 3*b*, *d*; Love's Labour's Lost 3*g*; Measure for Measure 3*a*

SELLÉ, William Christian. *See* Twelfth Night 3*f*

SÉMÉLADIS, M. *See* King Lear 1

SERPETTE, Henri Charles Antoine Gaston (1846–1904). *See* General Seyfried, Ignaz Xavier von (1776–1841). *See* Julius Caesar 2*a*

SHAKESPEARE, William (1849–1931). *See* Hamlet 2*b*

SHAPORIN, Yuri Alexandrovich (1889– ). *See* Comedy of Errors 2*a*; King Lear 2*a*

SHARMAN, Cecil. *See* Henry VIII 3*a*; Love's Labour's Lost 3*f*, *g*; Merchant of Venice 3*g*; Midsummer Night's Dream 3*f*

SHARP, Cecil James (1859–1924). *See* Midsummer Night's Dream 2*a*

SHAW, Geoffrey Turton (1879–1943). *See* As You Like It 3*h*; Love's Labour's Lost 3*g*; Merchant of Venice 3*g*; Midsummer Night's Dream 3*n*, *t*; Much Ado About Nothing 3*c*; Tempest 3*g*; Twelfth Night 3*c*, *j*

SHAW, James. *See* As You Like It 3*f*

SHAW, Martin Fallas (1875–1958). *See* As You Like It 3*b*, *f*; Love's Labour's Lost 3*f*; Midsummer Night's Dream 2*b*, 3*f*, *t*; Much Ado About Nothing 3*c*; Richard II 2*a*; Tempest 3*f*; Twelfth Night 3*b*, *j*; Winter's Tale 3*d*

SHEBALIN, Vissarion Yakovlevich (1902–63). *See* Taming of the Shrew 1

SHELLEY, Harry Rowe (1858–1947). *See* Romeo and Juliet 1

SHIELD, William (1748–1829). *See* Henry IV 3*c*; Midsummer Night's Dream 3*g*; Othello 3*b*; Passionate Pilgrim 7, 8

SHOSTAKOVICH, Dimitri (1906– ). *See* Hamlet 2*a*, *b*; King Lear 2*a*; Othello 2*a*; Sonnet 66

SIBELIUS, Jean [Johan] Julias Christian (1865–1957). *See* Tempest 2*a*, *b*; Twelfth Night 3*b*, *j*

SILVER, Charles (1868– ). *See* Taming of the Shrew 1

SIMMONDS, Thomas F. *See* As You Like It 3*b*

SIMON, Antoine [Anton Yulievich] (1851–1916). *See* Merchant of Venice 2*a*

SIMPSON, Frederick James. *See* Love's Labour's Lost 3*g*

SIMPSON, Richard ( ? –1876). *See* Love's Labour's Lost 3*f*; Tempest 3*d*; Twelfth Night 3*j*; Lucrece 3; Passionate Pilgrim 4, 5; Sonnets 5, 6, 7, 27, 58, 59, 63, 71, 73, 81, 96, 110

SKERJANC, Lucijan Marija (1900– ). *See* General

SLATER, Gordon Archbold. *See* Winter's Tale 3*e*

SLINN, Edgar Beck. *See* As You Like It 3*b*, *d*; Henry VIII 3*a*; Merchant of Venice 3*g*; Much Ado About Nothing 3*c*; Tempest 3*k*; Twelfth Night 3*h*

SMALE, Percy W. de Courcy. *See* As You Like It 3*d*

SMETANA, Bedřich (1824–84). *See* Macbeth 2*b*; Richard III 2*b*; Twelfth Night 1; General

SMITH, Alexander Brent (1889–1950). *See* Cymbeline 3*a*

SMITH, David Stanley (1877–1949). *See* Henry IV 2*b*

SMITH, Edwin. *See* Tempest 3*f*

SMITH, Hugh Priestley. *See* Twelfth Night 3*b*

SMITH, John Christopher (1712–95). *See* Henry VIII 3*a*; Love's Labour's Lost 3*d*; Midsummer Night's Dream 1, 3*b*, *d*, *h*, *k*, *l*, *r*, *t*; Much Ado About Nothing 3*c*; Tempest 1

SMITH, John Stafford (1750–1836). *See* As You Like It 3*f*, *h*; Love's Labour's Lost 3*f*; Measure for Measure 3*a*

SMITH, Walter Ernest. *See* Merchant of Venice 3*c*

SMYTH, Dame Ethel Mary (1858–1944). *See* Antony and Cleopatra 2*b*

SOBOLEWSKI, Eduard (1808–72). *See* Cymbeline 1

SÖDERMAN, Johan August (1832–76). *See* Coriolanus 2*a*; Richard III 2*a*; Timon of Athens 2*b*

SOKOLOV, Nikolai Alexandrovich (1859–1922). *See* Winter's Tale 2*a*

SOLLA, Isidore de. *See* Two Gentlemen of Verona 3*c*

SOMBRE, Hon. Mrs. Dyce- [Hon. Mary Ann Jervis]. *See* As You Like It 3*b*

SOMERVELL, Sir Arthur (1863–1937). *See* As You Like It 3*b*, *f*, *h*; Henry VIII 3*a*; Measure for Measure 3*a*; Twelfth Night 3*h*; Winter's Tale 3*e*, *g*; Sonnet 71

SOWERBUTTS, John Albert. *See* Much Ado About Nothing 3*c*

SPEAIGHT, J. *See* Midsummer Night's Dream 2*b*; Tempest 2*b*; Twelfth Night 2*b*

SPOHR, Louis (1784–1859). *See* Macbeth 2*a*, *b*

STADTFELD, Alexandre (1826–53). *See* Hamlet 1

STANFORD, Sir Charles Villiers (1852–1924). *See* Much Ado About Nothing 1; Twelfth Night 3*b*, *h*, *j*

STANISLAUS, Frederick. *See* As You Like It 3*d*; Much Ado About Nothing 3*c*; Twelfth Night 3*h*

STEGGALL, Reginald (1867–1938). *See* Cymbeline 3*b*; Henry VIII 3*a*; Measure for Measure 3*a*; Two Gentlemen of Verona 3*c*

STEGMANN, Carl David (*c*. 1751–1826). *See* King Lear 2*a*; Macbeth 2*a*

STEIBELT, Daniel (1765–1823). *See* Romeo and Juliet 1

STEINKÜHLER, Emil (1824–72). *See* Twelfth Night 1

STENHAMMAR, Wilhelm Eugen (1871–1927). *See* Hamlet 2*a*; Romeo and Juliet 2*a*; Twelfth Night 2*a*

STERNDALE-BENNETT, T. C. and W.
See Bennett, T. C. and W. Sterndale-

STERNEFELD, Daniël (1905– ). See
Twelfth Night 2a

STEVENS, Richard John Samuel
(1757–1837). See As You Like It
3b, d, h; Hamlet 3a; Henry VIII
3a; Merchant of Venice 3g;
Midsummer Night's Dream 3j, t;
Much Ado About Nothing 3c;
Tempest 3c; Twelfth Night 3b, h;
Two Gentlemen of Verona 3c;
Passionate Pilgrim 3

STEVENS, William P. See Love's
Labour's Lost 3d

STEVENSON, Frederick. See Tempest
3k

STEVENSON, Sir John Andrew (1761–
1833). See Hamlet 3a, c, l;
Measure for Measure 3a; Merchant of Venice 3g; Taming of
the Shrew 2a; Tempest 3d;
Twelfth Night 3f, j; Passionate
Pilgrim 1

STEWART, Sir Robert Prescott (1825–
1894). See General

STOESSEL, Albert Frederic (1894–
1943). See As You Like It 3d

STONE, Norman Murray (1890– ).
See As You Like It 3b; Cymbeline
3a; Love's Labour's Lost 3g;
Twelfth Night 3b

STORACE, Stephen (1762–96). See
Comedy of Errors 1

STRAUSS, Richard (1864–1949). See
Hamlet 3c, g, i; Macbeth 2b

STRAVINSKY, Igor Feodorovich (1882–
). See Love's Labour's Lost
3f; Tempest 3f; Sonnet 8

STREET, Joseph. See Two Gentlemen of Verona 2b

STRELEZKI, Anton [Arthur Bransby
Burnand]. See Measure for Measure 3a

STUCKEN, Frank Valentine van der
(1858–1929). See Tempest 2a

SUK, Josef (1874–1935). See Winter's Tale 2b

SULEK, Stjepan (1914– ). See
Coriolanus 1

SULLIVAN, Sir Arthur Seymour
(1842–1900). See As You Like
It 3c, d; Henry VIII 2a, 3a;
Macbeth 2b; Merchant of Venice
2a, 3c, d; Merry Wives of Windsor 2a; Much Ado About Nothing
3c; Othello 3b; Tempest 2a, b,
3d, f, g, k, l; Timon of Athens 2b;
Twelfth Night 3h

SULLIVAN, T. D. See Love's Labour's Lost 3d

SUPPÉ, Franz von [Francesco Ezechiele Ermenegildo Suppé Demelli] (1819–95). See Midsummer
Night's Dream 1

SUTERMEISTER, Heinrich (1910– ).
See Romeo and Juliet 1; Tempest 1

SUTOR, Wilhelm (c. 1774–1828).
See Macbeth 2a

SVENDSEN, Johan Severin (1840–
1911). See Romeo and Juliet 2b

SYKES, Harold Hinchcliffe. See
As You Like It 3f

SYMONS, Thomas. See Twelfth Night
3b

TANEIEV, Alexander Sergeievich
(1850–1918). See Hamlet 2b

TARPEY, W. Kingsley. See Twelfth
Night 3h

TAUBERT, Karl Gottfried Wilhelm
(1811–91). See As You Like It
3d; Love's Labour's Lost 3f;
Macbeth 1; Merchant of Venice
3g; Midsummer Night's Dream
2b, 3t; Othello 2b; Tempest 2a
and 3d, f, k; Twelfth Night 1 and
3b, h

TAUBMANN, Otto (1859–1929). See
Merchant of Venice 1

TAUSCH, Julius (1827–95). See As
You Like It 2a; Twelfth Night 2a

TAYLOR, E. D. See Merchant of
Venice 3c

TAYLOR, J. A. See Measure for
Measure 3a

TAYLOR, Samuel Coleridge- (1875–
1912). See Othello 2b and 3b;
Twelfth Night 3h

TAYLOR, Mrs. Tom [Laura W.

VAN ETTEN, Jane. *See* As You Like It 3*d*

VAUGHAN WILLIAMS, R. *See* Williams, R. Vaughan

VERACINI, Francesco Maria (1690–*c.* 1750). *See* As You Like It 1

VERDI, Giuseppe Fortunino Francesco (1813–1901). *See* Macbeth 1; Merry Wives of Windsor 1; Othello 1

VERNON, Joseph (*c.* 1738–82). *See* Twelfth Night 3*j*; Two Gentlemen of Verona 3*c*

VICARS, George Rayleigh. *See* Tempest 3*f*; Twelfth Night 3*h*

VIERLING, Georg (1820–1901). *See* Tempest 2*b*

VINCENT, Charles John. *See* Othello 3*b*; Twelfth Night 3*h*

VLAD, Roman (1919– ). *See* Romeo and Juliet 2*a*; Twelfth Night 2*a*

VOGLER, Georg Joseph (1749–1814). *See* Hamlet 2*a*

VOLKMANN, Friedrich Robert (1815–1883). *See* Richard III 2*a, b*

VOWLES, William. *See* As You Like It 3*b*

VREULS, Victor (1876–1944). *See* Midsummer Night's Dream 1

WADDINGTON, Sidney Peirce (1869–1953). *See* Twelfth Night 3*h*

WADELY, Frederick William (1882– ). *See* Twelfth Night 3*h*

WAGENAAR, Johan (1862–1941). *See* Taming of the Shrew 2*b*; Twelfth Night 2*b*

WAGNER, Jacob Karl (1772–1822). *See* As You Like It 2*b*

WAGNER, Wilhelm Richard (1813–1883). *See* Measure for Measure 1

WAITHMAN, R. H. *See* Two Gentlemen of Verona 3*c*

WALFORD DAVIES, H. *See* Davies, H. Walford

WALKER, Ernest (1870–1949). *See* As You Like It 3*d, f*; Cymbeline 3*b*; Henry VIII 3*a*; Love's Labour's Lost 3*g*; Tempest 3*d, f*; Venus and Adonis 6

WALLBANK, Newell S. *See* As You Like It 3*d*

WALLIS, Arnold J. *See* Twelfth Night 3*h*

WALTHEW, Richard Henry (1872–1951). *See* As You Like It 3*d*; Twelfth Night 3*j*; Sonnet 29

WALTON, Sir William Turner (1902– ). *See* As You Like It 2*a* and 3*f*; Hamlet 2*a*; Henry V 2*a*; Macbeth 2*a*; Richard III 2*a*

WAREING, Herbert Walter. *See* As You Like It 3*f*; Love's Labour's Lost 3*g*; Twelfth Night 3*h, j*; Winter's Tale 3*f*

WARLOCK, Peter [Philip Heseltine] (1894–1930). *See* As You Like It 3*d*; Love's Labour's Lost 3*f*; Measure for Measure 3*a*; Much Ado About Nothing 3*c*; Twelfth Night 3*h*; Winter's Tale 3*f*

WARRELL, Arthur Sydney. *See* As You Like It 3*d*

WARREN, Arthur M. *See* Tempest 3*f*

WASSALL, Grace. *See* As You Like It 3*b, d, f*; Love's Labour's Lost 3*d*; Merchant of Venice 3*g*; Passionate Pilgrim 3; Sonnets 18, 29, 30, 65, 90

WATERS, Charles Frederick (1895– ). *See* Midsummer Night's Dream 3

WATERS, Hugh, *see* Gavall, J.

WATSON, Geoffrey. *See* Othello 3*b*

WATSON, Henry. *See* Twelfth Night 3*h*

WATSON, William Michael. *See* As You Like It 3*d*; Othello 3*b*; Romeo and Juliet 2*b*; Tempest 3*k*

WEBBE, Samuel *the elder* (1740–1816). *See* Macbeth 3*c*; Passionate Pilgrim 8

WEBBE, Samuel *the younger* (*c.* 1770–1843). *See* As You Like It 3*b*; Merchant of Venice 3*c*; Twelfth Night 3*b*; Two Gentlemen of Verona 3*c*

WEBER, Bernhard Anselm (1766–1821). *See* Coriolanus 2*b*; Merchant of Venice 3*g*

WILSON, Henry James Lane. *See* Othello 3*b*

WILSON, John (1595–1674). *See* Measure for Measure 3*a*; Tempest 3*k*; Winter's Tale 3*e*

WILSON, Stanley. *See* Richard II 3*a*

WILSON, W. *See* Midsummer Night's Dream 3*n*

WINTER, Peter von (1754–1825). *See* Tempest 1; Twelfth Night 3*a*

WIRÉN, Dag Ivar (1905– ). *See* King John 2*a*; Merchant of Venice 2*a*; Midsummer Night's Dream 2*a*

WISSMER, Pierre (1915– ). *See* Antony and Cleopatra 2*b*

WISTER, Owen (1860–1938). *See* As You Like It 3*b*; Love's Labour's Lost 3*g*; Much Ado About Nothing 3*c*; Tempest 3*d, f*

WOLF, Ernst Wilhelm (1735–92). *See* Midsummer Night's Dream 1

WOOD, Charles (1866–1926). *See* As You Like It 3*b, d, f*; Henry VIII 3*a*; Merchant of Venice 3*c*; Tempest 3*f*; Two Gentlemen of Verona 3*c*

WOOD, Frederic Herbert. *See* As You Like It 3*g, h*; Love's Labour's Lost 3*f, g*; Merchant of Venice 3*g*; Midsummer Night's Dream 3*f, t*; Tempest 3*d, f, g, l*; Twelfth Night 3*e, j*

WOOD, Ralph Walter (1902– ). *See* As You Like It 3*d*; Love's Labour's Lost 3*g*; Measure for Measure 3*a*; Tempest 2*a*; Sonnets 64, 97

WOOLLEY, Charles. *See* Two Gentlemen of Verona 3*c*

WORDSWORTH, William Brocklesby. *See* Sonnet 33

WORSLEY, Frank Wallis. *See* Sonnet 100

WOYRSCH, Felix (1860–1944). *See* Hamlet 2*b*

WURM, Marie J. A. *See* As You Like It 3*f*

YATES, Edmund. *See* Twelfth Night 3*h*

YOUNG, Arthur. *See* As You Like It 3*b, d, f*; Measure for Measure 3*a*; Midsummer Night's Dream 3*t*; Much Ado About Nothing 3*c*; Twelfth Night 3*h*

YOUNG, William James. *See* Tempest 2*b*; Twelfth Night 3*h*; Two Gentlemen of Verona 3*c*

YRVID, Richard d'. *See* Ivry

YUFEROV, S. V. *See* Antony and Cleopatra 1

ZAFRED, Mario (1922– ). *See* Hamlet 1

ZANDONAI, Riccardo (1883–1944). *See* Romeo and Juliet 1

ZILCHER, Hermann (1881–1948). *See* As You Like It 2*a*; Comedy of Errors 2*a*; Taming of the Shrew 2*a*; Winter's Tale 2*a*

ZILLIG, Winfried. *See* Troilus and Cressida 1

ZIMMERMANN, Agnes Marie Jacobina (1847–1925). *See* As You Like It 3*b*

ZINGARELLI, Niccolò Antonio (1752–1837). *See* Romeo and Juliet 1

ZUMSTEEG, Johann Rudolph (1760–1802). *See* Macbeth 2*a*; Othello 2*a*; Tempest 1

# INDEX

(This index, of literary and musical works and of persons, is for pp. 3-241 only. For further information, consult also the Catalogue of Musical Works based on Shakespeare (pp. 243-290) and the Check-List of Composers (pp. 291-321). Where the title of a musical work based on a Shakespeare play differs from that of the play, Shakespeare's title is given in brackets. Page references to musical works based on the plays are given also under the play-title. Figures in bold type indicate something more than a passing reference.)